"*A Practical Guide to Teaching Research Methods in Education: Lesson Plans and Advice from Faculty* is an example of university faculty identifying and resolving a problem found in their practice of teaching. The book offers a wealth of pedagogical lessons that connect the concepts, processes, and tools of research methodology to student backgrounds and needs to enhance understanding and success. Every teacher of research methods will benefit from this professional development."

-- Jill A. Perry, PhD (she/her/hers), Associate Professor of Practice, Dept of Educational Foundations, Organizations, and Policy Studies, University of Pittsburgh, USA

"*A Practical Guide to Teaching Research Methods in Education: Lesson Plans and Advice from Faculty* is an essential contribution to the toolkit of education faculty. This volume spans qualitative, quantitative, and mixed methods, and provides faculty with expert advice and plans to engage students. From the classroom novice to seasoned faculty, *A Practical Guide to Teaching Research Methods in Education: Lesson Plans and Advice from Faculty* is a welcome addition to the library of educators invested in instructing students embarking on their research journeys."

-- Richard J. Reddick, Senior Vice Provost for Curriculum and Enrollment, and Dean of Undergraduate Studies, Distinguished Service Professor, Department of Educational Leadership and Policy, The University of Texas at Austin, USA

"As someone who has extensively studied effective teaching across research universities and community colleges, I believe this book serves as an exemplary resource for any faculty member who has struggled with how to get across complex ideas to novice and aspiring researchers. The unique combination of providing a lesson plan that instructors can pick up and immediately use with the discussion of the intellectual journey of developing the lesson is exactly what we need to improve teaching and learning in higher education research classes, dissertations, and research projects."

-- Audrey J. Jaeger, Executive Director, Belk Center for Community College Leadership and Research, W. Dallas Herring Professor of Community College Education, USA

"A Practical Guide to Teaching Research Methods in Education: Lesson Plans and Advice from Faculty **is bound to be a seminal resource for faculty and students alike. The book goes step-by-step through the research process. It starts with when students are working on getting clear about the problem they are researching and works its way to when scholars are identifying the implications of their findings for research, practice, and policy. The inclusion of lesson plans will provide faculty with an incredible resource as they teach and guide their students through the research process. This is the type of book that one can use during a course and subsequently return to again and again as a resource."**

-- Milagros Castillo-Montoya, Associate Professor of Higher Education and Student Affairs, Co-PI, Bill and Melinda Gates Foundation Grant, USA

A Practical Guide to Teaching Research Methods in Education

A Practical Guide to Teaching Research Methods in Education brings together more than 60 faculty experts. The contributors share detailed lesson plans about selected research concepts or skills in education and related disciplines, as well as discussions of the intellectual preparation needed to effectively teach the lesson.

Grounded in the wisdom of practice from exemplary and award-winning faculty from diverse institution types, career stages, and demographic backgrounds, this book draws on both the practical and cognitive elements of teaching educational (and related) research to students in higher education today. The book is divided into eight sections, covering the following key elements within education (and related) research: problems and research questions, literature reviews and theoretical frameworks, research design, quantitative methods, qualitative methods, mixed methods, findings and discussions, and special topics, such as student identity development, community and policy engaged research, and research dissemination. Within each section, individual chapters specifically focus on skills and perspectives needed to navigate the complexities of educational research. The concluding chapter reflects on how teachers of research also need to be learners of research, as faculty continuously strive for mastery, identity, and creativity in how they guide our next generation of knowledge producers through the research process.

Undergraduate and graduate professors of education (and related) research courses, dissertation chairs/committee members, faculty development staff members, and graduate students would all benefit from the lessons and expert commentary contained in this book.

Aimee LaPointe Terosky is Professor of Educational Leadership, Director of the Interdisciplinary Doctor of Educational Leadership program, and university liaison to School District of Philadelphia at Saint Joseph's University, USA. Her expertise in K–12 and higher education is in teaching/learning, urban principal and faculty careers, and qualitative research.

Vicki L. Baker is the E. Maynard Aris Endowed Professor in Economics and Management at Albion College, USA. She currently serves as the faculty director of the Albion College Community Collaborative. Her most recent book is *Managing Your Academic Career: A Guide to Re-Envision Mid-Career* (Routledge 2022).

Jeffrey C. Sun is Professor of Higher Education and Law and distinguished university scholar at the University of Louisville, USA. Dr. Sun's research examines the extent to which policy instruments, other legal actions, and innovative interventions advance or inhibit academic operations through college teaching, learning, and knowledge creation.

A Practical Guide to Teaching Research Methods in Education

Lesson Plans and Advice from Faculty

Edited by Aimee LaPointe Terosky, Vicki L. Baker and Jeffrey C. Sun

LONDON AND NEW YORK

Designed cover image: tadamichi / Getty images

First published 2023
by Routledge
4 Park Square, Milton Park, Abingdon, Oxon OX14 4RN

and by Routledge
605 Third Avenue, New York, NY 10158

Routledge is an imprint of the Taylor & Francis Group, an informa business

© 2023 selection and editorial matter, Aimee LaPointe Terosky, Vicki L. Baker, and Jeffrey C. Sun; individual chapters, the contributors

The right of Aimee LaPointe Terosky, Vicki L. Baker, and Jeffrey C. Sun to be identified as the authors of the editorial material, and of the authors for their individual chapters, has been asserted in accordance with sections 77 and 78 of the Copyright, Designs and Patents Act 1988.

All rights reserved. No part of this book may be reprinted or reproduced or utilised in any form or by any electronic, mechanical, or other means, now known or hereafter invented, including photocopying and recording, or in any information storage or retrieval system, without permission in writing from the publishers.

Trademark notice: Product or corporate names may be trademarks or registered trademarks, and are used only for identification and explanation without intent to infringe.

British Library Cataloguing-in-Publication Data
A catalogue record for this book is available from the British Library

ISBN: 978-1-032-18673-3 (hbk)
ISBN: 978-1-032-18675-7 (pbk)
ISBN: 978-1-003-25568-0 (ebk)

DOI: 10.4324/b23320

Typeset in Minion Pro
by SPi Technologies India Pvt Ltd (Straive)

Contents

List of Contributors	*xiii*
Foreword	*xvii*
Catherine Hill	
Introduction	1
Aimee LaPointe Terosky	

SECTION I
Topics, Problems, and Research Questions   7
Section Editor: Katie Conway

1   Introduction to Section I: Research Topics, Problems, and Questions   9
    Katie Conway

2   From Personal Passion to Hot Topics: Selecting a Topic to Research   11
    Sosanya Jones

3   Articulating a Research Problem and its Rationale: Using Graphical
    Depictions, Exemplars, and Students' Own Work   19
    Rebecca S. Natow

4   Branch Out: Using Tree Diagrams to Select and Develop Research Questions   27
    Vikash Reddy

SECTION II
Literature Review and Theoretical/Conceptual Framework   35
Section Editor: Leslie D. Gonzales

5   Introduction to Section II: Literature Review and Theoretical/Conceptual
    Framework   37
    Leslie D. Gonzales

viii CONTENTS

6 Connecting Pieces to the Puzzle: Finding and Maintaining Resources 39
Christa J. Porter and Janice A. Byrd

7 The Candy Sort: Organizing the Literature Review 46
Aimee LaPointe Terosky

8 Theoretical and Conceptual Frameworks: Understanding the Role of Theory in
Congruent Research Designs 52
Penny A. Pasque and Chelsea Gilbert

SECTION III
Research Design 63
Section Editor: Jeffrey C. Sun and Ishwanzya Rivers

9 Introduction to Section III: Research Design 65
Jeffrey C. Sun and Ishwanzya Rivers

10 Visualize Your Research Design: Moving from Research Questions
to Research Design 68
Ishwanzya Rivers and Jeffrey C. Sun

11 Let's Road Trip: Aligning Theoretical Frameworks, Research Questions and
Research Design 77
Aurora Kamimura

12 The Self and Research: Positionality through Artifacts 86
Beth E. Bukoski

13 Trustworthiness and Ethics in Research: Using Reflexivity to See the Self in
Ethical Research 94
G. Blue Brazelton and Ijeoma Ononuju

SECTION IV
Quantitative Methods 101
Section Editor: Willis A. Jones

14 Introduction to Section IV: Quantitative Methods 103
Willis A. Jones

15 Making Sense of Multivariate Analysis: Real-world Applications 106
Courtney S. Thomas Tobin

16 Linear Regression: A Student-driven Application of Team-based Learning 113
Amber D. Dumford

CONTENTS   ix

17   Hands-on Application of Exploratory Factor Analysis in Educational Research   120
Soyeon Ahn and Beck Graefe

18   Trending Topic: Teaching Difference-in-differences in a Quasi-experimental
Methods Course   131
R. Joseph Waddington

SECTION V
Qualitative Methods   141
Section Editor: David Pérez II

19   Introduction to Section V: Qualitative Methods   143
David Pérez II

20   Listening Deeply: Preparing to Facilitate Interviews and Focus Groups   146
Tricia R. Shalka

21   Write What You See, Not What You Know: Learning the Method of
Observation Through the Visual Arts   154
A. Emiko Blalock

22   On the Recovery of Black Life: A Holistic Approach to Document Analysis   163
Wilson Kwamogi Okello

23   Emerging Approaches: Ensuring a Pyramid of Congruence When Using
Critical and Poststructural Theories in Qualitative Educational Research   171
Antonio Duran and Alex C. Lange

24   Exploring How Epistemologies Guide the Process of Coding Data and
Developing Themes   179
Kari B. Taylor

SECTION VI
Mixed Methods   189
Section Editor: Chris Heasley

25   Introduction to Section VI: Mixed Methods   191
Chris Heasley

26   Low Hanging Fruit, Ripe for Inquiry: Considering the Quantitative
Dimensions of Mixed Methods Research   194
Kayla M. Johnson and Frank Fernandez

x CONTENTS

27 Creating your Masterpiece: Applying Brush Strokes to Qualitative
   Exploration of Mixed Methods Research   202
   Chris Heasley

28 Presenting and Visualizing a Mixed Methods Study   210
   Hugo A. García and Xinyang Li

SECTION VII
Findings and Discussion   221
Section Editor: Erin Doran

29 Introduction to Section VII: Findings and Discussion   223
   Erin Doran

30 An Introduction to Regression Using Critical Quantitative Thinking   225
   *Terrace Ewinghill, Adam Lazarewicz, Cindy Meza, Brent Gambrell,
   Diana Guerrero and Jameson Lopez*

31 Show the Story: Presenting Qualitative Findings   234
   Meghan J. Pifer

32 Block by Block: Building the Discussion Section   241
   Maire Brandenberg, Tamara Hoffer, McKenzie Rabenn and Cheryl Hunter

33 Making the Theoretical Practical: Implications for Theory   249
   James C. Coviello

34 The Donut Memo: Writing for Policymakers and Practitioners   256
   Christopher R. Marsicano, Rylie Martin, Ann F. Bernhardt and Emilia G. Rounds

SECTION VIII
Special Topics   265
Section Editor: Vicki L. Baker

35 Introduction to Section VIII: Special Topics   267
   Vicki L. Baker

36 Scholarly Identity Development of Undergraduate Researchers:
   A Lesson Plan for Professional Development   270
   Vicki L. Baker and Vanessa McCaffrey

37 Developing Students' Cultural Competence through Video Interviews   277
   Laura Lunsford and Jutta Street

38 Preparing Students for Community-engaged Scholarship: A Lesson Plan for
   Collaborative Inquiry Grounded in Awareness of Self and Others   285
   Gene Corbin, Vialla Hartfield-Méndez and Elaine Ward

CONTENTS   xi

39 Teaching Policy Implications: Can You Have Your Cake and Eat It Too?   293
    Jason E. Lane

40 Introducing Scholars to Public Writing   300
    Erin A. Hennessy

    Closing Words: Helping Students to Learn Research and Become Researchers 307
    Anna Neumann and Aaron M. Pallas

    Index   313

Contributors

Soyeon Ahn, University of Miami, Coral Gables, FL, USA

Vicki L. Baker, Albion College, Albion, MI, USA

Ann F. Bernhardt, Texas A&M University, College Station, TX, USA

A. Emiko Blalock, Michigan State University, East Lansing, MI, USA

Maire Brandenberg, University of North Dakota, Grand Forks, ND, USA

G. Blue Brazelton, Northern Arizona University, Flagstaff, AZ, USA

Beth E. Bukoski, Virginia Commonwealth University, Richmond, VA, USA

Janice A. Byrd, Pennsylvania State University, State College, PA, USA

Katie Conway, Columbia University, New York, NY, USA

Gene Corbin, University of Massachusetts, Boston, MA, USA

James C. Coviello, Saint John's University, Queens, NY, USA

Erin Doran, Iowa State University, Ames, IA, USA

Amber D. Dumford, University of South Florida, Tampa, FL, USA

Antonio Duran, Arizona State University, Tempe, AZ, USA

Terrace Ewinghill, University of Arizona, Tucson, AZ, USA

Frank Fernandez, University of Florida, Gainesville, FL, USA

Brent Gambrell, University of Arizona, Tucson, AZ, USA

Hugo A. García, Texas Tech University, Lubbock, TX, USA

Chelsea Gilbert, Ohio State University, Columbus, OH, USA

Leslie D. Gonzales, Michigan State University, East Lansing, MI, USA

Beck Graefe, University of Miami, Coral Gables, FL, USA

Diana Guerrero, University of Arizona, Tucson, AZ, USA

Vialla Hartfield-Méndez, Emory University, Atlanta, GA, USA

Chris Heasley, Saint Joseph's University, Philadelphia, PA, USA

Erin A. Hennessy, TVP Communications & Georgetown University, Washington, DC, USA

Catherine Hill, American University of Dubai, Dubai, United Arab Emirates

Tamara Hoffer, University of North Dakota, Grand Forks, ND, USA

Cheryl Hunter, University of North DakotaGrand Forks, ND, USA

Kayla M. Johnson, University of Kentucky, Lexington, KY, USA

Sosanya Jones, Howard University, Washington, DC, USA

Willis A. Jones, University of Miami, Coral Gables, FL, USA

Aurora Kamimura, Washington University, St. Louis, MO, USA

Jason E. Lane, Miami University of Ohio, Oxford, OH, USA

Alex C. Lange, Colorado State University, Fort Collins, CO, USA

Adam Lazarewicz, University of Arizona, Tucson, AZ, USA

Xinyang Li, University of Kansas Medical Center, Kansas City, KS, USA

Jameson Lopez, University of Arizona, Tucson, AZ, USA

Laura Lunsford, Campbell University, Buies Creek, NC, USA

Christopher R. Marsicano, Davidson College, Davidson, NC, USA

Rylie Martin, Davidson College, Davidson, NC, USA

Vanessa McCaffrey, Albion College, Albion, MI, USA

Cindy Meza, University of Arizona, Tucson, AZ, USA

Rebecca S. Natow, Hofstra University, Hempstead, NY, USA

Anna Neumann, Teachers College, Columbia University, New York, NY, USA

Wilson Kwamogi Okello, Pennsylvania State University, State College, PA, USA

Ijeoma Ononuju, Northern Arizona University, Flagstaff, AZ, USA

Aaron M. Pallas, Teachers College, Columbia University, New York, NY, USA

Penny A. Pasque, Ohio State University, Columbus, OH, USA

David Pérez II, Syracuse University, Syracuse, NY, USA

Meghan J. Pifer, University of Louisville, Louisville, KY, USA

Christa J. Porter, Kent State University, Kent, OH, USA

McKenzie Rabenn, University of North Dakota, Grand Forks, ND, USA

CONTRIBUTORS xv

Vikash Reddy, Campaign for College Opportunity

Ishwanzya Rivers, University of Louisville, Louisville, KY, USA

Emilia G. Rounds, Duke University, Durham, NC, USA

Tricia R. Shalka, University of Rochester

Jutta Street, Campbell University, Buies Creek, NC, USA

Jeffrey C. Sun, University of Louisville, Louisville, KY, USA

Kari B. Taylor, Springfield College, Springfield, MA, USA

Aimee LaPointe Terosky, Saint Joseph's University, Philadelphia, PA, USA

Courtney S. Thomas Tobin, University of California, Los Angeles, CA, USA

R. Joseph Waddington, University of Kentucky, Lexington, KY, USA

Elaine Ward, Merrimack College, North Andover, MA, USA

Foreword

Among all the lessons we can draw from John Dewey's classic work on *How We Think* (1910) is the simple yet profound observation that, yes, everyone thinks, but not everyone thinks well. Learning and relearning how to think well is becoming increasingly difficult in today's highly technological world.

Digital distractions abound. A number of scholars and experts in the fields of neuroscience, psychology, and education agree that, in general, people are experiencing an overload of stimuli, causing us to be less patient, more impulsive, less reflective, often unable to concentrate and think clearly (Bowen, 2021; Carr, 2020; Turkle, 2017; Wolf, 2018). While the concept and the process of learning to think well developed over hundreds of years, it wasn't until the mid-20th century that the now ubiquitous term "critical thinking" came into use. As defined by the National Council for Excellence in Critical Thinking (1987), critical thinking is based on universal intellectual values, such as clarity, accuracy, precision, consistency, relevance, sound evidence, good reasons, depth, breadth, and fairness. It is a disciplined process of evaluating the quality of evidence, detecting the presence of error, hypocrisy, manipulation, and bias – all of which are essential elements of the research process. As Robert Stake reminded us in *The Art of Case Study Research* (1995), good research is less about good methods than it is about good thinking.

When Aimee LaPointe Terosky envisioned this project, she was acting in response to a painfully familiar scenario—seemingly endless hours of reading poorly written, not very well-organized literature reviews, attempted by relatively smart and successful educators who happened to be doctoral students. So, what were they thinking? Good question. Being the consummate educator, she knew it was more important to ask, what more can I do to meet them where they are and lift them higher—not as a class but as individuals with varying degrees of prior knowledge, as well as different cultural, personal and academic backgrounds. As an internationally recognized and widely respected academic, Aimee LaPointe Terosky, as well as the chapter authors are well aware that those of us who have had the privilege of teaching research methods have ways of working that differ from one colleague to another. Then why not gather the collective wisdom of education scholars and expert methodologists and make it visible for those who seek to discover truth and sincerely desire to think well? Indeed, her approach to the design of this project reminded me of C.W. Mills' chapter on Intellectual Craftmanship in *The Sociological Imagination* (1959): Only by conversations in which experienced thinkers exchange information about their actual ways of working can a useful sense of method and theory be imparted (p. 195).

What resulted is an edited volume that is at once practical, intellectual, and uniquely designed to make our shared thinking about the research process visible and accessible. It is practical in that it provides detailed lesson plans on how to teach research concepts and skills. It is intellectual in its systematic approach to why and how education faculty can motivate students of research to make analytic connections and discover insights. A key takeaway for every reader is that learning to do research is a lifelong skill just as surely as learning to think well or critically is a lifelong endeavor.

Producing such a project was an enormous collaborative undertaking. For the benefit of current and future generations of scholars, the experts who contributed to this volume generously shared their distinctive ways of thinking and working—ways, that in many cases, were learned and adapted from those who came before them. As a sourcebook for the teaching of research methods, it will stand out as unique in its class for its practical advice and intellectual import.

When Johnny Saldana was commissioned to update the seminal work on *Qualitative Data Analysis* by the now deceased Matt Miles and Michael Huberman, he said, "I am a privileged guest in the academic house they built." Before concluding this foreword, I want to acknowledge how honored I am to have contributed this small piece to such a meaningful endeavor—like a privileged guest among so many outstanding scholars. Another privilege of my life was that of teaching Aimee LaPointe Terosky when she was studying for her Master's in education at Villanova University. That was almost 25 years ago. Even then, she was a strong independent thinker who understood that teachers really can change lives.

Catherine Hill
Dean, School of Education
American University in Dubai

BIBLIOGRAPHY

Bowen, J. A. (2021). *Teaching Change: How to Develop Independent Thinkers Using Relationships, Resilience, And Reflection*. JHU Press.

Carr, N. (2020). *The Shallows: What the Internet Is Doing To Our Brains*. WW Norton & Company.

Dewey, J. (1910). *How We Think*. Courier Corporation.

Mills, C. W. (2000). *The Sociological Imagination*. Oxford University Press.

Miles, M. B., Huberman, A. M., & Saldaña, J. (2018). *Qualitative Data Analysis: A Methods Sourcebook*. Sage Publications.

Stake, R. E. (1995). *The Art of Case Study Research*. Sage Publications.

Turkle, S. (2017). *Alone Together: Why We Expect More from Technology and Less from Each Other*. Hachette UK.

Wolf, M. (2018). *Reader, Come Home: The Reading Brain in A Digital World* (p. 54). Harper.

Introduction

Aimee LaPointe Terosky

As I sit bleary-eyed, frantically marking up a student's poorly written literature review, I reach for a second chocolate bar to dip into peanut butter in hopes of soothing my crushed teacher ego (note: bad grading experiences are correlated to high levels of chocolate consumption). I wonder why, despite my many attempts to get across how to write a quality literature review, my students – who are extremely bright and successful educational and social impact leaders – continue to struggle with writing a well-organized literature review.

If you're like me and countless other undergraduate and graduate faculty members in education (and related disciplines), you face the daunting task of teaching research concepts and skills to students with little more than your own research training and with limited time to deeply analyze why you do what you do. The higher education literature notes that most faculty members receive little to no pedagogical training for teaching, including teaching research skills (American Academy of Arts and Sciences, 2017; Austin et al., 2008; Pallas et al., 2017). As such, faculty members are charged with preparing the next generation of scholars and scholar-practitioners with a constrained toolkit. This is particularly troubling considering the significance of the task – developing those who will seek out new knowledge and solutions to society's needs.

Unfortunately, my chocolate and peanut butter strategy did not magically improve my students' literature reviews; however, it did result in a call to action. I decided to intentionally apply my own 20 years of expertise in the field of teaching and learning to enhance my ability to teach educational research. Through this intentionality, I learned a great deal from master-scholars on conceptualizations of good teaching and how to teach research methods to others, including across student demographics, institutional types, and course objectives. Through this endeavor, I also realized that other faculty would benefit from what I was learning and hearing, especially in terms of creating purposeful and equitable learning spaces for all students. It is in this spirit that this edited book was born, which invites faculty experts to: (a) provide practical, detailed *lesson plans* on how to teach research concepts and skills to undergraduate and graduate students, and (b) talk through the relevant *intellectual preparation* needed to effectively implement their lessons.

DOI: 10.4324/b23320-1

The intellectual preparation aspect of this book is guided by literature on conceptualizations of good teaching, particularly the work on pedagogical content knowledge by Lee Shulman (1986) and on convergent teaching by Aaron Pallas and Anna Neumann (2019). Although originally written for K–12 audiences, the field of higher education has also benefited from Shulman's concept of pedagogical content knowledge. This is notable for its integration of subject matter knowledge, or the core ideas of a discipline, and general pedagogical knowledge, or the instructional strategies implemented by teachers to manage and guide learning. In short, pedagogical content knowledge emphasizes how teachers design learning experiences based on how particular students learn specific subject matter (Shulman, 1987, 1999, 2004). Neumann and Bolitzer (2014) capture the meaning of pedagogical content knowledge by writing:

> …in learning, the onus is not and cannot be only on the learner. To learn, a person must have an opportunity to do so, ideally with a teacher (or teacher figure) who deeply understands the learner and the stuff being learned, and who creates bridges between the two.
>
> (p. 98)

The second concept guiding the authors' reflections on their lessons is convergent teaching, a concept introduced by Aaron Pallas and Anna Neumann (2019). Convergent teaching is defined as a teacher's simultaneous and enveloping attention to subject matter, the learner, and the context in which learning takes place. Convergent teaching is realized through three elements: (a) *targeting core ideas* (i.e., identifying the foundational content of a discipline or field), (b) *surfacing students' prior knowledge vis-à-vis their contexts* (i.e., locating students' prior knowledge from their cultural, personal, and academic background), and (c) *navigating prior knowledge and new knowledge* (i.e., identifying linkages and working through the differences between prior knowledge and new knowledge, ideas, and perspectives) (Pallas & Neumann, 2019). In sum, good teaching in the convergent model is depicted as faculty members creating learning environments that are grounded in core ideas and in an awareness of how students' backgrounds and prior knowledge (cultural, personal, and academic) shape and connect to new knowledge acquisition.

In thinking through my own doctoral teaching, and in consulting with national experts, I became increasingly aware of the untapped pockets of practical wisdom on how to effectively teach research concepts and skills to undergraduate and graduate students. As such, this edited book brings together noted college and university professors to share detailed lesson plans about selected research concepts or skills, as well as their own inner logic regarding their intellectual preparation to do what they do. Although this book is targeted at education professors and undergraduate and graduate students, I believe that other practitioners who rely on education and social science research could also benefit from this book as their own learning of research could be enhanced through the lesson plans and analytic commentary available in each chapter.

FORMAT OF THE BOOK

The purpose of this edited book is to provide practical, detailed lesson plans on how to teach specific concepts and skills relevant to the research process in education (and relevant disciplines), as well as a means of hearing exemplary teachers talk through what they

INTRODUCTION

do and why they do it. The editor and the section co-editors are all experts in teaching and learning, research methods, and/or faculty in higher education and we have collaboratively vetted the lesson plans included in this book. Our vetting criteria included:

- The author(s) are noted for their effectiveness in pedagogical approaches, especially in the teaching of research.
- Each chapter follows a two-part structure, including a detailed, step-by-step lesson plan, followed by a discussion of the authors' responses to a consistent set of prompts about their intellectual preparation for the lesson.
- The lesson has been successfully applied to real-world practice (e.g., higher education courses, professional development sessions, individualized research trainings) and formally and informally evaluated as effective by students and/or the author(s) themselves.
- In hopes of addressing systemic and historical inequities in preparing students and future researchers, each chapter highlights ways to create more equitable learning spaces.
- The lesson includes, when possible, face-to-face and virtual teaching options.
- The lesson is grounded in education research, but generalizable to various disciplines/fields so that it is accessible regardless of the professor's discipline, training, or disposition.
- The full set of co-editors and authors represent diverse demographics, including disciplinary expertise, institutional type, geographical location, race/ethnicity, age, gender/gender identity, and years of experience.

This edited book contains eight sections, organized in a way that matches, albeit imperfectly, the process of conducting an education research study. In *Section I: Topics, Problems, and Research Questions*, the chapter topics include selecting a research topic through reflexivity and alignment exercises, articulating a problem and its rationale, and developing research questions. In *Section II: Literature Review and Theoretical/Conceptual Framework*, the lessons and analytic commentary examine how to: find and maintain resources through a puzzle metaphor, organize literature reviews into categories or themes, and align a theoretical or conceptual framework congruently in research. In *Section III: Research Design*, topics include moving from research questions to research designs, aligning theoretical frameworks and research designs, and establishing positionality and trustworthiness. *Section IV: Quantitative Methods* highlights lessons and commentary on quantitative methodology, including: applying basic multivariate analysis to real world situations, linear regression through student-driven, team-based learning, experiential learning of Exploratory Factor Analysis, and Difference-in-Differences models in quasi-experimental methods. Subsequently, *Section V: Qualitative Methodology* reviews skills in deep listening in interviews and focus groups, applying the visual arts to observations and fieldnotes skill development, elevating holistic approaches to document analysis, fostering theoretical congruence in critical and post-structural studies, and using epistemologies to guide coding and theme development. In *Section VI: Mixed Methods*, authors provide lessons and discussions of the intellectual preparation relevant to developing quantitative research questions and methodological choices in mixed methods studies, to moving from qualitative to quantitative approaches using a self-portrait exercise, and to presenting mixed methods findings through an integrated approach called Joint Display Analysis. *Section VII: Findings and Discussions* focuses on presenting quantitative and qualitative findings coherently, including through critical quantitative methods and qualitative visual storytelling, presenting the discussion through a block-by-block metaphor, developing skills in writing implications for theory and practice through hands-on graphic organizers, and writing for policymakers and practitioners (through donut memos!) respectively. *Section VIII: Special Section* highlights traditional and contemporary means of research dissemination and audience engagement, individualized research settings, community-engaged scholarship, and virtual support throughout the research process, including topics such as professional development opportunities to develop portfolios that demonstrate scholarly development, facilitating cultural competency through cross-cultural videos and story circles, fostering deep understanding of the role of research with policy decision-making, and promoting public writing among scholars. The *Conclusion* provides a summative analysis of the various chapters' contributions to conceptualizations of good teaching of social science research.

FORMAT OF EACH CHAPTER

Each chapter will follow a standard two-part structure that addresses the following sections:

- In the *first section of the chapter*, the author(s) will briefly introduce the topic and purpose of the lesson and then provide a detailed lesson plan that follows a standard template: (a) topic, (b) learning objectives, (c) materials required, (d) pre-class preparation for student and/or teacher, (e) description of lesson activities, (f) virtual adaptations, when possible, and (g) assessment.
- In the *second section of the chapter*, authors share their intellectual preparation for the lesson through a series of consistent prompts:

Core Ideas:

- What are the core ideas or foundational concepts of the lesson?

Learners:

- What previous learning do students bring to the concept/skill that might positively or negatively impact the teaching?
- What are possible misconceptions about the concept/skill that students might bring into the lesson?
- How does the lesson foster an equitable learning space (e.g., accounts for culturally-relevant teaching, reciprocal learning/funds of knowledge, etc.)?

Context (Bridging Core Ideas and Learners)

- How does the lesson find connections and work through differences between students' prior knowledge and/or misconceptions, and the new knowledge being presented?

INTRODUCTION

- How does the lesson foster an equitable learning space (e.g., accounts for alternative perspectives, reciprocal learning/funds of knowledge, etc.)?

HOW TO USE THIS BOOK

One of the strengths of this book is its versatility, not only in who benefits from the experts' lessons and subsequent commentary, but also in how to apply these to individual needs and contexts. Covering significant elements of the research process, the overlying structure of the book mirrors the structure of research reports, articles, and dissertations. With this structure, the book can be read and applied in its entirety as a general guide for the full research process (from the first to last chapter). However, the book's design also allows for each chapter to be standalone, thereby affording faculty members or students, according to their needs, to pull from the most relevant sections requiring reinforcement or modification to enhance their current lessons and practices. Although every researcher – and, as such, every chapter author – brings their own epistemological views into the research process, we have intentionally designed this book as an adaptable resource that can resonate with a variety of perspectives.

CONCLUSION

Learning how to create knowledge through research is not an easy task; teaching others how to do so is an equally challenging task. With this book's lessons plans and reflections from exemplary teachers of research as their own personal toolkit, it is my hope that teachers of education (or relevant disciplines) research methods – or students and practitioners – can feel equipped to effectively teach and/or learn research skills and concepts without relying on mass ingestion of chocolate dipped in peanut butter!

BIBLIOGRAPHY

American Academy of Arts and Sciences. (2017). *The future of undergraduate education: The future of America*. A report by the American Academy of Arts and Sciences. Retrieved online at https://www.amacad.org/cfue

Austin, A.E., Connelly, M.R., & Colbeck, C.L. (2008). Strategies for preparing integrated faculty: The Center for the Integration of Research, Teaching, and Learning. *New Directions for Teaching and Learning, 113,* 69–81.

Neumann, A. & Bolitzer, L. (2014). Finding and fostering learning: What college and university leaders need to know and what they can do. *New Directions for Higher Education,* No. 165. Wiley Periodicals.

Pallas, A.M., & Neumann, A. (2019). *Convergent teaching: Tools to spark deeper learning in college.* Johns Hopkins University Press.

Pallas, A. M., Neumann, A., & Campbell, C. M. (2017). *Policies and practices to support undergraduate teaching improvement.* An occasional paper for the American Academy of Arts and Sciences Commission on the Future of Undergraduate Education.

Shulman, L. (1986, Spring). Those who understand: A conception of teacher knowledge. *Educational Researcher, 15*(2), 4–14.

Shulman, L. (1987). Knowledge and teaching: Foundation of the new reform. *Harvard Educational Review, 57*(1), 1–22.

Shulman, L. (1999). Taking learning seriously. *Change, 31*(4), 10–17.

Shulman, L. (2004). Problem-based learning: The pedagogies of uncertainty. In P. Hutchings (Ed.). *Teaching as community property: Essays on higher education,* (pp. 49–62). Jossey-Bass.

Section I

Topics, Problems, and Research Questions

Section Editor: Katie Conway

1

Introduction to Section I

Research Topics, Problems, and Questions

Katie Conway

Identifying and honing research topics and research questions are foundational skills in the practice of research; without getting these pieces right, the rest of the puzzle rarely fits together. Yet novice researchers often struggle with these skills: being focused and specific enough in their topics to craft answerable questions, while staying true to their own interests. The chapters in this section provide a scaffolding to demonstrate how to help students do just this. The exercises build on one another, allowing for students to: consider what they as individuals bring to their field of study, practice focusing their gaze on defined and contained topics, and design and select research questions from the many possibilities within a given topic.

At the end of each semester of an introductory course on the teaching of research methods in higher education, my students have a poster session; even though they have not collected data that semester, they go through the practice of sharing their research topic, questions, literature reviews, and proposed methodologies with their classmates and other visitors. During that session, I pull up the students' initial discussion board postings from the first weeks in the semester where they describe their research interests. I read out loud, standing in front of each poster, the initial topic and the final one. Almost without exception, the students began with broad, amorphous topics – often divorced from their personal interests because of prior beliefs that they must be "objective" in their research and interpreting that to mean they cannot bring themselves into it at all – and ended with specific, actionable research questions that they care deeply about. Their proposed methodologies at this stage may be squishy or inappropriate, but that's fine: to do research, they will need to go on to do much more study. My intent in this first semester – as in this first section of this book – is to drive home the foundational idea that a researcher must marry their own interest (and, indeed, perspectives) with a commitment to being precise, specific, and far narrower than they may initially wish.

I have found that my students arrive with topics that *sound* important – often because of their breadth. I ask them to imagine sitting at an extended family gathering where their fictional "Aunt Edna" (everyone has one, whether an actual relative or not) asks them what they're studying. When they reply with a broad topic – "I am studying how to increase

DOI: 10.4324/b23320-3

opportunities in higher education for historically marginalized students!" – Aunt Edna is THRILLED. They're going to solve this huge problem! But, we realize in class, those topics are not – in that form – researchable and that, in order to get to a real research problem, they must get to something *so much narrower*, so that their response to Aunt Edna will invariably result in her scratching her head and saying, "Well, THAT doesn't sound like it's that important." I tell them that it is in that moment – when they've disappointed Aunt Edna (or the fictional one in their mind) – when they know they have gotten narrow enough to actually have an answerable question.

CHAPTER OVERVIEWS

Although the chapters that follow bring different perspectives to bear on their topics, several threads run through them: passion and its role in choosing a topic, the need to vigorously narrow a topic to make it answerable, and the acknowledgement that any topic encompasses many possible research questions – not all of which can be studied at once.

In her chapter, Jones discusses the role of the personal, and indeed of personal passions, in the choosing of an area to study. She states that, "empathy, patience, and encouragement are key in supporting students who may have been socialized not to think of their own interests and passions as acceptable considerations for research"; the same could be said for many of us teaching this topic.

Natow's chapter provides a framework for "students to articulate their understanding regarding key concepts of **narrowing, alignment, evidence**, and **importance**." She acknowledges the challenge students often have in moving from a broad topic of personal interest (or a "passion," to use Jones' term) to a contained, studyable topic. The lesson plan in Chapter 3 provides a solid scaffold to help students disappoint their own Aunt Ednas.

Reddy's chapter notes that, "students struggle to move from an interest – what Jones calls in Chapter 2 a 'personal passion' – and a narrowed version of that topic (as scaffolded by Natow in Chapter 3) to actionable, studyable research questions," and "suggest[s] in this chapter a visual relationship between these concepts, with the topic conceived of as the trunk of a tree – providing the core strength to their work – and branches as individual research questions that may be related to the tree itself and to one another in different ways

COLLECTIVE CONTRIBUTION

The lesson plans in the next three chapters provide a clear map for teaching students how to narrow their topics to something researchable – all while respecting the individual interests they bring and the rigor of the field.

2

From Personal Passion to Hot Topics

Selecting a Topic to Research

Sosanya Jones

INTRODUCTION

So often, research methods are taught as if the practice exists in the absence of individual perspectives and students are taught that reflecting on their own experiences should not be a part of the process. But part of the journey toward developing your identity as a researcher – and of selecting which topics you will spend your time dedicated to studying – is becoming aware of yourself and how your background experiences and perspective can shape your interests in different topics. This **reflexivity** is an interactive process, meaning, it is something you will return to and engage in again and again throughout the life of a research project. Reflexivity will be discussed in more detail later in this chapter, but for now, take a few moments to ask yourself, "What topics light a fire under my feet, get my blood pumping, and pique my interest when I talk to my friends, colleagues, and family?"

This chapter will highlight the role of reflexivity – of considering yourself and your own passions – in selecting a research topic. Included are notes on the countervailing tension that pulls scholars away from those topics that call them toward so-called hot topics, defined as a highly covered and discussed topical issues or problems. This chapter's lesson focuses on a scaffolded process of bringing reflexivity into research in a way that foregrounds the researcher's own experience while ensuring rigor and relevance (Neumann & Pallas, 2006).

DOI: 10.4324/b23320-4

LESSON PLAN

Topic	*Selecting and Making Relevant a Research Topic*
Learning Objectives	• Understanding the role that reflexivity plays in identifying topics and problems that can be examined using research. • Understanding how a researcher's background experiences and role in the research process can help to identify topics/problem to study. • Findings ways to highlight the relevance and need for a researcher's topic of choice.
Needed Materials	Depending on the selected format of instruction, the instructor should have pre-prepared: • Online discussion section on the course's learning management system (for use with a laptop, desktop, tablet, phone). • Printed questions for a guided writing exercise. • Overhead slides listing each set of questions (see Activities section) for a guided face-to-face exercise (individually, one on one, or in a group).

Pre-lesson Preparation	• Before utilizing this activity, instructors may want to engage students in a discussion about the importance of a researcher's positionality (i.e., how the social-historical-political location of a researcher influences their orientations) and reflexivity to the research process. Suggested readings on reflexivity can be found below.
	• This lesson may be enhanced after a discussion about the concept of research paradigms and how paradigms shape the way researchers look at problems, but this is optional.
	• A discussion of positionality would also be a good segue into this lesson, but it is not necessary.
	• Suggested reading, but not required:
	   ◦ Ettl, K. (2020). Be passionate about your research topics and share this passion. In *How To Make Your Doctoral Research Relevant* (pp. 104–105). Edward Elgar Publishing.
	   ◦ Peshkin, A. (1988). In search of subjectivity: One's own. *Educational Researcher*, 17 (7), 17–22.
	   ◦ Sandberg, J., & Alvesson, M. (2013). Constructing research questions: Doing interesting research. *Constructing Research Questions*, 1–152.
	• All activities suggested can be done before, during, and after class. It could be helpful to do all three to emphasize the iterative nature of choosing a topic and to affirm that it is part of the process for students to change their minds, brainstorm, and adjust.
	• Having students do a brief annotated bibliography of topics of interest to their "hot topics" list may be helpful in providing examples of how they can create meaningful rationales for topics of interest to them.

Activities	**Reflexivity Exercises**:
	The instructor highlights the following points and provides time for students' questions:
	• Reflexivity is the process and awareness of your effect on the research process and outcome.
	• Researchers should engage in reflexivity throughout the entire research process, including identifying a topic and problem, designing their research project, engaging in data analysis, and reporting.
	• There are three types of reflexivity to be considered when thinking about problems that can be researched:
	   ◦ **Personal**: considering the ways in which individual researchers are influenced by their own beliefs and opinions.
	   ◦ **Epistemological**: considering the ways in which knowledge has been generated in the study.
	   ◦ **Positional**: examining the researcher's social place in relation to the research and those researched (i.e., asking questions about one own's social status in terms of class, education, race, ethnicity, nationality, religion, sexuality, gender, and ability).

FROM PERSONAL PASSION TO HOT TOPICS

Topic	Selecting and Making Relevant a Research Topic
	Next, the instructor guides the student(s) through a three-part exercise that asks them to reflect on their own personal, epistemological, and positional reflexivity.

1. The first exercise is the **Personal Reflexivity Exercise**, which helps students identify potential topics and problems for a research study. Students first independently write their responses for 10–15 minutes, and then share in pairs/small groups, or to the whole class. The questions include:
   - What topics do you believe need to be investigated, understood, or conceptualized better within your topical area(s) of interest?
   - How do these topics affect you personally? Professionally?
   - What are your assumptions, experiences, and biases about these topics?
   - What do you hope to contribute to the field and your own understanding regarding these topics?
2. Following the **Personal Reflexivity Exercise**, the instructor will lead the class in an **Epistemological Reflexivity Exercise**, which includes questions for identifying potential problems and evidence. Students first independently write their responses for 8–10 minutes, and then share in pairs/small groups or to the whole class for approximately 10–15 minutes. The questions include:
   - What is known about the identified topics you listed above?
   - What do you consider to be the sources of knowledge about these topics?
   - What do you consider valid evidence about these topics?
   - Why do you consider these sources of knowledge and evidence valid and credible?
   - What is still unknown, poorly understood, or misunderstood about the topics you listed?
3. Following the **Epistemological Reflexivity Exercise**, the instructor will lead the class in a **Positional Reflexivity Exercise**, which includes questions for identifying how students' own social markers influence their approach to research studies. Students first independently write their responses for 10 minutes, and share in pairs/small groups or to the whole class. The questions include:
   - Describe yourself in terms of your social markers (i.e., socioeconomic background, religion, gender, race, ethnicity, nationality, sexual orientation, professional role, age, and ability, etc.).
   - How have these social markers shaped your values and experiences with the issues you listed?
   - How do these social markers inform how you understand the issues, challenges, and unknowns you listed?

Following the three-part reflexivity exercise, the instructor then asks students to rank their top three topics for a research study. With each of the top three ranked topics, students will fill in the following script:

Within the topical area of **[insert name of topical area]**, I am interested in examining the issue of **[insert issue name]** more closely because **[insert what remains unknown, understudied, under conceptualized, or misunderstood]**, and understanding this issue better can help inform **[the larger, abstract problem it can address]**.

With three topics identified (in the above script), students now turn to articulating a researchable problem which will be reviewed in Chapter 3. In order to do so, the instructor guides students in an activity to ensure their topics/problems are relevant.

Topic	Selecting and Making Relevant a Research Topic
	Making Your Topic "Hot" Exercise: The instructor will note the following points: • Just because a topical area of interest may not be "hot" right now does not mean it will remain that way. National research agendas shift with time, political climate, social movements, and the emergence of new problems, but part of a researcher's job is to raise awareness and communicate why their research matters now. • Researchers can elevate awareness and concern about issues that were previously unknown. They can also disrupt devaluation, marginalization, and ignorance about a topic/problem or group of people by connecting them to a phenomenon of current interest. • One of the best ways of teasing out what may be "hot" about your topic to others is to begin to look at how your topic is connected or contradicts the hot topic list. The instructor guides students in a reflective exercise on "hot topics" by asking students to consider their three ranked topics. Students first independently write their responses for 5 minutes, and then share in pairs/small groups, or to the whole class, for approximately 10–15 minutes. The questions include: • What are "hot topics" in your field of study right now? • How do the issues you identified relate, however close or tangentially, to any of these hot topics? • Is there a way you can utilize one of the hot topic areas to help frame why your topic of interest is important or should be considered in understanding that topic?
Virtual Adaptations	• This lesson can be adapted for use in an asynchronous online discussion board format found on the learning management systems of most higher education courses. • The four sets of reflective questions can be used in virtual break-out groups (for example, on Zoom) consisting of pairs or groups of three–four people. • If students are stuck or unsure about topics of relevance to them and of interest to the public and policymakers, they can scan popular trade periodicals to their field and the press. This can be done both in face-to-face classroom time or asynchronously.
Assessment	• Instructors can assess students in multiple ways, depending on their instructional preferences and considering student's learning styles. Formative responses in class promote group engagement and sharing of ideas. They also model the importance of receiving feedback at all phases of the research process. However, instructors may also prefer to write up scripts for each activity so that students can have time to think through their ideas, read the work and ideas of others, and provide written comments. • In addition to the above assessments, I strongly suggest that instructors employ a culturally responsive framework for assessing this assignment. An example is located at the Center for Assessment: https://www.nciea.org/blog/classroom-assessment/culturally-responsive-classroom-assessment-framework.

INTELLECTUAL PREPARATION FOR LESSON

Core Ideas

This lesson homes in on two core ideas: the idea that reflexivity has a role in research, and the skill of aligning one's research passion to current "hot topics" when applicable. These are both discussed as follows.

Understanding Positionality as a Mechanism for Balancing Reflection and Relevance
The first core idea of this lesson, as represented by the three reflective exercises that ground the lesson, emphasizes honoring one's authentic self, interests, and own ways of knowing and learning, and in turn, how to converge and align research topics and problems with relevant personal and professional goals (see Fattore, 2021). Toward this end, this chapter will help instructors consider how to: (a) engage students in reflexivity in order to begin the process of cultivating a researcher identity; (b) help students reflect on their epistemic positionality and how it may inform the selection of their research topics and problems (Sandberg & Alvesson, 2013); and (c) enhance students' understanding of the importance of considering the range of factors that inform the way problems are viewed and framed. These include: the way the literature defines the problem, the way contemporary practices define or refer to the problem, personal experiences with the topic, theoretical conceptualizations of the problem, and the identification of research gaps (Grieshaber, 2022).

Historically, researchers, and researchers in training, have been taught that research is separate from the person doing the research and that including one's own positionality or research interests/passions is unacceptable and amounts to a failure to remain objective. However, one of this lesson's core goals is to help students unlearn this belief by embracing reflexive aspects of research to inform the research design process. In particular, this lesson will highlight how attending to one's positionality plays a valuable role in the research design. Namely, being able to draw upon one's own experiences when choosing a topic can provide students with helpful and healthy examples of engaging in the process of aligning one's interests and questions with research goals and later developing good research questions. Instructors should also consider their positionality in terms of knowledge acquisition. Although instructors may now be seasoned researchers, or at least be more experienced, their students are likely novices who have never engaged in the process of research or have only worked on an established research project developed by a faculty member. Empathy, patience, and encouragement are key in supporting students who may have been socialized not to think of their own interests and passions as acceptable considerations for research.

On the Role of "Relevance"
One of the most insidious and detrimental adages about conducting research is the advice, so often given to new scholars, that they must find a "hot topic" to study. Make no mistake about it: understanding the relevance and need for a given research topic is critically important in framing the rationale for research and appealing to those who may not realize its significance. Understanding what makes a topic relevant can open minds and funding opportunities that support your work. But – here's the rub – the topical areas we think are important may be worlds apart from the topical areas other people think are worthwhile to study. Policymakers, foundations, government agencies, and the media often shape discourse about what research is needed, which also informs and shapes funding priorities for research. This, in turn, can determine which topics are considered a priority for professional associations, journals, and conferences.

For those who wish to conduct research, this can create a real tension that cannot be ignored. Researchers may feel pressured or compelled by the necessity to stay relevant to abandon the interests that led them to pursue research and instead search for a "hot topic." But this approach to identifying research topics is shortsighted and a recipe for a career of dissatisfaction. At best, jumping on every hot topic just to chase funding and fame can lead to shallow and shortsighted engagement in an area of study, and at worst, it can result in disingenuous and disconnected research that has little meaning and/or misinforms policy and practice.

As clichéd as this may sound, it is also true that as a researcher, you should stay true to yourself and your research goals. Remember the topics and questions that excite you, that led you to your pursuit of knowledge and interest in research. These topics and questions are important, even if the rest of the world may not yet realize it. When we give in to the fervor to research "what's hot" without regard to the things we truly care about, we can sabotage the very goals that brought us to engage in research in the first place and thwart our potential contribution to the field. Our desire to shed light on issues we know in our bones are important can lead us down a path toward deep reflection and discovery that can ultimately glean new knowledge and improved policy, practice, and theory.

Learners

Prior to this lesson, students are likely to have confronted ideas that could help or hinder their own learning of reflexivity in the research process, and their own skill development in appropriately aligning their research to current hot topics.

In terms of helping learning, students probably already have lived experiences and perspectives that can inform their ability to identify viable research topics and problems. For example, many great dissertation topics are derived from personal practical and professional experiences within education, either as a teacher or as a student. Additionally, students are probably already aware of the importance of making research relevant and applicable to real world problems and this can be an asset in engaging in this topic. Students are often pursuing degrees so that they can make a difference or impact. Many may see their research as an opportunity to put research to good use to address a problem.

In terms of hindering learning, students may enter into this lesson with preconceptions about what topics and problems are appropriate and acceptable to be considered for research. For example, students are often taught to distance themselves from research by writing in the third person, to exclude their own positionality and interests in the topic, not understanding how these things can strengthen their rationale for the topic. Students may also come to this lesson with previous training on specific approaches to research (such as the scientific approach) and this consideration of their own interests, experiences, and perspectives may be confusing or seem contrary to their previous understanding.

Additionally, there are also a few possible misconceptions about the concepts/skills that students might bring into the lesson. For instance, students may be socialized to believe they have to have a hot and relevant topic and that their own research interests are not important or irrelevant. Furthermore, this assignment may be difficult for some students because they are not used to thinking about the framing of problems as malleable and dependent on multiple factors. Finally, students may struggle with moving from

FROM PERSONAL PASSION TO HOT TOPICS

conceptualizing large abstract problems they want to address to more concrete researchable problems.

This lesson fosters equitable learning by embracing and encouraging students to embrace their own interests and experiences as a way of informing their selection of topics and problems. This includes embracing their own cultural understanding, experiences, and ways of knowing (De Bie et al., 2019).

Context

The lesson finds connections and works through differences between students' prior knowledge and/or misconceptions and the new knowledge being presented, encouraging students to embrace their own interests and experiences as a way of informing their selection of topics and problems. This includes valuing their own cultural understanding, experiences and ways of knowing (Hunter, 2002).This lesson fosters an equitable learning space by emphasizing the importance of listening to different and devalued experiences, ways of knowing, and perspectives in order to identify topics and problems that can be researched (Fine, et al., 2021).

The activities in this lesson are valuable regardless of the research paradigm. Both qualitative and quantitative researchers can benefit from engaging in reflexive exercises that heighten their awareness of why they want, and ought, to research a particular topic.

I hope this exercise helps students identify a few key topical areas of interest to them, important issues they want to examine further related to those topics, and potential ways they can connect these topics and issues to current hot topics to emphasize the relevance of their research interests. The next two chapters will assist students in identifying and articulating a researchable problem as well as a problem statement that includes a strong and compelling rationale for why a research question is important. The reflexivity practiced in this chapter will be useful in enabling students to refine their interests into researchable problems, as well as to connect those problems to rationales that matter to them and the world.

BIBLIOGRAPHY

Agee, J. (2009). Developing qualitative research questions: A reflective process. *International Journal of Qualitative Studies in Education*, 22(4), 431–447.

De Bie, A., Marquis, E., Cook-Sather, A., & Luqueño, L. P. (2019). Valuing knowledge (s) and cultivating confidence: Contributions of student–faculty pedagogical partnerships to epistemic justice. In J. Hoffman, P. Blessinger, & M. Mokhanya (Eds.), *Strategies for fostering inclusive classrooms in higher education: International perspectives on equity and inclusion* (pp. 35–48). Bingly, UK: Emerald Publishing Limited.

Ettl, K. (2020). Be passionate about your research topics and share this passion. In David Urbano & Friederike Welter (Eds.), *How to make your doctoral research relevant* (pp. 104–105). Northampton MA: Edward Elgar Publishing.

Fattore, C. (2021). Teaching research design with authenticity. In Daniel J. Mallinson, Julia Marin Hellwege, & Eric D. Loepp (Eds.), *The Palgrave handbook of political research pedagogy* (pp. 141–149). Palgrave Macmillan, Cham.

Fine, M., Torre, M. E., Oswald, A. G., & Avory, S. (2021). Critical participatory action research: Methods and praxis for intersectional knowledge production. *Journal of Counseling Psychology*, 68(3), 344.

Flick, U. (2018). Chapter 6. In *An introduction to qualitative research*, 6th Edition. SAGE Publications, Inc. ISBN-13: 978-1526445650.

Grieshaber, S. (2022). Equity and research design. In S.A. Rolfe & I. Siraj-Blatchford (Eds.), *Doing early childhood research* (pp. 177–191). Routledge.

Hunter, M. (2002). Rethinking epistemology, methodology, and racism: Or, is White sociology really dead?. *Race and Society*, 5(2), 119–138.

Maxey, I. (1999). Beyond boundaries? Activism, academia, reflexivity and research. *Area*, 31(3), 199–208.

Maxwell, J. (2013). Chapter 4 and Exercise 4.1. In *Qualitative research design: An interactive approach* (*Applied social research methods*) (p. 84), 3rd Edition. San Francisco: SAGE Publications, Inc. ISBN-10: 1412981190; ISBN-13: 978-141298119

Neumann, A., & Pallas, A. M. (2006). Windows of possibility: Perspectives on the construction of educational researchers. In C.F. Conrad & R.C. Serlin (Eds.), *The SAGE handbook for research in education* (pp. 429–449). San Francisco: Sage.

Peshkin, A. (1988). In search of subjectivity: One's own. *Educational Researcher*, 17(7), 17–22.

Sandberg, J., & Alvesson, M. (2013). Constructing research questions: Doing interesting research. *Constructing Research Questions* (pp. 1–152). San Francisco: Sage.

Themelis, S. (2009). Sage handbook for research in education. *Educate*, 9(1), 48–49.

3

Articulating a Research Problem and Its Rationale

Using Graphical Depictions, Exemplars, and Students' Own Work

Rebecca S. Natow

INTRODUCTION

Articulating a research problem and its rationale can be a challenge for novice researchers. Often, students arrive at graduate school with particular academic interests and an idea, even if vague, of the research topic they would like to pursue. Once students have reviewed relevant literature and narrowed their topic to a particular area of inquiry, it becomes time to state the research problem and demonstrate its importance. Articulating a specific research problem involves not only identifying an issue in need of further research, but also justifying that research by explaining the topic's importance and implications – that is, answering the *So What?* question (e.g., Selwyn, 2014). A well-articulated problem statement presents evidence of a need for research, helps the researcher to articulate a study's purpose, and provides context and framing for particular research questions (Merriam & Tisdell, 2016).

My experience teaching research methods has shown that demonstrating research problems through graphical depictions and examples helps students to understand the process of how to articulate the problem and its rationale. Asking students to write problem and purpose statements based on their own research topic or area of academic interest can help bring this process to life. This chapter provides a sample lesson plan for helping students learn to articulate a research problem using graphical depictions, examples, and students' own work.

DOI: 10.4324/b23320-5

LESSON PLAN

Topic	*Articulating a Research Problem and Its Rationale*
Learning Objectives	• Students will distinguish between a problem statement and a purpose statement. • Students will explain the *So What?* question with regard to their research topic. • Students will read, write, and critique research problem and purpose statements. • Students will identify and articulate a research problem and purpose statement that will precede their study's specific research questions.
Needed Materials	• Projector, interactive white board, or similar device. • Examples of exemplary problem and purpose statements in actual published studies from research within the students' field of study (e.g., educational research when teaching in a school of education; a nursing study when teaching nursing students). These examples should represent the diversity of subjects and cultures in the field. • Classroom space for students to discuss problem and purpose statements in small groups.

Pre-lesson Preparation	• Students should be assigned reading materials to prepare them for identifying and articulating a research problem and drafting problem and purpose statements. Examples include: Baldwin (2018), Chapter 4 of Booth et al. (2016), Chapter 6 of Creswell and Poth (2018), Fain (2017), Irlbeck and Thornton (2012), Merriam and Tisdell's (2016) section on "The Research Problem" (pp. 76–82), and Newman and Covrig (2013).
	• Prepare several discussion questions to share with students prior to class. These discussion questions will help frame students' reading of assigned resources and prepare them for class-wide discussion. Examples of discussion questions include:
	  ○ What do we know about the process of articulating a research problem? What are the steps in doing this, and what factors should we be thinking about?
	  ○ How do scholarly literature and theory help us to think about possible research problems?
	  ○ What is a problem statement?
	  ○ What is a purpose statement?
	  ○ How do the problem and purpose statements help with framing research questions?
	• This lesson plan assumes students have at least a general idea for a topic they would like to research and that they have reviewed at least some scholarly literature related to that topic.
	• Prior to class, students should be assigned to write a first draft of problem and purpose statements based on their topic of interest, literature they have read related to the topic, and assigned readings regarding articulating a research problem (such as those identified above). Students should be informed that this will be a first draft and that they will be permitted to revise and resubmit the assignment after the class session. Students should be instructed to have a copy of their problem and purpose statements available during the class session.

Activities	The in-class activities are divided into five parts: (1) introduction and class-wide discussion; (2) graphical depictions; (3) examples; (4) small-group discussion; and (5) reports from small-group discussions and closing questions. At the heart of this lesson are graphical depictions, examples, and students' own work. **Introduction and class-wide discussion**: Begin with a class-wide discussion guided by the discussion questions provided to the students before class – see questions in Pre-lesson Preparation section. This should be an interactive dialogue, engaging as many students as possible in the class-wide discussion.

ARTICULATING A RESEARCH PROBLEM AND ITS RATIONALE

Topic	Articulating a Research Problem and Its Rationale
	Use the discussion questions as a guide to move the conversation forward regarding identifying and articulating a research problem, providing students with key information from the methodological literature, and getting the conversation back on track if it should wander off course. Talking points about each of the discussion questions include the following:

- *What do we know about the process of articulating a research problem? What are the steps in doing this, and what factors should we be thinking about?*
  - The process involves: First, identifying a general topic of interest to the researcher; second, narrowing the topic to a specific area capable and worthy of research; and third, articulating the purpose of the study (Baldwin, 2018; Merriam & Tisdell, 2016).
  - Research problems may be identified by consulting prior literature and theory, considering problems in professional practice or current events, and asking people who have knowledge about the topic (Booth et al., 2016; Fain, 2017; Irlbeck & Thornton, 2012). Researchers should also consider factors such as the policy and practice implications of a potential research problem.
  - A vital factor to consider is a research topic's importance (Baldwin, 2018; Booth et al., 2016). The researcher must articulate a justification for moving forward with the research – to answer the *So What?* question (e.g., Selwyn, 2014).
- *How do scholarly literature and theory help us to think about possible research problems?*
  - Reviewing the literature helps a researcher to understand a research topic better, to learn what is already known about a particular topic, to understand what is not yet known, and to identify areas in need of future research (Booth et al., 2016; Fain, 2017; Irlbeck & Thornton, 2012).
  - Merriam and Tisdell (2016) note three important aspects of a research problem: (1) context, or background of the general research topic; (2) gap in the literature, or an under-researched topic; and (3) significance, or a problem that is important. Prior literature and theory can provide information about these aspects.
  - Concepts from the theoretical literature can help a researcher consider how theories may be applied to particular problems of practice or explain a process or phenomenon within the researcher's topic area (Fain, 2017).
- *What is a problem statement?*
  - Students should define "problem statement" in their own words; however, having definitions from the methodological literature available during this exercise can provide the instructor with prompts and follow-up questions to ensure students identify all important aspects of the definition.
  - For example, Fain (2017) writes that a "problem statement makes a case for conducting the study" and that in citing relevant literature it presents "a significant researchable problem" (p. 78).
  - Merriam and Tisdell (2016) write that the problem statement "lays out the logic of the study," and is often constructed with "a funnel shape – broad at the top and narrow at the bottom," with the "top" being a "general area of interest" and the bottom becoming narrower, "directing the reader toward the specific question you have" (p. 77).
  - Research problems may not be problematic in the common sense of the word. Creswell and Poth (2018) write that rather than thinking of the problem statement as a "problem," it should be conceived as "the need for the study or creating a rationale for the need for the study" (p. 129).
- *What is a purpose statement?*
  - As with the problem statement, students should define a *"purpose statement"* in their own words, but having definitions from the methodological literature available during this exercise can provide the instructor with prompts and follow-up questions to ensure students identify all important aspects of the definition.
  - For example, Baldwin (2018) defines the purpose statement as "a clear, concise statement of what the study will accomplish, usually in one sentence" (p. 10).
  - Purpose statements often begin with the phrase, "The purpose of this study is…" and then state the study's goals (Baldwin, 2018, p. 10; Merriam & Tisdell, 2016, p. 77).

Topic	Articulating a Research Problem and Its Rationale

	• *How do the problem and purpose statements help with framing research questions?*
	  ◦ Although this lesson plan does not include research questions, the problem and purpose statements give rise to research questions, so it is appropriate to ask students to consider how the problem and purpose statements do this.
	  ◦ Emphasize the importance of aligning the study's research questions with the problem and purpose statements, such that a reader of those statements can see how the research questions logically flow from the problem and purpose statements (Baldwin, 2018; Creswell & Poth, 2018; Newman & Covrig, 2013).
	Graphical depictions:
	• Present graphical depictions of the relationship between research problems, purpose statements, and research questions. Graphical depictions are particularly useful for visually demonstrating the importance of *narrowing* and *alignment* in articulating a research problem: As the researcher moves from problem statement to purpose statement to research question, the focus becomes narrower, and all three components must be aligned with each other (Creswell & Poth, 2018).
	• Some methodological books and articles contain graphical depictions that are useful in this regard. For example, Creswell and Poth (2018) provide a graphic of narrowing a study's focus from a research problem to a purpose statement to research questions. Their graphic entitled "Interrelating Study Research Problem, Purpose, and Questions," is an upside-down triangle, with the research problem depicted at the top (in the largest third of the triangle), the purpose statement in the middle (where the triangle begins to narrow), and the research questions in the lowest third, demonstrating how these questions are even more narrow and precise than the purpose statement (p. 129). This graphic is useful in showing students how a research problem narrows to focus on a study's purpose, and then narrows further to arrive at specific research questions.
	• Instructors may also develop their own graphical depictions to illustrate the relationship between problem statements, purpose statements, and research questions. Similar to Creswell and Poth's (2018) triangle, funnel-shaped graphics (Merriam & Tisdell, 2016) or concentric circles are other examples of useful depictions.
	Examples:
	• Provide several examples of exemplary problem and purpose statements and discuss them with the class before convening small-group discussion. According to Creswell and Poth (2018), a problem statement should present "a rationale for the need for the study," explaining what the study is about and why it is important (p. 129). An ideal purpose statement succinctly states "the major objective or intent" of the research (Creswell & Poth, 2018, p. 132). Clear problem and purpose statements that reflect these characteristics may be used as examples in class, preferably in the students' field of study. For instance, when teaching doctoral students in educational leadership and policy, one text I use for this purpose is Hollingworth's (2012) article "Why leadership matters."
	Small-group discussion:
	• Divide students into small groups to share and discuss their previously drafted problem and purpose statements. Instruct students to provide each other with feedback based on the following factors: (1) Are the problem and purpose statements clear? (2) Does the problem statement present an important research problem in need of study? (3) Is the problem statement grounded in prior literature and/or theory? (4) Does the purpose statement follow logically from the problem statement?
	• The instructor should monitor small-group discussions and answer any questions students may have.
	Reports from small-group discussions and closing questions:
	• Resume discussion with the class. Ask students to report to the full class on how well they believe the small-group discussion went with respect to understanding problem and purpose statements and providing feedback on each other's drafts. Answer any remaining questions from students before dismissing class.

ARTICULATING A RESEARCH PROBLEM AND ITS RATIONALE

Topic	Articulating a Research Problem and Its Rationale
Virtual Adaptations	<u>Synchronous online adaptations</u>: These discussions and activities can easily be converted to a synchronous online course, using an internet video-conferencing platform such as Zoom or Microsoft Teams. Pre-lesson preparation remains the same for students and faculty. Class-wide discussion can occur with the discussion questions as a guide and students responding via a "raise hand" or similar feature. Small-group discussion can occur in online breakout rooms. <u>Asynchronous online adaptations</u>: Asynchronous classes often consist of "modules" that include certain activities to be completed within a set period of time. Class-wide discussion is not held in real time in an asynchronous class; therefore, this lesson's class-wide and small-group discussions would need to be adjusted for an asynchronous environment. Class-wide discussion may involve the instructor posting questions on a discussion board or as part of an online presentation that allows commenting, and asking students to respond to the questions and to each other's comments. The instructor should actively monitor and participate in this discussion, using the talking points provided above as a guide. Small-group discussions in an asynchronous environment may involve asking students to write a first draft of their problem and purpose statements toward the beginning of the module, and asking students to post their draft on a discussion board that will be accessible to other students in their small group. Students should then read other students' drafts, provide feedback on those drafts, and engage in discussions around those drafts. Again, the instructor should play an active role in these discussions.
Assessment	<u>Formative assessment</u>: Students' first drafts of the problem and purpose statements should be a formative assessment. It will be important for students to complete this assignment prior to attending class, and the instructor should provide feedback on the draft. However, this draft should not be graded, and students must be given an opportunity to revise and resubmit the statements. <u>Summative assessment</u>: Students' subsequent drafts of the problem and purpose statement may be graded. Another option is to have students include their revised problem and purpose statements as part of a full research proposal due later in the term.

INTELLECTUAL PREPARATION FOR LESSON

Core Ideas

The core concepts that are foundational to this lesson are *narrowing, alignment, evidence,* and *importance.*

Articulating a research problem involves *narrowing* a topic area and body of literature to a particular problem. This lesson will encourage students to focus on a particular issue as the research problem. Reading assignments such as Merriam and Tisdell (2016) specifically state that describing a research problem is a process that begins "broad" and ends "narrow" (p. 77). Discussion questions as above will help students think about how a research problem is informed by, but a narrow segment of, broader literature. Graphical depictions such as Creswell and Poth's (2018) upside-down triangle reinforce how a study's purpose is narrowed from the problem statement.

A research problem must *align* with a study's purpose and, ultimately, its research questions (Newman & Covrig, 2013). Asking students to read and discuss the methodological literature on problem and purpose statements, and to discuss the questions above, will help students understand the relationship between a research problem, a study's purpose, and research questions. The same graphical depiction described in the previous paragraph will reiterate this point, as should the instructor when providing feedback on students' first drafts of their problem and purpose statements.

Students must also provide *evidence* to support the assertions they make about the research problem – to describe it, to demonstrate its importance, and to show it is a "problem" in need of research (Creswell & Poth, 2018, p. 129). The discussion question above prompts students to think about how scholarly literature contributes to articulating a research problem. Additionally, the assignment to write a draft problem statement before class will have students engage with the literature to provide support for their statements of fact.

Finally, students must articulate the *importance* of a research problem – to answer the *So What?* question. In the conversations about discussion questions above, it must be emphasized that a study's importance is a critical factor to be considered when articulating a research problem. The assignment to write problem and purpose statements will provide students with the experience of justifying the importance of their chosen topic. Should students not do so in their initial draft, feedback from small-group discussion and the instructor on the formative assessment should alert students to the need for stating the research topic's importance.

Learners

Previous Learning and Possible Misconceptions
Students are likely to arrive at this class with a general idea of what they want to study. They may have reviewed literature related to their topic of interest. This lesson asks students to write problem and purpose statements based on a research topic of their choice, which is designed to enhance students' interest in the assignment. Students will therefore bring their prior knowledge of the topic with them to this lesson. This prior knowledge may be helpful, as familiarity with the topic and its prior literature can help students formulate the research problem and identify evidence from previous research to support the problem statement.

However, students' own biases about a topic of their choice may negatively influence the lesson plan. For example, bias may prevent students from seeing particular aspects of the problem, or make them believe something is a problem when it is not, or not view something as problematic when it may be. Additionally, students may have misconceptions that a research problem must be something troublesome or severe. The word "problem" has negative connotations, whereas a research problem may not be negative at all, but something important and in need of new research (Creswell & Poth, 2018, p. 129).

Context

Prior Knowledge and Possible Misconceptions
This lesson plan both builds upon students' prior knowledge and helps to address misconceptions about research problems.

ARTICULATING A RESEARCH PROBLEM AND ITS RATIONALE

Again, this lesson invites students to write problem and purpose statements on research topics of their choice. This assignment builds on students' prior knowledge about the research topic and challenges them to use evidence to articulate the research problem and develop a clear statement of purpose. The core concept of *narrowing* their topic area to particular problem and purpose statements – as emphasized by discussion questions and graphical depictions – prompts students to take their prior knowledge of a topic and focus on an area that is perhaps most in need of research.

Regarding misconceptions about research problems, this lesson specifically addresses the fact that research problems need not be negative in the traditional sense of the word "problem" in response to discussion question (b) above. Assigned readings may also address this point. An example is the chapter in Creswell and Poth (2018) that also contains the graphical depiction of the upside-down triangle to demonstrate the narrowing relationship between purpose and problem statements. Bringing this possible misconception to students' attention through reading assignments and specifically addressing it during class-wide discussion may help to correct the misconception.

Equitable Learning Space

This lesson makes an effort to foster an equitable learning environment. Different types of activities – most prominently graphical depictions, examples, and students' own work – are included, which are useful for reaching different kinds of learners (Sankey et al., 2011). The examples of problem and purpose statements from a variety of published studies should represent the diversity of subjects and cultures within the field, as this is a strategy used by teachers who employ culturally relevant practices (Ladson-Billings, 2014). Fostering collaboration among classmates – as through this lesson's small-group discussions – is another practice that aligns with equitable learning environments (Morrison et al., 2008).

Allowing students to choose their own research topic and work on it throughout the course enables students to select a topic that is meaningful to them, including studies of a student's own culture or personal context. This also builds on students' prior learning and connects to their "funds of knowledge," which is another practice in keeping with culturally relevant pedagogy (Morrison et al., 2008, p. 438).

BIBLIOGRAPHY

Baldwin, L. (2018). *Research concepts for the practitioner of educational leadership*. Brill Sense.

Booth, W. C., Colomb, G. G., Williams, J. M., Bizup, J., & Fitzgerald, W. T. (2016). *The craft of research* (4th ed.). The University of Chicago Press.

Creswell, J. W., & Poth, C. N. (2018). *Qualitative inquiry and research design* (4th ed.). Sage.

Fain, J. A. (2017). *Reading, understanding, and applying nursing research* (5th ed.). F. A. Davis Company.

Hollingworth, L. (2012). Why leadership matters: Empowering teachers to implement formative assessment. *Journal of Educational Administration, 50*(3), 365–379.

Irlbeck, S. A., & Thornton, N. (2012). Defining research problems: Processes for beginning researchers. In *Instructional technology research, design and development: Lessons from the field* (pp. 25–42). IGI Global.

Ladson-Billings, G. (2014). Culturally relevant pedagogy 2.0: Aka the remix. *Harvard Educational Review, 84*(1), 74–84.

Maxwell, J. A. (2013). *Qualitative research design: An interactive approach* (3rd ed.). Sage.

Merriam, S. B., & Tisdell, E. J. (2016). *Qualitative research: A guide to design and implementation* (4th ed.). Jossey-Bass.

Morrison, K. A., Robbins, H. H., & Rose, D. G. (2008). Operationalizing culturally relevant pedagogy: A synthesis of classroom-based research. *Equity & Excellence in Education, 41*(4), 433–452.

Newman, I., & Covrig, D. M. (2013). Building consistency between title, problem statement, purpose, & research questions to improve the quality of research plans and reports. *New Horizons in Adult Education and Human Resource Development, 25*(1), 70–79.

Sankey, M., Birch, D., & Gardiner, M. (2011). The impact of multiple representations of content using multimedia on learning outcomes across learning styles and modal preferences. *International Journal of Education and Development using ICT, 7*(3), 18–35.

Selwyn, N. (2014). 'So What?'… a question that every journal article needs to answer. *Learning, Media and Technology, 39*(1), 1–5.

4

Branch Out

Using Tree Diagrams to Select and Develop Research Questions

Vikash Reddy

INTRODUCTION

Narrowing a research topic to actionable research questions can be a challenge; this chapter provides instructors with a lesson plan that uses accessible readings to illustrate the difference between topic questions and research questions. It then has students work to create sets of research questions related to their study's topic. The chapter will draw distinctions between descriptive, relational, and causal research questions, as well as quantitative and qualitative questions, noting that research projects may seek to address multiple questions.

Generating and refining the research questions for a study is a critical part of a researcher's journey. The process of creating a bona fide research question is not so simple, however, with students often struggling to move from a topic or general question to an actionable question or set of questions (Booth et al., 2016; Luker, 2008). Even experienced researchers need to think carefully about their research questions as they formulate them.

In my experience teaching research methods to novice researchers (often practitioners and policymakers experienced in their own fields but new to the practice of scholarly research), I have found that students struggle to move from an interest to actionable, studyable research questions. I suggest in this chapter a visual relationship between these concepts, with the topic conceived of as the trunk of a tree – providing the core strength to their work – and branches as individual research questions that may be related to the tree itself and to one another in different ways. I find this representation effective, as it helps maintain the concept of the narrowing that takes place as a researcher moves from topic to question that others, such as Creswell and Poth (2018) describe using inverse triangles. This visual, however, allows students to see that topics can yield multiple related questions that cannot be addressed by a single study.

By now students have selected research topics and identified problems that are worth further investigation. In the tree and leaf analogy used for this lesson, the topic can be thought of as the trunk, problems as the various major branches. At this point, students should look to further narrow their research projects by generating focused research

DOI: 10.4324/b23320-6

questions that they can address in their own projects. Research questions tell us the specific relationship or phenomenon that the researcher is looking to explain.

This lesson helps students understand how research questions differ from broader topic questions by having them read an article about "good teaching." The lesson begins with general discussion related to the assigned article, before moving to small group discussions in which additional research questions related to good teaching are generated and categorized. The lesson concludes with instructions for students to complete a similar task for their own projects – either as part of class or assigned work following class.

LESSON PLAN

Topic	Generating Research Questions
Learning Objectives	• Students will understand the relationship between a general research problem and focused research questions. • Students will understand the differences between descriptive, relational, and causal research questions. • Students will understand the differences between quantitative and qualitative research questions. • Students will generate research questions and hypotheses for a research problem and select a research question, or set of questions, to pursue for their own research topic.
Needed Materials	• Chart paper/board with drawing of tree and branches • Sticky notes
Pre-lesson Preparation	How can I scaffold this lesson? • The lesson assumes students selected research topics and read relevant literature in prior class sessions. Because research questions and research methods are fundamentally linked, students should be encouraged to consider their own methodological backgrounds, even if they do not settle on the specific methodology of their own studies until later. Subsequent lessons on study design (both quantitative and qualitative) should emphasize the importance of a study's research questions in designing data collection and analysis procedures. • Students should read the article, "What is good teaching" by Kristina Rizga. In this *Atlantic* article, Rizga draws on interviews conducted with veteran educators across the United States. I like this article because the title sounds a lot like the research questions that students so often start out with. It has the allure of something you can find out through a research project, and it sounds like an interesting question! Those who study teaching and learning, however, will quickly recognize that this question needs to be narrowed and refined before an actionable research study can be imagined around it.
Activities	This lesson comprises three main elements. The first is a discussion of the article "What Is Good Teaching?" The second is a more general discussion about research questions, focusing on two dimensions along which research questions can be conceived, namely causality and methodology. The lesson applies those concepts to the article "What Is Good Teaching?" Finally, students generate lists of research questions that fit their own topic, selecting the appropriate questions for the project they are undertaking. **Class Discussion – "What Is Good Teaching?"** • Begin the lesson with a discussion that recaps topic selection and problem definition. • How would students define the topic of this article/research? ◦ Note that even within the context of defining a topic, we can get quite specific. The title suggests the article is about good teaching, but the focus is clearly on K–12 education rather than higher education. The degree of specificity for topic definition is up to the instructor.

BRANCH OUT

Topic	Generating Research Questions
	• What problem does this article address and what is the purpose or rationale for studying them? ◦ The average teacher today is much less experienced than the average teacher in 1988. ◦ Test-preparation has taken priority over more authentic educational activities. • Ask the class: Does this article tell us the answer to the question, "What is good teaching?" ◦ Ask for a few suggestions for what the article does tell us, and what questions are addressed. For example: ▪ Good teachers get to know their students and their families. How do effective teachers approach students and families? ▪ Good teachers reflect on their practice. How do effective teachers… • At this stage, instructors may choose to divide students into small groups to discuss the following questions. Students should discuss the specific questions embedded within the article about good teaching. ◦ What more specific questions does the article address? ▪ For example: How do good teachers learn new teaching strategies? ▪ For ecample: What strategies do effective teachers use to reach different sets of students? ▪ For example: How do teachers and schools close racial/ethnic gaps in access and achievement? ◦ Beyond the questions that are immediately apparent from the article, what other questions can we ask regarding the topic of effective teaching? ▪ This may also require students to think about problems and rationales beyond those already identified. This should be encouraged. • Students should write their questions on sticky notes in preparation for the sharing portion of the exercise. ◦ SCAFFOLDING OPPORTUNITY. Depending on the prior experience of the course participants as well as the number of course sessions available for the development of the topic, problem, and research questions, instructors may want students to attempt to classify their questions as quantitative and qualitative, with a different color sticky note for each type. This will lend itself to the visual impact of the tree, with each branch having (hopefully!) notes representing both types of questions. More advanced students may sort potential research questions into those better suited to descriptive, correlational, and causal. ◦ Descriptive questions simply ask the researcher to describe the context or data. For example: ▪ How many years of experience does the average teacher have? ▪ How many teachers have less than three, five, or ten years of teaching experience? ▪ How are experienced teachers distributed across schools or grade levels? ◦ Correlational questions ask whether there is a relationship between two things, even if one doesn't necessarily cause the other ▪ Do students with more experienced teachers get higher test scores? (Note: This question does not attribute any higher test scores to teacher experience. Such differences may be caused by other factors.) ▪ Do teachers from different teacher training programs see different outcomes with their students? ◦ Causal research questions ask whether there is a cause-and-effect relationship between two variables. Sticking with the teacher experience set of questions, some potential causal questions are: ▪ Do additional years of teaching improve teacher effectiveness? ▪ Does a certain teacher training program create more effective teachers, as measured by student test scores?

Topic	_Generating Research Questions_

Introduction of Research Tree
- If students were working in groups or pairs, bring them back to a class discussion. Before asking students to share the more detailed questions, introduce the concept of the tree to help organize research questions related to a particular topic.
- Reference the concept of the inverted triangle – starting broad, narrowing down to research questions. Some questions are too broad. By now they have realized that – like the question of "What is good teaching?" – we must narrow them down. We are doing the same thing here. Starting broad and narrowing down. The tree allows the researcher to visualize clusters of questions within a problem area of a topic.
- After a brief discussion with the class about the topic, write a topic on the tree trunk. If using the Rizga article, this will be something like "Good teaching in K–12 schools."
- The next step is narrowing down the problems. This article deals with a number of different problems. Students may want to write out one-to-two-sentence problem statements that can go on the branches. In this exercise, a single level of branches will suffice, but in their own thinking, students should be encouraged to include as many branches as they think are truly necessary. Any of the larger branch topics suggested here could be subdivided into a number of subtopics. Note that students will be sharing their questions, written on sticky notes, so encourage them to share problem statements/areas where their question would fit. Potential problem areas to prompt discussion include:
  - Workforce experience
  - Testing mandates
- Ask students for the questions their group created. Sticky notes can be placed on the appropriate branch of the tree – with sufficient questions, the quantitative/qualitative color notes should help students see there are different ways to study a certain problem.

Discussion of Research Questions
- At this stage, either ask students to volunteer a research question or refer to the sticky notes that have been placed on the tree. Note that most of the questions that are on the sticky notes will need to be revised before they are good research questions, while others might not be suitable at all.
- In reflecting on questions, there are a number of considerations and explanations. In keeping with the theme, this lesson asks students to think about the BRANCH OUT questions. While there may be some overlap, these should help students evaluate their questions after they have created them.
  - **B**readth – The questions need to be narrow enough to focus the researcher and the study, but broader than the instrument questions that belong on the survey or protocol.
  - **R**easonable – Aside from being actionable, is this study reasonable from intellectual and ethical points of view?
  - **A**ctionable – Can you obtain data on this topic, either data that has been collected and can be used for secondary analysis, or original data? Do you have the capacity (the requisite skills, access, time) to conduct the analysis indicated by this question?
  - **N**ovel – Has anybody asked this already? If so, what makes your question different?
  - **C**oncise – Can you state each question in a single sentence that ends with a question mark? Ensure that the question does not elicit a yes/no answer.
  - **H**elpful – Are these questions relevant to your topic and problem? Do they help you address the purpose of the study?
  - **O**riented to the method – Above, the exercise instructions note that instructors can have students use different colored sticky notes to distinguish quantitative and qualitative research questions. Encourage students to think about how they will answer the question as they refine their question.

Topic	Generating Research Questions

	• ○ **U**nbiased – Researchers approach their work with their own lenses and biases, but researchers should be careful to create questions that will not lead to a predetermined conclusion.
	 • ○ **T**hought-provoking – Boring questions will lead to boring research, and questions with simple yes/no answers are not likely to yield interesting projects.
	 • As the instructor leads the class through the questions on the sticky note, consider how they do against the BRANCH OUT criteria.
	 • When it comes time to select a research question for a student's own project, concepts like novelty and actionability will become more important. While brainstorming potential research questions, however, including questions that have been addressed and those that might be too complex or costly for the current study is fine.
	 Class Exercise – Formulating Research Questions
	 • At this stage, students can then have time to work on their own Research Project Tree. Before doing so, however, a few concepts should be covered that might not surface during the "Good Teaching" exercise.
	   ○ Creating research questions is an iterative process. Upon digging into a topic, researchers may change their approach as they narrow down to their own research questions.
	   ○ Even after the initial set of questions is defined, researchers revisit their questions throughout the research process. These questions will evolve as the researcher becomes more familiar with the existing literature and the available data.
	 • Begin by having students reiterate their own topics and problems that they have refined over their first few classes.
	 • Some students may have only just begun thinking about narrowing down their questions, while others may be further along. Students, both those who are further along and those in the earlier stages, should be encouraged to come up with additional questions, classified with regard to any problems and rationale statements they have written that are related to their topic, even those they know they won't be studying. The larger visual of the tree with multiple questions can help students better understand how their study will fit within the topic.
	 • In small groups, have students share and discuss their initial research questions. Through the course of these discussions and discussion with the instructor, students should arrive at a research question or set of questions that they will work to address over the remainder of the course.

Virtual Adaptations	This lesson is easily adaptable to synchronous virtual platforms, like Zoom. A Google Slide with a picture of a tree can be used in place of the tree drawn on the classroom board or chart paper. Student comments can be added to the slide as sticky notes would be added to a chart pad.
Assessment	<u>Formative assessment</u>: Students' research question lists can be used for formative assessment purposes, allowing the instructor to see whether students are generating appropriate questions in real time. Given the generative nature of the exercise, however, they should not be used for summative purposes. <u>Summative assessment</u>: Either as part of the session or subsequently, students should consider the research question(s) that best represent the study they intend to pursue over the course of the term. These questions should be submitted for feedback and assessment purposes.

INTELLECTUAL PREPARATION FOR LESSON

Core Ideas

Generating research questions is an essential step in helping researchers narrow their focus from a general topic to a study they can execute. Traditional depictions of the initial stages of the research problem often discuss the narrowing or focusing of a topic down to a problem, and subsequently to a research question, illustrated with an inverse triangle. Although this depiction is helpful in explaining the process of narrowing down to a question, it is highly focused on the single research question. The tree diagram used in this lesson stays true to the idea of narrowing from a topic to a research question, but it gives students an alternative visual for the way in which researchers move from topic to research questions.

A benefit of this visual is its potential to help students understand that their research question – like a leaf on a tree – is one question amid a large set of questions that stem from a given topic. A topic is the collection of a number of problems and questions, and one of the challenges for researchers is identifying which tree limb they want to climb. Related to this is the important job of deciding which questions to leave out. Visualizing the questions of interest among the larger set of research questions can be an effective reminder that the project at hand is not designed to cover the entire topic, but rather a well-defined space within the topic.

More generally, research questions must reflect the topic and rationale identified by the researchers in the phases of inquiry discussed in the two preceding chapters. After identifying a problem, and stating why it's important, the researcher must get specific about what they want to study. Although there is no definitive checklist for the ideal research question, the BRANCH OUT list, drawn from various sources (Booth et al., 2016; Gerring, 2007; Mattick et al., 2018; Maxwell, 2013; O'Leary, 2020; Vanderbilt Writing Studio, 2007), is a helpful mnemonic that offers a thematic set of considerations to help direct students in their research process.

One topic not addressed in the tree exercise concerns distinctions between causal and descriptive research questions. Though students may frame questions as causal or descriptive, the lesson assumes a more novice researcher who is yet to grapple fully with causal versus descriptive interpretations. Instructors adapting this exercise for students with greater prior research sophistication can incorporate dimensions of causality into the tree exercise using approaches similar to those for scaffolding in qualitative and quantitative research questions.

Learners

Although asking or coming up with questions is not a new exercise, crafting good research questions is much more difficult than most people realize. As the lesson shows, a good discussion question and a good research question are two different things. By this stage, students have a topic, and they have articulated their reasons for wanting to pursue this topic. This lesson requires them to become more specific about the direction of their own study.

Previous Learning Misconceptions
Distinguishing between interesting questions and research questions can be difficult. Indeed, the title to the article featured in the class discussion might initially strike many as a reasonable research question. Moving from a general topic to a research question or a set of questions that guide a study is difficult, with most initial attempts yielding questions that are too broad and/or infeasible for students, such as "What is good teaching?"

At the other end of the spectrum are questions that are too narrow. In these cases, questions might be grouped together to help identify the overarching question that ties them together. Narrow questions may also be better suited for inclusion in survey instruments or interview protocols, to help the researcher build towards their research question.

A final set of misconceived questions involve those that are better suited to follow the research and address the implications of the research findings. In the context of Rizga's article, larger questions related to improving teacher pipelines and preparation programs are an example of questions better kept for the interpretation of the study's findings.

Context

Scaffolded Learning

Rather than asking students to immediately identify their own research questions, this lesson begins with a discussion of how a published study's general question differs from the research questions that underlie the research project. Students then categorize the questions according to the subtopics. This allows students – in particular students with limited experience generating novel research questions – a chance to see how questions narrow and branch out until a researcher arrives at an actionable research question before attempting to distill their own topics down to their finer research questions. The instructor may, as noted in the lesson plan, introduce ways for students to distinguish between qualitative and quantitative questions, or causal and descriptive questions, depending on students' prior familiarity with these concepts.

The lesson is also designed to build on prior chapters, with the final product for the lesson being a set of research questions that are specific to students' previously articulated research topics, problems, and rationales.

Confidence Building

This lesson begins with the premise that writing good research questions is tricky, and even writers for the *Atlantic* do not always write their research questions with the appropriate level of precision. Instructors should assure students that the process of forming research questions is a difficult and iterative one. Further, students should come away understanding that these questions, and the rationales behind them, should be revisited frequently throughout the research process.

BIBLIOGRAPHY

Booth, W. C., Colomb, G. G., Williams, J. M., Bizup, J., & Fitzgerald, W. T. (2016). *The craft of research* (4th ed.). The University of Chicago Press.

Creswell, J. W., & Poth, C. N. (2018). *Qualitative inquiry and research design* (4th ed.). Sage.

Gerring, J. (2007). *Case study research*. Cambridge University Press.

Luker, K. (2008). *Salsa dancing into the social sciences: Research in an age of info-glut*. Harvard University Press.

Mattick, K., Johnston, J., & de la Croix, A. (2018). How to…write a good research question. *The Clinical Teacher, 15*(2), 104–108. https://doi.org/10.1111/tct.12776

Maxwell, J. A. (2013). *Qualitative research design: An interactive approach* (3rd ed.). Sage.

O'Leary, Z. (2020). *Checklist for 'Good' questions*. SAGE Publishing. https://study.sagepub.com/oleary3e/student-resources/forming-research-questions/checklist-for-%E2%80%98good%E2%80%99-questions

Vanderbilt Writing Studio. (2007). *Formulating Your Research Question (RQ)*. Retrieved from: https://www.vanderbilt.edu/writing/resources/handouts/

Section II

Literature Review and Theoretical/ Conceptual Framework

Section Editor: Leslie D. Gonzales

5

Introduction to Section II

Literature Review and Theoretical/Conceptual Framework

Leslie D. Gonzales

Every year or so, I have the privilege of teaching a doctoral-level qualitative research methods course. And every year, students and I return to a similar set of conversations: *How does one go about crafting a literature review? How is it possible to manage all that I am learning from the scholarship? What in the world is a conceptual framework and how does it differ from a theoretical framework? Oh yeah, and where do we find these frameworks, anyways?*

These conversations are as challenging as they are exciting because they are opportunities to work with students at the very point they are digging into the hearts of their projects. We work through the pragmatic, such as how to reach out to the very generous librarians at our institutions, how to develop search terms and search processes, and how to identify quality sources. We work through the conceptual, including unpacking the fundamental assumptions and concepts that undergird their work and figuring out how those assumptions and concepts map onto theoretical traditions. Yet, as generative as these conversations and exercises are, I have continuously searched for materials that would allow me to better support my students in their journeys.

The contributors in this section may have brought my search to a close. In this section, the authors offer thoughtful advice for developing, organizing, and articulating literature reviews and conceptual and/or theoretical frameworks. As a collective, these authors encourage researchers to slow down and take the time that is necessary to design systems rather than haphazardly applying strategies and practices. For example, in the Porter and Byrd chapter, readers will learn how to set up a systematic approach to searching for literature and how to manage the wonderful fruits of their labor with reference management tools. In the Terosky chapter, readers will be nudged to think deeply about the possible patterns in their literature and how to leverage these patterns, so that future consumers of their work will experience a well-organized literature review. And finally, in the Pasque and Gilbert chapter, readers learn that conceptual and theoretical frameworks are not mere last-minute sections to throw on to a research project, but that they are actually operating underneath our thinking all of the time. Our task is to unpack that thinking in service of our readers.

DOI: 10.4324/b23320-8

In Chapter 6, Drs. Christa Porter and Janice Byrd draw on their award-winning article "Understanding Influences of Development on Black Women's Success in College: A Synthesis of Literature" (Porter & Byrd, 2021) to describe how to conduct a rigorous and inclusive literature review. After modeling for readers the importance of naming and unpacking one's fundamental starting point as researchers, Porter and Byrd take readers through a "metaphorical puzzle." Through this metaphor, the authors encourage researchers to reflect and identify the key pieces of their respective study puzzle as well as its boundaries. The authors then provide concrete advice on how to find out more about these key puzzle pieces (e.g., how to source literature) and strategize for organizing the pieces (e.g., arranging the literature review). Researchers seeking creative yet pragmatic advice about how to source, organize, and present scholarship in service of their projects will find this chapter invaluable.

In Chapter 7, Dr. Aimee LaPointe Terosky provides further support to researchers with respect to the literature review process. Specifically, Terosky helps researchers think through an array of possibilities for organizing the massive amounts of scholarship one reads while conducting research. Terosky highlights the value of synthesizing and "categorizing" literature into piles – and eventually themes – through a delightful lesson called the "Candy Sort." This chapter may be especially helpful to those embarking on their first literature review.

In Chapter 8, Dr. Penny Pasque and doctoral candidate Chelsea Gilbert urge readers to take seriously the role *and* power of theoretical and conceptual frameworks. After providing helpful vocabulary and scaffolding and distinguishing between theoretical and conceptual frameworks, Pasque and Gilbert lead readers through a lesson that teaches them how to recognize the assumptions, orientations, and values that are already implicitly holding the work together. This contribution will be of great help to researchers striving to align the ideational underpinnings of their work with its practical design and mechanics.

The contributors in Section II will have you making puzzles, eating candy, and thinking hard about theory all in service of research that is as transparent and rigorous, as it is creative.

BIBLIOGRAPHY

Porter, C. J. & Byrd, J. A. (2021). Understanding influences of development on Black women's success in college: A synthesis of literature. *Review of Educational Research*, *91*(6), 803–830.

6

Connecting Pieces to the Puzzle

Finding and Maintaining Resources

Christa J. Porter and Janice A. Byrd

INTRODUCTION

Your students have decided on a topic of study, potentially drafted some research questions, and perhaps can articulate a compelling purpose statement. The next step (or maybe not necessarily in that order) is to find literature that will help them piece together and make sense of their topic in the broadest sense. In other words, at this point in the research process, your students must explore various possibilities of word combinations and search terms to compile a listing (or multiple lists) of scholarship to review. Think about their search as connecting pieces to a puzzle; each piece (or set of articles found through a particular key term) is valuable to the larger picture illustrated within the puzzle (their research project). How they "piece" together the appropriate scholarly works – or find and maintain the resources – affects their ability to effectively progress to the next phase of thoughtfully reviewing and integrating the literature.

The purpose of this chapter is to guide your students' search for resources by finding and connecting the puzzle pieces. Before they begin to read through literature and establish themes, they must first: (1) understand what each piece entails, (2) clarify boundaries of what pieces to include and exclude, and (3) understand how each piece could potentially create and/or enhance the puzzle. We recognize that each institution and institutional library provides varied resources to students and they/we are socialized into and through research processes differently. In this chapter, we offer specific examples as well as encourage possibilities for you as the instructor and students to find and maintain resources.

DOI: 10.4324/b23320-9

LESSON PLAN

Topic	*Finding and Maintaining Resources*
Learning Objectives	• Students will conduct an introductory online search through the institutional library database, Google Scholar and ResearchGate, and discipline-specific journals (i.e., to locate results inaccessible through institutional libraries). • Students will identify key terms and practice engaging search functions to compile an initial list of search results. • Students will clarify boundaries of what results to include and exclude based on briefly reviewing abstracts.
Needed Materials	• Students should have access to a laptop, desktop, or tablet with internet access. • Instructors should plan to use the classroom computer to guide students through the search. • If your institutional or college-specific librarian offers a resource guide, upload it to the course site as a supplement to this activity.

Pre-lesson Preparation	• If applicable, invite your institutional or college-specific librarian to give a brief tutorial to familiarize students with the library database (i.e., including an explanation of indexes or publication sources such EBSCOHost, JSTOR, APAPsycInfo, etc.). Your pre-lesson planning will depend on how much the librarian details and explains for the students within their tutorial. However, use the librarian's tutorial as a guide or supplement, not as the complete lesson. Walking through this activity with students offers a collaborative experiential learning opportunity with their peers.
	• Prepare a topic (inclusive of key terms and search functions) in advance so students can engage the same online institutional search experience.
	• Identify examples of discipline-specific journals inaccessible or not indexed through the library. Prepare a mini lesson on use of search functions (i.e., using AND, OR, NOT to specify search terms or keywords, "phrase searching," and use of the asterisk symbol * (NIH, 2021)). Review several institutional search guides and tools available online for assistance with the mini-lesson preparation.
	• Prepare a Google Scholar and ResearchGate search for the topic or specific author to highlight journal articles, books, and book chapters. Prepare to demonstrate how to navigate scholar pages, download and request scholarly works from authors.
	   ○ To search Google Scholar, view: https://scholar.google.com/
	   ○ To search ResearchGate, view: https://www.researchgate.net/
	• Prepare examples of reference management software (i.e., Zotero, Mendeley, EndNote) and identify free resources your institution provides to students. For those not interested in reference management software, prepare a template of how students can compile/chart resources in an excel or Google spreadsheet (i.e., demonstrate how to effectively organize columns and rows) or a Word document.
	• Determine whether all students have a personal laptop (or access to share with a partner). If not, reserve a computer lab for class so all students can engage independently in the activity.

Activities	• Guide students through accessing the institutional library page. • Determine terms and search functions (i.e., if the topic is development of women and girls in sport, the key terms could be development, college, youth, girls, athletics, intramural, professional, united states); demonstrate how to use AND, OR, NOT, "phrase searching," or the asterisk symbol * in the search boxes. Be as specific as possible with search functions to result in publications most relevant to the search. For example, use the NOT feature to eliminate publications and studies that sample men or boys. Use the asterisk (*) to widen results if you are not completely sure of which search terms to use (i.e., women in sports* or girls in sport*).

CONNECTING PIECES TO THE PUZZLE

Topic	Finding and Maintaining Resources
	• Narrow, filter, or refine results by year of publication or date range, document or source type (book or article), discipline or field, subject/genre, location, or database. Your institutional database/search page should permit you to limit or refine your search based on certain factors such as publisher, language, database, and/or timeframe.
	• After using the same types of search functions, filters, and key terms, compare the search results of your students. Direct students to follow your search and then perform the same search on their device, then share the number of results they ascertain. Are the titles the same or different? What differences are there in the number of results? Have students think of ways to narrow (or broaden) the results further. Walk students through how to save their search and receive search alerts. Refer to your institutional/college-specific librarian if you are not as familiar with the process of saving searches.
	• Open additional tabs to replicate the search through Google Scholar and ResearchGate (e.g., online indexes of scholarly work). Similarly, open another tab to replicate the search through a discipline-specific journal.
	• Allow at least 45–60 minutes for students to review abstracts in the various platforms (institutional database, Google Scholar, ResearchGate, and discipline-specific journal). Allocated time will depend on the number of students in the course, length of the course, diversity of learning styles and accommodations, and whether all students have access to engage the activity. Have students review at least 5–10 abstracts. Help them identify how to eliminate an article based on the abstract and reflect on their perceptions of whether the article/work should be included or excluded based on the topic. Ask students to:
	◦ Reflect on what each piece (search result) entails.
	◦ Clarify boundaries of what pieces to include and exclude.
	◦ Discuss the role of the search process and whose voices/writings are included/excluded in theirdiscipline/field specifically, and literature canons in general (use intellectual preparation sections below to guide the discussion).
	◦ Identify how each piece could potentially create and/or enhance the larger puzzle (why the search result should be included in the next phase – reading full published pieces as part of the literature review).
	• After the exercise, offer your template/example of how to compile citations by using reference management software, a spreadsheet, or a Word document.
	• Frequently check in with students throughout the activity. Once completed, facilitate a class debrief. Decide upon an individual reflection exercise, assignment, or group discussion (see assessment section).
Virtual Adaptations	• To conduct this activity virtually, you would need to confirm (1) whether all students in the course will be able to "see" your shared screen, and (2) whether students will be able to engage individually on their computer or device during the allocated work time.
	• In either case, you should prepare to move through each step in "real time" or "in front of" students. Create screenshots as guides to assist students at each step of the activity based on the selected topic of study (i.e., screenshots of the institutional library search page with key terms included and a results list based on certain inclusion/exclusion criteria).
	• Prepare to visit a discipline-specific journal web page, display the example spreadsheet template of how to organize results, demonstrate how to navigate your/someone's Google Scholar page, and share your/someone's ResearchGate page.
	• Based on their level of accessibility, decide whether to demonstrate each part of the activity or allot time for them to individually conduct the online searches in the same way they would if in person.

Topic	Finding and Maintaining Resources

Assessment	You can assess student learning from this activity in three ways based on learning objectives of the activity:
	1. Have students record and submit their results list (5–10 citations) in an Excel or Google spreadsheet or Word document. Then review and compare the results as a class. Specifically highlight differences and similarities across results and discuss how students made meaning of their decisions to include/exclude based on the topic. Lead students in a discussion of how they made meaning of their decisions.
	2. Have students individually reflect on their search experience via a for-credit assignment they submit to you (i.e., an electronic discussion post) or as a not-for-credit post within their personal researcher journal. Example prompts include:
	   a. Describe your overall impressions of the search activity?
	   b. Describe your understanding of different search platforms (i.e., Google Scholar, institutional database, and/or discipline-specific journals).
	   c. In what ways will this search activity assist you in finding and maintaining resources for your research study?
	   d. Explain how you made meaning of your decisions about what to include/exclude concerning results.
	3. You could also encourage students to reflect on their experience as a class or in pairs, using the same or similar prompts.

INTELLECTUAL PREPARATION FOR LESSON

As Black women qualitative researchers, who utilize critical methodological approaches in our research, we are aware that our thoughts and values about research are invariably linked with how we teach related processes. For example, in our article, "Understanding Influences of Development on Black Women's Success in College: A Synthesis of Literature" (Porter & Byrd, 2021), we intentionally grounded our literature synthesis in a Black feminist/intersectional framework to critically discuss how Black undergraduate women experience identity development and success. We acknowledged our approach to the literature synthesis was tied to our own lived experiences as Black women as well as our desire to combat racism and sexism (Evans-Winters, 2019). We believe all research regardless of methodological approach (e.g., quantitative, qualitative, mixed methods) is subjective and influenced by one's socialization, worldview, and positionality (Bhattacharya, 2017). To mediate these influences, all researchers are encouraged to engage in ongoing critical self-reflexivity (DeCuir-Gunby, 2020; Williams et al., 2021) to explore our relationship to the topic; we must also identify and reflect upon the lenses (or frames) through which we examine, interpret, and analyze data.

Core Ideas

We offer the following core ideas to think about when approaching this lesson/chapter: institutional databases, key terms and language, inclusionary and exclusionary boundaries, Google Scholar and ResearchGate, and when to stop searching.

Institutional Databases
Access to journals and scholarly sources within institutional databases varies from institution to institution. Visit your institutional library website and search accessible journals to determine whether your discipline-specific journals are available to you. If not, speak

CONNECTING PIECES TO THE PUZZLE

with a librarian on staff about gaining access, interlibrary loans, and how your search is influenced by journals inaccessible at your institution.

Key Terms and Language
Key terms vary across time; changes in legislation, participant identities, and context differently influence how and why researchers examine topics. Before you begin searching key terms related to your inquiry, spend time journaling the history and breadth of language used to describe the concept, issue, or population. For example, when searching for scholarship exploring the mental health of adolescents, you should also search for other language used to describe this population such as youth or high school students. If you are exploring the experiences of trans*gender students across the educational pipeline, avoid conflating gender with sexuality. The acronym "LGBTQ+" has been historically used to name students with varying sexualities (lesbian, gay, bisexual, queer), yet has not necessarily accounted for/included students identifying as trans*. If you are unaware of the language used to describe your topic of inquiry, spend time reading the introductory paragraphs or literature reviews of a few articles or chapters on the topic to learn more about how other scholars describe the concept/population/issue.

Inclusionary and Exclusionary Boundaries
As you are connecting pieces of the puzzle, you will need to clarify boundaries of what to include and exclude (Haynes et al., 2020; Porter & Byrd, 2021). Ask yourself specific questions as you are beginning to search for resources. For example, if you are examining the experiences of Black women's access to health care, are you interested in empirical studies wherein the participant sample includes only Black women? Are you interested in scholarship that compares Black women's experiences to Black men, to other women of Color, or to white women? Are you considering intersections of identities beyond race and gender (Esposito & Evans-Winters, 2022)? Is there a particular time frame, age range, or geographic location you desire to include as boundaries of the study (i.e., a twenty-year time span, geriatric adults, or within the United States)? Understanding your boundaries – what to include or exclude – during the process of finding resources will help you refine the search results and maintain clarity when reviewing abstracts.

Google Scholar and ResearchGate
Before manuscripts are published as journal articles or book chapters, most are shepherded through a peer-reviewed process, also known as a masked peer review by a committee of scholars. Peer-reviewed journals are valuable to the broader academic enterprise and bodies of literature, yet there is also a breadth of scholarship published outside of academic journals as edited/authored books or monographs, book chapters, and opinion editorials. Google Scholar and ResearchGate are online platforms that index scholarly work as it becomes available through various outlets. In other words, once a book or book chapter is published, Google Scholar picks up the reference information and makes the citation available. Similarly, through ResearchGate researchers can update and upload various works and make them accessible for others to request and/or download.

When to Stop Searching

The search process can quickly become a never-ending rabbit hole of discovery or dismay. When you begin to see the same articles, books, and scholars within your results (e.g., library database or Google Scholar), you have probably carried out due diligence to best represent scholarship on the topic. If you are missing key works, spend time looking up scholarship referenced in the articles you identified to learn what other researchers have published on the topic. You may also search a seminal piece in Google Scholar and use the "Cited By" feature to acquire a list of scholarship citing this work. If you are conducting a qualitative research inquiry such as a systematic literature review, content analysis, or critical discourse analysis, adhere to procedural guidance relative to the respective methodology.

Learners

Individual understandings of research, rigor, and quality of academic scholarship, differ. Our socialization to/of research in graduate and professional school (and undergraduate programs for some individuals) often influences how we learn about and have access to particular topics, populations, and data, as well as our exposure to the publication process.

Throughout these orientation processes, students should be encouraged to think critically about why certain sources (and types) of scholarship are held in higher esteem (i.e., qualitative vs. quantitative, identity-based journals). Higher value or perceptions of quality are influenced by multiple factors including one's academic program/discipline and socialization around research. For example, students may place higher value on certain types of research methodologies and publication venues because they have been taught to publish in, read from, and cite a particular 'canon' of academic journals (Williams et al., 2021).

(Mis)perceptions may influence students' approach to finding, including, and/or excluding resources. For example, a journal's ranking, impact factor, and/or prestige within their discipline may influence their decision to include an article in their results (i.e., as opposed to also including an article published in a lower tier, open-access journal with a broader practitioner-based audience). The activity encourages students to broaden how scholarship is defined by illuminating published works beyond peer-reviewed academic journals. Thus, it may be helpful to discuss with students what they deem as "valuable," "rigorous," and "critical" scholarship and how they came to their understanding. Encourage students to reflect on how their understanding of research could influence or hinder their ability to locate appropriate resources.

Context

Students come to research with varying levels of familiarity and exposure. Inviting a librarian to the course session or meeting as a class in the institutional library is valuable, yet providing a hands-on, real-time activity for students fosters an equitable learning environment because everyone is engaging in the same search, at the same time, and with the same resources.

BIBILIOGRAPHY

Bhattacharya, K. (2017). *Fundamentals of qualitative research: A practical guide*. Routledge.

DeCuir-Gunby, J. T. (2020). Using critical race mixed methodology to explore African Americans in education. *Educational Psychologist*, 55(4), 244–255. https://doi.org/10.1080/00461520.2020.1793762

Dillard, C. B. (2008). When the ground is Black, the ground is fertile: Exploring endarkened feminist epistemology and healing methodologies in the spirit. In N. K. Denzin, Y. S. Lincoln, L. Tuhiwai Smith (Eds.) *Handbook of critical and indigenous methodologies* (pp. 277–292). Sage. https://dx.doi.org/10.4135/9781483385686.n14

Esposito, J., & Evans-Winters, V. (2022). *Introduction to intersectional qualitative research*. Sage.

Evans-Winters, V. E. (2019). *Black feminism in qualitative inquiry: A mosaic for writing our daughter's body*. Routledge.

Haynes, C., Joseph, N. M., Patton, L. D., Stewart, S., & Allen, E. L. (2020). Toward and understanding of intersectionality methodology: A 30-year literature synthesis of Black women's experiences in higher education. *Review of Educational Research*, 90(6), 751–787. https://doi.org/10.3102/0034654320946822

National Institutes of Health [NIH]. (2021, August 27). *Literature Search: Databases and Gray Literature*. https://www.nihlibrary.nih.gov/services/systematic-review-service/literature-search-databases-and-gray-literature

Porter, C. J., & Byrd, J. A. (2021). Understanding influences of development on Black women's success in college: A synthesis of literature. *Review of Educational Research*, 91(6), 803–830. https://doi.org/10.3102/00346543211027929

Williams, J. M., Byrd, J. A., & Washington, A. R. (2021). Challenges in implementing anti-racist pedagogy into counselor education programs: A collective self-study. *Counselor Education and Supervision*, 60, 254–273. https://doi.org/10.1002/ceas.12215

7

The Candy Sort

Organizing the Literature Review

Aimee LaPointe Terosky

INTRODUCTION

We have all seen, and have often even been the overwhelmed researcher looking at endless piles of articles (or files on a screen), armed with little more than a highlighter or a spreadsheet…desperately trying to make sense of what has already been said – and what still needs to be said – on a topic. "Scholars must say something new while connecting what they say to what's already been said," notes Howard Becker (2007), "and this must be done in such a way that people will understand the point" (p. 141). Thus, it is no surprise that examining and articulating the literature is challenging, as it is often vast and potentially unwieldy. As a professor teaching an introductory research course to doctoral students in education, I witness, year after year, students struggling with the literature. My ongoing efforts to better support my students' skills in writing literature reviews led to this "Candy Sort" lesson. The purpose of the "Candy Sort" lesson is to provide a relatable and hands-on approach to organizing a literature review around key themes and supporting evidence. And what better way to do that than with candy?

LESSON PLAN

Topic	*Organizing the literature review around key themes and supporting evidence*
Learning Objectives	• Students will create and organize relevant literature into categories of themes. • Students will articulate the rationale for their categories of themes, as well as their reasoning for including certain pieces of literature into each category. • Students will recognize multiple perspectives around how to create and organize relevant literature into categories of themes, thereby stressing the point that there is not "one right way" to present a literature review (Becker, 2007, p. 43).
Needed Materials	• Bags of assorted candy (preferably with different types and sizes of candy, different colors of wrappers) – you will want approximately 20–30 pieces of candy per group of students. • Small buckets or large cups. • Sticky notes. • For prior homework, students select, read, and take notes on the key ideas from five scholarly journal articles on a topic/problem of their choice.

DOI: 10.4324/b23320-10

THE CANDY SORT
47

Topic	*Organizing the literature review around key themes and supporting evidence*
Pre-lesson Preparation	• *How can I scaffold this lesson?* I use the "Candy Sort" in the first introductory research course in our doctoral program. My faculty colleagues who teach the advanced methods courses in later semesters also refer to the "Candy Sort" to continually reinforce these ideas. • *Do all students have the cultural context to appreciate the "Candy Sort"?* The "Candy Sort" is grounded in the act of sorting trick-or-treat candy after the United States' holiday of Halloween. For international students or those unfamiliar with the American tradition of Halloween trick-or-treating, I provide a video link about the tradition for students to view before class or use other visualizations, such as sorting clothes/accessories in a closet.

Activities	• Divide class into groups of 3–5 students.
	• Based on the number of students/groups in your course, distribute piles of candy (approximately 20–30 pieces) onto group's tables
	• Start the class by stating that we will engage in a United States holiday experience – that of sorting candy following Halloween trick- or-treating. Explain the experience if there are students who are not familiar with Halloween and trick-or-treating. If needed, connect the concept of sorting to other activities, such as organizing a kitchen cabinet, a closet, bookshelf, and so on.
	• On the board or screen, have the following prompt posted: "Sort your candy into categories that make sense to you. Be prepared to provide a rationale for your group's decision-making around your candy categories."
	• After 5–10 minutes of students sorting the candy, call on one person per group to explain the groups of candy and their rationale for grouping the candy in that way. (Typically, the different groups have different methods and categories for their candy piles.) Some examples of sorting including:
	  ◦ by color of wrapper – all the red wrappers together, all the blue together;
	  ◦ by texture of candy – chewy candy, hard candy, melting candy;
	  ◦ by size – large candy, small candy;
	  ◦ by personal likes and dislikes of the candy.
	If needed, ask relevant probing questions to each group, for example:
	  ◦ Can you tell us why you sorted the candy in this way?
	  ◦ What other variations did you consider?
	  ◦ Can you explain why this sorting schema makes sense to you and your group members?
	• Next, ask the groups to create a label or name for each of their categories of candy and to write it on the provided sticky notes and place the sticky note on a bucket or cup; then have students place the candy that corresponds with the label into the respective bucket or cup. Some examples of sticky note labels include:
	  ◦ by color: red wrappers, blue wrappers;
	  ◦ by texture of candy – chewy, hard, melting;
	  ◦ by size – large, small;
	  ◦ by personal likes and dislikes – favorite, least favorite.
	• After 5–10 minutes of students creating labels and filling buckets/cups, ask one representative from each group to share their labels/names. If needed, ask probing questions, such as:
	  ◦ How does this label capture your category of candy?
	  ◦ How does this label make sense for you when categorizing this candy theme?
	  ◦ Is there a way to clarify your label to fully capture your category of candy?
	  ◦ Could other categories fall into this label?
	• After all groups present their labels, ask students the following question
	  ◦ Why do you think we are doing this activity in a course focused on research (or writing)? You can either ask all students to think about this question independently for 1–3 minutes (to allow for all students to formulate an answer) and then call on students to share their thoughts, or have students pair up with a partner to discuss this question collaboratively.

Topic	*Organizing the literature review around key themes and supporting evidence*
	• After 1–3 minutes of independent reflection or student paired reflection, call on students to hear their responses to the question, "Why do you think we are doing this activity in a course focused on research (or writing)?" 　○ Typical responses include: 　　▪ Learning how to categorize and organize multiple things. 　　▪ Learning that other groups view the same candy/topics in different ways. • Then provide a mini-discussion/lecture around the alignment between this activity and literature reviews. Explain the following: 　○ A quality literature review organizes the literature around themes and categories and then pulls in previous scholarship (e.g., analytic commentary, empirical studies, etc.) as evidence to support the theme/category. 　○ That each piece of candy could represent a piece of scholarship or study or finding. 　○ This theme/category approach strives to avoid two common mistakes in literature reviews: 　　▪ The "book report" or "annotated bibliography" approach, which is akin to an annotated bibliography in which each paragraph is a summary of one article or author's views. 　　▪ The "scattered paragraph approach," in which many ideas/themes/categories are thrown into one paragraph/section without any sense of order. • Next, ask students to consider their current academic papers for which they are conducting literature reviews. 　○ Ask them to think through the five journal articles they read and took notes on for homework and now create themes/ categories (buckets/cups), and names/ labels for their articles. 　○ Ask them to write the author or the key finding on a slip of paper to be symbolic of a piece of candy going into a bucket • After 15–20 minutes of students applying the candy sort to their own academic papers or literature review, call on one or two volunteers to share their work. • Homework: Students create an outline for their literature review based on the labels/ names and rationale they created on their five articles. Note: In drafts of their final literature reviews in my introductory research class, I often have students put the applicable label from their "cups/buckets" (in a highlighted color) at the beginning of each paragraph in their literature reviews to help them learn how to organize their writing. Note: The "Candy Sort" lesson can also be used to demonstrate the process of coding and theme development in qualitative data analysis. Rather than evidence from the literature, students sort, categorize, and label segments from interview, focus group, observation, or document data to move from codes to themes.
Virtual Adaptations	During the Covid-19 Pandemic, I had to transition to a synchronous Zoom class setting. Fortunately, the "Candy Sort" was easily adaptable, especially with the help of the Learning Design team at my university. • Prior to class, add stock images (from unsplash.com; creativecommons.org) of different types of candy into a Google Slide; make a copy of the Google Slide for each group. • Students sort (click on the candy image and drag with their mouse/ trackpad) the images of candy into categories just like they would in the face-to-face classroom. • Each group shares their Google Slide by using the Share Screen Zoom feature. • For labeling the categories of candy, students draw boxes around their sorted groups and add a textbox to write the category's name/label.
Assessment	• Formative Assessment: During independent work time, move about the room and assess students' ability to connect the candy sort to their own academic paper's literature review. • Formative Assessment: Review homework which requires students to create an outline for their literature review based on the labels and rationale created in class. • Summative Assessment: Grade the final academic paper following a rubric requiring organization around themes/categories and appropriate labels for themes/categories/ paper sections.

THE CANDY SORT

INTELLECTUAL PREPARATION FOR THE "CANDY SORT" LESSON

According to numerous methodology books, the purposes of a quality literature review are threefold: (1) provide an overview of the existing scholarship on a topic/subject, (2) ground the new study in the existing literature, and (3) highlight the gaps in the literature to represent the new study's contribution to the field. Although this definition reads simply, in fact, organizing a literature review is anything but simple, as generations of novice and veteran researchers have struggled with finding and articulating key ideas and gaps in the vast literature on most topics. To help alleviate these challenges, I next examine my intellectual preparation for the "Candy Sort" by discussing the core ideas of the lesson's topic, the learners, and the context of bridging core ideas and learners.

Core Ideas

The "Candy Sort" lesson is anchored in two core ideas for effectively organizing and articulating a literature review: creating and naming categories of themes found in the literature, and drawing a researcher's awareness to alternative possibilities and contributions to the literature. I will discuss each next.

Creating and Naming Categories of Themes

Although novice and veteran researchers can become overwhelmed by the vast literature on any given topic, a core idea of the "Candy Sort" lesson is to demonstrate that relevant literature can be effectively organized – or sorted – into coherent categories based on common characteristics or meanings, much like the examples in the lesson explained around sorting candy by wrapper color, size, or texture. By first focusing on finding common themes across different elements of the literature or data sources (i.e., scholarly and practitioner articles, books, reports, transcripts, etc.), novice researchers learn how to create an organized structure that effectively tells the story of what has already been said, as well as what still needs to be said on a topic ("the gaps in the literature"). Moreover, the "Candy Sort" calls on students to develop category names, thereby capturing the essence of a theme or idea, an essential skill throughout the entire research process.

Drawing Awareness to Alternative Perspective and Contributions

A second core idea of the "Candy Sort" is drawing awareness to alternative perspectives and contributions. Typically, as groups share their candy sorting strategies and labels, it is clear that each group has a unique approach and rationale to the sorting of their candy. This outcome highlights how researchers can organize and represent literature in a number of ways, all of which can be correct if accompanied by a clear and coherent rationale. Moving students beyond thinking there is only one "right way" to organize and communicate the salient elements of the literature provides a valuable lesson on the role of the researcher and the value of alternative perspectives in research.

The Learner

An effective lesson needs to take into consideration the learners, including the background and prior knowledge they bring with them into the learning situation. When preparing for the "Candy Sort", I reflect on the previous learning, as well as possible misconceptions, around writing and research that might shape how my students engage with this lesson.

Previous Learning and Misconceptions
Prior to the "Candy Sort" lesson, the learners (i.e., students) will likely have entered the course with previous experiences (i.e., term papers, thesis) and ranges of preparation in outlining, organizing, and writing literature reviews. In my experience, it is likely that many students will hold tightly onto two forms of organizing a literature review. The first form is what I refer to as the "book report" format, which structures a literature review similar to an annotated bibliography with each paragraph "covering" a different author's work in a stand-alone, disjointed fashion. The second form is what I refer to as the "stream of consciousness" approach, in which students cover numerous themes and references in one, largely disorganized, paragraph. I have found that novice researchers/academic writers struggle with crafting their literature review around categories of themes with evidence from references/studies to back up each theme. As such, the "Candy Sort" strives to hone in on the art and science of finding categories of themes, labeling the categories concisely and clearly, and articulating the rationale and justification for the categories by linking back to the relevant literature.

Beyond past experiences with the book report and stream of consciousness formats, it is also likely that students will bring with them the notion of "one right way" to structure a literature review, and may even desire predetermined categories of themes. The "Candy Sort" strives to counter the "one right way" narrative of research by illustrating how different groups of students decided to sort their candy in different ways, and yet, each group was correct in assuming they could justify their organizational schema. It is my hope that, by demonstrating that literature reviews – and academic writing – are part science and part art, students will assume more agency in their own writing voices, especially as we prepare them to incrementally advance in their own academic writing toward a unique dissertation study.

The Context

Conceptualizations of good teaching call on faculty members to create a bridge between a lesson's core ideas and learners' prior knowledge. As Ken Bain (2004), author of the award-winning book, *What the Best College Teachers Do*, points out, previously held mental models and misconceptions are often the hardest things for students to unlearn. In order to form this bridge and push students' learning toward new knowledge, there are two key strategies built into the "Candy Sort" lesson: scaffolded learning and confidence building.

Scaffolded Learning
The "Candy Sort" lesson is based on the premise that students will best grasp the core idea of developing and labeling categories of themes from the literature if they can mitigate feeling overwhelmed by the literature. Many novice researchers gather endless articles, books, and resources for their literature reviews only to find themselves unsure of what to

include and how to present it in a way that guides the reader. As such, the "Candy Sort" begins with the familiar practice of sorting candy (or similar activity) – a lower-level skill most students mastered as children – and then slowly builds from the familiar to increasingly complex skills, such as categorizing ideas in the literature, labeling the categories, identifying evidence that supports the categories, and articulating the organizational structure and rationale. The lesson's strength comes in connecting a past skill – sorting candy – to a comparable, more complex skill – sorting the literature – all the while requiring students to justify their organization. The ability to analyze literature (or data) and articulate themes is one of the most valuable skills of a researcher, as this is a similar skill set for more advanced research skills such as coding and identifying the findings of a study.

Confidence Building

By teaching introductory research to new doctoral students, I have come to realize that many students employ the book report or stream of consciousness formats because it feels safe – it allows them to avoid inserting their own voice into the structure of the literature review. Through its scaffolded approach of sorting candy, something that appears on the surface unrelated to literature reviews, the "Candy Sort" lesson pushes students to stake a claim around what they see as categories of themes in the candy, and eventually, in the literature. The ability to stake, articulate, and justify a claim – namely identifying categories of candy/themes – is an important disposition and skill set for a budding scholar.

In closing, the "Candy Sort" strives to engage students in a lighthearted, experiential lesson that uses the power of sorting candy to foster deeper connections to categorizing, labeling, and justifying core ideas in the literature, while honoring, and as needed, countering students' prior learning and contexts. Oh, and the benefit of leftover candy for a post-class feast isn't so bad either!

BIBLIOGRAPHY

Bain, K. (2004). *What the best college teachers do*. Harvard University Press.
    Shares strategies for teaching effectiveness from noted college professors; includes discussion of students' background knowledge and mental models.
Becker, H.S. (2007). *Writing for social scientists: How to start and finish your thesis, book, or article* (2nd ed.). University of Chicago Press.
Reflects on common challenges in academic writing faced by novice and experienced writers and researchers.

8
Theoretical and Conceptual Frameworks

Understanding the Role of Theory in Congruent Research Designs

Penny A. Pasque and Chelsea Gilbert

INTRODUCTION

Brayboy (2005) asserted, "Stories are not separate from theory. They make up theory" (p. 439). Before we discuss pedagogy and theory, we invite you to first take a moment and consider yourself in relationship to theory – what are your stories? To what theories do your stories connect? And when did you make these connections? Perhaps you connect your stories to theory through formal classroom readings, or perhaps you found your way to theories that resonate with you and your life experiences in a less formal way.

Although theories may at times feel obtuse or challenging to understand, they provide important ways for us to make sense of our experiences and the experiences of those around us. For example, bell hooks (1994) explained that "I came to theory because I was hurting …. I came to theory desperate, wanting to comprehend—to grasp what was happening around and within me…. I saw in theory then a location for healing" (p. 59). hooks found theories that resonated with her experience and how she experienced the world.

In a similar fashion, Sara Ahmed (2017) asserted that "theory can do more the closer it gets to the skin" (p. 10). Here, Ahmed encourages us to utilize theory to dive deeply into the content and make changes that physically and emotionally matter to people <u>and</u> to herself. In this way, theory – and, by extension, our research – has the potential to impact people's daily lives, whether through recommendations for changes in policy, programs, or other areas (insert any research topic here!).

The purpose of this lesson is to (re)orient students learning the basics of research to the central role of theory in their research design decisions, including congruent choices about methodology, methods for collection, analysis, and trustworthiness. We provide an example grounded in qualitative research for illustrative purposes; quantitative and mixed methods stem from positivist and post-positivist approaches and this lesson plan includes and extends beyond those paradigms. By grounding themselves in theory in an accessible way, emerging scholars may craft more congruent – and, therefore, more impactful – studies.

DOI: 10.4324/b23320-11

THEORETICAL AND CONCEPTUAL FRAMEWORKS

QUALITATIVE LESSON PLAN

Topic	*Understanding the purpose of a theoretical framework and its use in informing congruent decision-making in qualitative research*
Learning Objectives	• Students will be able to define and distinguish between theoretical and conceptual frameworks. • Students will be able to explain the ways to utilize a theoretical framework in a congruent way throughout a qualitative research study. • Students will be able to apply a theoretical framework in qualitative data analysis through theoretical coding.
Definitions	To begin, we thought it might be helpful to define a few words from the exercise; however, note that each term is far more complicated than described here (also see Pasque et al., 2012). • "Epistemology" – knowing. • "Ontology" – being. • "Onto-epistemology" – knowing and being, intertwined. • "Axiology" – valuing, including values and criteria of values. • "Praxiology" – doing. • "Paradigm" – a collection of beliefs and concepts; a philosophical and practical way of thinking, knowing, being, and doing. Examples include: ○ Used in quantitative and mixed methods research: ▪ "Positivism" – seeks "Truth" ○ Used in qualitative research: ▪ "Post-positivism" – seeks "truth" (lower case) while acknowledging that the researcher makes a difference with the questions they ask, and methods they choose. ▪ "Constructivism" – acknowledges the nature of both knowledge and reality as socially constructed; the researcher is seen as the instrument for the research. ▪ "Interpretivism" – seeks multiple perspectives of reality from participants; the researcher perceived as instrument. ▪ "Post-structural" – challenges traditional concepts of truth, including through deconstruction of language and power. ▪ "Critical" – unapologetically interrogates and upends constructions of hegemonic power, inclusion/exclusion of voices, and individual and systemic oppression.
Needed Materials	• Short explanations of 3–4 theories drawn from different paradigmatic / onto-epistemological perspectives. • Copies of an example transcript from a qualitative study (1 transcript for each group). • Sticky notes or notecards labeled with a variety of options for the following categories (if possible, each category should be denoted by a separate color; 1 set for each group): ○ Paradigmatic / onto-epistemological approaches, such as: ▪ Post-positivist ▪ Constructivist ▪ Interpretivist ▪ Poststructural ▪ Critical ○ Theoretical frameworks, such as: ▪ Black Feminist Thought ▪ Intersectionality Theory ▪ TribalCrit

Topic	*Understanding the purpose of a theoretical framework and its use in informing congruent decision-making in qualitative research*
	<ul><li>Sense-making</li><li>Racial Battle Fatigue</li><li>Sense of Belonging</li><li>Queer Theory</li></ul><ul><li>Research questions (tailored to the example transcript)</li><li>Research methodologies, such as:<ul><li>Narrative inquiry</li><li>Ethnography</li><li>Phenomenology</li><li>Grounded theory</li><li>Discourse analysis</li></ul></li><li>Data collection methods, such as:<ul><li>Interview videos and transcripts (e.g., semi-structured, conversational, walking interviews, oral history)</li><li>Observations</li><li>Documents and/or artifacts</li><li>Participant diaries</li><li>Photo elicitation or drawings</li><li>Focus groups (e.g., semi-structured, talking circles, sister circles)</li><li>Researcher memos</li></ul></li><li>Data analysis methods that match the methodologies selected, such as:<ul><li>Deconstruction (see Allan, 2009)</li><li>Line-by-line coding (see Saldaña, 2021)</li><li>Thematic coding (see Saldaña, 2021)</li><li>Open & axial coding (see Corbin & Strauss, 2007)</li><li>Character mapping, plot, and/or time analysis (see Dauite & Lightfoot, 2003)</li><li>Messy, ordered, and political mapping (see Clarke et al., 2017)</li></ul></li><li>*Note*: Ensure that there are multiple congruent options for qualitative research studies represented amongst the notecards.</li></ul>
Pre-lesson Preparation	<ul><li>*Timing and scaffolding*: This lesson is designed to fall at the latter point of an introductory masters- or doctoral-level course on research methods or qualitative research. Prior to this lesson, students should understand the basic aspects of qualitative research design, paradigmatic and onto-epistemological approaches to qualitative research, and common methodologies and methods used in qualitative research.<ul><li>If possible, the class period prior to this lesson should utilize the example transcript to increase students' familiarity with the content. Subsequent class periods should refer to the activities undertaken in this lesson to reinforce the content and further illustrate the myriad uses of theory in qualitative research.</li></ul></li><li>*Prior homework*: Students should be familiar with the concept of congruence in qualitative research (YouTube video: Linder et al., 2017).</li></ul>
Activities	*Note*: This lesson is designed to fill an entire class period (approximately two hours). If needed, the lesson can be separated into two (approximately 60 minute) periods by pausing after the first small group activity. **Part I**<ul><li>Introductory discussion: What is theory? (10–15 minutes)<ul><li>Open by asking the class, "What is theory?" Take a few responses.</li><li>Share the <u>Brayboy quote</u> from the beginning of the chapter on a board/screen. Ask students – is this how they think about theory? Is their story of theory similar or different? How so?</li></ul></li></ul>

THEORETICAL AND CONCEPTUAL FRAMEWORKS

Topic	*Understanding the purpose of a theoretical framework and its use in informing congruent decision-making in qualitative research*

- ○ Share the bell hooks quote. Ask students to respond to this perspective on theory – does it align with their own? Why or why not?
- ○ Explain that, although theories may at times feel obtuse or challenging to understand, they provide an important way for us to make sense of our experiences and the experiences of those around us.
- ○ Use the Ahmed quote to illustrate this further. In qualitative research, we are aiming to better understand our lives and the lives of others, and theory is an important way that enables us to move toward making a difference.
- Theoretical vs. Conceptual Frameworks (10 minutes)
  - ○ Explain that one way theory is used in qualitative research is through a theoretical or conceptual framework.
  - ○ A theoretical framework is the perspective through which your research questions will be answered, and functions to provide "a clearly articulated signpost or lens for how the study will process new knowledge" (Collins & Stockton, 2018, p. 2). Generally, a theoretical framework comes from one existing theory.
  - ○ A conceptual framework "categorize[s] and describe[s] concepts relevant to the study and the many relationships among them" (Rocco & Plakhotnik, 2009, p. 122). It "best functions as a map of how all the literature works together in a particular study" (Collins & Stockton, 2018, p. 5). Conceptual frameworks often bring together two or more existing theories or models. At times, it is helpful for scholars to draw a figure of a conceptual framework.
  - ○ Ask students, "Why do we use frameworks in qualitative research?"
    - Answers may include: to provide focus and organization in a study, to connect the study to existing scholarship, or to aid in sense-making of the topic being studied (Collins & Stockton, 2018).
  - ○ Give an example of a theoretical framework and a conceptual framework, either from the literature or from your own research.
  - ○ *Note*: It is important to share with students that, even in a grounded theory approach, "theory-free research does not exist" (Collins & Stockton, 2018, p. 2).
- Theory Nuggets (10 minutes)
  - ○ Transition by sharing that theoretical and conceptual frameworks are not isolated parts of a qualitative research study (for doctoral students – they show up in and beyond "Chapter 2"). Before moving into an activity that illustrates this further, explain that you are going to introduce the students to a few key theories by sharing some "theory nuggets." *Note*: This is especially important if your students are from different disciplines, have varying levels of exposure to theory, or are generally uncomfortable talking about theory.
  - ○ Choose 3–4 theories and spend 2–3 minutes reviewing the core tenets of each. Some examples include Black Feminist Thought, TribalCrit, Intersectionality Theory, Racial Battle Fatigue, Sense-Making, and Queer Theory. *Note*: The activity will illustrate the broadest range of perspectives if you intentionally choose theories from a range of paradigmatic / onto-epistemological perspectives (i.e., try not to just choose critical or constructivist theories).
- Congruence Review (5 minutes)
  - ○ Finally, spend a few moments asking students to share the meaning of congruence in qualitative research, building on their homework (Linder et al., 2017, video). Ensure that students recognize "congruence" means that all parts of a study are in alignment with one another.
  - ○ It may be helpful to illustrate an example of incongruence, such as a student who wishes to use transcendental (post-positivist) phenomenology as her methodology while drawing from constructivist grounded theory to code her data. *Note*: The exception to this is the advanced concept of bricolage with critical inquiry (Kincheloe, 2005), which you may want to introduce to students along with further readings.

Topic	*Understanding the purpose of a theoretical framework and its use in informing congruent decision-making in qualitative research*

- Small Group Activity 1: Congruence in Theoretical Decision-making (25 minutes)
  - Split students up into groups of 3–4.
  - Assign each group one theory that you reviewed earlier in the class during "theory nuggets" as their <u>theoretical framework</u>.
  - Explain that the students will have approximately 20 minutes as a group to craft a congruent study based on the "pieces" before them – notecards previously created with options for paradigmatic / onto-epistemological approaches, theoretical frameworks, research questions (crafted based on the example transcript), esearchh methodologies, collection methods, and analysis methods.
  - As a group, students should discuss the ways that a congruent study might be crafted based on the theoretical framework that they have been given. Let students know that there are many "right" or congruent answers and some incongruent answers. The goal of this activity is for them to be able to justify their decisions. *Example*: Some sections, such as methods for data collection, may have more than one correct answer (for example: focus groups and interviews).
  - Make your way to each group to assist as needed. Students may need coaching in the following areas:
    - How to determine the paradigmatic / epistemological approach of a particular theory.
    - How to choose a congruent methodology from different types of research questions.
    - Methods for data collection, data analysis, and trustworthiness that correspond to different methodologies.
- Debrief (15 minutes)
  - Have each group present their congruent study.
  - Discuss the elements of the activity that were most challenging for the students. Ask: "What is difficult about maintaining congruence in a qualitative study?" and "Why is it important?"
  - As time allows, have a discussion with the group about how students think their assigned theoretical framework might impact a) data collection, b) analysis were they to conduct this study, and c) the congruent steps for trustworthiness (e.g., member checking, audit trails, researcher reflexivity, researcher positionality, bridling, bracketing).

Part II
- Explanation of Theoretical Coding (5 minutes)
  - Focus students' attention back to the example transcript and explain that they are now going to practice one method of using theory during the data analysis phase of a study.
  - Explain that "theoretical coding" is a form of "deductive" (or "etic") coding where the researcher structures codes from their theoretical framework and looks at the data through the lens of those codes.
  - Let students know that theoretical coding can be used with most methodological approaches with the exception of grounded theory.
  - Finally, offer the metaphor of using theoretical concepts as organizers; Collins and Stockton (2018) "a high-level theory, like a coat closet, can provide a framework through which to organize data" (p. 4).
- Small Group Activity 2: Theoretical Coding (20 minutes)
  - Place students back into their same small groups of 3–4. Using the example transcript, instruct them to practice theoretical coding using their previously assigned theory.

THEORETICAL AND CONCEPTUAL FRAMEWORKS

Topic	*Understanding the purpose of a theoretical framework and its use in informing congruent decision-making in qualitative research*
	○ As a group, students should first decide on several concepts relevant to their theory that they might look for in the transcript. If the transcript is especially long, encourage the students to practice coding one section of the transcript. *Note*: Students do not need to emphasize a particular methodological approach at this stage; the goal is simply to get a sense for how theory might be "plugged in" (Jackson & Mazzei, 2011, p. 725) to data. ○ Make your way to each group to assist as needed. Students may need coaching in the following areas: 　▪ Theoretical coding also known as deductive (etic) coding versus inductive (emic / emergent) coding. 　▪ Identification of a concept within a theory and applying it to data. 　▪ Disagreements amongst students about codes (note that these can be important and rich conversations, much like in research teams). • Debrief (15 minutes) ○ Have one representative from each theory share a one-minute overview of their group's "findings." ○ Reflect on the ways that theory impacts data analysis. What did students notice through this activity that they may not have noticed without theory? ○ Ask students to imagine what it might be like to put their assigned theory in "conversation" with another. For example, what might happen if Black Feminist Thought and Queer Theory were combined to create a new conceptual framework? How might this impact coding of the data? • Close (5 minutes) ○ Return to the initial discussion about theory and its role in qualitative research. Reminder: just like qualitative research, theory can be highly personal. Encourage students to begin with their own storied lives as an entry point and connect them with existing theory.
Virtual Adaptations	This activity can easily be adapted into a synchronous virtual class meeting by utilizing Jamboard (Google, 2022), a free digital whiteboard resource. (See Figure 8.1). • Create a separate Jamboard for each small group of students. • Create sticky notes of different colors (each color to correspond to a different aspect of a qualitative research study) and pre-populate the sticky notes with the multiple options for each category (as described above; use one color of sticky note for each paradigmatic approach, one color for research questions, one color for methodology, etc.). Organize these into "piles." • If desired, use the functionality on Jamboard to create "boxes" that students can use to organize their sticky notes / drag and drop. • Use a video conferencing platform to separate students into small groups with each group in a separate breakout room.
Assessment	• Formative assessment: While the small groups engage in activities, move around the room and assess students' ability to apply the concepts. • Formative assessment: As each group of students shares with the large group, assess their understanding of the concepts and any areas where confusion or misconceptions arise. • Formative assessment: During the closing portion of the lesson, ask students to share one key takeaway and one concept they are still unclear about. Use these to adjust future lessons. • Summative assessment: Grade the students' final assignment with attention to the use of theory as well as congruence between theory, methodology, collection, analysis, and trustworthiness.

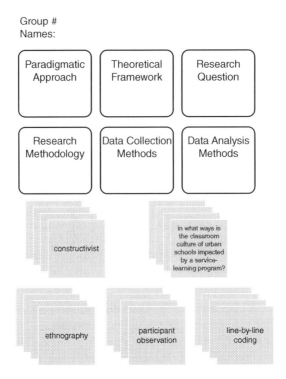

FIGURE 8.1 Example Setup for Google Jamboard Activity

Note. The boxes in the upper half of the board correspond to the varying aspects of a qualitative research study, while the piles of sticky notes (Jamboard has fun colors!) in the lower half of the board comprise options for each category. In the activity, each group would be given a different theoretical framework, and would work to "fill in" the boxes with options that are congruent with that framework. Some categories, such as data collection methods, may allow for more than one "correct" response. See: https://jamboard.google.com/

INTELLECTUAL PREPARATION FOR LESSON

As a faculty member, I/Penny have taught qualitative research for more than 15 years and the topic of my scholarship is qualitative inquiry. In addition, I have taught research design for quantitative, qualitative, and mixed methods courses. As a graduate student with years of practitioner experience and an aspiring researcher with expertise in qualitative and quantitative methodologies, I/Chelsea have facilitated many engaging activities that center student learning and have explored numerous theories. Together, we have designed, taught, and revised this lesson, and we reflect on core ideas in this section. Our goal is to make theory accessible to instructors and students because we find that theory is extremely beneficial and is always present in research whether or not scholars recognize this.

Core Ideas

Beyond the learning outcomes described above, the core ideas that anchor this lesson include the pervasiveness of theory in research and the importance of theoretical congruence. We briefly describe each.

The Pervasiveness of Theory in Qualitative Research

Theory is deeply personal but is not always recognized as such. Early career scholars often fear it – and this is not surprising because it is often inaccessible. That said, theory is a part of our own stories and students have already been engaging in theory work all their lives, often without recognizing it. Regardless of paradigmatic approach, researchers – and the theories to which they knowingly or unknowingly subscribe – make a difference in the research process. This is true of positivist approaches, which seek to reduce or even eliminate researcher "bias," as well as of constructivist or interpretivist approaches, which embrace the researcher's perspective as a core element of a study design. In all cases, the theory a researcher chooses should reflect understanding of the context under exploration.

Theory is also pervasive throughout a research design and should not be limited to "Chapter 2" or the review of literature. Students should take up the theoretical or conceptual framework (e.g., two or more theories/models connected conceptually) throughout a research design (e.g., problem statement, rapport with participants, collection, etic/deductive analysis when warranted, findings, trustworthiness decisions, and beyond). The lesson also illustrates that, for qualitative researchers, the process is iterative; students can be taught to reflect on – and revise – theoretical and conceptual framework choices based on new knowledge from their study.

The Importance of Theoretical and Research Design Congruence

The exercise demonstrates the ways that different theoretical frameworks may drastically alter a qualitative study, from beginning to end. It may be instructive for some quantitative and mixed methods scholars as well. The exercise above is split into two parts and focuses on two core concepts: congruent design decisions and theoretical coding.

First is the important use of a *theoretical framework in making congruent research design decisions* in every area of the study. We expand upon the exercise above with an illustrative example. We remind instructors that there are many "right" or congruent answers and some incongruent answers.

A group focused on qualitative research was assigned the theoretical framework of "Sense of Belonging," which describes the ways that college students come to feel at home in their campus environments (see Strayhorn, 2019). The students chose the answers:

- Paradigmatic/onto-epistemological approach: Interpretivist.
- RQ: What stories do collegiate women of color share about their experiences within a STEAM undergraduate research opportunity program (UROP)?
- Methodology: Narrative inquiry.
- Data collection methods: Sister Circles, a variation on focus groups centered on Black women's experiences (see Evans-Winters and Esposito, 2018), and journals.
- Data analysis methods: Plot analysis, which involves seeing the data through the lens of a story and analyzing crucial elements of the plot of that story (see Dauite & Lightfoot, 2003), and theoretical coding,
- Trustworthiness: Researcher positionality (if included).

Note that Sense of Belonging (Strayhorn, 2019) can align with an interpretivist or a constructivist approach (it could also be coupled with additional theories or models to create a conceptual framework). Also notice how narrative inquiry is the methodology chosen, and data collection methods align with the theory and the methodology.

The second concept is that of "theoretical coding." Narrative inquiry is often inductive, but in this example, the scholar deductively codes for the elements of Sense of Belonging (i.e., cognitive elements, affective elements, alienation). As stressed already, the theory of Sense of Belonging is reflected in collection and analysis, but also in establishing trustworthiness and writing up the findings, discussions and implications for change.

Learners

Students often use theory in their jobs or lives without recognizing it. Encourage students to trust their intuitive knowing and seek existing theories that resonate with their perspective. Most students can understand theory if they find the right texts and/or the theories that align with their worldview. Much already exists from western/white perspectives, so as instructors, it may be helpful to encourage students to consider theories that come from the margins to foster equitable learning spaces.

Also, scaffold the learning. Start with the easier renditions of theory, then move to the more complex. It does take time for students to read and learn, but that is the privilege of graduate school and one reason they will be considered an "expert" moving forward (if not already).

Context

Theory plays a central role in qualitative, quantitative, and mixed methods research, although some graduate programs are void of theory and some require specific theories. Thus, it is important that instructors scaffold understandings of theory – and its multiple uses – into discussions with students. We understand this may require significant intellectual preparation to hone one's own understanding of theory and, often, students want an easy way to understand the depth of theory, but that is not always possible.

We find that connecting theory to students' own existing stories and honoring their past content knowledge are ways to provide comfort that they have already engaged with theory. Further, we often learn western/white knowledge in doctoral programs; thus, minoritized theories/perspectives are important to center. This helps minoritized students to understand the theories available already as well as offers a way to introduce theories that many students have not yet been exposed to in their studies. This is only an introduction; from here, students must engage deeply with the existing literature – and (excitingly!) their own research study – to manifest new understandings of theory.

BIBLIOGRAPHY

Ahmed, S. (2017). *Living a feminist life*. Duke University Press.

Allan, E. J. (2009). *Feminist poststructuralism meets policy analysis: An overview*. Routledge.

Brayboy, B. M. J. (2005). Toward a tribal critical race theory in education. *Urban Review, 37*(5), 425–446. https://doi.org/10.1007/s11256-005-0018-y

Clarke, A. E., Friese, C., & Washburn, R. S. (2017). *Situational analysis: Grounded theory after the interpretive turn* (2nd ed.). Sage.

Collings, P. H. (2000/2009). *Black feminist thought*. Routledge.

THEORETICAL AND CONCEPTUAL FRAMEWORKS

Collins, C. S., & Stockton, C. M. (2018). The central role of theory in qualitative research. *International Journal of Qualitative Methods, 17*, 1–10. https://doi.org/10.1177/1609406918797475

Corbin, J., & Strauss, A. (2007). *Basics of qualitative research* (3rd ed.). Sage.

Dauite, C., & Lightfoot, C. (2003). *Narrative analysis: Studying the development of individuals in society.* Sage.

Evans-Winters, V., & Esposito, J. (2018). Researching the bridge called our backs: The invisibility of "us" in qualitative communities. *International Journal of Qualitative Studies in Education, 31*(9), 863–876. https://doi.org/10.1080/09518398.2018.1478152

Google. (2022). *Google Jamboard.* https://jamboard.google.com/ *This is a great resource for this exercise or other exercises, particularly for online courses or an online discussion board that supplements in-class activities.*

hooks, b. (1994). *Teaching to transgress.* Taylor & Francis. *This is a seminal teaching textbook for the field of education and beyond.*

Jackson, A. Y., & Mazzei, L. A. (2011). *Thinking with theory in qualitative research: Viewing data across multiple perspectives.* Taylor & Francis.

Kincheloe, J. (2005). On to the next level: Continuing the conceptualization of the bricolage. *Qualitative Inquiry. 11*(3). 323–350.

Linder, C., Jones, S. R., Pasque, P. A., & Stewart, D-L. (2017). On congruency in qualitative research. https://www.youtube.com/watch?v=Qfq49zKsMqk

Dr. Linder brought together this group of national award-winning qualitative scholars to talk with the graduate students in her qualitative research course about the concept of "congruency."

Pasque, P. A., Carducci, R., Kuntz, A. K., & Gildersleeve, R. E. (2012). Qualitative inquiry for equity in higher education: Methodological innovations, implications, and interventions. *ASHE Higher Education Report, 37*(6). Jossey-Bass.

Rocco, T. S., & Plakhotnik, M. S. (2009). Literature reviews, conceptual frameworks, and theoretical frameworks: Terms, functions, and distinctions. *Human Resource Development Review, 8*(1), 120–130. https://doi.org/10.1177/1534484309332617

Saldaña, J. (2021). *Coding manual for qualitative researchers* (4th ed.). Sage.

Strayhorn, T. (2019). *College students' sense of belonging* (2nd ed.). Routledge.

Section III

Research Design

Section Editors: Jeffrey C. Sun and Ishwanzya Rivers

9

Introduction to Section III

Research Design

Jeffrey C. Sun and Ishwanzya Rivers

A successful research project requires a suitable research design. The research design is the plan, structure, or outline that achieves the research objective. Research design is concerned with the aims, uses, purposes, intentions, and plans within the practical constraint of location, time, money, and the researcher's availability (Hakim, 2000). With those ends in mind, researchers are faced with integrating a lot of pieces of their study, and often, we are faced with few techniques in conveying memorable and meaningful ways to achieve this (Becker, 1998). For instance, they must contemplate the role of the extant literature, the study framework, unit(s) of analysis, phenomena of interest, the research questions, and a handful of practical considerations including data access, methods, cost, ethics, and other logistics. Those elements are the starting point or perhaps what some researchers might call the inputs to the design. Then, researchers contemplate and eventually select from among the three major categories of research design: quantitative (e.g., experimental – true and quasi-experiments and non-experimental), qualitative (e.g., case studies, narrative research, phenomenological research, grounded theory, and ethnography), and mixed method research design (e.g., convergent parallel mixed method, explanatory sequential and exploratory sequential mixed methods) (Creswell, 2014; Creswell & Creswell, 2017; Jongbo, 2014).

In Chapter 10, "Visualize Your Research Design: Moving from Research Questions to Research Design," Ishwanzya Rivers and Jeffrey Sun present a lesson to guide researchers on the research design process by building onthe study framework and research questions as well as connecting the research questions and the projected research outputs. Specifically, after a basic review of research methods, the lesson employs a mind mapping exercise asking critical questions such as what the researchers need, want, and are required to conduct the research, as well as considering what it costs and how/in what ways theory informs the study. It also incorporates peer feedback to avert the feeling of research isolation, which new researchers sometimes report as an undesirable experience. Further, the peer reviews encourage a research team mindset and support reflective practice for both the presenting student and the reviewing student.

DOI: 10.4324/b23320-13

Aurora Kamimura reminds us that the alignment of each section of a research study – especially when building from the topic, literature review, framework, hypotheses, and research questions – allows one section to inform the next. These building blocks ensure intentionality, focus, and coherency as design aspects to the study. Accordingly, Chapter 11, "Let's Road Trip: Aligning Theoretical Frameworks, Research Questions and Research Design," takes an illustrative approach for new researchers to identify different trails that a study design takes, much like travelers selecting a route to reach certain destinations on a map. The traveling route metaphor works well as Merriam and Tisdell (2015) aptly noted,

> Rarely would anyone starting out on a trip just walk out the door with no thought of where to go or how to get there. The same is true when beginning a research study…This map…is a *logical plan for getting from here to there*.
>
> (p. 73)

The "Let's Road Trip" lesson allows us to digest the logical plan of a research design through imagery and practical recall.

Whether quantitative, qualitative, or mixed methods, our positionality as researchers influences and shapes our studies. Certainly, other factors come into play such as the topic to be studied, sampling techniques, and the data analytic approach have some impact on the research design, but researcher positionality largely accounts for how we structure our studies and look at our data. In Chapter 12, Beth Bukoski offers "The Self and Research: Positionality Through Artifacts" as a series of symbolic imagery to show how researchers represent their social identities (e.g., gender, race/ethnicity, professional role at work), which are salient to the research project.

To examine the appropriateness and consistency of our data analysis, a research design aspect includes how we think about study trustworthiness. In Chapter 13, "Trustworthiness and Ethics in Research: Using Reflexivity to See the Self in Ethical Research," G. Blue Brazelton and Ijeoma Ononuju explore that value of the data, which quantitative researchers often reference as examining measurement, reliability, and validity. Specifically, the lesson involves constructing a rubric to establish evaluation criteria and descriptions through a guided exercise. This activity offers a collaborative approach where the students anchor key components of reflexivity and connect it to trustworthiness.

In conclusion, the lessons on research design present activities on mapping, routing, reflecting, and evaluating. These approaches to learning research design are shared from experienced researchers, and integrate memorable and practical lessons. Indeed, researcher learning literature, such as Cliff Adelman's *Lessons of a Generation*, in which he shares his struggles tackling a large national dataset and coding decisions, and Annette Lareau's (2011) appendix in *Unequal Childhoods*, in which she journals the challenges and decision points she faced while conducting her study, are wonderful gifts to emerging and experienced scholars. They remind us that we will encounter unexpected events, we are imperfect, and we must not forget the roles of planning and pivoting (when needed) to ensure logic, consistency, focus, coherency, alignment, and planning. Threaded among these chapters are tools and insights that elucidate these interests, and they have students engaged so the lessons are both memorable and meaningful.

BIBLIOGRAPHY

Becker, H. S. (1998). *Tricks of the trade: How to think about your research while you're doing it*. The University of Chicago Press.

Creswell, J. W. (2014). *Educational research: Planning, conducting, and evaluating quantitative and qualitative research*. Sage.

Creswell, J. W., & Creswell, J. D. (2017). *Research design: Qualitative, quantitative, and mixed methods approaches* (5th ed.). Sage Publishing.

Hakim, C. (2000). *Research design: Successful designs in social and economic research*. Routledge.

Jongbo, O. C. (2014). The role of research design in a purpose driven enquiry. *Review of Public Administration and Management 3*(6), 87–94.

Lareau, A. (2011). *Unequal childhoods: Class, race, and family life* (2nd ed.). University of California Press.

Merriam, S. B., & Tisdell, E. J. (2015). *Qualitative research: A guide to design and implementation* (4th ed.). John Wiley & Sons.

10

Visualize Your Research Design

Moving from Research Questions to Research Design

Ishwanzya Rivers and Jeffrey C. Sun

INTRODUCTION

In 1971, sociologist Walter Wallace illustrated research design considerations for the growing presence of what was known as "scientific sociology." His processing offered an accessible, relational examination of research design. Even today, developing a research design often leaves students fearing and dreading the research process because of its overwhelming set of constructs and conceptual elements involved. As Groenewald (2004) notes, "Aspiring scholars need a grasp of a vast range of research methodologies in order to select the most appropriate research design, or combination of designs, most suitable for a particular study" (p. 42). This agonizing step of choosing the "right" design may leave students stuck spinning their mental wheels by consulting literature, commiserating with their peers, and spending endless hours conversing with their advisors. "Visualize Your Research Design" assists students in moving from their research question(s) to a research design. "Visualize Your Research Design" helps students to visualize the connections between their research questions, research design, and their projected research outcomes.

LESSON PLAN

Topic	*Sorting through multiple research design options, but ultimately visualizing and selecting a research design based on the research question(s)*
Learning Objectives	• Students will identify the research design process. • Students will differentiate between research design options. • Students will pose a research design to their research question(s). • Students will critique the rationale for choosing a research design.

DOI: 10.4324/b23320-14

VISUALIZE YOUR RESEARCH DESIGN

Topic	Sorting through multiple research design options, but ultimately visualizing and selecting a research design based on the research question(s)
Needed Materials	<ul><li>Large sheets of paper (e.g., butcher block).</li><li>Colored markers/pencils (multiple colors for each student).</li><li>Post-it notes.</li><li>Lecture/Mini-Discussion on Research Design.</li><li>For prior homework, students will have read:<ul><li>Abutabenjeh & Jaradat, 2018.</li><li>Creswell & Creswell, 2017, Chapters 1, 5 and 6.</li></ul></li><li>From prior lessons, students will need:<ul><li>Their finalized research question(s).</li><li>The study's conceptual or theoretical framework.</li><li>Research notebook (electronic or physical).</li></ul></li></ul>
Pre-lesson Preparation	<ul><li>*How may I scaffold this lesson?*<ul><li>This lesson is based on students finalizing their research question(s) in previous sessions using an exercise connected to research outputs, study framework, and future research goals. This lesson leads to a formal writing assignment where students will interview an expert researcher in their chosen research design on how to structure and complete research projects utilizing that research design.</li></ul></li><li>*Do all students have the cultural context to appreciate this lesson?*<ul><li>"Visualize Your Research Design" requires knowledge of mind mapping, which some students may confuse with concept mapping. Although illustratively similar in many cases to concept and argument mapping, mind mapping involves pictures and a non-linear connection of ideas. For those students unfamiliar with mind mapping, outline the instructions as provided below and offer an example of a mind map for the activity.</li><li>Students may resist mapping or visualizing their research and sharing those maps with the class. They may feel that mapping does not connect with the research process and may struggle to make the connection. Facilitate a discussion about how powerful illustrations tell stories, depict relationships, or connect ideas, so they grasp the significance of this lesson.</li></ul></li></ul>
Activities	**Opening** <ul><li>Aligned with Robert Gagné's (1965) instructional events, we always start class with an activating activity that allows students to check in and orient themselves to the space, the learning, and each other. To check in, students are asked to share:<ul><li>What's new in their life/world?</li><li>What have they thought about since the last class?</li><li>Then, using an audience response technology (e.g., Mentimeter), state in a phrase or sentence an "aha" point or message from the readings. After that, another response is requested where students present a question or an area of clarification needed.</li></ul></li><li>The opening activity primes learners to share and engage in the course activities, tie in past lessons and current course readings/preparation materials, and prompt areas of student learning assessment for us as instructors.</li></ul>**Activity 1: Reading Discussion** <ul><li>To scaffold learning, provide a discussion of the readings and concepts. The key concepts to cover are:<ul><li>The definition of research design and its connection to research questions, research outcomes, literature, and frameworks as well as preview researcher positionality.</li><li>The three types of research design (e.g., quantitative, qualitative, and mixed method).</li><li>The types of research processes inherent to each research design. Providing examples of each type of research design would be helpful.</li></ul></li></ul>

Topic	*Sorting through multiple research design options, but ultimately visualizing and selecting a research design based on the research question(s)*

Quantitative
- Experimental
  - ◇ Randomized experiment with comparisons
- Quasi-experiment
  - ◇ Survey research, not randomized but comparison group
  - ◇ Casual-comparative research
- Non-experimental
  - ◇ Correlation design
  - ◇ Descriptive studies

Qualitative (as illustrations)
- Case studies
- Narrative research
- Phenomenological research
- Grounded theory
- Ethnography

Mixed Method
- Action Research
- Convergent parallel mixed method
- Explanatory sequential mixed methods
- Exploratory sequential mixed methods

Activity 2: Visualizing and Mind Mapping
- Explain the process of mind mapping. A mind map is an illustration with a keyword or phrase in the middle, lines connecting from the center to a main idea, and even more lines connecting from the main ideas to details.
- Using your mind map as an example, explain the directions for learners:
  - Students choose the mind map topic and place it in the middle of the drawing (e.g., their research question).
  - Students come up with 3–5 main ideas, then evenly space them in a circular formation around the mind map topic (e.g., sampling, research site, materials, theoretical framework).
    - Students will be familiar with theories from prior work, particularly theories related to their research questions.
    - They will have completed an exercise and reading on theory prior to this lesson.
  - Draw a line from the mind map topic to each main idea.
  - Brainstorm supporting details such as ideas, tasks, and questions for each main idea.
  - Draw lines connecting each main idea to its supporting details.
- Inform students they will create a mind map to visualize their research design.
- Hand each participant a large sheet of paper (butcher block) along with Post-it notes.
- Pass around a container of multicolored markers/pencils (*Note*: you will need multiple colors for each student).
  - Advise students to take four different colors.
- On the board or screen, post the following prompt: "We are going to visualize our way to a research design by mind mapping the research design concepts." Display an image of the mind map with the following labeled sections:
  - Central theme or center idea: Your research question. Encourage students to draw an image representing their research question.
  - Four main ideas: sampling, research site, materials, and theoretical framework.
- Inform students their mind maps should have those labeled central themes and four main ideas, but they are to brainstorm supporting details such as ideas, tasks, and questions for each main idea. Students are often hesitant to "commit" the words/phrases onto the large sheet of paper, so encourage them to use Post-it notes as the warm-up or practice activity.

VISUALIZE YOUR RESEARCH DESIGN

Topic	*Sorting through multiple research design options, but ultimately visualizing and selecting a research design based on the research question(s)*

- As students are creating their mind maps, display the following questions to prompt their creations:
  - What do you need to conduct your research?
  - Where do you want to conduct your research?
  - Who else is required to conduct your research?
  - What does it cost to conduct your research?
  - How does theory inform your research?
  - What theory informs your research?
- Give students ~20 minutes to map their concepts. After students complete their mind maps, invite individual students, perhaps 4–5 from across the various study design categories (e.g., quantitative, qualitative, and mixed method), to share their maps with the class.
- *Optional*: as students share their maps, make connections of their examples to the 3 research designs. Reference key concepts, when possible, from the reading discussion. Also, create an atmosphere in which the presenting student may pose questions in an agile learning manner. Likewise, encourage other students to raise questions and offer practical considerations as if they were on the research team with the presenting student.
- Inform students that they may continue to add to their mind maps as they move through the remainder of the lesson, but complexity is not the goal, but rather the primary interest is a 50,000-foot view of the research project.

Activity 3: Research Design Speed Interview

- Arrange the class in paired pods with chairs and tables in a straight row or an arrangement that your room will accommodate (if there is an odd number of students, one group will have three students). The goal is to allow for easy pairing of students and students' ability to switch groups easily.
- On the screen or board, display the following prompt(s):
  - What is the subject of your research?
  - What do you need to conduct your research?
  - Who do you need to conduct your research?
  - Where will your research happen?
  - Why is your research important to you as a researcher?
- Explain that the students, who will role-play as members of the other student's research team, will spend 10 minutes in each round of the Speed Interview asking and answering the displayed questions. Use 7 or 12 minutes depending on the number of students in the course and the direction of the conversation; allow a shorter time if they appear to be off task and longer if they seem to struggle with the questions.
  - Let paired students know they should take turns asking and answering the displayed questions.
  - When the timer sounds, students switch partners, with the front row of partners moving one seat to the right.
    - As the instructor, determine which row rotates and which row remains stationary. Display instructions for student movement on the board.
  - Switch groups 6 times for a total of 60 minutes.
    - Run a timer for 10 minutes with an audible sound indicating the end of each 10-minute round.
    - You should also verbally let students know when they need to switch partners.

Topic	*Sorting through multiple research design options, but ultimately visualizing and selecting a research design based on the research question(s)*

	• After ~60 minutes, ask one student from the last pair to share what they have learned about their current partner's research from the interview. Have groups share out their observations. To accomplish this, ask for volunteers or cold-call students.
	   ○ As students share their observations, make notes and connections to one of the research processes inherent to each research design discussed above.
	   ○ Examples might include:
	      ▪ a large number of participants answering questions (i.e., quantitative survey research).
	      ▪ Individual interviews at a school (i.e., qualitative phenomenological research)
	      ▪ Observations of policy implementation and analysis of survey data (i.e., convergent parallel mixed method).
	• Give students ~5 minutes to add to their mind maps, explaining that the Speed Interview might have resulted in new ideas and if so, they should add details to their mind maps.
	• Close the activity by discussing with the students how, in answering the questions during the Speed Interview, they have identified what data is required, the method they would like to use to collect and analyze data, and how they will answer their research questions. Ultimately, they have visualized a research design. The next step is to identify and finalize a research design by articulating and critiquing their justification for the specified research design.
	Activity 4: Journaling Your Decision
	• As a closing activity, inform students they will Journal in their research notebooks for 10–15 minutes to finalize their research design.
	• Ask students to take out their research notebooks (physical or electronic).
	• Display the following prompt on the board or screen: "Using your mind map and the observations from the Speed Interview, outline your research design for your research questions and choose one of the research processes from one of the three research designs (e.g., quantitative, qualitative, mixed methods). List the rationale for choosing that research design, making connections to your researcher positionality and your research outcomes."
	   ○ Refer students back to the homework reading and the reading discussion.
	• Display a timer for 5 minutes.
	• Call time when the timer ends.
	• Homework: Students will submit their journals for feedback on the feasibility of the chosen research design and their research questions.

Virtual Adaptations	Adapting this lesson for an asynchronous or synchronous lesson requires additional formatting but transitions well to the online environment.
	• **Activity 1: Reading Discussion**
	   ○ As an asynchronous session, you must record a content video addressing the core concepts.
	• **Activity 2: Visualizing and Mind Mapping**
	   ○ As a synchronous and asynchronous session, students can utilize MindMeister (www.mindmeister.com) to create their mind map.
	      ▪ Synchronous: as homework before the lesson, instruct students to create a free account at MindMeister as they will need to access the account during the session.
	      ▪ Explain the steps for creating a mind map in MindMeister.

Topic	*Sorting through multiple research design options, but ultimately visualizing and selecting a research design based on the research question(s)*
	<ul><li>Asynchronous: Assign the visualizing and mind mapping activity as a discussion board prompt instructing students to create a MindMeister account. Outline the steps for creating the mind map through a recorded video that provides detailed instructions.<ul><li>Students will share their mind map screenshots with classmates in the discussion board forum.</li><li>Provide feedback making connections to the reading concepts.</li></ul></li></ul><ul><li>**Activity 3: Research Design Speed Interview**<ul><li>Synchronous: create breakout rooms for each pair of students. Move students in and out of the breakout rooms during the 6 rounds of the Speed Interview, changing partners.<ul><li>Debrief as a whole class.</li></ul></li><li>Asynchronous: pair students using the Group tool in your learning management system and create a written peer interview assignment where students interview one another.<ul><li>Include a self-observation section that students could then use for Activity 4: Journaling</li><li>Provide feedback on the submitted written assignment, making connections to the various research processes.</li></ul></li></ul></li><li>**Activity 4: Journaling Your Decision**<ul><li>Synchronous or Asynchronous<ul><li>Set up the Journal tool in your learning management system.</li><li>Set the parameters of the journal to only allow access for 5 minutes from when students open the assignment.</li><li>Display the journal prompt.</li><li>Provide instructions outlining the purpose of the journal assignment and the connection to finalizing a research design choice.</li></ul></li></ul></li></ul>
Assessment	Formative Assessment:<ul><li>During the reading discussion, assess students' ability to identify the various research designs and their ability to discuss the concepts.</li><li>During the Mind Mapping activity, assess students' ability to list the main ideas of their research questions.</li><li>During the Speed Interview discussion, assess students' observation of their classmates' answers and the connection to research designs.</li></ul>Summative Assessment:<ul><li>Review students' research journals and assess students' ability to identify a research design and provide a rationale for choosing a research design.</li><li>Grade the researcher interview following a rubric requiring articulation of research design rationale and connection of research design to research questions.</li></ul>

INTELLECTUAL PREPARATION FOR "VISUALIZE YOUR RESEARCH DESIGN"

Moving from a research question to a research design is a critical step for a researcher because it determines the feasibility and outcomes of the research project. Seemingly a straightforward process, conceiving of a research design requires sufficient knowledge of research design and its relationship to appropriate data collection, organizing and analyzing techniques, and interpreting results and findings. To connect research questions to research design, we discuss our intellectual preparation for "Visualize Your Research Design" by examining the core ideas of the lesson's topic, the learners, and the context for bridging core ideas and learners.

Core Ideas

"Visualize Your Research Design" is grounded in two core ideas for choosing a research design: connecting and seeing relationships between concepts, and reflection.

Connecting and Seeing Relationships Between Concepts
Choosing a research design can be a daunting task for novice researchers; however, a core idea of the "Visualize Your Research Design" lesson illustrates that connecting and seeing relationships between concepts aids in identifying a research design. By identifying and differentiating between research designs and research processes, novice researchers learn of the intrinsic relationship between the research question, research outcomes, and the research design. Mind mapping makes remembering information easier, creates connections uniquely, and allows students to become more actively involved in the learning process. Using all the ways the brain processes information – words, images, logic, color, and spatial awareness – novice researchers connect and see the relationship between the research question and research design, bringing clarity and ease to the research design decision-making process.

Reflection
Reflection is the second core concept of the "Visualize Your Research Design" lesson plan. Reflection requires novice researchers to examine how and why they chose their research design. Reflecting on the connection of their research questions to a specific research design highlights for novice researchers that choosing a research design is a deliberate process. Reflection serves to identify assumptions, choices, experiences, and actions during the research design choice process. Reflection requires researchers to think through their decisions, highlighting the experiences, opinions, throughs, and feelings in navigating the research design process.

The Learner

Students bring their past experiences, prior knowledge, and current selves to each lesson. In preparing this lesson, we must reflect on the learners' previous knowledge and possible misconceptions about choosing a research design and conducting research that might shape how students respond to this lesson.

Previous Learning and Misconceptions
Prior to the "Visualize Your Research Design" lesson, students will have encountered research designs and research studies through articles, readings, and prior hands-on

experience. Some students may have pre-formed their research design based on a desire to conduct a particular research design before aligning their research questions with the design. Additionally, many students attend the university to work with a specific researcher and often choose their research design based on the advisor's research design without consideration of their positionality, research questions, or research outcomes. The "Visualize Your Research Design" lesson plan moves students away from these set ideas of what their research should be by requiring them to visualize and reflect on the connection of the research design to their research questions and their desired research outcomes.

The Context

"Visualize Your Research Design" hinges on the idea that students need to connect and see relationships between concepts and reflect to translate their research questions into a research design. We ask students to visualize their research questions through a mind map of four key ideas and to connect those concepts to a potential research design. Through reflection, they critique that connection and discuss the intentionality of choosing a research design that aligns with their research questions. Active learning and critical thinking are the key strategies threaded into "Visualize Your Research Design" to connect the lesson's core ideas and learners' prior knowledge.

Active Learning and Critical Thinking

"Visualize Your Research Design" utilizes active learning or intentional engagement, purposeful observation, and critical reflection to engage novice researchers in identifying meaning-making during the research design choice process. "Visualize Your Research Design" begins with an activating activity to orient learners to the intellectual environment and encourage them to reflect on who they are and what they bring to the learning space, priming learners for critical reflection. "Visualize Your Research Design" utilizes mind mapping as a tool to facilitate critical thinking. Mind mapping promotes critical and creative thinking and encourages brainstorming, signaling to novice researchers that choosing a research design is a deliberate iterative process.

In closing, "Visualize Your Research Design" requires novice researchers to think about meaning-making and the intentionality of choosing a research design as well as highlight the relationship between their research questions and their research design. In short, learners are tasked with engaging, observing, and reflecting on the progress of their research process.

BIBLIOGRAPHY

Abutabenjeh, S., & Jaradat, R. (2018). Clarification of research design, research methods, and research methodology: A guide for public administration researchers and practitioners. *Teaching Public Administration, 36*(3), 237–258. https://doi.org/10.1177/0144739418775787

Budd, J. W. (2004). Mind maps as classroom exercises. *Journal of Economic Education, 35*(1), 35–46. https://doi.org/10.3200/JECE.35.1.35-46

Creswell, J. W. (2014). *Educational research: Planning, conducting, and evaluating quantitative and qualitative research.* Sage.

Creswell, J. W., & Creswell, J. D. (2017). *Research design: Qualitative, quantitative, and mixed methods approaches* (5th ed.). Sage Publishing.

Davies, M. (2011). Concept mapping, mind mapping and argument mapping: What are the differences and do they matter? *Higher Education, 62*, 279–301. https://doi.org/10.1007/s10734-010-9387-6

Farrand, P., Hussain, F., & Hennessy, E. (2002). The efficacy of the "mind map" study technique. *Medical Education, 36*(5), 426–431. https://doi.org/10.1046/j.1365-2923.2002.01205.x

Flynn, S. V. (2021). *Research design for the behavioral sciences: An applied approach.* Springer Publishing.

Gagné, R. M. (1965). *The conditions of learning.* Holt, Reinhart & Winston.

Hakim, C. (2000). *Research design: Successful designs in social and economic research.* Routledge.

Wallace, W. (Ed.) (1971). *The logic of science in sociology.* Routledge.

Weathington, B. L., Cunningham, J. L., & Pittenger, D. J. (2017). *Research methods for the behavioral and social sciences.* Wiley.

Wheeldon, J., & Faubert, J. (2009). Framing experience: Concept maps, mind maps, and data collection in qualitative research. *International Journal of Qualitative Methods, 8*(3), 68–83. https://doi.org/10.1177/160940690900800307

11

Let's Road Trip

Aligning Theoretical Frameworks, Research Questions and Research Design

Aurora Kamimura

INTRODUCTION

"*El viaje es más importante que la meta.* / The journey is more important than the destination." – Constantino Cavafis

[*traslado de griego* / translated from Greek]

I see my path, but I don't know where it leads. Not knowing where I'm going is what inspires me to travel it.

– Rosalia De Castro

Many of us have taken road trips, and some of us may even have heard versions of these quotes that speak to the value of the journey, but does that have anything to do with research? Oftentimes, as we begin to design our research study, it is important to pause and ensure that all of the *dots* are connecting. Much like a road trip, we must always plan out each stop to ensure that we are on the correct path toward our destination. Although, as easy as it is to become shortsighted in planning a road trip by only focusing on the destination; we, as researchers, can also become short-sided by only focusing on what we anticipate finding.

The Greek poet, Contantino Cavafis, reminds us to enjoy the journey, not simply the destination. Using the image of a road trip, we too can view our research as a journey to be enjoyed, one with multiple destinations, possibilities, and new discoveries. Like a road trip, with our research, we can travel down unimagined roads and gain inspiration by allowing the journey to organically propel us to our destination. Isn't that what we all, as researchers, seek: the joy of discovery? So, let's take a road trip as we help our graduate students map the various paths of discovery available when connecting frameworks, hypotheses, and research questions to our research design.

DOI: 10.4324/b23320-15

LESSON PLAN

Topic	*Road Mapping the connection between the theoretical/conceptual framework(s), hypotheses (if applicable), research question(s), and research design of a study*
Learning Objectives	Students will: • Connect research pieces, particularly the theoretical framework(s), hypotheses (if applicable), research question(s), and the research design of a study. • Articulate the rationale for decisions made between connection points: theoretical framework(s), hypotheses (if applicable), research question(s), and research design. • Recognize the value that multiple perspectives have on *roads* taken and *destinations* reached, varying by decision-making processes.
Needed Materials	• US Planning Road Maps (preferably large folded hard copy maps so the entire continental US appears on one image) – you will want one map per group of students. • 3 highlighters (different colors) per group. • 3 Sticky notes per group. • *For prior homework*: This assumes a prior set of assignments in which the learners, at some point in the course, have conducted a literature review (Chapter 7), have identified theoretical/conceptual framework(s) in an assignment (Chapter 8), and have constructed their study research question(s). • *For instructor*: In your syllabus, delineate that the final project for the class will be a research proposal, inclusive of all research design sections, for a future "pilot study." This research proposal will be the accumulation of multiple assignments throughout the course. Therefore, have clear deadlines for the prior assignments (see prior homework), giving sufficient time for students to reflect and make adjustments on each. Ensure that students have received prompt and proper feedback on the prior assignments.
Pre-lesson Preparation	• *How can I scaffold this lesson?* I use the "Let's Road Trip" exercise in a couple of different courses, including an introductory research course primarily for masters and doctoral students, to talk about the strength of research design in creating trustworthiness of the findings and proposed conclusions. • *Do all students have the cultural context to appreciate this exercise?* "Let's Road Trip" is grounded in the American tradition of cross-country road trips. Although most graduate students probably learned how to read maps in primary school, I recognize that it has been many years since most of the students have used a hard copy map, so I recommend drawing on YouTube videos on map reading as a supplement.

Activities	• Share that for today's "warming up our voices" we will be mapping out a cross-country road trip.
	• Divide class into groups of 3–5 students, preferably by having students count off to create diverse groups or pre-arrange the groups to ensure a cross section of backgrounds and interests. *If the class is small, students can also work independently.*
	• Before handing out the materials to each group, ask if anyone has questions or concerns using or reading a hard copy map of the US. Once questions are answered, ask for a "thumbs up/thumbs down" to signal if students feel ready to receive the directions for today's "warming up our voices" exercise.
	• Distribute the following materials to each group: (1) 1 US Planning Road Map per group; (2) 3 highlighters (different colors) per group; and (3) 3 sticky notes per group.
	• On the board or screen, have the following prompt posted:
	  ◦ "Let's Road Trip: Overall Directions" *[Slide 1]*
	    ▪ The goal of this exercise is to map 3 different routes from your assigned start point, which will be a location on the west coast, to a destination on the east coast. Even though each group will be assigned a distinct start location, all start locations are on the west coast.

LET'S ROAD TRIP

Topic	Road Mapping the connection between the theoretical/conceptual framework(s), hypotheses (if applicable), research question(s), and research design of a study

- Your group must begin from the assigned location (i.e., Route 1: San Francisco, CA; Route 2: Seattle, WA; Route 3: Portland, OR).
- In each of your 3 mapped routes, you *must* pass through Chicago, IL.
- You will use the highlighters to mark each of your 3 routes. Use a different color for each distinct route (from start to finish).

○ "Let's Road Trip: Part I Directions" *[Slide 2]*
- Before your group starts mapping, come to a consensus on 3 different rationales for selecting distinct routes between your start location and Chicago, IL.
  Hint: Be creative and interesting! See bullet 3 (below) for examples of possible rationales.
- Once your group has come to a consensus for all 3 routes, highlight each route from your designated start to Chicago, IL with a different color highlighter.
- On each of the 3 sticky notes, write the rationale used for mapping each distinct route. One rationale per sticky note. Then place the sticky notes next to the matching route. Some examples of sticky note labels may include:
  ◇ Quickest route (by time).
  ◇ Quickest route (by number of freeway transitions).
  ◇ Longest route (by time).
  ◇ Longest route (by number of road transitions).
  ◇ Most scenic route.
  ◇ Stops where friends live.
  ◇ Visiting type of locations (e.g., best bars, famous diners, colleges).
- Groups will have 10 mins to complete this first phase of the road trip mapping. (*If more time is needed, provide an additional 5 minutes to avoid rushing through this process.*)
- After the groups have mapped their road trip to Chicago, IL, bring them back together as a whole class to share one rationale with the class explaining their travel route from their designated start to Chicago. Ask them to share and justify their favorite or most exciting route.

○ "Let's Road Trip: Part II Directions" *[Slide 3]*
- You will have 10 mins to complete this second phase of the road trip mapping. (*Again, if more time is needed, provide an additional 5 minutes as the discussion piece is very important.*)
- Now, use the *same 3 rationales* that you used for the first half of your road trip (i.e., your assigned starting point to Chicago) to help you traverse from Chicago to 3 destinations so long as they fall within an east coast state. *Hint: Since each rationale was different, each route new route should land in different locations.*
- Map each route from Chicago to the east coast individually to ensure that your group is holding true to the original rationale.
- Discuss the following questions, and be prepared to share when we return to a whole class discussion:
  ◇ What was the most exciting part of mapping each road trip?
  ◇ What was most challenging about mapping each road trip?
  ◇ If you could go back and change anything, what would that be? Why?
  ◇ What do you wish you had known at the beginning that would have helped you on your journey?

○ "Let's Road Trip: Discussion" *[Slide 4: sequentially animate these questions for the discussion]*
- Have students share each of the 3 rationales they used for each route from the west coast departure to Chicago and on to the east coast destination. Also, explain why this rationale made the most sense for the route. *If time is running short, maybe have each group highlight one route.*
  ◇ What other rationales did you consider?
  ◇ What was most exciting about this exercise? Or most frustrating?

Topic	*Road Mapping the connection between the theoretical/conceptual framework(s), hypotheses (if applicable), research question(s), and research design of a study*

- For 2 minutes, students will journal about this question: In your opinion, how do you think road trip mapping relates to today's class topic of "aligning theoretical frameworks, research questions and research design?"
- Next, ask several students to share some of their thoughts. Typical responses include:
  ◊ Learn how early decisions impact our final destination.
  ◊ Help us think about our research design as a journey with multiple options.
  ◊ Learn how each of us can study similar phenomena, make different decisions at different points, and end up with very different research designs.
- At this point in class, transition to a mini-lecture and engaged discussion regarding this exercise and the alignment between theoretical/conceptual framework(s) assignments, research questions, and research design. The focus should contain the following:
  ○ Much like a road trip, where you have to drive to and through each point to make the connection, in a research study, the alignment must be present from beginning to end. For example, your literature review and theoretical framework must point directly to your line of inquiry as stated in your research question(s). Subsequently, in order to properly answer the question(s) posed, the research design must align to produce the data to answer such question(s).
  ○ In a quality empirical research study, you are able to easily map the flow from the literature review and theoretical framework to the research question(s), to the research design (and eventually through to the findings and discussion conclusion). *Note*: Remind students of previous class exercises where they examined published studies for this alignment.
  ○ Explain that each decision made in developing the routes on the road map represented the decisions made throughout a research study design. As each rationale shifted, so did the trajectory of the road trip. Likewise, as pieces of your study change, so should the alignment with the proper research design.
  ○ The road map approach aims to reinforce two main concepts in research design:
    - Connectivity via alignment: If a research study does not have strong alignment from beginning to end, the conclusions cannot be validated or trusted. Much like the road trip, you must traverse all routes by ground and cannot skip over locations or take differing modes of transportation to complete the road trip, as this will cause major disconnections and complications.
    - The literature review (and the highlights/gaps discovered) can be considered the starting destination (i.e., west coast starting point) on your road trip. The theoretical framework is used to analyze the identified gap, thus representing the rationale used to get to "Chicago, IL." Chicago essentially represents the research question(s). Returning to the rationale previously identified is the alignment that is necessary to ensure the connectivity between the research question(s) and the research design; thus, representing returning to the original rationale to help designate how to reach the destination (i.e., the research design).
    - Minimize bias in research instruments: If the goal is to find inspiration and enjoy the journey on the road trip, then similarly the goal should be to find inspiration in the organic process of data finding. When we tailor our research designs in preconceived ways, we limit, and often bias, the findings that will arise within a study. We must remember to be invested in the journey not the destination, as this will also help us reduce possibilities where bias can enter our design process.

Topic	Road Mapping the connection between the theoretical/conceptual framework(s), hypotheses (if applicable), research question(s), and research design of a study

- Next, ask students to consider their current alignment within their literature review, theoretical/conceptual framework(s), research question(s), and research design for their own study.
  - Ask them to journal for 7–10 minutes regarding their alignment. Here are the questions to focus on in this journal reflection period (post these on the board or screen):
    - When you reflect upon the multiple aspects of this exercise, do you see any alignments with aspects of a research study If so, what are the alignments you see?
    - *Note*: some alignments could include: the starting point on the west coast location is like a literature review, route to Chicago is like research questions, selected routes to east coast location are like research design)
    - What are the highlights and gaps you've identified in the literature on your topic?
    - How does your proposed theoretical or conceptual framework(s) help analyze this/these gap(s)? Are there specific operationalizations of these frameworks that best help analyze this/these gap(s)?
    - Do(es) your research question(s) distinctly and only address these gaps and theoretical/conceptual operational approaches?
    - Based on your research question(s), does your proposed research design align?
      - ◊ Does your proposed sample help you answer your research question(s)?
      - ◊ Does your proposed methodology help you answer your research question(s)?
      - ◊ Do you need to broaden or narrow any of the design aspects to help you precisely answer your research question(s)?
      - ◊ Do you see any necessary changes or adjustments to ensure alignment within your study? If so, what are they?
- After journaling, ask students to create a *Crosswalk* table to ensure alignment between all aspects, that is: literature review, theoretical/conceptual framework(s), research question(s), and research design.
  - This double check on alignment will allow students to move forward smoothly and more successfully as they implement their research design.
  - The Crosswalk table will include (broken out in detail; see sample Crosswalk document in Appendix):
    - X-axis: thematic highlights/gaps from the literature review, operationalized components of the theoretical/conceptual framework(s), and research question(s) (main RQ and any sub-RQs as applicable).
    - Y-axis: (Quantitative studies) Hypotheses; (Qualitative studies) Interview/focus group/observation/other protocol questions or prompts.
    - In the middle, cross-section area, students should place a check mark or "x" where the x-axis and y-axis concepts align. For example, if one of the interview protocol questions helps answer RQ sub-question 1, then the student would place an "x" in that cross-section area.
- *Homework*: Students will submit a completed Crosswalk table displaying alignment of all aspects that is: literature review, theoretical/conceptual framework, research question(s), and research design. If any adjustments or changes were made to any of the aforementioned sections following this activity, students should attach an addendum with the new, adjusted research sections.

Virtual Adaptations	The "Let's Road Trip" exercise is easily adaptable for synchronous and asynchronous learning, whenever necessary. The difference in modality only requires a shift in materials provided for the exercise.

- Prior to class, create PDF documents with US road maps that contain as many highways and side roads as possible (some examples include: Amazon, TripInfo, YellowMaps). Make a copy of the PDF for each cluster.

Topic	Road Mapping the connection between the theoretical/conceptual framework(s), hypotheses (if applicable), research question(s), and research design of a study
	• *Synchronous*: In Zoom breakout rooms, each cluster would access the PDF map, follow the same directions as designed for in-person by using the highlight and post-it functions on Adobe. • *Asynchronous*: Create the clusters prior to the class session. Share clear step-by-step directions, as outlined for in-person, asking them to find a time to conduct the exercise together during a time that works best for all. • Create a discussion post where all clusters can upload their marked-up PDF, so all can view. • *Synchronous*: Each cluster shares their PDF by using the Share Screen Zoom feature, and invites peers to also view on discussion posts if Share Screen poses any viewing challenges. • *Asynchronous*: Ask each cluster to share their rationale for each of the 3 routes they selected, and responses to the discussion questions during Part II Discussion of the exercise. Clusters should post these insights under their respective PDF of their map.
Assessment	• Formative Assessment: During cluster work time, stop into each cluster discussion and assess students' ability to connect the road map exercise to their own research study alignment (and topic for the day). • Formative Assessment: Review homework assignment which requires that students submit a completed Crosswalk table ensuring alignment between all areas of the research study leading up to and through the research design. • Summative Assessment: Grade the final "pilot study" paper following a rubric requiring all aspects of the study to align from literature review to conclusions.

INTELLECTUAL PREPARATION FOR "LET'S ROAD TRIP" LESSON

Core Ideas

The "Let's Road Trip" lesson is centered around two core ideas: (1) ensuring alignment between theoretical/conceptual framework(s), research question(s), and research design, and (2) minimizing bias through research design.

Ensuring Alignment

Although even the most experienced researcher might be driven to jump to the research design part of a study, the extant literature on effective research skills reinforces that a quality study must allow each step of the design to align and direct the next step. Accordingly, the theoretical/conceptual framework of a study should "draw upon the concepts, terms, definitions, models, and theories of a particular literature base" (Merriam & Tisdell, 2016, p. 86). This framework, comprised collectively through the lens of the conceptual framework[1] and theoretical perspective[2], in turn will engender specific research question(s) (Merriam & Tisdell, 2016). Subsequently, the research design[3] inextricably should be designated by the research question(s), as failure to do so will result in a shortage of data or improper data collection in responding to the main study inquiry. The "Let's Road Trip" lesson allows students to create their own "road map" of their research study to ensure alignment.

The Learner

The "Let's Road Trip" lesson preparation and execution takes into consideration diverse learners' experiences and prior knowledge. This is with the understanding that prior knowledge is inclusive of both prior learning and misconceptions regarding research design.

Previous Learning and Misconceptions

As with any graduate level course, learners (i.e., masters and doctoral students) enter the learning environment with prior knowledge, drawn from diverse experiences in life, work, courses, and research. More specifically, since educational research is frequently learned through an apprenticeship model, learners who have conducted prior research come with substantial knowledge depending on how they have been trained (formally and informally), regarding the alignment (or therefore lack of) of theoretical framework(s), research question(s), and research design. As we are aware, education does not have formal disciplinary requirements for structured teaching of research design for research teams/projects. Therefore, prior learning ranges significantly, from minimal understanding of the research design process to in-depth training from the principal investigator of the research team/project. However, regardless of depth of training, all learners enter "Let's Road Trip" with lived experience that contributes to the multiple perspectives informing the exercise.

Due to the diverse learners' experiences and backgrounds, misconceptions may also be present. One that was previously mentioned relates to training that research design should be guided by methodology or access to data sources. If learners have only experienced this type of environment, freeing themselves of these misconceptions can be challenging; however, mapping the driving route on the map can help them understand how we have to begin the trip (and the study) at the beginning and not in the middle (i.e., methodologies, methods). Furthermore, since not all learners have experienced a cross-country road trip through the US, they can be invited to draw from similar experiences where mapping is required, such as subway rides, bus routes, bike routes, walking or hiking paths, and multi-destination flights. The opportunity of drawing from one of these proxy experiences is that each of these mapping mechanisms has its own nuances specific to the method. Therefore, "Let's Road Trip" will challenge these learners to consider how to adjust these nuances to become functional for a driving route.

The Context

A successful lesson plan should consider the diversity of the learners, including background and prior knowledge grounded in education and lived experiences, regional and global perspectives, learning perspectives and styles, and much more. With this in mind, creating a lesson that allows each learner to contribute fully, inclusive of background, social identities, and experiences, may allow for the greatest learning to transpire. "Let's Road Trip" was developed with this premise in mind, in order for all learners to find a space to contribute to the creativity of the exercise.

Fostering Equitable Learning Spaces

Scholars have asserted that pedagogies aiming for the strongest learning should aim to create assessments and engaged exercises that allow learners to draw from diverse backgrounds and experiences (Lawrie et al., 2017). "Let's Road Trip" intentionally builds in various opportunities for all cluster members to contribute and for their perspectives to be valued. For example, during Part I, learners are asked to come up with three distinct and creative rationales for their mapped routes, while coming to consensus. These directions are purposeful to foster an equitable learning space where all cluster members can contribute ideas to the discussion, and share how they came to that rationale. While sharing the rationale, learners often share experiences that have informed the contribution. In coming to a consensus, the goal is to validate others' perspectives and experiences while learning from them.

In conclusion, "Let's Road Trip" provides a low-stakes opportunity for developing scholars to strengthen their research design and ensure alignment between theoretical/conceptual framework(s), research question(s), and research design. In turn, the goal is that graduate students will move forward with more confidence and success as they collect data. The Crosswalk table they will develop as an assignment/assessment will also serve as a great checks-and-balance to ensure alignment as they produce quality empirical research...even better!

APPENDIX

Crosswalk Table for Quantitative Research Study

	Hypothesis 1	*Hypothesis 2*	*Hypothesis 3*	*Hypothesis 4*	*Hypothesis 5*
Literature Gap 1					
Literature Gap 2					
Literature Gap 3					
Theory Operationalization 1					
Theory Operationalization 2					
Theory Operationalization 3					
Main RQ					
Sub-RQ 1					
Sub-RQ 2					

Crosswalk Table for Qualitative Research Study

	Interview Q1	Interview Q2	Interview Q3	Interview Q4	Interview Q5
Literature Gap 1					
Literature Gap 2					
Literature Gap 3					
Theory Operationalization 1					
Theory Operationalization 2					
Theory Operationalization 3					
Main RQ					
Sub-RQ 1					
Sub-RQ 2					

NOTES

1 The conceptual framework includes the literature review, theory, and theory regarding the phenomenon of inquiry (Jones, Torres, & Arminio, 2022).
2 While conceptual framework and theoretical perspectives/frameworks are often used interchangeably in educational research, Jones, Torres, and Arminio (2022) posit that theoretical perspective refers to the researcher paradigmatic (i.e., epistemological and ontological) assumptions undergirding the study.
3 The research design is comprised of two main components: (1) methodology ("a process that guides [the] study design, implementation, data collection, data analysis, and interpretation"); and (2) method ("how data are collected") (Jones, Torres, & Arminio, 2022, p. 14).

BIBLIOGRAPHY

Creswell, J. W., & Creswell, J. D. (2021). *Research design: Qualitative, quantitative, and mixed methods approaches* (5 th ed.). Sage Publications.

Jones, S. R., Torres, V., & Arminio, J. (2013). *Negotiating the complexities of qualitative research in higher education: Fundamental elements and issues* (3rd ed.). Routledge.

Lawrie, G., Marquis, E., Fuller, E., Newman, T., Qiu, M., Nomikoudis, M., Roelofs, F., & Van Dam, L. (2017). Moving towards inclusive learning and teaching: A synthesis of recent literature. *Teaching & Learning Inquiry*, 5(1), 9–21.

Merriam, S. B., & Tisdell, E. J. (2016). *Qualitative research: A guide to design and implementation* (4th ed.). John Wiley & Sons.

12

The Self and Research

Positionality through Artifacts

Beth E. Bukoski

INTRODUCTION

Who the researcher is and how they come to the research are intrinsic to the research process. Put another way, the researcher and their understanding of the world and how it should be studied (i.e., epistemology or paradigm) have an inextricable relationship to study design and interactions with participants and other researchers. A common way researchers share how their ways of knowing influence the study is through a positionality statement, which should describe "a critical understanding of the role a scholar's background and current (socially constructed and perceived) position in the world plays in the production of academic knowledge, particularly in qualitative research" (Garcia, 2014. p. 794). Researchers' experiences, values, social identities, and location in time and space influence every research project including study design, relationship with participants, and ethics of the study.

Positionality work is self-analysis and the positionality statement in a manuscript or presentation reflects the product of that self-analysis. The process and product of positionality work are distinct but co-dependent, meaning a quality statement is the product of an engaged process. The researcher must practice intentional, iterative, and recursive reflexivity (think of a spiral here) throughout a research project, involving activities such as journaling, debriefing, and bracketing. Product work involves the researcher developing a concise and clear positionality statement to explain the researcher's role in the project, which bolsters the study's rigor and credibility.[1] The statement itself is usually brief, detailing the researcher(s)'s multiple identities, how they "come to" the work, and strategies used to grapple with their relationship to the research and participants. The seeming simplicity and brevity of a positionality statement is, however, misleading.

Beginning researchers may see the "the self and research" relationship as oppositional (i.e., subjectivity, or bias, is bad), as completely separate (i.e., unrelated because self is irrelevant to research), or as synonymous (a form of researcher identity politics). None of those stances is wholly accurate since all knowledge is partial. The purpose of this lesson is to provide an individualized approach to help students to understand their own

DOI: 10.4324/b23320-16

THE SELF AND RESEARCH

subjectivities and their relative insider and outsider statuses related to the research project, and to learn the skill of reflexivity.

LESSON PLAN

Topic	*The Self and Research: Positionality through Artifacts*

Learning Objectives	• Students will
	  ○ identify social identities salient to their positionality.
	  ○ document salient insider and outsider statuses in relation to the participants.
	  ○ learn strategies for engaging reflexively with their identities throughout the research process.
	  ○ articulate how their identities have informed their project (i.e., draft a positionality statement).

Needed Materials	• Student-provided: artifacts (objects, pictures, clippings, etc.) representing social identities salient to their research project (e.g., gender, sexuality, race/ethnicity, ability status, etc.).
	• Prior homework/reading:
	  ○ Garcia, 2014, pp. 794–796
	  ○ Patel, 2016, pp. 57–62
	  ○ Hill Collins, 2012, pp. 3–16
	  ○ Pillow, 2003, pp. 175–196 (optional; helpful for post-[2] oriented students)

Pre-lesson Preparation	How can I scaffold this lesson? • As other research elements are covered, ask questions such as: "Tell me where you see yourself in design decisions," and "How does who you are inform what you're choosing to study and how you study it," etc. Do all students have the cultural context to appreciate the activity? • Students only need their experiences, but may or may not feel comfortable sharing depending on classroom culture and norms. • Some students may resist engaging, believing their identities do not matter or do not shape their access to power and privilege. Resistance is most common with researchers who adhere to an objectivist epistemology. Be prepared to discuss how experimental, quasi-experimental, and mixed-methods research also require positionality work (e.g., operationalization of variables, access to data, how research is received). Quantitative work, for example, can unintentionally recenter Whiteness; positionality work can address such bias.

Activities	Opening
	• I start this lesson class with an intention-setting such as, "I invite you into our shared learning space. What's a word that can anchor you today? You might choose words such as curious, non-judgmental, engaged."
	Activity 1[3]: Lecture-Chat
	• Provide a lecture-chat on the readings and relevant concepts and language to scaffold learning:
	  ○ Definition of positionality, including subjectivity, insider/outsider status, and reflexivity.
	  ○ Positionality is contextual, relational, constantly changing.
	  ○ Researcher positionality can affect various parts of study design, including examples.
	  ○ Strategies for working through positionality.
	  ○ Elements of a positionality statement.

Topic	The Self and Research: Positionality through Artifacts

Activity 2: Subjectivity, Power, and Politics
- Post this prompt: "In Patricia Hill Collins' speech "Why Black feminist thought?", she neither uses the word positionality, nor does she speak directly to research design. How does this piece help us make sense of what positionality is and how it can be explored?" Allow students a few minutes to think-pair-share and then facilitate discussion.
  - Some key ideas likely to come up include: identities implicate power, politics, and ethics; identities are contextual and relational; our understanding of ourselves and how we relate to others and our work change over time, knowledge claims are always partial and situated, epistemic privilege.

Activity 3: Subjectivity
- Groups of 2–4 students with their artifacts. Prompt: "Take turns sharing an artifact, saying what it is/represents about you, and how the identity (-ies) have influenced your research project thus far. Consider both design choices (e.g., problem definition, literature organization) and interactions with participants or researchers (e.g., entering the field).
- After 15–20 minutes of sharing, invite discussion with the entire class. Help students move from naming the identity to explaining ways their positionality has informed their work and access to power/knowledge.
- Ask relevant probing or connective questions, for example
  - Identity X seems important in your problem definition, can you tell us more about how your identities (this or another) informed your site selection or sampling procedure?
  - Student Y just shared about two identities she could not separate. Did anyone else have two or more identities they felt they could not separate? Tell us about that.
  - Student Z was able to gain clarity on their epistemology (or other design element) through reflexivity work. Did anyone else have an "ah-ha" moment regarding their study design?
- Note: often every student wants to share, which I encourage as it reinforces how all researchers must grapple with positionality.

Activity 4: The Politics and Ethics of Positionality
- Ask students to reflect or think-pair-share for 2–3 minutes in response to the following prompt: "When you think of your project – why you, why this, why now and here?"
- Typical (more generic) responses include:
  - I have some connection to this issue/population.
  - I have access to the key people/data and I know the context.
  - I'm too close to the project.
  - I know my identity is going to make this project challenging, how do I cope with implicit bias?
  - My identities and history position me as an insider. I wouldn't trust someone else to do this research as well as me.
- Optional: Students take 5–10 minutes to make a table or figure of their key insider and outsider knowledges and how their status may help or hinder their work. (See Table 1 for a template with examples.)
- Note: A Venn diagram can be useful to help students think through their relationships with those encountered in the field (e.g., gatekeepers, participants). A table can be useful for exploring their relationship to research design elements. The template provided does a bit of both, so instructors should adapt as needed for their students.

THE SELF AND RESEARCH

Topic	The Self and Research: Positionality through Artifacts
	Closing: • Option: Ask each student to place one of their artifacts on a desk or table and take a picture to share with the class as a reminder of their work (include students or not). • Thank them for their engagement and openness, solicit final questions, reflections, ah-ha moments, and/or appreciative comments for peers. • For homework, students should draft or finish drafting their positionality statement.
Virtual Adaptations	• If you teach online and have synchronous sessions, you can do this activity relatively easily by using breakout rooms. • Activity 1 can be a pre-recorded lecture or just find some good YouTube videos. • Activities 2 and 4 can be discussed as a whole group or done in breakouts then as a whole group depending on class size and time constraints. • For Activity 3, students should still gather their artifacts, then they can share via video. Students can also be encouraged to take pictures of artifacts or find relevant clip-art so they can share their screen if they prefer not to reveal their actual background, or you can ask students to place pictures/symbols of their artifacts into a Mural space (https://www.mural.co/).
Assessment	Formative Assessment: • Move around the room and assess students' ability to connect their artifacts to positionality (naming) and elements of their research design (explanation). Formative Assessment: • Provide feedback on the assignment after this lesson. Summative Assessment: • Grade the final research paper, consider a rubric including identification of salient identities, explanation of how those identities shaped the study, and reflexive strategies used during the project.

TABLE 12.1
Positionality Table with Examples

General Research Topic: Researcher interviewing and surveying 9th grade English teachers about literature choices and culturally relevant teaching

Study Element	Insider/Outsider	Potential Issues	Strategies
e.g., Access to participants and their context, Developing rapport, etc.	I was an English teacher for 10 years before pursuing a PhD. Most participants are White and the researcher is Latina; the researcher taught in a different area of the state.	There may be unfamiliar language or acronyms. There may be cultural disconnects (race/ethnicity but also regionalism, SES, education, etc.). They may feel I am there to judge or critique them, etc.	Daily reflexive journal. After-interview memo to capture field notes, journal to capture personal reflections and musings (e.g., two-column journal). Review websites for key acronyms and leaders at the school; do an informational interview with someone at the school ineligible to participate but who holds contextual and procedural knowledge. Focus on how participants are the knowledge-holders and I am there to learn; there are no right or wrong answers.

INTELLECTUAL PREPARATION FOR "POSITIONALITY ARTIFACT" LESSON

Core Ideas

Subjectivity

All knowledge is partial and all knowledge is situated, informed by the lived realities of the knowledge-producer (Haraway, 1988). Subjectivity cannot be explored without understanding how our subjectivities relate to power, or how subjectivity is intersectional (Crenshaw, 1989). Intersectionality also draws attention to the importance of anti-essentialism, or the idea of within-group diversity. This key move – leaning away from subjectivity as neutral and either essentialized or individual (e.g., I love to travel, or all middle class/White people love to travel) and leaning toward how identities shape access to and relation to power – is critical. For example, yes, I love to travel, but that orientation is shaped by my socio-economic status, which makes travel possible, the ease with which I can move among regions/countries as a documented, White, cis, able-bodied person, and fear about possible treatment as a queer woman in some spaces. This example illustrates how subjectivity is temporal, relational, spatial, and contextual.

Insider-Outsider Knowledges

Every researcher holds multiple positionings and each can be mapped onto a relative insider or outsider status. Insider and outsider statuses reside on a spectrum that is fluid (see Table 12.2); there are advantages and disadvantages to the various positions, and insider/outsider status relates to access. The researcher should consider how they will interact with participants or others in the field and how their subjectivities may give or preclude access to certain kinds of knowledge, that is, what knowledge may be intelligible to the researcher, and what knowledge might be unintelligible to the researcher.

In addition, researchers must think critically about how their relative insider and outsider statuses position them as more or less suited to do the work well (ethically, credibly, rigorously). Only the researcher can determine if they, specifically, are well-suited to this problem, with these people, and in this context. Writing, discussion, and engagement with reflexive practices can aid the researcher in making this determination and in developing their project with intentionality.

TABLE 12.2
Spectrum of statuses

Insider	Insider and/or Outsider	Outsider
Researcher is a member of the group and/or has direct experience with the phenomenon under study and has deep and wide knowledge of the group/phenomenon.	Researcher has some insider knowledge/experiences and some outsider lack of knowledge/experiences. Researcher may have once been an insider but is no longer, or may have proximate experiences that aid in their understanding of the group and/or phenomenon.	Researcher is not a member of the group or has no/limited experience of the phenomenon under study and has more limited knowledge of the group/phenomenon.

THE SELF AND RESEARCH

Reflexivity

Reflexivity moves beyond reflection and is the key tool for the process work of positionality. Pillow (2003) describes reflexivity as a methodological tool, which qualitative researchers can use to examine the various relationships implicated by qualitative research projects – self, power, ethics, data analysis, data representation, politics, and so forth. Reflexivity is also dynamic. For example, a researcher can influence and be influenced by the research project. A mirror is helpful for explanation. Reflection is the researcher looking in a mirror, meaningful for understanding self but limited in its field of reference. Reflexivity uses the same mirror but adds background, context, and relationships that contribute to the image (which may themselves have mini-reflections) and adds one or more additional mirrors, such that the person gazing into the mirror is now refracted. The gaze has multiple focal directions, and the "viewer" must engage with reflection and the act of reflection itself. Chiseri-Strater (as cited in Pillow, 2003) offers this distinction: "to be reflective does not demand an 'other,' while to be reflexive demands both another and some self-conscious awareness of the process of self-scrutiny" (p. 130). To simplify, reflexivity is a kind of meta-reflection.

The Learner

Prior to this lesson, students will be familiar with the major design elements of research but may or may not have prior experience with epistemology and positionality. Students will have a range of reactions. Some students have deep-seated beliefs that subjectivity is bad. Some students will have had educational experiences where their positionality was actively dismissed, discouraged, or rendered invisible. Students who hold marginalized identities often find positionality work validating. Rarely, a student thinks their insider status means only another insider can critique their work. Engage students in thinking about the different purposes of research designs, the value of research projects across the spectrum of epistemologies and techniques, and how self and relationships influence all research projects in some way. The best tools an instructor has are questions and curiosity. Most students will immediately grasp insider-outsider status as it bears a similarity to in-group and out-group ideas. Drawing students' attention to cultural knowledge, experiential knowledge, and implicit versus explicit knowledge can be helpful. Students often have an easier time grappling with positionality as it relates to more concrete areas of research design (e.g., interviewing) and a harder time with the more abstract areas (e.g., theoretical framework choice, data analysis). If you find this the case, pushing them to use a Venn diagram or table to write through the issues can be helpful. In addition, positionality work can be heady, theoretical, and hard. Bring students back to questions of "Who are you?" and "How are you influencing the study in conscious and unconscious ways?" as well as Patel's "Why me? Why this? Why now and here?" Students also have preconceptions and misconceptions about positionality as process and product. Isolating positionality as a lesson can lead students to thinking it is a singular act rather than an ongoing process. Consider scaffolding the lesson further by having students keep a reflexive journal throughout the semester. Regarding product, I encourage students to seek a "right sizing" in relation to the ethical issues implicated by positionality, how much the audience needs to understand, and the desired length of the manuscript. If clear guidance is needed, I offer 2–3 paragraphs or about a page double-spaced for an 18–20 page final pilot study paper.

Occasionally, a student decides a positionality statement is unnecessary and potentially oppressive labor. Insider researchers may feel a positionality statement as justifying who they are. Borrowing from Tuck and Yang (2014), this is a valid political move; the choice itself reflects their work regarding positionality. Have the student(s) submit a brief rationale for why a positionality statement is not included instead of the statement itself.

The Context (Bridging Core Ideas and The Learner)

Students need to engage iteratively and recursively with their positionality as it relates to research design, field work, and data analysis, and representation – in short, the entire research endeavor. In this activity, I ask students to share some pieces of their own identity and experiences and to discuss how who they are influences study design and relationships. I also ask them to consider how their identities may provide opportunities and challenges to accessing knowledge and presenting data ethically.

Students have the opportunity to process their experiences through sharing artifacts, in-class reflection, and specific activities requiring them to connect their positionality to the research design and relationships. If one activity does not resonate, likely another will. Giving students the space and encouragement to show up as they are is vital to learning about positionality as process and product. By working individually and collectively through the activities, students will engage in shared meaning-making, engage their own subjectivities, and learn about their peers' various subjectivities.

Confidence Building

On the one hand, doctoral students, particularly those who hold one or more marginalized identities, often find thinking through positionality quite powerful. They finally have license to do research that resonates with their insider knowledges and to consider their insider status as legitimate. On the other hand, some terms – such as intersectionality – have become a buzzword, the simplicity of identity politics is alluring, reflection is much easier than reflexivity, and the cognitive dissonance that can manifest from grappling with one's privilege and oppression can be heavy work. Some students may resist the work because they (consciously or subconsciously) do not want to acknowledge their privileges, and/or do not want to broadcast their trauma or use their trauma in their research (which may indicate the need for a different topic or problem definition).

Encourage students to gain confidence by asking open-ended questions (e.g., Tell me more about how you came to this decision; what prior experiences do you have that relate to this idea? What assumptions do you hold about X? What does this section communicate about your values as a researcher?). Be prepared for unexpected moments of vulnerability; encourage students to sit with their discomfort, and remind them that positionality work is iterative and reflexive (again, think of a spiral). The journey to understanding one's positionality is never "done," and the relational nature of research is negotiated, fluid, and complex – embrace the ambiguity.

NOTES

1 While a researcher's positionality can influence any aspect of the research process, it links specifically to issues of trustworthiness, which will be covered in other texts.
2 "Post-" meaning postmodern, post-structural, deconstructionist, etc.
3 I use the label activity instead of steps since the instructor may choose to order these a different way.

BIBLIOGRAPHY

Crenshaw, K. (1989). Demarginalizing the intersection of race and sex: A Black feminist critique of antidiscrimination doctrine, feminist theory and antiracist politics. *University of Chicago Legal Forum*, 139–167.

García, M. (2014) Positionality. In S. Thompson (Ed.), *Encyclopedia of diversity and social justice* (pp. 794–796). Lanham, MD: Rowman & Littlefield.

Haraway, D. (1988). Situated knowledges: The science question in feminism and the privilege of partial perspective. *Feminist Studies, 14*(3), 575–599.

Hill Collins, P. (2012). Chapter 1: Why Black feminist thought? In P. Hill Collins (Ed.), *On intellectual activism* (pp. 3–16). Philadelphia, PA: Temple.

Merriam, S. B., Johnson-Bailey, J., Lee, M-Y., Kee, Y., Ntseane, G. & Muhamad, M. (2001). Power and positionality: negotiating insider/outsider status within and across cultures. *International Journal of Lifelong Education*, 20(5), 405–416. https://doi.org/10.1080/02601370120490

Patel, L. (2016). Excerpt from Chapter 3: Research as relational. In L. Patel (Ed.), *Decolonizing research: From ownership to answerability* (pp. 57–62). New York, NY: Routledge.

Pillow, W. (2003). Confession, catharsis, or cure? Rethinking the uses of reflexivity as methodological power in qualitative research. *International Journal of Qualitative Studies in Education*, 16(2), 175–196. https://doi.org/10.1080/0951839032000060635

Tuck, E., & Yang, K. W. (2014). Unbecoming claims: Pedagogies of refusal in qualitative research. *Qualitative Inquiry*, 20(6), 811–818. https://doi.org/10.1177/1077800414530265

13

Trustworthiness and Ethics in Research

Using Reflexivity to See the Self in Ethical Research

G. Blue Brazelton and Ijeoma Ononuju

INTRODUCTION

We wrote this chapter during the peak of the United States' Omicron variant infection wave of the COVID-19 pandemic which was exacerbated by an epidemic of misinformation and distrust in research, scholarship, and virtually any information tied to divisive topics (and even some innocuous-seeming topics). While distrust fueled by misinformation varies based on personal, philosophical, and political ideologies, educators are on the front lines of teaching others how to share knowledge that is credible regardless of the level of scrutiny. What we have learned as educators, researchers, and consumers of knowledge during this time, is that scrutinizing and critiquing the researcher (whether with legitimate criticisms or false/specious claims) is an effective strategy to spur misinformation and its reach and impact. However, engaging in such critical examination of ourselves or others as researchers requires structure and clear expectations so as to mitigate potential negative and less-than-productive effects such as experiences of imposter syndrome. In our teaching, we use rubrics to provide such structure for students. Traditionally, rubrics have been defined functionally to describe the "expectations of an assignment by listing the criteria, and describing levels of quality from excellent to poor" (Reddy & Andrade, 2010, p. 435), but for our chapter we have included Reddy and Andrade's (2010) extension that "rubrics have the potential to help students understand the targets for their learning and the standards of quality, as well as make dependable judgments about their own work" (p. 437). As such, we offer a lesson centered on creating and applying a rubric to guide current and future researchers toward developing and expressing the need to be thoughtful in the interpretation of research data via reflexivity; a tool we see as valuable in qualitative and quantitative research.

DOI: 10.4324/b23320-17

TRUSTWORTHINESS AND ETHICS IN RESEARCH

LESSON PLAN

Topic	*Writing a Rubric and Prompt for a Researcher Reflexivity Statement*
Learning Objectives	• Students will learn principles of researcher reflexivity. • Students will apply the principles of researcher reflexivity to develop a rubric used to evaluate their own researcher reflexivity statement. • Students will be exposed to other elements of researcher trustworthiness (as defined by the readings and other course materials related to the day's lesson).
Needed Materials	• Physical or virtual avenues for collaboration (white boards/poster board; breakout rooms in video chat software, Google docs, etc.). • Blank rubric template options (hardcopy or digital). • For prior homework, students will have completed required reading from the course research text (or selected individual readings) on research trustworthiness. • Three sample researcher reflexivity statements (consider asking research colleagues for examples or pull from published research appropriate for the course topic if applicable). • While we defer to the teacher's curricular autonomy, we recommend Diane Watt's 2007 article "On becoming a qualitative researcher: The value of reflexivity" as appropriate pre-reading for teacher and learner.
Pre-lesson Preparation	• This activity relies upon students engaging with the need to be present in their research by requiring them to evaluate themselves as emerging researchers. Thus, the instructor should prepare to help students to "desterilize" their research contexts via acknowledging the relationship between researcher reflexivity and power. • The lesson should be situated appropriately in the course when learners have read about and engaged with general goals and principles of research ethics and trustworthiness. • Ideally, the instructor will have already facilitated a community capable of collaboration and dialog as part of the preparation for this lesson. • The instructor should also be ready to discuss power in relation to research, and be willing to share that power with the learners by allowing them to design an actual rubric that will be used to evaluate an assignment related to writing a reflexivity statement (possibly in connection with an actual or hypothetical research project as part of the course).
Activities	• Using the "think, pair, share" model of your choosing, ask students to first think about the prompt "How do we know if research is trustworthy?" for no more than 10 minutes in total (timetable is flexible). • Transition the discussion towards the concept of research reflexivity as one important way to assess the trustworthiness of a particular research study for no more than 5 minutes. • Ask the students to break into groups of 3–4. • Provide sample reflexivity statements (we recommend requiring them as pre-reading as well), and ask them to spend the next 5–8 minutes in comparig/contrasting the reflexivity statements including: What do they have in common? How do they differ? What would be the general objective of these reflexivity statements? (If possible, consider leaving the room during part of this discussion.) • When discussion seems to be waning, keep the groups intact but begin a group discussion and ask for takeaways based on the prompts and debrief the process of evaluating reflexivity statements.

Topic	Writing a Rubric and Prompt for a Researcher Reflexivity Statement
	• After a few minutes of group discussion, ask students to return to their small groups and begin to write a rubric for evaluating reflexivity statements for their (actual or hypothetical) research projects. Provide a digital copy and hardcopies of a rubric grid. Remind students to use course readings, previous discussion of the day, and any online resources they have been provided with or may have found. • Each group should report out their rubric to the rest of the class (may need to adapt group sizes, timetable, and so on to fit) and explain their rationale for the evaluation categories and descriptions. Remind non-presenting students to look for how their rubrics compare. • Facilitate a discussion where students build a master rubric for the class based on what groups have provided. Ideally, the group will reach consensus in the discussion. 　　We recommend using the finished rubric as the actual evaluation tool for grading any reflexivity statements that the students may be writing in the course. Alternatively, the rubric can also be used to evaluate the sample reflexivity statements used earlier in the activity as a potential follow up to this lesson.
Virtual Adaptations	This lesson can transition easily into virtual learning environments, as it is high-touch as opposed to high-tech. Synchronous Learning: • When using conference/video call software, the lesson can be run without much adaptation by using breakout rooms or equivalent. Also, online polling tools can be used for voting toward consensus. Asynchronous Learning: • This activity can easily replace other asynchronous activities (such as responding to a weekly discussion board prompt) by asking students to report out (including infographic, audio/visual, or standard document sharing tools), and then engaging in a conversation via collaboration platforms (such as the learning management system).
Assessment	• Formative: Circulate amongst the groups, in-person or digital breakout rooms, and listen to the concepts being used to create and justify rubric categories and score descriptions. • Formative: Occasionally ask a group about what ethical considerations they are making regarding inclusivity of perspectives within the rubric discussions. • Summative: Use the rubric to evaluate reflexivity statements (if applicable) or, if no reflexivity statement will be required in the course, then evaluate the final rubric made by the class for key components of reflexivity and its relationship to trustworthiness (potentially for participation points or another formal grade category).

INTELLECTUAL PREPARATION

The body of scholarship on research trustworthiness and ethics is substantial, and there is no shortage of advice for educators and researchers. For those conducting research on human subjects as part of their degree, a review by an institutional research board (IRB) is required to compel responsible and ethical decisions in the research process. Essentially, there are multiple sources of knowledge available to support a researcher producing research that is credible. At the heart of this conversation on ethical and trustworthy research is the need to prioritize honesty and transparency at all stages of a study, but especially when disseminating knowledge in teaching and publishing. As such, the lesson above and subsequent discussion of the lesson begin (or continue, depending on the timing of the lesson) an authentic conversation about being honest in one's own research by using reflexivity as a practice for being present in the study and transparent about one's lived experience.

Reflexivity as a Practice

> Learning to reflect on your behavior and thoughts, as well as on the phenomenon under study, creates a means for continuously becoming a better researcher. Becoming a better researcher captures the dynamic nature of the process. Conducting research, like teaching and other complex acts, can be improved; it cannot be mastered.
>
> (Glesne & Peshkin, 1992, p. xiii)

Glesne and Peshkin (1992) establish for us the idea of unmastery being a static state, while the pursuit of mastery is dynamic. In fact, Paolo Friere (1972) provides a similar sentiment in *Pedagogy of the Oppressed* when he rebukes the narrative of teachers no longer being learners. In fact, he challenges teachers to readily seek out the position of learner and opportunities to learn alongside their students, in the process of facilitating their student's education. Even in our teacher preparation programs, we often require our students to enroll in an action research course. Why? So that as educators, they can live out the most quintessential element of education and that is learning. Always pushing the envelope to learn more about your profession, your practice, yourself, all in pursuit of this idea to do better and to know better.

As researchers, we can base the idea of trustworthiness on the mandate to Do No Harm. That's the job. Can you learn, without creating harm? A simple concept in theory, but not as simple in application. We are preparing our students to be professional learners, and as learners, they will make important contributions to the world. In theory, this sounds feasible, but it is much more difficult because we are simultaneously training our students to be experts in their field. That is the power of the lesson plan outlined here. By having our students create a rubric for reflexivity, we establish for them the responsibility and checks and balances that come along with conducting research. The lesson plan is designed to normalize reflexivity so that our students can become better and more trustworthy researchers. Reflexivity as a practice teaches you to continuously ask yourself, in a loop, "How can I show up better?" Developing a rubric to monitor your own reflexivity contributes directly to the overall trustworthiness of the research. Also, we believe that, as scholars, we should routinely engage in the process of using rubrics to critically reflect on who we are as researchers and the ways in which we make sense of the world. Rubric-focused continual re-evaluation of a scholar's reflexivity and other research-related statements may help us to continue with ethical and trustworthy research.

As teachers ourselves, we know that sometimes we teach practices that we ourselves struggle to follow (at least from time to time). The lesson requires the teacher to believe in both the potential of sharing power with the learners, and that it is through reflexivity that we can moderate discussions about how who we are influences our research and scholarship. So, we see these two paths as parallel, if not overlaid upon each other: reflexivity as necessary for the researcher's credibility; and reflexivity as a strength for the teacher's credibility. Boyer's model of scholarship established that when we examine, critique, and certainly reflect upon our teaching, that teaching is scholarship.

The Learner

As we mention above, it is important to acknowledge that while the topic of bias is significant in the context of research trustworthiness and ethics, we do not view the idea of bias to be inherently negative. Instead, we suggest using lived experience as a better way of framing how who we are affects the ways in which we conduct and interpret research. This lesson requires that the learners be made aware and further assured of that distinction, which itself is an important aspect of teaching reflexivity in general. For this lesson, the learner is required to use their agency to both synthesize and contextualize the concept of reflexivity as an individual, while also being asked to share that agency in community with their classmates. Both of us make small changes to the lesson based upon what we have learned about the learners, so as to empower both individual and community engagement with the lesson activity and content.

The Individual Learner

Individual learners bring to the classroom many preconceived notions and assumptions about research trustworthiness and ethics, whether learned from previous courses or from their readings of research articles that offer sections on reliability, validity, generalizability, and so forth. While these concepts are important for all research, we find that overcoming these assumptions is one of the main considerations we must prioritize when preparing to teach this lesson. Many students feel that their research perspective must be sterile and distant from their data (which is almost certainly impossible, yet the attitude persists). They are often prepared to defend their actual or hypothetical research as unaffected by their bias/lived experience, and sometimes as free from all bias because the study is quantitative. Our advice to the instructor using our lesson is to be prepared for this conversation and to acknowledge these perspectives as valid to the learner as an individual, but in need of examination via reflexivity.

The Learning Community

For the class as a learning community, we could offer an entire volume on the considerations we find potentially relevant for teacher preparation. In practice, we suggest offering this lesson only after the learning community has been established with expectations for civil discourse and when the teacher feels capable of addressing the potential disagreement about the role of reflexivity in research. While the lesson requires that the teacher should offer some of their power to the class to encourage agency, it is important that the teacher still exercises some control through moderation of the activity discussions.

The Context

We built this lesson from the advice of James Lang in his 2016 book *Small Teaching: Everyday Lessons from the Science of Learning*, which encourages all teachers to see the beauty and potential even in the smallest incremental units of learning by framing the lesson around knowledge (predicting, retrieving, interleaving), understanding (connecting, practicing, explaining), and inspiration (belonging, motivating, and finally learning). Lang's model is straightforward, yet expansive in the ways it includes theories of cognition in each preparatory step, as he argues for a somewhat common-sense perspective that it is by making small changes in both how we prepare for and deliver our lessons that we build the potential for powerful learning. Within this model, it is the teacher's perspective and thoughtful preparation, even as simple as establishing the first five minutes of every class as an opportunity to engage the learner and give them an opportunity to prepare themselves for the day's learning, where we can demonstrate good practice of reflexivity toward trustworthiness of our teaching. And we can accomplish this learning without having to redesign toward innovative or state-of-the-art teaching strategies and activities. While we do not have the space to fully describe Lang's model here, at the heart of his model is how continuing to teach in our current landscape can itself be radical and revolutionary.

Our lesson seeks to leverage every individual component of Lang's model. For example, to engage both retrieval and prediction by allowing students time to reflect upon the class readings, review any notes they may have, and begin to create knowledge by making educated guesses as to what reflexivity is in practice via the first several minutes of the lesson. Next, students will have the opportunity to understand reflexivity in action by drawing connections between their ideas and those of their classmates. And while it may be difficult for some teachers to initially relinquish some of their power by allowing students to write an assignment rubric that will be the official grading mechanism for their reflexivity statements, such an action allows for both practice and self-explanation to help ground the learning. Finally, as our lesson on reflexivity argues that honesty, transparency, and lived experience are not only welcome, but necessary when establishing trustworthiness in research, we can motivate students to see that even our own perspectives as teachers are limited and in need of enrichment from their ideas. While our argument that centering and empowering the learner in the learning experience is far from an original one, in the pursuit of preparing the next generation of scholars for the ways in which their words may be dissected, we believe in encouraging this self-reflective and intentional practice of sharing power early, often, and consistently.

While our lesson leverages both the theory and application of reflexivity toward a deeper understanding of trustworthiness and ethics and research, it is just one part of a bigger conversation in developing the next generation of researchers. As the Watt (2007) quote we used to begin this chapter illustrates, the development of a researcher identity is a continual process and being reflexive alone does not an ethical researcher make. However, we believe that the lesson itself encourages the kinds of conversation that can serve as a foundation to additional discussions, such as understanding the nature of harm in research, the need to speak from and not beyond one's data, and more. While being transparent and open about reflexivity will not solve all issues of misinformation in our current landscape, we can at least encourage these good habits as a way of acknowledging that the "who" of the source does matter when vetting information. Turning the classroom over, regarding the rubric preparation, may yield some discomfort initially, but we find the practice effective. It is also nice to have someone else write a rubric for a change and to use students' own words to defend our assignment scoring for a change!

BIBLIOGRAPHY

Boyer, E. (1990). *Scholarship reconsidered: Priorities of the professoriate*. Princeton University Press.

The foundational document on Boyer's model of scholarship encourages us to think of scholarship more holistically and thoroughly.

Freire, P. (1972). *Pedagogy of the oppressed*. Herder and Herder.

This text addresses how the oppressed can fight for their humanity within the classroom context, and how educators can participate in the humanizing process.

Glesne, C., & Peshkin, A. (1992). *Becoming qualitative researchers: An introduction*. Longman.

This text offers a look into what it means to become a qualitative researcher. Though dated, its core principles remain true.

Lang, J. M. (2016). *Small teaching: Everyday Lessons from the science of learning*. Jossey-Bass.

Offers a rich description of how to build conditions for learning through planning in small increments, using theories of cognition, and many examples to help teachers think about planning and adapting teaching for various audiences.

Reddy. Y. M. & Andrade, H. (2010). A review of rubric use in higher education. *Assessment & Evaluation in Higher Education, 35*(4), 435–448. https://doi.org/10.1080/02602930902862859

A relatively comprehensive review of the empirical research regarding the use of rubrics in higher education.

Watt, D. (2007). On becoming a qualitative researcher: The value of reflexivity. *Qualitative Report, 12*(1), 82–101. https://eric.ed.gov/?id=EJ800164

Discusses the potential of reflexivity as a compass to guide the researcher through the process of qualitative research toward trustworthy and ethical scholarship.

Section IV

Quantitative Methods

Section Editor: Willis A. Jones

14

Introduction to Section IV

Quantitative Methods

Willis A. Jones

Many of us who have taught quantitative methods courses share the experience of walking into a classroom where students are staring at us with a unique blend of fear and anxiety. Many of these students have convinced themselves that they are not "math" people and question their ability to learn the ideas/concepts underpinning quantitative methods. Fortunately, scientists have yet to find a "math gene." There is no evidence that some people are born with a fixed ability to do math or other mathematics-related activities. Through practice and persistence, any student can learn the skills used to conduct high-quality quantitative educational research.

Faculty play an essential role in facilitating the practice and persistence needed for students to learn quantitative methods. However, teaching quantitative methods in education can be challenging. Faculty must balance statistical depth with practical applicability. Faculty must balance facilitating student memorization of techniques with developing their critical thinking skills. Faculty must consider how to allocate time between data collection versus data analysis. From the perspective of students, learning quantitative methods can also be challenging. As Schleutker (2022) points out, the learning goals of quantitative methods courses (applying, analyzing, evaluating, and creating) are complex and cognitively demanding in terms of Bloom's Taxonomy for categorizing educational goals (Armstrong, 2010).

Many faculty have developed creative pedagogical techniques and lesson plans to address the challenges of teaching quantitative methods. Unfortunately, the sharing of effective pedagogical strategies among faculty who teach quantitative methods is limited. In this section, four highly acclaimed professors share analytical commentary and lesson plans for teaching some commonly used quantitative data collection and analysis approaches.

In Chapter 15, Dr. Courtney S. Thomas Tobin discusses a strategy she uses to teach students basic multivariate analysis. This strategy is based on the core idea that students best learn bivariate and simple multivariate methods by collecting their own data and analyzing that data in a real-world scenario. Dr. Thomas Tobin's approach involves students being presented with a real-world scenario where they assume a particular role, engage

DOI: 10.4324/b23320-19

in group work, develop and disseminate surveys, analyze data, and present findings. For students who are new to quantitative research, this lesson plan offers a non-intimidating way to apply the basic analytic skills they are acquiring. This approach is great for students learning about correlations, t-tests, ANOVA, and other basic bivariate and multivariate techniques.

In Chapter 16, Dr. Amber Dumford shares a lesson plan she uses when teaching students about linear regression. The goal of the lesson is for students to understand the basic components of simple and multiple linear regression such as independent/dependent variables, R^2, regression coefficients, and so on. Dr. Dumford's lesson plan also involves students collecting and analyzing data in real time. By allowing students to select their own research questions and variables, students experience a fun way to use regression to get to know each other better. The team-learning approach used by Dr. Dumford stimulates engagement and follows a 4S (significant, same problem, specific choice, and simultaneously report) approach to team-based learning advocated by Michaelsen and Sweet (2008).

Chapters 17 and 18 provide lesson plans for teaching more advanced quantitative methodologies. One of the bigger challenges for students learning quantitative methods within the social sciences is understanding how to measure abstract constructs such as anxiety, satisfaction, or institutional support. Given the prevalence of such concepts in educational research, most graduate students in education are expected to be familiar with a family of multivariate statistical methods known as factor analysis. One of the more common types of factor analysis is exploratory factor analysis. In Chapter 17, Dr. Soyeon Ahn and graduate student Beck Graefe describe a lesson plan they use for teaching students exploratory factor analysis (EFA). The lesson plan is centered around three blocks of activities (article critique, instructor demonstration, and student application) that students engage in over the course of one to two class periods. Instructor scaffolding and support for students are key to effectively implementing this lesson. Professors using this lesson plan should be very comfortable with the various concepts associated with EFA. Ahn and Graefe provide several appendices in their chapter with code for data analysis and a flowchart of questions students should consider when deciding how to use EFA. Arguably the most helpful aspect of their appendices is the template for writing about the results of an EFA. Writing up findings from complex quantitative methodologies can be tricky. The template provided by Ahn and Graefe will help faculty teach students the often neglected step of effectively communicating results from quantitative research.

In the final chapter of this section (Chapter 18), Dr. R. Joseph Waddington describes a lesson plan he uses to teach difference-in-differences estimation. Difference-in-differences is a popular quasi-experimental technique designed to help researchers make causal inferences out of naturally occurring events. Students in this lesson are asked to review and discuss foundational papers using difference-in-differences and data from one of those studies to practice estimating a difference-in-differences model using Stata statistical software. Dr. Waddington describes the various key concepts that faculty must understand to effectively teach about difference-in-differences. This chapter provides professors with an easy-to-follow strategy for teaching an essential qualitative technique for the applied educational scholar.

I hope professors who teach quantitative methods can take all or parts of these lesson plans and incorporate them into their own teaching. The authors of these chapters have shared invaluable teaching knowledge and experiences in the following pages. I am confident that if other professors study these lesson plans, they will become better, more impactful teachers of quantitative research methods.

BIBLIOGRAPHY

Armstrong, P. (2010). *Bloom's Taxonomy*. Vanderbilt University Center for Teaching. Retrieved June 17, 2022 from https://cft.vanderbilt.edu/guides-sub-pages/blooms-taxonomy/

Michaelsen, L. K., & Sweet, M. (2008). The essential elements of team-based learning. *New Directions for Teaching and Learning, 2008*(116), 7–27.

Schleutker, E. (2022). Seven suggestions for teaching quantitative methods. *Political Science & Politics, 55*(2), 419–423. doi:10.1017/S1049096521001426

15

Making Sense of Multivariate Analysis

Real-world Applications

Courtney S. Thomas Tobin

INTRODUCTION

While teaching numerous courses on quantitative research methods and social statistics, I have witnessed a range of student responses to learning about multivariate analysis (i.e., the study of relationships between multiple factors within a sample to gain insights into those relationships among a broader population). For many, just the *thought* of learning statistics is unappealing at best and terrifying at worst. These students often attribute such feelings to a "math phobia" or fear of the unknown. At the same time, I have fielded questions from students such as, "When are we ever going to use this?" This has prompted me to seek strategies to alleviate their anxieties and convey that statistical methods, and particularly basic multivariate analysis skills, can be accessible and relatable. At the end of the day, I want my students to understand that these skills have numerous real-world applications that can be useful no matter what career path they plan to pursue. To this end, I have increasingly integrated traditional pedagogical techniques (e.g., lectures, textbook readings, practice questions) with more hands-on activities that allow students to extend their knowledge and practice their new skills with realistic applications. The goal of this chapter is to share some of these activities and to provide instructors with fun, effective strategies for teaching foundational skills in multivariate analysis. This activity is designed to be facilitated over multiple (likely two) class periods.

DOI: 10.4324/b23320-20

MAKING SENSE OF MULTIVARIATE ANALYSIS

LESSON PLAN

Topic	*Using real-world scenarios to apply basic multivariate statistics skills.*
Learning Objectives	<ul><li>Students will learn the purposes of multivariate analysis in the context of real-world scenarios.</li><li>Students will build on their knowledge of the research process by developing and testing an original research question that can be addressed using multivariate analysis.</li><li>Students will consider challenges associated with the quantitative data collection process by (a) crafting and administering a short survey to address their research question, and (b) preparing their data for analysis.</li><li>Students will distinguish between and determine the appropriateness of various statistical tests used to conduct basic multivariate analysis (e.g., t-test, χ^2, ANOVA).</li><li>Students will work collaboratively and demonstrate their mastery of multivariate analysis by presenting their results with appropriate statistical and substantive explanations.</li></ul>
Needed Materials	<ul><li>Scenario description [see "Developing the Scenario" below]</li><li>Statistical software (e.g., STATA, SPSS, R). Many universities have site license agreements that allow students to use software such as STATA and SPSS for free. R is an open-source statistical tool available for free.</li><li>Textbook to provide students with foundational knowledge and opportunities to practice statistical skills. I recommend is *Statistics and Data Analysis for Social Science* by Eric J. Krieg, ISBN-10: 0205863655, and the associated workbook *SPSS Technology Manual for Statistics and Data Analysis for Social Science*.</li><li>Spreadsheet program (e.g., MS Excel, Google Sheets)</li><li>Online survey platform (e.g., Google Forms, SurveyMonkey, Qualtrics). As with statistical programs, many institutions have license agreements that give students free access to online survey platforms.</li></ul>
Pre-lesson Preparation	**Developing the Scenario**. An essential part of the success of these activities is the scenario, which sets the stage by providing context and an overarching rationale for the tasks that your students will complete. So, before getting started, you will want to choose a "real-world" scenario that makes sense and is interesting for your class. I try to tailor this scenario for each group of students because it helps to make the experience more relatable. I find it especially helpful to consider my students' varied background, including their ages, cultural or religious backgrounds, hometown or country of origin, preferred hobbies, academic major, and career goals. Since I typically implement these activities well into the term, I have often gleaned such information from conversations with my students. However, you might choose to administer a brief survey to learn more about your students as well. In any case, you can use this information to develop a scenario in which a researcher or research team would need to conduct multivariate analysis. Examples of scenarios include: **Scenario A**: A team of market researchers want to learn the public's opinion about a specific product. **Scenario B**: A group of researchers from the city's department of public health seeks to identify the factors that influence a neighborhood's health behaviors or outcomes. **Scenario C**: A team of political consultants for a local campaign (e.g., city council, school board, or mayoral race) want to better understand the issues that are most important within this community.

Topic	*Using real-world scenarios to apply basic multivariate statistics skills.*

	Note: *Potential Adaptations*: These activities may be adapted for your class size or other considerations. In my experience, developing a single scenario works especially well for smaller classes (~20 students). For larger classes, however, a more effective strategy might be to put students into groups of 5–7 individuals and to assign a slightly different version of the scenario to each group. This would help you to avoid significant overlap in students' research questions and survey items. For example, if you are implementing Scenario A, all groups would still play the role of market researchers, but each group would focus on a different product (chosen by you or each team). Class size notwithstanding, this adaptation might be preferable if you would like there to be greater diversity of group topics. This approach may also be utilized if having your students work independently is preferred. With this adaptation, each student would "customize" the scenario. For instance, with Scenario A, this option would involve individual students selecting their own product of interest.
	
	 Group Assignments. After considering these potential adaptations, divide your class into your preferred group size (or determine that they will work independently).
	
	 Scenario Description: Prepare and provide students with a written description providing background information regarding the chosen scenario. This is a great opportunity to be creative and give students information that will get them engaged. Scenario descriptions should include key information such as:
	 • Role
	  ○ *Who are the students supposed to "be" in this scenario?* Provide information about (or allow students to determine) their background and credentials.
	 • Problem
	  ○ *What is the question or issue they are trying to address? What is their motivation?* It will also be helpful to specify the details of your scenario, so make sure to fully explain what students are trying to find out and why. For instance, when describing Scenario A noted above, I would specify the product of interest, provide some details about what the product is, why it is important, a challenge or issue the company wants to address, and so on. This information will help your students to craft better survey items during the data collection process.
	 • Other relevant information
	  ○ *What information would be helpful to know?* Additional details, such as their location, target population, or other conditions/constraints you want students to keep in mind should also be provided. Continuing with Scenario A as an example, let's say that the product of interest is a new family board game. In this case, specifying that students are market researchers trying to learn what low-income families in the midwestern United States think about their board game product, and board games in general, provides important additional context that students need to know for data collection and the interpretation of their results.

Activities	**Activity #1: Data Collection** In this activity, students will work together to craft a survey and collect original quantitative data to address research questions and test hypotheses based on a real-world scenario. Each small group will propose a unique research question and hypothesis; groups will also generate their own set of survey items that will be compiled into a single survey to be administered to the entire class. Data from this class survey will be used in Activity #2. • Start the session by (a) sharing the group assignments, and (b) asking students to sit with their groups. • Explain the chosen scenario (see *Scenario Description* above) to your students.

MAKING SENSE OF MULTIVARIATE ANALYSIS

Topic	*Using real-world scenarios to apply basic multivariate statistics skills.*
	<ul><li>Provide a brief overview of the data collection process, highlighting the following:<ul><li>Forming a strong research question and hypothesis</li><li>Creating survey items</li></ul></li><li>Ask students to brainstorm potentially important demographic characteristics; write a list on the board/screen.<ul><li>Examples might include characteristics such as age, sex/gender, race/ethnicity, hometown. Encourage them to also identify characteristics that would be relevant for the scenario.</li></ul></li><li>Have a group discussion to illustrate the various ways we might ask questions in a survey and how that leads to different types of variables. Review and contrast variable types such as continuous vs. categorical variables, nominal vs. ordinal variables, etc.<ul><li>As a class, finalize the survey items that you would like to include to assess demographics.</li></ul></li><li>Within their small groups, students should complete the following:<ul><li>Form a research question and hypothesis based on the provided scenario. Each group should craft a unique research question and hypothesis.</li><li>Generate survey items to test their hypothesis. Each group should propose 5–10 survey items with a variety of variable types. In other words, the items should be a mix of continuous and categorical (nominal and ordinal) variables.<ul><li>*Note*: The number of survey items that each group generates can be adjusted based on the number of groups in the class. For instance, in a class of 20 students, you might have 5 groups consisting of 4 students each. In this case, each group can generate 5 survey items, resulting in 25 survey questions, which would be compiled with the demographic items generated during the full group discussion.<ul><li>Groups may exchange their survey items to provide peer feedback.</li><li>This part of the activity can be completed during class time or outside of class, depending on the amount of time available.</li></ul></li></ul></li></ul></li><li>Compile each group's survey items, along with the demographic items crafted during the group discussion, into a single questionnaire, using Google Forms or a similar platform.<ul><li>Ask students to complete the survey.</li></ul></li><li>Facilitate a discussion to review the results of the survey, considering issues such as:<ul><li>Challenges of developing a survey; make sure to discuss this within the context of the scenario (e.g., What are some strategies that we, as "market researchers" [in Scenario A], can use to get at the information we really want to know?)</li><li>Operationalizing variables (e.g., deciding the best format for certain survey items; What process might we use to decide whether we should make a variable continuous or categorical?)</li><li>Distribution of survey responses; students can also calculate simple univariate statistics (e.g., mean, median, mode) for their group's variables as an additional exercise (see Assessment below). This can also be used as part of a review of these earlier concepts. Depending on the class length, Activity #1 might be completed during class 1 of a 2-class session sequence.</li></ul></li></ul>

Topic	*Using real-world scenarios to apply basic multivariate statistics skills.*

	Activity #2: Analyzing the Data
	In this activity, students apply their multivariate analysis skills by analyzing the data collected in Activity #1.
	• Provide a lecture/discussion of basic multivariate methods, including:
	   ◦ The purpose of multivariate analysis.
	   ◦ A review of statistical tests (t-test, χ^2, ANOVA) and the conditions in which they should be utilized.
	   ◦ Creating and interpreting graphical representations of multivariate associations, such as line graphs and bar charts.
	• Within their same small groups, ask students to revisit their research question from Activity #1 and complete the following:
	   ◦ Identify the variables from the class survey data that can be used to address this research question.
	   ◦ Form a hypothesis and specify the expected relationship between the two variables.
	   ◦ Determine which statistical test (t-test, χ^2, ANOVA) would be most appropriate to analyze the relationship between variables.
	   ◦ Use statistical software to run the statistical test.
	   ◦ Present the output and write a brief explanation (3–5 sentences) that uses appropriate statistical terminology (i.e., denotes whether the association is statistically significant, and the magnitude and direction of the association) but also includes a more accessible, substantive conclusion about the "meaning" of the results within the context of the scenario.
	• Groups should then repeat the previous step with two additional research questions, generating research questions and selecting variable pairs that will allow them to use each of the following statistical tests: t-test, χ^2, ANOVA.
	• Provide each group with feedback along the way (see Assessment below).
	• Groups should present their findings to the class during brief presentations, making sure to stay in character based on the provided scenario (see Assessment below).
	   ◦ Encourage students to use appropriate graphics (e.g., line graphs, bar charts) to illustrate their findings to the class.
	• Conclude the activity with a group debriefing session that covers:
	   ◦ Recap: The purpose of multivariate analysis
	   ◦ Lessons learned from each activity
	      ▪ Prompt: What are some effective strategies for collecting quantitative data?
	      ▪ Prompt: What have you learned about the data analysis process that you didn't know before?
	The goal should be to complete Activity #2 during one class period. This would give students the experience of compiling and presenting data in a short time window.

Virtual Adaptations	These activities can be easily adapted for a virtual classroom environment. Small group interactions may occur via Breakout Rooms. Instructors may also ask students to complete group assignments within Google Docs. This not only allows students to work collaboratively, but it also allows the instructor to monitor each group's progress and to provide feedback in real time. For presentations, students may prepare slides and images to share with the class via the Zoom Screen Share feature.

Topic	*Using real-world scenarios to apply basic multivariate statistics skills.*
Assessment	**For Activity #1**: • Assessment #1.1. Survey items for each group. • Assessment #1.2. Estimating univariate statistics for group variables. **For Activity #2**: • Assessment #2.1. Analysis and results for each group. • Assessment #2.2. Group presentations.

INTELLECTUAL PREPARATION FOR THE LESSON

Core Ideas

Two interrelated core ideas provide the foundation for these activities: (1) Data collection as an integral part of the multivariate analysis process; and (2) the real-world applicability of multivariate analyses.

Although many students come in with a general understanding of what a survey is or may have even collected similar types of survey data in other courses, it has been my experience that few students recognize the integral role of data collection in multivariate analysis. Activity #1 emphasizes the significance of the quantitative data collection process by getting students engaged and focused on a specific problem/issue that they need to address. By crafting their own research question, hypothesis, and survey items, students are encouraged to be intentional and think critically about the decisions they are making. This provides an important lesson, mainly that in the analysis process, there are often multiple ways to solve a problem and there is not necessarily a "right answer." Instead, they begin to see that research is often a more reflexive process during which they need to understand *why* they might make certain choices, like deciding the best way to ask questions in a survey to address their research questions. These critical thinking skills are further developed through Activity #2, in which students are asked to integrate their understanding of the substantive challenge (i.e., the issue presented in the scenario) with their methodological knowledge of multivariate statistical tests. This link is critical, as it demonstrates for students that our methodological choices are not made in a vacuum but are based on the context of the issue (or scenario) we face.

This also reflects the second core idea of the real-world applicability of basic multivariate methods. Grounding these activities within detailed scenarios forms the context in which students can practice making these types of decisions. More specifically, by asking students to consider these issues within small group and larger class discussions, these activities provide numerous opportunities for them to think through this process, which takes their learning to a higher level and enhances their ability to utilize these skills beyond the classroom. Furthermore, presenting their findings with an emphasis on both statistical and substantive interpretations ensures greater comprehension of these concepts and shows students the importance of translating their research findings.

Learners

As previously noted, fear of statistics and the misconception that "Statistics is math. I'm no good at math, so I must be bad at stats" is relatively common among students. For many students, my class is their first exposure to social statistics and data analysis, while others may have some experience from other classes. Managing students' anxieties and the diversity of experience are often more challenging than teaching the content itself. I have found that acknowledging students' perceptions and addressing them head on at the start of the class is most effective, as it helps to allay their fears and fosters some degree of openness about learning the subject.

For instance, I often explain to students that while memorization might have been an effective learning strategy in their previous math classes, the goal in our class would be to develop their critical thinking skills so they are prepared to apply their statistical skills to a wide range of issues.

Context

The impact of the activities is further amplified by the way they are integrated into the class. Specifically, the activities are intended to be completed after students have learned the fundamentals of quantitative data analysis (e.g., univariate analysis, hypothesis testing). The activities presented here should be implemented over multiple class sessions and work best when integrated with other teaching methods (e.g., textbook readings, quizzes, lectures/discussions) to facilitate student learning. This approach allows for flexibility in the class schedule, which is helpful when I find that I need additional time to review/discuss certain topics with students. The activities also focus on helping students to connect the dots between their previous statistical knowledge, and by working in groups, the goal is that students gain important collaborative research skills and benefit from these reciprocal learning experiences.

Through the activities presented in this chapter, my hope is that students have more opportunities for fun, experiential learning to apply their knowledge of basic multivariate statistics.

16

Linear Regression

A Student-driven Application of Team-based Learning

Amber D. Dumford

INTRODUCTION

Every semester, graduate students come into my courses on educational research, assessment, big data, or predictive analytics with great apprehension about how data and statistics will be used in these classes. The students often dread these courses because collecting and analyzing data can be intimidating. Where these fears seem to culminate is in the topic of linear regression. I have found that walking them through the process step by step, from the question that you are interested in answering to the results from the actual regression model, can help students grasp the topic. Additionally, allowing students to make choices about the variables used in the example model and be participants in the data collection can make it more relatable and fun. The purpose of this lesson on linear regression is to present a complex statistical topic in a way that is more digestible for all students, even those who might "fear" numbers.

LESSON PLAN

Topic	Linear Regression Model
Learning Objectives	• Students will understand both the components of a simple linear regression and multiple linear regression (e.g., dependent variable, independent variables, R^2, regression coefficients). • Students will be able to describe the association between variables in a linear regression model. • Students will develop a deeper understanding of the linear regression model and its limitations.

DOI: 10.4324/b23320-21

Topic	Linear Regression Model
Needed Materials	- A statistical software package (e.g., SPSS, SAS, R, Minitab). - Software for collecting survey data (e.g., Qualtrics, SurveyMonkey). - *Note*: For statistical and survey software, most universities have site licenses, and you will need to check with your IT team. - For prior homework, have students read two research articles that use linear regression. Typically, the articles that I choose have simpler regression models and cover topical areas that might be interesting or timely. For example, during COVID, I selected one of my own research articles that used linear regression models to explore the relationship between student engagement and number of courses taken online (Dumford & Miller, 2018). Another article presenting regression results well and on a topic that interested students was one on the association between social media use and social adjustment to college (Yang & Lee, 2020).
Pre-lesson Preparation	- *How can I scaffold this lesson?* This lesson typically comes later in the semester after we first covered simpler quantitative analyses (e.g., descriptive statistics, correlations). Understanding the process and concepts used in linear regression is built upon in some of my courses when we discuss predictive learning analytics tools, which typically use machine learning algorithms (one of which is linear regression). - If you are not a survey wiz – get to know your survey software. Go ahead and create the template for your survey: Create a name for your survey and input some basic (and tested) student demographic survey questions (i.e., gender, age, race/ethnicity) to get it started and save time during class. Note: Qualtrics has a support section on their website and there is a getting started module here: https://www.qualtrics.com/support/survey-platform/survey-module/survey-module-overview/. SurveyMonkey also has a section on their website with tutorials and videos here: https://help.surveymonkey.com/en/create/creating-a-survey/.

Activities	- Set up the lesson: Give students the plan for the lesson.
	  - Example: We will be doing an exercise today to get to know each other better and learn about linear regression.
	- Let students pick the dependent variable for the model indirectly by asking them what question that they would like to know about each other (Note: be sure to steer them towards a continuous variable). Some examples that classes have chosen in the past:
	  - How many concerts have you been to?
	  - How much time per day do you spend listening to music?
	  - How much time per day do you spend on TikTok?
	  - How many times per week do you visit Starbucks?
	  - How many times have you watched your favorite TV series?
	- Let the students pick the independent variables indirectly by asking them "What do they think might be some characteristics or behaviors that are related to the chosen dependent variable?" In addition to typical demographics (e.g., gender, age, race/ethnicity), some examples that classes have chosen in the past:
	  - How many hours do you watch TV?
	  - How many hours do you spend studying or reading for classes?
	  - What is your favorite movie genre?
	  - How much do you like coffee?
	- Develop the survey questions with the students – just a few questions based on the variables that students discussed and picked. You want a question for each of the dependent and independent variables (limit to 4–5 including demographics). You do not want to make the survey too complicated or long, but you do want to try to make sure to include some variables/questions that might be related to your dependent variable.

LINEAR REGRESSION

Topic	Linear Regression Model
	<ul><li>Once the survey is created, have all the students take the survey. Give them 10–15 minutes.</li><li>Once all students have taken the survey, download the data from the survey software into your chosen statistical software package.</li><li>Next, review the data with the students. Start by just looking at the descriptive statistics/frequencies of your survey questions with the class. Let them discuss the answers from their fellow classmates. For example, are they surprised by how many times they visit Starbucks per week? Are there any issues that you need to consider or fix? Are there variables with little or no variance? NOTE: Again, relate this back to the students themselves – if there is little or no variance then everyone in the class answered exactly the same and that variable will not be helpful in predicting the answer to the question that they picked.</li><li>After you have a good feel for the data, choose one of the independent variables and run a simple linear regression. Choose the independent variable that they were most interested in understanding the relationship with the dependent variable.</li><li>Before you review the results, have the students predict what they think the relationship will look like.</li><li>Discuss the results. Be sure to talk about the relationship in ways that answers the question that they posed (not just as the statistical components). Some examples:<ul><li>Variance explained: R^2</li><li>Regression coefficient (both unstandardized and betas)</li></ul></li><li>Next, put all the variables into the model and run a multiple regression.</li><li>Discuss these results. Again, be sure to talk about the relationships in ways that answer the questions that they posed (not just as the statistical components). Some examples:<ul><li>Variance explained: R^2</li><li>Regression coefficients for all the included variables (both unstandardized and betas)</li></ul></li><li>After the fun conversation about what all the components meant, discuss the assumptions of linear regression. Point out the importance of checking the assumptions before looking at results and this is one of the most often skipped steps when researchers are conducting linear regressions. Assumptions to check:<ul><li>Linear relationship between the independent and dependent variables: Review the scatter plots and discuss.</li><li>Variables are normally distributed: Review the histogram for each variable.</li><li>No multicollinearity: Run a correlation matrix (Pearson's bivariate correlation) among all independent variables. Check to make sure there are no correlations $r = 0.70$ or higher. In general, a correlation coefficient close to 0.80 suggests collinearity exists (Young, 2017). You can also review the variance inflation factors (VIF). VIF > 5 indicates that multicollinearity may be present and if the VIF > 10 there is certainly multicollinearity among the variables (Belsley, 1991; Field, 2017).</li><li>Homoscedasticity: Check the scatter plot (making sure the residuals are equal across the regression line).</li></ul></li><li>Additionally, review some of the cautions to use with linear regression. These include:<ul><li>Correlation does not mean causation</li><li>Sample size can impact statistical significance (with large sample sizes everything can be statistically significant), SO both statistical significance and practical significance are important</li><li>The number of participants within each subgroup can get small sometimes (e.g., race/ethnicity groups), so important to look at those numbers when interpreting betas</li></ul></li></ul>

Topic	Linear Regression Model
	• TEAM BREAKOUTS: Now have students apply what they learned here to the two articles they read for homework. Have them break into groups and identify the different components AND talk about the relationships. Make a list of the pieces of information that you want them to find and interpret (e.g., R^2, unstandardized regression coefficients, betas coefficients). During the team discussions, you should walk around to each group to clarify any confusions that they might have about the tasks at hand, while allowing them to struggle with the problem. • Then all groups come back together and share their results – have them put them on the board in a table OR try the alternative adaptation used in the virtual environment.
Virtual Adaptations	Students often find learning linear regression online hard, but this lesson can translate into a synchronous virtual session seamlessly. • Go through all the same steps • Use share screen option to show the process • Team breakouts can be done through virtual breakout rooms on most synchronous platforms (or by creating specific chat sessions for each group ahead of time). • One adaptation that I have used in the virtual environment was to implement GooseChase (https://www.goosechase.com/) to create a scavenger hunt where the teams could input the various linear regression components from the articles. The students seemed to enjoy this because it was "competitive" (the students get points for entering in each requested component). NOTE: This technology could be used in a face-to-face setting as well.
Assessment	• Formative Assessment: During the entire lesson, you are checking in with students to make sure that they are understanding and engaging with the concepts. This is a very discussion-based activity. • Formative Assessment: During team breakouts, move about the room and assess students' ability to connect the class example to the linear regression in the two research articles that they read for homework. • Summative Assessment: Grade the final class project where students use these techniques in their own mini research project.

INTELLECTUAL PREPARATION FOR LESSON

Most graduate students in the social sciences, not just in the United States but also world-wide, are required to take at least one statistics or quantitative methodology course. The thought of these classes often causes anxiety for students as they find it hard to understand the statistical concepts that are presented in class (Onwuegbuzie, 2003). This anxiety has been shown to negatively influence both attitude toward statistics and academic performance in several disciplines, including education (Finney & Schraw, 2003; Onwuegbuzie et al., 2000). In response to students' anxiety over statistics, I have tried to invent "fun" and practical ways to teach complex statistical concepts. Although this lesson is not ground-breaking, it is one where I have seen students engage in the components of one of the more complex statistical methods taught in most required quantitative methods courses – linear regression.

Core Ideas

Linear regression at its core is all about relationships. Simple linear regression is the statistical method for calculating the relationship between two variables. Multiple linear regression, what we see more commonly in research articles, takes that a step further and calculates many relationships in one model – those between multiple variables and one outcome/dependent variable. This specific lesson focuses on the most commonly discussed and core concepts of linear regression (e.g., variance explained or R^2, unstandardized regression coefficients, and beta coefficients), the assumptions of linear regression, and cautions to take when using linear regression. The premise behind the lesson is that students learn better when they can relate to the material being taught to them and since they cannot relate to statistics itself, you must improvise and use techniques that focus on questions/topics that interest them in teaching the core concepts of linear regression.

Learners

When designing any lesson, you need to consider the learners themselves. They will bring to the classroom their previous learning, preconceived notions, and learning differences. In this section, I will reflect on how these ideas helped me create this lesson.

Previous Learning and Misconceptions

Many students, especially those in the social sciences, come to graduate school having taken few, if any, statistics courses. Often the only course that they may have taken was a large introductory course, which relied on lecturing. This lesson is designed to try to avoid lecturing when discussing linear regression. Ideally, the students are creating this learning experience and you are just facilitating the technical aspects. The focus is on topics of interest to the students rather than the technical aspects of linear regression. The students are designing the questions that they want to ask and the relationships that they want to explore. The instructor is just putting all of that within the steps and context of linear regression. Students can see how everyone in the class fits into the linear regression model and how their characteristics and behaviors might predict their behavior on the dependent variable question.

Learner Differences

As previously mentioned, graduate students often have anxiety concerning statistical concepts. In particular, this anxiety seems to be heightened in certain students. Older students report experiencing significantly higher levels of anxiety around statistics concepts when compared to their younger peers (Baloğlu, 2003) and male students have also been found to experience higher levels of anxiety when seeking statistics when compared to their female counterparts (Edirisooriya & Lipscomb, 2021). African American graduate students report higher levels of statistics anxiety than their White counterparts, even after controlling for the number of statistics courses previously taken (Onwuegbuzie, 2004). Finally, students in online classes have been found to report more statistics anxiety than their counterparts taking traditional face-to-face courses (DeVaney, 2010). This lesson tries to alleviate anxiety for all groups by creating a discussion around a complex statistical topic that is about more than just numbers and terminology. It uses the linear regression technique to discuss topics that are relevant to the students.

Context

This linear regression lesson is built upon two core tenets of teaching: (1) students learn better when they are applying the concept that they are trying to learn, as they are learning it, and (2) team-based learning is best for developing students' ability to solve complex problems. I will discuss both of these components in the next sections.

Experiential Learning and Application

In the past, linear regression has often been taught with a focus on giving students information and then hoping that they retain it. This has often been done through lecturing techniques. Engaging students in the learning process through "learning by doing" and reflecting on the experience is at the heart of experiential learning. The teacher's role moves from the giver of knowledge to a facilitator in the learning process. This process is at the core of the current lesson on linear regression. Students are active participants in every step of the learning process, not disengaged bystanders. They are given the agency to choose the questions and relationships that will be explored.

Team-based Learning

According to the 4S framework (Sibley & Ostafichuk, 2015), team-based learning should include four different components. First, the problem given to the team should be *significant* and complex. Second, you should give all teams the *same problem* to work on at the same time. While they are working, you move around to each team to track student progress and resolve any confusion that they might have, but you also need to remember to let students struggle with the problem itself on their own. Third, you should require each team to come to consensus on their responses and express their *specific choice(s)*. Finally, all teams should reveal their answers *simultaneously*. Any differences in answers can ignite a spirited discussion. All four of these components can be found in this lesson during the team breakouts.

CONCLUSION

This linear regression lesson strives to create an entertaining and relaxed learning experience for students, where students can learn a complex statistical technique without anxiety. Students who participate in this lesson create the questions (so they care about the questions and ultimately the results), see themselves in the data (they are after all the survey participants), and ultimately grasp how everything fits together (since they have navigated the process holding the steering wheel through the whole process). Conducting a lesson on linear regression in a way such that the topics, concepts, and process are all controlled by the students, helps students to recognize the relevance of what they are doing. They appreciate the application of linear regression in a real way and this discovery has, at least for my classes, increased student engagement.

BIBLIOGRAPHY

Agresti, A. (2018). *Statistical methods for the Social Sciences* (5th ed.). Pearson.

Baloğlu, M. (2003). Individual differences in statistics anxiety among college students. *Personality and Individual Differences, 34*(5), 855–865.

Belsley, D. A. (1991). *Conditioning diagnostics: Collinearity and weak data in regression.* John Wiley & Sons, Inc.

Creswell, J. W., and Guetterman, T. C. (2019). *Educational research: Planning, conducting, and evaluating quantitative and qualitative research* (6th ed.). Pearson.

DeVaney, T. A. (2010). Anxiety and attitude of graduate students in on-campus vs. online statistics courses. *Journal of Statistics Education, 18*(1). DOI: 10.1080/10691898.2010.11889472

Dumford, A. D., and Miller, A. L. (2018). Online learning in higher education: exploring advantages and disadvantages for engagement. *Journal of Computing Higher Education, 30*, 452–465. DOI: 10.1007/s12528-018-9179-z

Edirisooriya, M. L., and Lipscomb, T. J. (2021). Gender influence on statistics anxiety among graduate students. *Journal of Research in Science Mathematics and Technology Education, 4*(2), 63–74.

Field, A. (2017). *Discovering statistics using SPSS* (5th ed.). Sage.

Finney, S. J., and Schraw, G. (2003). Self-efficacy beliefs in college statistics courses, *Contemporary Educational Psychology, 28*, 161–186.

Nilson, L. B. (2016). *Teaching at its best: A research-based resource for college instructors.* John Wiley & Sons.

Onwuegbuzie, A. J. (2003). Modeling statistics achievement among graduate students. *Educational and Psychological Measurement, 63*(6), 1020–1038.

Onwuegbuzie, A. J. (2004). Academic procrastination and statistics anxiety. *Assessment & Evaluation in Higher Education, 29*(1), 3–19.

Onwuegbuzie, A. J., Slate, J. R., Paterson, F. R. A., Watson, M. H., and Schwartz, R. A. (2000). Factors associated with achievement in educational research courses, *Research in the Schools, 7*, 53–65.

Shrestha, N. (2020). Detecting multicollinearity in regression analysis. *American Journal of Applied Mathematics and Statistics, 8*(2), 39–42, DOI: 10.12691/ajams-8-2-1

Sibley, J., and Ostafichuk, P. (2015). *Getting started with team-based learning.* Stylus Publishing, LLC.

Yang, C., and Lee, Y. (2020) Interactants and activities on Facebook, Instagram, and Twitter: Associations between social media use and social adjustment to college, *Applied Developmental Science, 24*(1), 62–78. DOI: 10.1080/10888691.2018.1440233

Young, D. S. (2018). *Handbook of regression methods.* Chapman and Hall/CRC.

17
Hands-on Application of Exploratory Factor Analysis in Educational Research

Soyeon Ahn and Beck Graefe

INTRODUCTION

Much research in educational research focuses on the interrelationships between and among constructs such as student performance, motivation, success, and satisfaction. These constructs are often measured by multiple variables, making statistical analysis daunting for students. An Exploratory Factor Analysis (EFA) is often used for measuring abstract constructs because of its ability to handle multiple variables, yet EFA requires users to make many statistical decisions to properly apply the technique to their data. In fact, multiple methods exist to perform an EFA (principal axis factoring, maximum likelihood estimation) and extract a set of coherent factors from variables using factor rotation methods (orthogonal and oblique). Users must carefully decide which method is most appropriate for their purposes. Students often feel overwhelmed or get lost when applying what they have learned to their own research when using EFA. This chapter provides a lesson plan that reduces students' frustration when performing EFA on their own data and further supports students in becoming effective users of and able to critique EFA. The chapter stresses the importance of instructional support and making statistical analysis relevant to student research, allowing them to develop genuine answers to important questions in educational research.

LESSON PLAN

Topic	*Hands-on application of EFA using a statistical software package and summarizing findings in line with academic writing requirements.*
Learning Objectives	By the end of this lesson, students will be able to • Understand "when" and "why" to apply EFA. • Describe step-by-step procedures for performing EFA. • Run EFA on their own data using statistical software. • Summarize EFA results. • Critically evaluate other educational research using EFA.

DOI: 10.4324/b23320-22

APPLICATION OF EXPLORATORY FACTOR ANALYSIS

Topic	*Hands-on application of EFA using a statistical software package and summarizing findings in line with academic writing requirements.*
Needed Materials	• Two peer-reviewed articles using EFA in educational research. • Flowchart that displays step-by-step EFA procedures (Appendix A). • SPSS and R syntax for EFA analysis (Appendices B-1 and B-2). • A template that allows students to copy and paste the required statistical information directly from the statistical software and fill in the blanks for interpreting EFA results (Appendix C). • An instructor-provided dataset (e.g., datasets including variables for students, teachers, and professionals in K–16, which were collected by the National Center for Educational Statistics [NCES] (https://nces.ed.gov/datalab/) for EFA demonstration. • A student-provided dataset for EFA. Dataset can be either collected by students or by other researchers. • Computers with installed statistical software packages such as SPSS, R, SAS, STATA. • The APA Publications and Communications Board task force report. *The American Psychologist, 73*(1), 3–25. https://doi.org/10.1037/amp0000191, providing standards for quantitative research in psychology.
Pre-lesson Preparation	• Ensure that students have their own datasets for practice, either original or from other sources. • Encourage students to review the previous EFA lecture and prepare questions for assessing their understanding of EFA. This lesson should follow a lecture that teaches students the basic conceptual and mathematical understanding of "why", "when", and "how" to use EFA. This lecture should be guided by the following questions: (1) When to use EFA? (2) What is the primary goal of EFA? (3) How is EFA different from PCA? (4) How to determine the number of factors? (5) What statistical information is needed to discuss the importance of factors?; (6) How to label the extracted factor(s)? and (7) What is the role of factor rotation?
Activities	**Review of EFA** • Review of previous EFA lecture (see Pre-lesson Preparation section). • Ask students to list EFA terminologies (10 mins.). EFA terminologies can be found in the textbook index. • Draw a cognitive concept map of terminologies and their relationships as a class (10 mins.). Example the use of a cognitive concept map for teaching statistics can be found in https://onlinelibrary.wiley.com/doi/epdf/10.1111/test.12083. **Group Activity: Apply EFA to Sample Peer-reviewed Articles** • As a whole class, review a sample article provided by the instructor, with the instructor helping students recognize how the article uses outputs, (direct quotations, tables, figures) to interpret EFA results (20 mins.). • Then, divide students into groups of 3–5. • Ask small groups to review the second sample article provided by the instructor and answer EFA interpretation questions. Sample questions for simple conceptual understanding of EFA include: (1) How many factor(s) were extracted?, (2) What criteria were used to extract the factor(s)?, (3) Which rotation method was used to identify the simpler structure?, and (4) What is the sum of squared loadings? (20 mins.). **EFA Procedures Review** • Review flowchart delineating detailed step-by-step EFA procedures (see Appendix A for an example flowchart) (10 mins.). • Demonstrate how to run EFA on a simple instructor-provided dataset using a statistical software package of choice. Let students know that vignettes are available for future use as needed (see Appendix B.1 for an example SPSS vignette) (20 mins.). • Complete a template for interpreting EFA results as a class together (see Appendix C for a template) (15 mins.).

Topic	*Hands-on application of EFA using a statistical software package and summarizing findings in line with academic writing requirements.*
	Group Activity: Applying EFA • Divide the class into groups of 3–5 students. • Ask small groups to repeat the steps on another research question using the same instructor-provided dataset (30 mins.). • Ask each student to perform EFA on their own datasets and summarize EFA findings in line with statistical reporting standards (30 mins). • After 30 minutes of each students' individual work on their own datasets, ask students to submit their syntax, outputs, and write up as homework by next class.
Virtual Adaptations	During the Covid-19 Pandemic the demonstration of EFA analysis using a statistical software package was easily adaptable to a synchronous Zoom class setting. • Prior to class, provide all class materials needed. • Instructors are encouraged to use a Zoom whiteboard for drawing a cognitive map together as a class. • Small groups share their work via the Share Screen Zoom feature.
Assessment	1. Formative Assessment: Review submitted syntax, outputs, and write-up for performing EFA on their datasets as homework. 2. Summative assessment: Test on students' understanding of EFA involving (1) interpret EFA results (i.e., communality, sum of squared loadings, # of items extracted, rotation method used, which items to keep based on factor loading), and (2) write statistical findings of EFA. 3. Summative assessments: Grade the final paper using a standard for reporting statistics (i.e., Appleman et al., 2018).

INTELLECTUAL PREPARATION FOR "HANDS-ON APPLICATION OF EFA" LESSON

One approach to teaching EFA is to lay out the multiple steps involved and guide students to choose the most appropriate method for each step. When interpreting EFA results, students must synthesize statistical information, while justifying their interpretation(s) based on theory. Such complexity often overwhelms students. To alleviate these challenges, careful instructional design that incorporates scaffolding can greatly increase students' understanding of EFA while reducing their anxiety, thus enhancing their statistical confidence in using EFA. In this section, we demonstrate examples of scaffolding for core ideas, learners, and context.

Core Ideas

This lesson is divided into three learning blocks: "Block 1: Students Critique Published Sample EFA Articles," "Block 2: Instructor Demonstrates the Application of EFA Using Instructor-provided Data," and "Block 3: Students Apply EFA to Their Datasets." In each block, instructors are encouraged to utilize various scaffolding methods, such as visual aids (e.g., flow charts), templates, mental maps (i.e., a cognitive map), vignettes, and verbalized thinking processes. Below, we will discuss the objective of each learning block and then demonstrate how each can be organized by employing different scaffolding methods.

APPLICATION OF EXPLORATORY FACTOR ANALYSIS

Block 1: Students Critique Published Sample EFA Articles
This block builds on students' understanding of a previous EFA lecture covering the theoretical and mathematical backgrounds of EFA. Block 1 includes three class activities that engage students: (1) review EFA terminology (e.g., communalities), (2) draw a cognitive map of EFA terms and their relationships (e.g., communalities vs. sum of squared loadings), (3) critique a sample article together, with the instructor helping students recognize the way the article uses outputs, such as direct quotations, tables, and figures, to interpret EFA results, and (4) work as a small group to review another sample article and answer questions related to EFA interpretation. An empirical example of EFA will reveal how the technique can be applied to solve problems in education.

The instructor is encouraged to provide cues, encourage students' think-out-loud processes, rephrase students' answers, revisit critical concepts, and actively correct students' misunderstandings as needed. At the end of this block, students will be able to connect previous knowledge to application, clarify their misunderstandings of EFA application, enhance their confidence in using EFA, and learn how to read, evaluate, and write EFA results.

Block 2: Instructors Demonstrate the EFA Application Using an Instructor-provided Dataset
In this block, instructors show students how to perform EFA using statistical software (SPSS or R) and provide clear guidelines for interpreting statistical information and formally writing the results. Instructors can use a flowchart delineating the detailed step-by-step procedures of EFA (Appendix A) and model how to run EFA on a simple instructor-provided dataset, using statistical software packages (Appendix B.1 and B.2). Instructors and students can populate a template using statistical information directly from the outputs and fill in the blanks for interpreting EFA results (Appendix C). Lastly, students can perform EFA for another research question using the instructor-provided dataset and filling in the template as a group.

In this block, the instructor will need to provide learning aids such as flowcharts, vignettes, and templates. A flowchart provides step-by-step guidelines for running EFA and should detail best practice guidelines for choosing a method when running EFA, making note of the theoretical justification for their choice. Vignettes need to be instructive and detailed; screenshots with commentary will help students turn to the vignettes when they get lost running EFA on their own data. It is ideal to provide vignettes for the application of statistical techniques using at least two statistical software packages for future reference. Templates will help students extract the necessary information and summarize conclusions in line with reporting standards.

When demonstrating statistical software applications, instructors should consistently ask questions and adjust pacing based on students' progress. While the instructor is presenting a software application to the class, a teaching assistant can provide additional individual support for students. When students are working on their group projects, the instructor can prompt discussion by providing cues and asking related questions. At the end of this block, students will be able to perform EFA on a dataset and properly write EFA results. In addition, students will have various learning materials that they can use in the future for their own research.

Block 3: Students Apply EFA to their Datasets
This block encourages students to perform EFA to answer their own research questions. In this block, the instructor first asks students to verbalize the step-by-step procedures for the EFA application. Then, students will use various materials such as the flowchart, vignette, and template and perform their own EFA.

The instructor can support students by providing cues, reminding students of missing steps, and asking related questions. At the end of this block, students will be able to perform EFA and summarize EFA results in line with academic reporting standards.

The Learner

Successful teaching requires educators understanding their students. Appropriate scaffolds are dependent upon prior knowledge and experience that students bring to a classroom (Bliss et al., 1996; Granott, 2005). Previous knowledge can misdirect learning, causing misconceptions, or be used advantageously, strengthening understanding. Understanding students' previous knowledge enables instructors to anticipate and address students' misconceptions.

Previous Knowledge to Assist in the Integration of EFA
Students learning EFA need competency in univariate statistics. Univariate statistics should be reviewed before commencing EFA instruction. Students also may not have a complete understanding of eigenvalues/eigenvectors of a matrix and are likely to benefit from additional support/practice. Students might be new to multivariate statistics and may be unpracticed in identifying appropriate methods given their research questions.

Common Misconceptions
Students often struggle to understand when to use EFA over Principal Component Analysis (PCA). PCA is dimension reduction to improve model parsimony and reduce the risk of multicollinearity. EFA analyzes variables that are not directly measurable. When deciding what method to use, students should discern if their goal is to determine the variability of a variable that cannot be directly measured, or to simplify their model by reducing the variables (Joliffe & Morgan, 1992; Suhr, 2005).

Another misconception is related to factor rotation. Explaining rotation using visual examples, such as a physical model, may support understanding. Provide students with many examples to practice determining the most appropriate rotation method; emphasize finding the method that produces the simplest results (Brown, 2009).

Many students have difficulty grasping that the eigenvalues of a matrix are a measure of factor variance. The number of eigenvalues above one frequently indicates the minimum number of factors present, although this method of determining the number of factors may result in biased results (Bandalos & Boehm-Kaufman, 2010). Each eigenvalue is associated with a percentage of the variance that is explained by the associated factor. Based on outputs produced by software, students should determine whether to retain a factor by calculating the percent of information that the factor produces within the model by hand.

APPLICATION OF EXPLORATORY FACTOR ANALYSIS

Students might mix up eigenvalues and factor loadings and may benefit from opportunities to critique the analyses of others and interpret their own results.

Opportunities for Inclusive Research Design
Inclusivity should start when designing research; It is important to consider in identifying and interpreting factor structure. Validity of EFA results depends on the generalizability of the variables measuring factors. To improve student interpretation, attention should be given to the cultural sensitivity of variables and to potential biases that can result.

The Context

Students often become disengaged in statistics classes, expressing frustration, confusion, anxiety, and boredom. The requirement to use numerous technical terms may overwhelm students. Students' anxiety about statistics creates unnecessary learning barriers. In many EFA lessons, little guidance is provided for delineating, performing, and summarizing EFA. Usually, students lack opportunities to work with their own datasets. This lesson is centered around instructional scaffolding to address these barriers and provide a supportive learning environment where students take an active role in their learning.

Instructional Scaffolding
Instructional scaffolding breaks complex materials into manageable units, providing specific instructional tools for each unit. When effectively implemented, it creates a supportive, collaborative, and equitable learning environment. Students engage with materials through inquiry and collaboration. Scaffolding requires the instructor to be a facilitator. For successful instructional scaffolding, an instructor must: (1) constantly be mindful of students' knowledge, skills, and comfort levels; (2) be patient as students vary in ability to understand new concepts; (3) understand where students need support and where they can accomplish tasks independently; and (4) reflectively evaluate which scaffolds are most helpful for students' learning and modify as needed. These practices empower an instructor to design activities and assessments that are tailored to individual student's needs, interests, and abilities.

Supportive Learning Environment
Students' learning is maximized when they feel valued, included, and empowered in the classroom. Such a learning environment is particularly important in statistics courses, where students are heterogeneous in terms of their knowledge and skills. To establish supportive sociocultural norms in the classroom, instructors must understand and honor students' prior knowledge and skills, actively listen to students' responses, encourage collaboration with diverse peers, and constantly monitor students' progress. The instructor can motivate by providing cues and asking challenging questions.

Finally, this lesson emphasizes the importance of student-centered instruction that supports differences in students' learning processes and builds their confidence and ability to use more advanced statistical techniques in educational research.

APPENDIX A

FLOWCHART

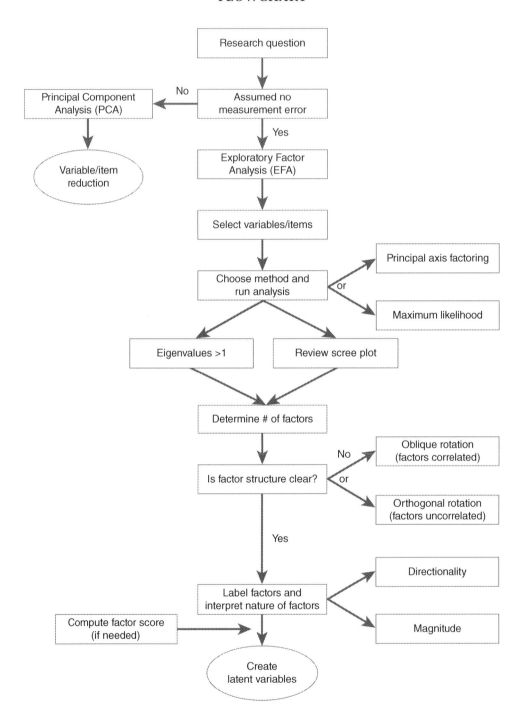

APPENDIX B.1

DEMONSTRATION OF EXPLORATORY FACTOR ANALYSIS (EFA) USING IBM SPSS 28

Run EFA using Principal Axis Factoring method

Step 1: Analyze -> Dimension Reduction -> Factor

Step 2: Move all variables into the "Variables" box

Step 3: Descriptives -> Select "Coefficients," "KMO, and Bartlett's test of sphericity" -> Continue

Step 4: Extraction -> use "Method" menu to select "Principal components" -> select "Scree plot" -> Continue

Step 5: Rotation -> select "Varimax" -> Continue

Step 6: Options -> select "Sorted by size" -> Continue

Step 7: Click "Paste". The syntax window will generate this code:

Step 8: Highlight code and click green "play" button

Step 9: Interpreting your output

- Assumptions – KMO, Bartlett's test, and Correlation Matrix
- Total Variance
- Scree Plot
- Pattern Matrices
- Component Transformation Matrix

APPENDIX B.2

DEMONSTRATION OF EXPLORATORY FACTOR ANALYSIS (EFA) USING R

```
#install R packages first
install.packages(c("foreign", "psych", "nFactors"),
dependencies=TRUE)

#load packages before running model.
require(foreign)
require(psych)
require(nFactors)

#Example dataset
#The data includes 11 variables from 100 college students (data
are listed in Appendix A in Thompson (2004)'s book). # Citation:
Thompson, B. (2004). Exploratory and confirmatory factor analysis:
Understanding concepts and applications. Washington, DC: American
Psychological Association.
```

```
#Read dataset and save as "EFA_data".
EFA_data=read.table(file="Appendix_Thompson.csv", header=TRUE,
sep=",")

#Step 1: run correlation among variables (per1 - per11) and test
whether correlation is identity matrix or not (KMO and Bartlett's
test)

EFA_cor = cor(EFA_data)
#correlation among 11 items included in "EFA_data" is saved as
EFA_cor.
EFA_cor
#Print correlation among 11 items included in "EFA_data".

#check whether correlation (EFA_cor) = I (all variables are
uncorrelated with each other)
#KMO (Kaiser-Meyer-Olkin Measure of Sampling Adequacy) varies
between 0 and 1 and values closer 1 are better.  A value of .6 is a
suggested minimum.
KMO(EFA_data)

#Bartlett's Test
cortest.bartlett(EFA_data, n=nrow(EFA_data))
#Bartlett's test examines whether correlation (EFA_cor) = I (all
varialbes are uncorrelated with each other).

#Scree Plot
plot(eigen(EFA_cor)$values) #EFA_cor is the correlation that was
saved before
abline(h=1.0)
# select # of factors based on eigenvalues

#rotation to be "varimax"
pa1= fa(EFA_cor, nfactors=3, fm="pa", rotate="varimax")
print(pa1) # print results
#commonality: % of variance in variable explained by three factors
#sum of squared loading:
#SSL for factor 1: 2.91, SSL for factor 2: 2.89, SSL for factor 3:
2.14.

#rotation to be "oblim"
pa2 = fa(EFA_cor, nfactors=3, n.obs=ncol(EFA_data), fm="pa",
rotate="oblimin")
print(pa2)

#Maximum Likelihood Factor Analysis
fact1 = fa(EFA_data, 3, rotate="varimax")
```

APPLICATION OF EXPLORATORY FACTOR ANALYSIS

```
print(fact1, digits=2, cutoff=.3, sort=TRUE)
fact2 = fa(EFA_data, 3, rotate="oblimin")
print(fact2, digits=2, cutoff=.3, sort=TRUE)
```

APPENDIX C

TEMPLATE FOR EFA

I. Check whether correlation matrix is an identity matrix or not

    1. Kaiser-Meyer-Olkin measure of sampling adequacy (KMO)

    2. Bartlett's test

    <u>Write up</u>

    The KMO value of _____ suggests that a correlation matrix is/is not an identity matrix, indicating that variables are/are not related each other. Similarly, the result from Bartlett's test suggests that a correlation matrix is/is not an identity matrix, indicating that variables are or are not related each other ($\chi^2(\quad) =$ _____, $p =$ _____).

II. Create a screeplot

    <u>Write up</u>

    As shown in Figure X, _____ number of factors have an eigenvalue greater than 1, suggesting that _____ number of factors are extracted from _____ number of variables (or items).

III. Sum of squared loadings

    <u>Write up</u>

    Sum of squared loading for each factor is _____ for factor1, _____ for factor2, _____ for factor3, _____ for factor4, suggesting that _____% of variance by factor1, _____ % of variance by factor2, _____ % of variance by factor3, were explained.

IV. Communality for each variable

    <u>Write up</u>

    Communalities are _____ for variable1, _____ for variable2, _____ for variable3, , ... These suggests that _____% of variance in variable1, _____% of variance in variable2, _____% of variance in variable3, ... was explained by _____ number of extracted factors.

V. Which variable belongs to each factor

    <u>Write-up</u>

    Variables _____ – _____ are loaded on Factor1, with its associated factor loadings ranged from _____ to _____.

    Variables _____ – _____ are loaded on Factor2, with its associated factor loadings ranged from _____ to _____.

    Variables _____ – _____ are loaded on Factor3, with its associated factor loadings ranged from _____ to _____.

VI. Label of factor

    <u>Write up</u>

    Factor1 is labeled as _____,

    Factor2 is labeled as _____,

    Factor3 is labeled as _____,

BIBLIOGRAPHY

Appelbaum, M., Cooper, H., Kline, R. B., Mayo-Wilson, E., Nezu, A. M., & Rao, S. M. (2018). Journal article reporting standards for quantitative research in psychology: The APA Publications and Communications Board task force report. *The American Psychologist, 73*(1), 3–25. https://doi.org/10.1037/amp0000191

Bandalos, D. L., & Boehm-Kaufman, M. R. (2010). Four common misconceptions in exploratory factor analysis. In C. E. Lance & R. J. Vandenberg (Eds.), *Statistical and methodological, myths, urban, legends* (pp. 81–108). Routledge.

Bliss, J., Askew, M., & Macrae, S. (1996). Effective teaching and learning: Scaffolding revisited. *Oxford Review of Education, 22*(1), 37–61.

Brown, J. D. (2009). Choosing the right type of rotation in PCA and EFA. *JALT Testing & Evaluation Newsletter, 13*(3), 20–25.

Granott, N. (2005). Scaffolding dynamically toward change: Previous and new perspectives. *New Ideas in Psychology, 23*(3), 140–151.

Joliffe, I. T., & Morgan, B. J. T. (1992). Principal component analysis and exploratory factor analysis. *Statistical Methods in Medical Research, 1*(1), 69–95.

Suhr, D. D. (2005). Principal component analysis vs. exploratory factor analysis. *SUGI 30 Proceedings*, 203–30.

18

Trending Topic

Teaching Difference-in-differences in a Quasi-experimental Methods Course

R. Joseph Waddington

INTRODUCTION

Difference-in-differences (colloquially, **diff-in-diff**, or abbreviated as **DiD** or **DD**) is one of the core techniques in the quasi-experimental methods toolkit. When used appropriately and satisfying key assumptions, difference-in-differences can yield powerful causal inferences about a naturally occurring treatment. It is arguably the most popular quasi-experimental research design in the social sciences (Cunningham, 2021).

The elegance of difference-in-differences lies within its simplicity and accessibility. Although it is an advanced technique building upon interaction terms in regression analysis, the mechanics of difference-in-differences hinge primarily on an interaction between a treatment indicator and treatment timing. Thus, a firm understanding of regression model interactions combined with a theoretical grasp of causal inference (especially the "counterfactual") is the requisite baseline knowledge a learner needs to begin engaging with difference-in-differences.

This chapter provides instructors with an overview of a unit for teaching difference-in-differences. This unit is geared towards learners who are engaging with this technique for the first time, perhaps in an introductory causal inference or quasi-experimental methods course. Although the technique builds upon basic regression analysis, this foray into difference-in-differences focuses on the conceptual design, empirical exposition, and threats to validity. After this unit, students should be able to develop a basic difference-in-differences research design, analyze data using a difference-in-differences empirical model, and consume research that uses difference-in-differences. I provide a detailed plan for a unit that spans two class periods, formatted specifically for a course that meets once weekly for two-and-a-half hours.

DOI: 10.4324/b23320-23

LESSON PLAN

Topic	*Difference-in-Differences Research Design*
Learning Objectives	Students who successfully complete the requirements of this unit should expect to be able to: • Develop a research design using a basic difference-in-differences approach with attention to research questions, empirical approach, and potential threats to validity. • Analyze data using difference-in-differences and communicate findings using written language specific to the social sciences and associated scholarly audiences. • Consume research that uses difference-in-differences with a critical lens and appropriately situate work using difference-in-differences within the extant literature.
Needed Materials	Required readings (see Bibliography): • Murnane & Willett (2011), Ch. 8, pp. 141–164. • Dynarski (2003). • Card & Krueger (1994). Supplemental readings (see Bibliography): • Cunningham (2021), Ch. 9. • Goodman-Bacon (2021). Statistical software: • Stata/BE (or equivalent software – I <u>do not</u> recommend SPSS). Please check with your institution as many universities have site license agreements that allow students and faculty to use STATA for free. Data: • Dynarski (2003) data via textbook examples from Murnane and Willett (2011) on UCLA Statistical Consulting website (https://stats.oarc.ucla.edu/other/examples/methods-matter/). • Data for assignment set up for using difference-in-differences. I have students use a hand-me-down data set to analyze the 1993 Earned Income Tax Credit (EITC) expansion using a similar approach as Eissa and Liebman (1996) did to analyze the 1987 EITC expansion.
Pre-lesson Preparation	• Faculty should review student background with interaction terms in regression analysis. Understand in what fields students learned about the topics. • Faculty should review required and supplemental readings, work through data sets and ensure code is updated. • This unit should be sequenced in the first half of the course, after covering experimental designs and natural experiments.
Activities	**Week 1** • In small group discussion, ask students to compare experiments with natural experiments. What are the similarities and differences? It is especially important for students to clearly understand that a natural experiment occurs when control and experimental groups are not artificially manipulated by researchers but instead are created by nature or factors outside of the researchers' control. • Ask students to discuss in small groups some of the takeaways from their reading about natural experiments, and especially difference-in-differences. What are the key considerations?

TRENDING TOPIC

Topic	Difference-in-Differences Research Design
	<ul><li>Lecture on difference-in-differences. The lecture should incorporate the following items:<ul><li>A review and example of interaction terms.</li><li>A discussion of the setup of the difference-in-differences, including the pre-post and treatment-comparison variables.</li><li>An example of difference-in-differences using the regression interactions framework. This should include calculation of the first and second differences and derivation of the difference-in-differences causal effect.</li><li>A discussion of the essential threats to internal and external validity of the difference-in-differences approach.</li></ul></li><li>Break.</li><li>Discuss in small groups the Dynarski (2003) paper. This discussion should incorporate the following questions, assigned to specific groups:<ul><li>What is the causal question of interest in the study?</li><li>What is the identification strategy or method used in the study? In other words, how does the study use observational data to approximate a randomized experiment?</li><li>What is(are) the estimated average effect(s) of the treatment on the outcome? What is the *statistical* and *practical* significance of this(these) estimated effect(s)?</li><li>What are the key threats to the internal validity of the study? In what ways could these threats bias the estimated average treatment effect(s)?</li><li>For what populations, programs, and places can the effect(s) be safely generalized?</li></ul></li><li>Report responses to the whole class for further discussion.</li></ul>**Week 2**<ul><li>The beginning of the session should feature time for questions from students in a whole group setting, regarding lingering confusing concepts about the difference-in-differences design, empirics, and validity issues from Week 1 activities.</li><li>Discuss with the whole group the Card and Krueger (1994) paper. This discussion should incorporate the following items:<ul><li>The key questions described above (in Week 1 discussion).</li><li>A discussion of the research setting.</li><li>Hand calculations of the descriptive difference-in-differences estimate of the minimum wage increase impact using the descriptive table in the paper – this is key for enhancing the soundness of the mechanics.</li></ul></li><li>Break.</li><li>Conduct Stata lab session using the Dynarski (2003) data. Be sure to demonstrate and discuss the following:<ul><li>Constructing the difference-in-difference interaction term.</li><li>Descriptive analysis.</li><li>Calculating the first and second differences.</li><li>Using a regression model to calculate and interpret the difference-in-differences estimate.</li><li>Provide an independent or small group second example with calculating and interpreting the difference-in-differences estimate. Report back to the whole group.</li></ul></li><li>Discuss any lingering questions about difference-in-differences.</li><li>Provide overview of assignment on difference-in-differences.</li></ul>

Topic	Difference-in-Differences Research Design
Virtual Adaptations	This unit is adaptable to either a fully synchronous format or a hybrid blend of synchronous and asynchronous activities. I would avoid teaching this topic in a purely asynchronous setting, as live discussion and engagement are essential for handling misconceptions or statistical software issues. A fully synchronous online adaptation would follow the activities above in nearly an identical manner. For example, an instructor could use Zoom (or other video conferencing software) with the whole group discussions, enabling the instructor's screen sharing for lecture and Stata lab components. Breakout rooms can be used for small group discussions. It is helpful for the instructor to have a device whereby "on-screen annotations" of key parts of lecture notes or research articles can be displayed, such as a tablet and stylus connected to the device through which Zoom is running. For a hybrid online adaptation, consider the following structure: • Week 1 (*asynchronous*): Students view a pre-recorded lecture video on a review of interaction terms and an overview of the empirical mechanics of difference-in-differences. The lecture video could be recorded via Zoom and uploaded to YouTube. Students should have access to a version of the lecture slides with equations unsolved and prompts unanswered so they can "fill in" as they are watching the video. The video should display the slides with on-screen annotations (see above note on suggested equipment for annotations), with video and audio of the instructor also visible. After viewing the video, students answer questions about the difference-in-differences approach from Murnane & Willett (2011) Chapter 8 and the Dynarski (2003) article via small group discussion posts. These questions can be taken from those described in the Week 1 activities. • Week 2 (*synchronous*): Follow lesson plan for the Week 2 activities and suggestions above for a fully synchronous online adaptation.
Assessment	• *Formative Assessment (Journal Article Discussion)*: Students discuss in small groups the methodological details of a paper (read prior to class) using difference-in-differences. Move about the room to assess students' understanding of the methodology while discussing in groups. After the small group discussion, students share their understanding through whole group discussion. • *Formative Assessment (Stata Lab)*: Students use Stata to independently (or in small groups) complete a data analysis exercise using difference-in-differences. Move about the room to assess students' understanding of the methodological application and use of data analysis software. After the independent/small group work, students share their understanding through whole group discussion. • *Summative Assessment (Independent Unit Assignment)*: Students write a structured, two-page policy brief after using Stata to conduct a difference-in-differences analysis. The brief should focus on and be graded through assessing the difference-in-differences approach, threats to validity, and results of the analysis. The brief should be written using language accessible to policymakers, who are the target audience. • *Summative Assessment (Final Course Project)*: Students produce a research proposal or data analysis on the topic of their choice incorporating a quasi-experimental approach discussed in the course (difference-in-differences is one example). Either option should focus on the methods. Grade projects with a focus on the identification strategy, empirical model, interpretation, and assessment of threats to validity.

INTELLECTUAL PREPARATION FOR UNIT

Successful instruction of difference-in-differences requires understanding the core ideas, learners, and learning context associated with this unit. The prerequisite knowledge of the instructor and the students alike is most important. This includes assessing students' prior knowledge of regression techniques acquired from previous coursework, with emphasis on interaction terms. Because learners from different disciplinary backgrounds may participate in such a course, knowing about each student's anchoring context is key for successful instruction and discussion. The next sections detail the preparation and expectations for this unit.

Core Ideas

I break down the core ideas for this unit into three parts. First, I discuss various foundational concepts for understanding difference-in-differences. Next, I describe the key difference-in-differences concepts covered in this unit before concluding with an overview of advanced topics not covered.

Foundational Concepts

Causal inference, or the framework for uncovering the effects of programs, policies, or interventions, is the first critical foundational concept for understanding and using difference-in-differences. Difference-in-differences is a quasi-experimental method within the broader causal inference framework. Prior to introducing quasi-experimental techniques, it is essential to have a working understanding of **experimental design** and the concepts of **treatment and control groups**. More specifically, students need to understand the **counterfactual**, or the hypothetical experience of an individual treatment subject in the absence of treatment. Once students have this theoretical background, difference-in-differences provides an excellent first foray into quasi-experimental methods as it relies on naturally occurring variation, or a **natural experiment**.

From an empirical perspective, difference-in-differences is a direct extension of **regression analysis** with **interaction terms**. Early in the course, it is essential to review the mechanics and interpretation of multiple regression models, including analyzing and interpreting a model in the statistical software package during a lab and/or an assignment. The mechanics and interpretation of interaction terms require their own review during the first week of this unit. Once complete, learners are primed to begin exploring key difference-in-differences concepts.

Key Difference-in-Differences Concepts

This unit explores several essential concepts for understanding difference-in-differences, each of which are highlighted in various parts of the lesson plan and activities as well as here. The overarching key causal inference concept is the **natural experiment**. This is an **exogenous change** whereby certain individuals (or other units) are exposed to a treatment, often a policy or intervention implementation. In the simplest scenario, this change takes place at a fixed point in time. From this, the essential treatment group and timing dimensions of the difference-in-differences framework arise.

Within this framework, learners must first define the **comparison group**. This is the group of individuals (or other units) who were observed in the same timeframe and setting but were untreated (i.e., not impacted by the exogenous change). As such, these individuals serve as the hypothetical counterfactual for the treated group. Second, learners must understand the significance of the **pre-treatment** period. This is the period immediately before the treatment whereby inherent differences between the treatment and comparison groups can be isolated.

Once these key concepts are established, the next step is discussing the empirics. The **first** and **second differences** can be framed as pre-post differences within the treatment and comparison groups. The first difference is the difference in the outcome before and after the exogenous change for the *treatment* group. It is essential to highlight that the first difference alone is a biased estimate of the causal effect. The second difference is the difference in the outcome before and after the exogenous change for the *comparison* group. Subtracting the second difference from the first difference yields the unadjusted **difference-in-differences** treatment effect estimate.

Before describing the difference-in-differences estimate as a causal effect, conversation should center on issues of **internal and external validity** and the underlying assumptions of the difference-in-differences approach. One key internal validity assumption to satisfy is the **parallel trend assumption**, whereby the outcomes of the treatment and comparison groups are trending in the same direction and at a similar rate in the pre-treatment period. Another key internal validity assumption to satisfy is that all treated individuals are treated at the same time. When treatment timing differs across units, the appropriate treatment effect is estimated only when weights are assigned based on treatment timing and time-varying controls are included. These advanced topics are outside the scope of this introductory unit (see Goodman-Bacon, 2021).

Advanced Concepts Not Covered
This unit is geared towards learners' first exposure to difference-in-differences. All learners should consider further study of this technique in a subsequent course and/or by engaging with supplemental materials to successfully implement an advanced research design using difference-in-differences. Key additional concepts needed to build mastery of this technique include using **placebo tests** to assess the parallel trend assumption, conducting **event studies** with longer time panels, and **weighting for differential treatment timing**.

Learners

The instructor must understand the various disciplinary backgrounds and quantitative methods experiences of learners in the course to successfully teach this unit. In this section, I provide some examples of past students to whom I have had the privilege of teaching this topic and how that has informed my preparation and instruction.

Learners Participating in this Course
At my institution, this course is an initial foray into causal inference and quasi-experimental methods. Most students taking this course are doctoral students and what I would call "eager methodologists, hesitant quants." Students across departments in the

TRENDING TOPIC

College of Education, other social sciences (e.g., sociology, social work), and some departments of the College of Business and Economics (e.g., accounting, management, and marketing) are attracted to this course. At my institution, there are causal inference courses in economics and public policy that provide a deeper and more sophisticated econometric-oriented dive into these techniques and are best suited for their students.

It is important to approach this unit (and course) with an insightful understanding of students' prerequisite training and methodological strengths. All students are required to have completed a course on regression analysis. Some may have taken other advanced quantitative coursework, such as multilevel models, network analysis, categorical data analysis, or measurement techniques. Knowing the depth of students' prior quantitative methods experiences helps to design a targeted review of regression techniques (especially interactions) used in this unit.

Learners' Misconceptions from Prior Knowledge

In the "Foundational Concepts" section, I described the background on causal inference and regression models with interaction terms with which students must be equipped before learning difference-in-differences. There are two critical misconceptions which may arise from these concepts, each of which need to be remedied to clearly understand difference-in-differences.

Exogenous Variation and Timing

In Kentucky, we have a popular saying: all bourbon is whiskey, but not all whiskey is bourbon. A similar idiom applies here: (nearly) all difference-in-differences designs use interactions, but not all interaction models use a difference-in-differences design. Difference-in-differences is a specific *concept* and *technique* employed to uncover causal effects, not merely to tease out an additive effect. One group must be impacted by an exogenous change outside the group's control at a specific point in time. In addition, there must be a contemporaneous comparison group not impacted by the exogenous change. The outcome must be measured before and after the change.

As these are essential components to the difference-in-differences framework, it is impossible for all interaction terms to fit a *difference-in-differences* quasi-experimental design. Learners may be inclined to connect difference-in-differences and interactions in contexts that are devoid of a treatment naturally occurring at a point in time.

Interpretation of Regression Models with Interaction Terms

Even when learners appropriately construct a difference-in-differences design, they may struggle with regression model interpretations. This often stems from a weak understanding of how to interpret the main effects in models with interaction terms.

Learners often forget that once two variables are interacted, the main, non-interacted effects of the two variables are interpreted in the context of the *reference group* of the other variable in the interaction. For example, consider the following basic difference-in-differences model:

$$Y_i = \alpha + \beta Treat_i + \gamma Post_i + \delta Treat * Post_i + \varepsilon_i$$

Here, the outcome (Y) for an individual (i) is a function of a random intercept (α), a treatment group status indicator $(Treat_i)$, a post-intervention time period indicator $(Post_i)$, an interaction for the treatment group in the post-intervention time period $(Treat_i)$, and a random error term (ε_i). The key interpretations here are β, γ, and δ.

In the absence of an interaction, β would represent the average difference in Y between the treatment and comparison groups. With an interaction in the difference-in-differences framework, this is no longer true. Here, it is the average difference in Y between the treatment and comparison groups *prior to the exogenous change*. It is the pre-treatment difference between treatment and comparison groups that needs to be accounted for to identify a causal effect.

Similarly, in the absence of an interaction, γ would represent the average difference in Y between the post- and pre-intervention time periods. Again, that is not the case with an interaction in the difference-in-differences framework. Instead, it is the average difference in Y between the post- and pre-intervention time periods *for the comparison group only*. It is the **counterfactual** difference before and after the timing of the intervention, another important factor to partial out to identify a causal effect.

Learners tend to correctly interpret the interaction term as the **additive impact**, and specifically in the difference-in-differences framework, the causal effect. Yet, the common misinterpretations surrounding the main effects can severely hinder a learner's understanding of *how* the difference-in-differences model yields causal effects. Thus, it is critical to understand how and why accounting pre-treatment differences and counterfactual trends lead to causal effects.

Context

The last piece for ensuring successful instruction of difference-in-differences is attending to the learning context. This means understanding where there is a common disciplinary background and using examples that appeal to students from different disciplinary backgrounds.

Connections with Prior Knowledge and Disciplinary Background

Learners will enter this course with varied regression training and research methodologies anchored in different disciplinary backgrounds. It is critical to have whole group and small group conversations about prerequisite methodological knowledge early in the course. Another important activity is to ask students to talk about examples in their field ripe for using difference-in-differences. This group conversation is embedded within the first week's activities. Although mixing and mingling learners from different disciplinary backgrounds is ideal for the course as a whole, this is an instance where shared background knowledge from similar disciplinary backgrounds may be helpful. Finding ways to foster clarity and confidence are important.

Fostering an Equitable Learning Space

While nailing down the conceptual framework and mechanics of difference-in-differences can be challenging, it is critical to use clear, easily digestible examples. I use

TRENDING TOPIC

the Dynarski (2003) and Card and Krueger (1994) examples because of the clear writing and scenarios to which difference-in-differences is applied. Take for example the Card and Krueger minimum wage article, which is a contemporary policy discussion. Most doctoral students, at least through their general education, understand basic supply-and-demand concepts, such that one would theorize increases in wages would lead to decreased employment. This Card and Krueger application of difference-in-differences provides students with the opportunity to both engage with the methodology and simultaneously challenge their peers while connecting with current issues. In general, avoiding examples laden with jargon and/or abstract concepts is critical to learners' success.

BIBLIOGRAPHY

Card, D., & Krueger, A. (1994). Minimum wages and employment: A case study of the fast-food industry in New Jersey and Pennsylvania. *American Economic Review, 84*(4), 772–793.

Cunningham, S. (2021). *Causal inference: The mixtape* (online version). Ch. 9: Difference-in-Differences. from https://mixtape.scunning.com/difference-in-differences.html (accessed February 4, 2022).

Dynarski, S. (2003). Does aid matter? Measuring the effect of student aid on college attendance and completion. *American Economic Review, 93*(1), 279–288.

Eissa, N., & Liebman, J. B. (1996). Labor supply response to the Earned Income Tax Credit. *Quarterly Journal of Economics, 111*(2), 605–637.

Goodman-Bacon, A. (2021): Difference-in-differences with variation in treatment timing. *Journal of Econometrics, 225*(2), 254–277.

Murnane, R.J., & Willett, J.B. (2011). *Methods matter: Improving casual inference in educational and social science research*. Oxford University Press.

Textbook examples for *Methods Matter: Improving Causal Inference in Educational and Social Science Research* by Richard J. Murnane and John B. Willett. Ffrom: https://stats.oarc.ucla.edu/other/examples/methods-matter/ (accessed February 4, 2022).

Section V

Qualitative Methods

Section Editor: David Pérez II

19

Introduction to Section V

Qualitative Methods

David Pérez II

Teaching students how to conduct qualitative research is complex. Whether you are teaching aspiring K–12 educators, social scientists, or future practitioners in student affairs and higher education (SAHE), instructing students on how to employ qualitative methodologies that center the lived experiences of minoritized communities presents challenges. Within the field of SAHE, individuals that aspire to serve as practitioners, scholars, and policymakers are expected to demonstrate competence in the area of Assessment, Evaluation, and Research (AER). According to ACPA and NASPA (2015), this competency focuses on:

> ...the ability to design, conduct, critique, and use various AER methodologies and the results obtained from them, to utilize AER processes and their results to inform practice, and to shape the political and ethical climate surrounding AER processes and uses in higher education.
>
> (p. 20)

Among the 33 foundational, intermediate, and advanced outcomes outlined by ACPA and NASPA, only one outcome centers on issues related to equity, diversity, inclusion, and accessibility (DEIA).[1] In full disclosure, I was not aware of this until I was tasked with revising the syllabus for an introductory graduate-level research course in the Higher Education department at Syracuse University. Given the emphasis placed on DEIA in education and the social sciences, it is imperative that we develop curricula that provides students with the foundational knowledge, skills, and resources needed to understand research that has resulted in educational [in]equities.

If you endeavor to engage students in similar discourse, I urge you "not to be constrained by the 'right' or 'appropriate' way of conducting qualitative research" (Nicolazzo et al., p. 15). To be clear, I am not suggesting that we approach this process haphazardly. Rather, I encourage you to go beyond exposing students to different qualitative methodologies and discussing methods to systematically collect and analyze data. These are essential, but nonetheless insufficient skills needed to navigate the complexities of conducting qualitative research.

DOI: 10.4324/b23320-25

In addition to providing insights about qualitative research processes (e.g., interviews, observations, document analysis, etc.), the contributors to this section draw attention to how our positionality[2] as scholars influences how we approach the collection and analysis of qualitative data. Moreover, the contributors invite readers to engage in inquiry that centers the experiences of the minoritized communities and that promotes educational equity.

In Chapter 20, Dr. Tricia Shalka invites readers to engage in *listening deeply*, which is strikingly different from hearing and simply rephrasing what research participants articulate during an interview or focus group. Listening deeply humanizes the process of conducting qualitative research which not only centers the experiences of research participants, but also encourages aspiring scholars to be fully present and to engage in ongoing self-reflection. Consequently, this fosters relationships with participants from minoritized communities that demonstrate care.

Dr. Emiko Blalock presents a *visual arts framework* in Chapter 21 to advance how aspiring scholars perform observations and craft field notes. Implied in the title of her chapter, she encourages readers to reconsider what they see based on prior knowledge. Stated differently, "who we are shapes how and what we see" (p. 160). Contrary to the field of education, visual arts help to broaden our understanding of what field notes represent – they are more than a written record of our observations. Field notes are visual records of our ever-changing social context.

After reading Chapter 22, I found myself pondering one question: How do aspiring scholars account for suppressed narratives that have been omitted from historical documents? In rich detail, Dr. Okello describes how *holistic document analysis* provides a critical account of history that challenges majoritarian narratives about Black people and raises new questions in order to document histories that have been suppressed, distorted, or omitted in other ways. By attending to these distortions and omissions, aspiring scholars can ethically contribute to research that centers the recovery of Black life.

Dr. Antonio Duran and Dr. Alex C. Lange introduce the *pyramid of congruence* to advance research using critical and poststructuralist theories in Chapter 23. Although their lesson plan was designed for aspiring scholars, the insights they offer are instructive for established scholars who seek to employ these emerging approaches to inquiry. Moreover, their pyramid provides the scaffolding to ensure that research outcomes, data collection methods, and data analysis procedures are congruent with the epistemic assumptions that undergird critical and post-structuralist theories, and ultimately increase educational equity.

In Chapter 24, Dr. Kari Taylor addresses how different epistemologies should guide how aspiring scholars code qualitative data and develop themes. Although she employs coding strategies that are typically associated with grounded theory, which provides students with the structure needed to identify preliminary themes, Dr. Taylor emphasizes that we must challenge and support aspiring scholars as they make sense of qualitative data. To this end, she draws on the *learning partnership model* to draw upon students' experiences, validate their scholarly aptitude, and collaborate with them in making meaning of qualitative data.

Collectively, the contributors to "Section V: Qualitative Methodology" offered valuable insights that underscore the importance of considering how one's positionality influences research processes. In addition, they center issues related to DEIA, which has been overlooked as an important outcome of research across all levels of education.

NOTES

1 Use culturally relevant and culturally appropriate terminology and methods to conduct and report AER findings (ACPA & NASPA, 2015, p. 20).
2 Positionality describes "the relationship between the researcher and his or her participants and the researcher and his or her topic" (Jones et al., 2013, p. 26).

BIBLIOGRAPHY

ACPA & NASPA. (2015). *Professional competency areas for student affairs educators*. Washington, DC: ACPA – College Student Educators International & NASPA - Student Affairs Administrators in Higher Education.

Jones, S. R., Torres, V., & Arminio, J. (2013). *Negotiating the complexities of qualitative research in higher education: Essential elements and issues* (2nd ed.). New York: Taylor & Francis.

Nicolazzo, Z., Jaekel, K., Tillapaugh, D., & Pérez II, D. (2021). Temporalities of [no] harm: Navigating trauma through research with minoritized populations in higher education. *International Journal of Qualitative Studies in Education*, *34*(1), 19–36. https://doi.org/10.1080/09518398.2020.1720851

20

Listening Deeply

Preparing to Facilitate Interviews and Focus Groups

Tricia R. Shalka

INTRODUCTION

While doing an interview in 1997, actress Gillian Anderson observed that, "There is a difference between being listened to and being heard." I can feel in my body that this is true. I am reminded of the intangible feeling I have when I know someone is deeply understanding me and what I am trying to convey, rather than simply going through the motions of listening more superficially. In relationships of all kinds in our lives, the difference between just "being listened to" and "being heard" often directly impacts the depth of trust, authenticity, and meaning that we experience with others. As I often remind my students, research, too, is a relationship we are building with others and one in which we need to be attentive to fostering a genuine sense of trust, safety, and compassion. One of the ways that interviewers create these kinds of conditions is by shifting beyond *just* seeking to listen to others and instead actually understanding and holding others' lived experiences with curiosity and care. In other words, we are committed as interviewers to seeking to understand others' experiences on their own terms and remembering that there is a real person in front of us, not just data to be collected.

To the novice researcher, facilitating an interview or focus group may seem like a straightforward task – you develop an interview protocol, you ask some questions, and you call it a day. For those of us who have had longer engagements as researchers, we know that what may, at face value, seem deceptively simple about interviewing is remarkably complex and difficult to do well. In articulating the relational accountability that is at the heart of Indigenous research methods, Wilson (2008) amplifies the "exquisite listening skills" (p. 113) that are part of this ethos of care and accountability to others. The ways in which we interact with fellow humans in the context of research matters and it specifically matters that we come to view these interactions beyond simply the mechanics of data collection and instead as relationships to be nurtured.

Although asking good questions is an important mechanism in getting useful data (Merriam & Tisdell, 2016), good questions, alone, do not ensure high quality interviews. In many ways, meaningful interviewing is less about devising the "perfect" questions, but rather about creating space for others to feel comfortable and held in a way that enables

DOI: 10.4324/b23320-26

them to bring their full selves to bear. What are some components of that way of being that I try to foster in students? First, I want students to engage in self-work to understand how their positionality affects how they interact with and understand others, while being attentive to how systemic oppression impacts individual experiences differently. Second, I want them to arrive with a sense of shared humanity rooted in respect and compassion for those with whom they will engage. Finally, I want them to learn how to get out of their heads, to be present, and to listen deeply. The purpose of the lesson that follows is to help students develop some of these ways of being and tools to engage in deep listening.

LESSON PLAN

Topic	*Learning to listen deeply in interviews and focus groups*
Learning Objectives	• Students will develop greater awareness about how their presence can foster (or detract from) safety and relationship. • Students will identify how systems of oppression impact interview interactions. • Students will develop awareness of their internal experiences as interviewers (i.e., their thoughts and feelings). • Students will use silence and restatement as skills towards deep listening.
Needed Materials	• Pen/pencil and paper • Moveable chairs to sit in groups
Pre-lesson Preparation	• Although this lesson engages students in self-reflection and conversations about power and privilege, there is an assumption that this is not the first or last time students would be exposed to these topics. Instead, these concepts would be scaffolded throughout a research methods course giving students multiple touchpoints to explore their positionality and talk explicitly about how oppression intersects research. • This lesson is intended as a deeper dive into interviews and focus groups and would follow an earlier session and/or mini lecture presenting basic interview facilitating skills (e.g., asking open-ended questions, developing an interview protocol, structured versus semi-structured versus unstructured designs, sampling, logistics, etc.).
Activities	**Grounding Practice** • Offer this grounding practice to start the class giving students the option to participate or not (options and choices are key in these types of activities through a trauma-informed lens[1]). • Invite students to find a comfortable seated position. Then invite students to either gently close their eyes if that is comfortable for them, or keep their eyes open with a soft gaze slightly forward and down. • Invite students to take three deep and slow breaths. Breathe in through the nose slowly and deeply. Exhale through an opened mouth slowly. • Next, invite students to let their minds wander; to think about all the things they have done that day. Prompt them to start with waking up and then just let their thoughts run through the day up until class. Offer them the opportunity to pause on any moments in the day they want to think a bit more about. • Then, invite students to bring their thoughts to the present moment and allow the rest of the day (both what has happened before and what is to come) to just slip away for this moment. As students bring their thoughts to the current moment, invite them to focus their attention to their feet and to feel their feet as heavy and rooting into the floor.

Topic	*Learning to listen deeply in interviews and focus groups*

- Close the activity with one final deep breath – in slowly through the nose, and out slowly through the mouth.
- Take a moment to process this grounding practice with an emphasis on the elements of being in the moment:
  - How are you feeling after that activity?
  - What did it feel like to focus your thoughts and sensations on the present moment?

Activating Prior Knowledge

- Provide students with the following prompt and ask them to free-write about it for 5 minutes: "What helps you to feel comfortable about sharing your experiences with others?"
- Ask for some volunteers to share.
- Facilitate a conversation about: (a) what we personally need to feel comfortable sharing in conversations, and (b) what others may do that contributes to our sense of safety or not. Make connections to the skill of facilitating interviews or focus groups – that we want to be attentive to creating conditions of safety and relationship for others to feel good about contributing and sharing. The following questions may be useful to prompt further thinking:
  - How have people in your life communicated to you (verbally or nonverbally) that they're genuinely interested in hearing you?
  - What does it feel like to be comfortable and/or safe in a conversation with someone? What might it feel like to be uncomfortable or unsafe? What conditions might contribute to these differences?
  - How might our social identities (e.g., race, class, gender, ability status, sexual orientation, etc.) impact what we share with others or not, and how? How do systems of privilege and oppression (e.g., racism, sexism, etc.) impact these interactions?
- Conclude with a few key points:
  - Similar to creating space for meaningful conversations with others, interviewing is also about thinking in terms of how we build rapport, relationship, comfort, and safety.
  - Safety and comfort are subjective and are intertwined with systems of power and privilege. Who we are in the world through the lens of our social identities and experiences impacts our interactions with others in interviews, which presents both opportunities and challenges.
- Transition: Let students know the remainder of the class will provide them opportunities to practice skills related to deep listening – silence and restatement.

Practicing Silence

- Ask students to pair up.
- Explain that the class will practice silence as a skill for deep listening. One person will be the interviewer and the other will be the interviewee. The interviewee will have 1–2 minutes to talk about any topic uninterrupted. The interviewer will be silent during that time, listening and using their body language and non-verbal communication to create a sense of support, safety, and interest with the interviewee.
- After the first round, provide these prompts and allow each pair 5 minutes to debrief:
  - What was it like to be the one talking? What was it like to be the one engaged in silence?
  - What did the interviewer do (verbal or non-verbal) that helped to establish rapport, support, safety and interest?
  - What did the interviewer do that distracted from those goals?
- Have the pair switch roles and repeat practicing silence and debriefing.

LISTENING DEEPLY

Topic	Learning to listen deeply in interviews and focus groups
	• Bring the class back together for group discussion. The goal of this debrief time will be to help students consider: (a) how their presence impacts others, and (b) how active listening and being present are key tools in effective interviewing. The following prompts can guide this discussion:

• Bring the class back together for group discussion. The goal of this debrief time will be to help students consider: (a) how their presence impacts others, and (b) how active listening and being present are key tools in effective interviewing. The following prompts can guide this discussion:
  ○ What did it feel like in your bodies to engage in this practice? (e.g., tightness or ease in muscles, butterflies in belly, posture, etc.).
  ○ What were you thinking about during the activity and/or afterwards?
  ○ What non-verbal responses helped to encourage a sense of comfort, willingness to share, and/or contributed to building a relationship?
  ○ What aspects of the **Practicing Silence** activity could be useful in facilitating interviews or focus groups (e.g., paying attention to non-verbal communication, listening without worrying about what to say next, giving space for interviewees to share without rushing them to the next topic, etc.)? What might not (e.g., need to ask questions at some point in interviews)?

Practicing Restatement
• Have students form groups of 3–4.
• Explain the next practice skill – restatement means that after you listen to what someone says, you paraphrase what you believe the person shared (either in terms of content or affect). Listening to restate or paraphrase is a way to begin practicing deep listening and understanding.
• Offer prompts that students can use as they begin working with restatement (can be shared on a PowerPoint screen, on a white board, etc.):
  ○ "It sounds like…"
  ○ "I hear you saying…"
  ○ "What stood out for me is…"
  ○ "You're [e.g., worried about…, busy, etc.] …"
• In each practice round, one person will be the interviewer, one person will be the interviewee, and the remaining participants will be observers. Interviewee will have 3–5 minutes to talk and during that time the interviewer will respond using restatements only. Observers will pay attention to the interactions between the interviewer and interviewee with attention to how safety, support, and deep listening are being enacted or not. After the round is completed, have small groups engage in a debrief guided by these prompts:
  ○ What was the experience like for members in the various roles from their vantage points?
  ○ What did the interviewer do that signaled deep listening and understanding? Safety and support? What did the interviewer do that distracted from those goals?
  ○ For the interviewer – what helped you to stay present while listening? What made it difficult to stay present?
• Continue with additional rounds as time permits, with group members shifting roles.
• Bring the full class back together for a large-group discussion. The following prompts can guide this discussion:
  ○ What does it mean to engage in deep listening in the context of interviews?
  ○ Interviewing can be a vulnerable space for both interviewees and the interviewer. As interviewers, how can we create conditions for safety, comfort, compassion, and relationship? How does privilege and oppression intersect this conversation?
  ○ What might get in the way of being able to accurately understand what someone is sharing in an interview?
  ○ What is one thing you have learned from our collective practices today that you want to keep in mind as you move forward facilitating interviews or focus groups?

Topic	Learning to listen deeply in interviews and focus groups
Virtual Adaptations	• This lesson can be transitioned online through a platform like Zoom where there is the ability to send students into breakout rooms for small groups.
Assessment	• Formative Assessment: During group time, move around the room and informally assess students' abilities to make connections between the practices and what they need to be attentive to as interviewers. • Summative Assessment: In final research proposal assignment, look for students' attention to incorporating principles highlighted in this lesson including how relationship, rapport, safety, and compassion will be prioritized and established in conducting interviews or focus groups.

INTELLECTUAL PREPARATION FOR THE LISTENING DEEPLY LESSON PLAN

This lesson is fundamentally about fostering ways of being in students. That requires a heavier lift than might be the case in presenting the more tangible skills of interviewing, such as creating open-ended questions. Below, I discuss the core ideas that support this engagement and some considerations for how students may arrive to this type of lesson.

Core Ideas

This "Listening Deeply" lesson plan has two aims. First, the instructor is helping students to foster ways of being as interviewers. Second, the instructor is helping students to develop tangible skills for deep listening, including silence and restatement. To that end, this lesson is organized around four core ideas that are at the heart of strong facilitation of interviews and focus groups: (1) being present, (2) engaging in self-reflection, (3) being attentive to shared humanity; and, (4) listening deeply.

Being Present

I distinctly remember one of my qualitative methods professors preparing our class for an interview activity. He told us that when we went into the interview, he wanted us to sit on top of our interview questions. At first, some of us thought he was joking. It turned out he was not. As we realized he was not joking, you could feel the palpable sense of terror rising in the room. "*But how will we know what to ask?*" "*What if we forget our questions?*"

My professor's point was dramatic enough that I remember it to this day, and it was a good one – Pay attention to the person and conversation in front of you. He did not want us stuck in our heads worried about the next question in our interview protocol. He did not want us scrambling to read our list of interview questions rather than listening. Instead, he wanted us to be present and listening to the person we were in conversation with. He wanted us to follow the conversation rather than staying fixated on our predetermined set of questions.

In full disclosure, I do bring my interview questions into interviews. But, that said, my professor's framing freed me up to realize that strong interviews and focus groups require

LISTENING DEEPLY   **151**

that researchers stay present with the people in front of them. That is an important idea to communicate in this lesson plan. The opening grounding activity can be a reference point to return to throughout the lesson to remind students what it feels like to be in the present moment as opposed to being preoccupied with thoughts about what has happened before or what may happen after an interview.

Engaging in Self-reflection

Something my students hear from me often and in varied ways is that who they are in the world is not separate from who they are as students – they bring their full, whole selves to the classroom space. This is true of research, also, and there is a dual responsibility in this respect as it relates to facilitating interviews and focus groups. Specifically, it is important that students engage in self-reflection about their positionality to understand how they may impact others in interview settings as well as how they themselves may be impacted by the encounters (Nicolazzo et al., 2020).

The free-writing, silence and restatement activities all offer opportunities to engage students in self-reflection. I am attentive in these conversations to make explicit how privilege and oppression are always already present as we enter into interview or focus group interactions. This is a critical point to make so that students can understand their impact and interpretations of others' experiences and how they are impacted in return in deep ways. Thus, I am explicit in helping students to consider what power dynamics might be at play in particular settings, for whom certain spaces and interactions may feel safe or unsafe, and how the constellation of our individual social identities may frame what we readily see and understand or do not.

Being Attentive to Shared Humanity

My primary research area is about how trauma impacts college students' experiences (e.g., Shalka, 2019, 2021). Thus, I readily bring a trauma-informed lens to both my pedagogy and research. Safety, control, and relationships are frequently compromised for those who have experienced trauma (Venet, 2021). Knowing that, I pay particular attention in research to recognizing the humanity in others and working towards establishing relationships that can foster a sense of safety and care. I work to help my students pay attention to these concerns, as well.

This lesson plan incorporates many moments in which students have an opportunity to pause and reflect on how they are building rapport, safety, connection, and care, which are all fundamental to facilitating interviews and focus groups. In particular, many of the debrief questions prompt students to consider these dimensions of their roles as interviewers in the context of power and oppression.

Listening Deeply

The primary theme of this lesson plan is about helping students listen deeply in interviews and focus groups. This is a fundamental capacity for students to nurture as they prepare to facilitate powerful interviews and focus groups. This lesson balances tangible skills to help students listen deeply using silence and restatement. At the same time, it emphasizes deep listening as a way of being. In other words, deep listening is as much about who we are, how we show up in the world, and the ways we stay present with one another, as it is about the specific listening skills we use.

There are many components to what listening deeply entails and several of these dimensions are highlighted throughout this lesson. Some of these elements include: being present, paying attention to non-verbals, listening in order to paraphrase, establishing safety and care, and probing the limits and potential of our own understanding in the context of systems of privilege and oppression.

Learners and Context

Much of this lesson is grounded in my previous experiences interacting with students who are early in their learning about qualitative methods. What I have observed is that students are frequently conditioned (often unknowingly and sometimes even in contradiction to how they otherwise make sense of the world) to approach research from postpositive paradigms. Specifically, I often see students convinced that the important thing to do in interviewing is to ask the exact same questions in the exact same way to everyone. Certainly, there are designs where that would make sense, but the broader issue is that students get stuck on issues of replicability and regimented methods as opposed to understanding some of the importance of embracing subjectivity in many qualitative designs. In this vein, I see students getting stuck on the questions themselves in an interview, sometimes at the expense of really hearing what the person in front of them is sharing.

This lesson attempts to help students get "unstuck" and released from these postpositive constraints, but that can be a challenging process for students. I have noticed that students get frustrated when I respond to their questions with "it depends" rather than being able to offer them a recipe about how to proceed. Students are sometimes worried about not getting the "right" data and want the definitive answer on how to make sure they do. This lesson has a lot of potential to dig into those desires and interrogate whether ideas of "right" or "perfect" are the goal or even possible. In helping students develop ways of being instead of following recipes, I am helping them to also commit to continuous learning and practice in refining their approaches and exploring alternate perspectives. I am asking them to hold firmly onto their research questions for guidance, but then to ease into the interview process focused on building relationships and creating space for mutually productive interactions to emerge. These are the kinds of interview interactions I want students to strive for that ultimately help them to get to the deeper kind of information they are likely after.

NOTE

1 Trauma-informed educational practices incorporate knowledge about trauma and traumatization into educational design and decision-making to support student success. See Venet (2021) for one example.

BIBLIOGRAPHY

Merriam, S. B., & Tisdell, E. J. (2016). *Qualitative research: A guide to design and implementation* (4th ed.). Jossey-Bass.

Nicolazzo, Z., Jaekel, K., Tillapaugh, D., & Pérez II, D. (2020). Temporalities of [no] harm: Navigating trauma through research with minoritized populations in higher education. *International Journal of Qualitative Studies in Education*, 1–18. https://doi.org/10.1080/09518398.2020.1720851

Shalka, T. R. (2019). Saplings in the hurricane: A grounded theory of college trauma and identity development. *The Review of Higher Education, 42*(2), 739–764. https://doi.org/10.1353/rhe.2019.0013

Shalka, T. R. (2021). Traversing the shadow space: Experiences of spatiality after college student trauma. *The Review of Higher Education, 45*(1), 93–116. https://doi.org/10.1353/rhe.0.0176

Stratton, S. (1997, March). Promotional interview with Gillian Anderson and HAL. https://www.gilliananderson.ws/transcripts/96_97/97extremis.shtml

Venet, A. S. (2021). *Equity-centered trauma-informed education*. W. W. Norton & Company.

Wilson, S. (2008). *Research is ceremony: Indigenous research methods*. Fernwood Publishing.

21

Write What You See, Not What You Know

Learning the Method of Observation through the Visual Arts

A. Emiko Blalock

INTRODUCTION

New artists learning to draw often hear the phrase "draw what you see, not what you know." This saying can also be applied to the method of observation, where researchers have opportunities to gain awareness of their knowledge and how that knowledge shapes what they see in the natural settings where observation research occurs. Perceptions, prior knowledge, and how we anticipate what we might see based on what we already know influence how observations are performed. In essence, our positionality or "accounting for the ways researchers' embodiment and social location matter in the process" of research and inquiry (Reich, 2021, p. 577), plays an important role in our ability to perform observations. This chapter advances an approach to research formed from visual arts (Blalock, 2019, see Figure 21.1). For observations, this visual arts framework highlights *seeing and doing* to foster student researchers' abilities to recognize what they know, make sense of what they see, learn to see in different ways, and write what they see.

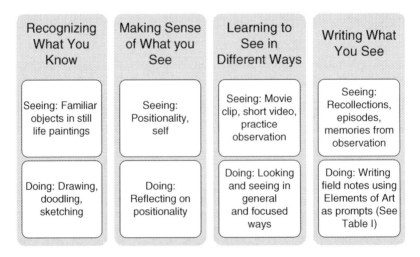

FIGURE 21.1 Observations and Field Notes Using a Visual Arts Framework

DOI: 10.4324/b23320-27

WRITE WHAT YOU SEE, NOT WHAT YOU KNOW

By using visual arts, students will be introduced to disciplines beyond their own fields of study that aid in learning and expanding knowledge. Additionally, this chapter provides a lesson for performing observations and writing up field notes that can be applied to in-person or adapted for online courses. Given the increased fluidity of in-person to virtual teaching and learning in recent years, virtual observations offer a unique opportunity to reframe how foundational qualitative methods are taught.

LESSON PLAN

Topic	*Performing general and focused observations and writing accompanying field notes using the visual arts*
Learning Objectives	• Students will learn to recognize and articulate their own positionality in performing observations. • Students will differentiate between types of observations. • Students will practice writing field notes. • Students will be exposed to cross-disciplinary learning using the visual arts.
Needed Materials	Classroom will need at least one shareable note-taking platform of instructor's choice, such as: • Large dry-erase board. • Large paper for writing. • Google Docs, Jamboard, or Padlet access if instructor prefers online media to share in the classroom. • Working Wi-Fi or Internet connection. • Access to Internet browser in classroom or personal computer. Students will need: • Paper and a writing utensil to hand-write notes. • Computers to log on to online learning forum. • Working Wi-Fi or Internet connection. • Access to Internet browser on personal computer.
Pre-lesson Preparation	*Are images appropriate for students?* Recommendations are provided in this lesson for images and paintings to display for students. Depending on the demographic of the classroom, faculty can select short movies or other video clips that might be more familiar to students, or more relevant to seminar topics or themes of the overall course.

Activities	**Recognizing What You Know**
	• Ask each student to take out a piece of paper and a writing utensil. Share with the students that this activity will be considered a "warm-up exercise" for performing observations.
	• Display a still life painting of your choosing. Consider these artworks if unfamiliar with still life paintings:
	    ○ Gwendolyn Knight *Still Life with Jug and Apples*
	    ○ Frida Kahlo *Still Life with Parrot and Fruit*
	    ○ Katsushika Hokusai *Still Life: Double Cherry-Blossom Branch, Telescope, Sweet Fish, and Tissue Case*
	    ○ Wayne Thiebaud *Cakes*
	    ○ Giorgio Morandi *Natura Morta*
	• Once the image is on display and all students can see it, ask each student to draw what they see. Provide 3–5 minutes for drawing time. After 3–5 minutes, remove the image.

Topic	*Performing general and focused observations and writing accompanying field notes using the visual arts*

Making Sense of What You See

- Begin a 10–15 minute discussion with the group by asking what they saw, then by probing for how they felt. Use any of the following prompts to help the conversation focus on seeing:
  - Share what you saw on the screen.
  - What did the image look like?
  - Can you describe the image in detail?
- Continue the discussion by inquiring about how they felt and what they thought while drawing:
  - How did it feel to draw?
  - What were you thinking about as you were drawing?
  - When you saw the image, what kinds of memories or feelings did you have, if any?
  - When you saw the image, what did you think about?
- During the group discussion, also probe about feelings of discomfort or when/ if students felt distracted.
- These questions serve two purposes: (1) To aid students in recognizing their own selves when they engage in seeing something closely, and (2) To help students "get out of their own way" when they perform observations.
- Although the still life images may at first glance appear benign, they are intended to provide close observation of objects that might be familiar, inviting a deeper reflexive opportunity for students to increase their self-awareness as they look upon images that they may take for granted.

Learning to See in Different Ways

- Once the discussion is finished, the class will move on to practicing *general observations* and *focused observations*. Describe to students that general observations are exploratory in nature and open-ended, and focused observations are more attentive to research questions. The clip below is a movie from the Museum of Modern Art in New York City, titled "Gave Away the Secret." The video is approximately 7 minutes long – see https://www.moma.org/magazine/articles/171.
- Explain to the students they will be completing two back-to-back observations of the same short movie. During both viewings students will take brief notes about what they see while the movie is playing.
- Prepare for the first viewing by recommending students try to take in as much as they can from the movie, observing all parts of interactions, movements, and short conversations. They should write short cues or notes about the movie to help them remember what they saw. This viewing serves as the general observation.
- At the end of the first viewing, provide 1–2 minutes for students to organize their notes.
- Reconvene the class and invite students to share parts of their notes such as key words or short sentences. Record some of these notes using the shareable note-taking platform.
- Forego a whole class discussion after students share their notes and immediately move on to the second viewing of the same short movie, and this time direct students to use a research question such as "How do museums portray work and occupations?" or "Why are museums an important part of people's lives?" This viewing serves as the focused observation.
- Again, reconvene the class and invite students to share portions of their notes and record some of these notes using the shareable note-taking platform.

WRITE WHAT YOU SEE, NOT WHAT YOU KNOW

Topic	*Performing general and focused observations and writing accompanying field notes using the visual arts*

- Using the two sets of notes, engage students in dialogue about the differences between their *general observations* and *focused observations*. Use the following probing questions:
  - What differences did you notice in the two kinds of observations?
  - Which kind of observation did you prefer? Why?
  - How did making a drawing help prepare you for your observation?
- After processing this activity, inquire about how students might envision themselves in the scene they observed. The questions offered below are intended to encourage students to articulate their positionality, how they might navigate place during an observation (such as a museum), and identify whether they might feel uncomfortable, uncertain, or unwelcome. Use the following questions as a guide:
  - How would you describe "culture" in the movie?
  - Can you describe any moments where you felt unsure or confused by what you observed? How would you navigate these feelings?
- Summarize this portion of the activity by discussing two important points about making observations:
  - General observations may still be "focused" depending on what the researcher may think is important in a scene and the experience they bring with them to the observation.
  - Focused observations guided by a research question can aid in taking account of what we see differently.
  - Multiple observations of the same scene or site (i.e., multiple site visits when performing observations as data collection) is often required to grasp a full picture of a scene.

Writing What You See

- To prepare the students to write field notes, consider sharing the following points from Emerson, Fretz, and Shaw (2011):
  - Field notes are subjective: "Whether it be an incident, event, routine, interaction, or visual image, ethnographers recreate each moment from selected details and sequences that they remember or have jotted down: words, gestures, body movements, sounds, background setting, and so on" (p. 46). Elaborate on this point by reminding students that observing is not a neutral endeavor, but one where having an awareness of our positionality aids in our observation skills and ability to write field notes.
  - Field notes are descriptive, and focused observations aid in description: "The writer selects details that most clearly and vividly create an image on the page; consequently, he succeeds best in describing when he selects details according to some purpose and from a definite point of view" (p. 58). Elaborate on this point by reminding students about general and focused observations, and any differences students described between their two observations of the short movie.
  - Field notes are made up of multiple episodes: "Unlike a sketch, which depicts a 'still life' in one place, an episode recounts action and moves in time to narrate a slice of life. In an episode, a writer constructs a brief incident as a more or less unified depiction of one continuous action or interaction" (p. 77). Elaborate on this point by referring back to the first exercise in drawing a still life, then viewing the short movie and how close observation of a still-life image may help students see details, and motion and action add depth to the story of an observation. Thus, performing observations and writing up field notes requires attention to details within a narration of life.

Topic	*Performing general and focused observations and writing accompanying field notes using the visual arts*

	• After completing the short talk, transition to writing field notes by sharing a selection of field notes using examples from Emerson et al. (2011) or Lareau (2021) so students can read and see completed field notes. In the spirit of using visual art for this lesson, use the elements of art to begin drafting field notes. Writing field notes for this portion of the lesson will occur in two parts. First, students will work as a class to identify moments and scenes that stood out to them. Second, they will each practice writing their own field notes based on their notes and the class discussion.
	  ◦ Step 1: The class will work together to create initial images and notes from the two movie observations.
	  Next, invite students to recall moments from their viewing by prompting them to describe a detail from the movie using an art element as a jumping off point. See Figure 21.2 at the end of this chapter for "Elements of Art," their descriptions and accompanying questions to use from each element to begin probing students' memories to construct field notes.
	  As students offer their descriptions, write these descriptions down with the corresponding art element on the shareable note-taking platform and reference these notes during the next step.
	  ◦ Step 2: Students will write field notes by hand or using their computers. They can select notes from their first or second viewing of the short movie.
	  Encourage students to use any additional notes they took during class discussions and/or notes from shared discussions via the shareable note-taking platform to draft field notes.
	  ◦ Grant students 10 minutes to practice writing field notes.
	• Afterwards, engage the entire class in discussion about the process of writing field notes using the following questions:
	  ◦ How did you feel writing field notes?
	  ◦ What images from the movie did you find easy and/or difficult to describe?
	  ◦ What did you think you forgot?
	• End the lesson with final questions to identify major takeaways from the previous exercises. Use the following prompts to guide this conversation:
	  ◦ Circling back to the still life images, what did you see that prompted you to draw what you did?
	  ◦ Remembering the "Gave Away the Secret" movie, what words might describe the movie's theme?
	  ◦ Finally recognizing ourselves, our observations, and our field notes, what more can we find? (Yenawine, 2013)

Virtual Adaptations	Moving this lesson to a virtual platform would not require a tremendous amount of change. Instructors would need to ensure access to the internet and sharing abilities for note-taking. Web-based images of still life and the movie clip with audio will need to be shared with the class using an online platform.
Assessment	• Formative Assessment: During collaborative note-sharing, students will display their notes, what they have observed, and descriptions of what they noticed. • Summative Assessment: The final class discussion will offer insights into pulling all the parts of the lesson together, and how students make connections between themselves, their observations, and their field notes.

Element	Description	Accompanying Probing Question
Line	A mark with greater length than width, defined by a point moving in space	Did you notice any lines in the observation, or instances in the movie when your attention seemed to be moving in a line, directed towards one thing or another?"
Shape	A closed line	What shapes did you see?
Form	Three-dimensional shapes expressing length, width, and depth	Were there expressions in people or objects? What sizes did you notice?
Space	In which positive and negative areas are defined	Describe the space, or the spaces 'in-between' what is seen or said
Color	Light reflected off objects. Color has three main characteristics: hue (the name of the color, such as red, green, blue, etc.), value (how light or dark it is), and intensity (how bright or dull it is)	Were there light or dark areas? How did these light or dark areas shift what you saw? What colors stood out?
Texture	surface quality that can be seen and felt.	What did the observation 'feel' like, were there notable textures?

FIGURE 21.2 Elements of Art and Questions to Prompt Writing Field Notes

Adapted from "Understanding formal analysis: Elements of art" from the Paul J Getty Museum.

INTELLECTUAL PREPARATION FOR "WRITING WHAT YOU SEE" LESSON

This lesson approaches the method of observations as an artform, where each step is one component of creating a larger scene, portrait, or painting of what a researcher sees and then records. During preparation for this lesson, it is important to note that observations are just one part of an entire process; observations require preparation of a site, gathering materials, then writing about what is seen. Furthermore, offering a lesson using visual art may require some level of experience with visual arts. Familiarity with creative and visual arts can come in the form of doodling, photography, drawing; even a faculty member's own daydreams and interest in the creative process will suffice to support implementing this lesson.

Core Ideas

Performing observations and writing field notes is not a neutral endeavor; rather, awareness of our experiences inform what we see, and eventually, our selectivity of scenes and observed details create larger narratives and stories. Two ideas aid in bolstering this theme. First, what we know can influence what we see. Perhaps a student visited or is from Japan, then Hokusai's *Still Life* may conjure much more than an image of fish and a telescope but an entire host of lived-experience. These salient memories and personal knowledge may inform how a student records certain accounts in their observations. Second, writing is the visual record of what we see. Physical jottings and fieldnotes are the material data representing images when those images are no longer available or in the past. Both of these core ideas aid in supporting students' ability to understand themselves as researchers conducting observations and writing field notes, as well as opening themselves to new ways of understanding the method of observation (Calarco, 2018).

Who We Are Shapes How and What We See
Often when making observations, one's memories, prior experiences, and social histories can be made present through what a researcher sees. A simple mug might spur someone to remember their morning cup of tea or coffee; a bowl of green apples may conjure an image of an agricultural landscape or the tastes of sweet and sour. An example of this is offered by Lareau (2021) who commented, "working with research assistants I was struck that the most important source of variation in the field notes was the individual field worker's own childhood experiences" (p. 151). Thus, prior knowledge and experiences influence how and what we see. Supporting students' awareness of how their prior knowledge and experience may shape how and what they see during an observation is important to help students recognize and acknowledge their positionality.

Writing is the Visual Record
Building from the awareness that our own knowledge and experience can inform observations, a researcher's field notes serve as a visual record of the context. As Lareau (2021) indicated, "the point of writing field notes is to create a portrait over time" (p. 163). Thus, written field notes are a picture, portrait, or landscape of one's observations. It is imperative that when writing field notes, students understand their task is to create this visual record in striking detail, with lively strokes of descriptive images. Just as students may have noticed small imperfections in a mug, crafting the visual record includes miniscule details in field notes, situating these writings among their broader recollections of the observation.

Learners

Connecting visual art to performing observations may feel awkward for many students, which might surface in one of two ways during class. First, students may have preconceived ideas about what drawing is for and "where it belongs" (i.e., art belongs in art class). However, visual arts and each student's creativity can be brought to this lesson, as well as what each student recognizes and perceives as art. Although this lesson largely uses more well-known forms of fine art, students can also draw on their own environments and backgrounds to understand the process of art-making, and in turn, seeing in new ways. For example, García's (2018) book, *La Lotería as Creative Resistance*, offers alternate examples of artwork.

Second, in my experience working with students both in higher education and in art classes, students may associate being able to draw with having to be "an artist," which can inhibit their openness to the process of drawing and creating. Students may feel discomfort and question their abilities. However, what grounds this lesson is the process of creating and inviting students to tap into their own forms of creativity; creativity as a broadly defined construct. The process of creating can be very personal, which requires instructors to encourage and affirm when they exercise personal creativity. This process will increase the likelihood that they tap into their personal creativity when they engage in fieldwork.

Context

Drawing and engaging in visual art is an important part of the lesson for this chapter, because it bridges students' prior knowledge and new knowledge. Viewing familiar objects such as the still life paintings and being asked to draw these objects invites students to notice minor details and see in new ways. Drawing also supports memory recall, offering students' ways to position their memories within larger contexts of what they see (Fernandes, et al., 2018). Moreover, engaging with visual arts and writing about the arts enhances critical thinking skills, particularly for students from underserved communities (Bowen, et al., 2014). Thus, the context for this lesson – our abilities to "see" during observations, understand how we see, and reflect on how our ability to see is an extension of what we know as well as what we could learn to know – is rooted in the same context of creativity that invites individuals to consider different perspectives, new questions, and unimaginable possibilities. Discussing the importance of visual arts as a catalyst to prompt aesthetic development and critical thinking, author Abigail Housen (2008) notes:

> Implementing [arts] in curriculum opens a number of opportunities for the teacher, the learner, and the subject…in the course of talking about an image, learners effectively teach each other, bringing new observations to light, offering opposing views, and ever widening the discussion.

(pp. 16–17)

This new way of seeing or experiencing qualitative methods begins with ourselves as researchers, and for students, it is important to bridge what they know and how they see by drawing on their current knowledge in order to engage in observational methods that increases awareness about their positionality and expands how they see the world.

BIBLIOGRAPHY

Blalock, A. E. (2019). *How forms of capital shape the teaching strategies of women in fixed-term faculty positions.* Doctoral Dissertation, Michigan State University.

Bowen, D. H., Greene, J. P., & Kisida, B. (2014). Learning to think critically: A visual art experiment. *Educational Researcher, 43*(1), 37–44. https://doi.org/10.3102/0013189X13512675

Calarco, J. (2018). Notes from the field: Show how you know what you know. *Scatterplot* Retrieved from https://scatter.wordpress.com/2018/11/06/notes-from-the-field-show-how-you-know-what-you-know/

Emerson, R. M., Fretz, R. I., & Shaw, L. L. (2011). *Writing ethnographic fieldnotes* (2nd ed). The University of Chicago Press.

Fernandes, M. A., Wammes, J. D., & Meade, M. E. (2018). The surprisingly powerful influence of drawing on memory. *Current Directions in Psychological Science, 27*(5), 302–308. https://doi.org/10.1177/0963721418755385

García, L. (2018). La lotería as creative resistance: The funds of knowledge, critical pedagogy, and critical race theory in art education In J. Marquez Kiyama & C. Rios-Aguilar, Eds.), *Funds of knowledge in higher education: Honoring students' cultural experiences and resources as strengths* (p. 67). Routledge.

Housen, A. (2008). Art viewing and aesthetic development: Designing for the viewer. In P. Villeneueve (Ed.), *From periphery to center: Art museum education in the 21st century* (1st ed., p. 172). National Art Education Association.

Kukielski, T. (Producer) Moreno, R.F. & Wiland, A. (Directors). (2020). *Art in the 21ˢᵗ Century: Borderlands*. [Video]. Retrieved from https://art21.org/watch/art-in-the-twenty-first-century/s10/borderlands/

Lareau, A. (2021). *Listening to people: A practical guide to interviewing, participant observation, data analysis, and writing it all up*. The University of Chicago Press.

Reich, J. A. (2021). Power, positionality, and the ethic of care in qualitative research. *Qualitative Sociology, 44*(4), 575–581. https://doi.org/10.1007/s11133-021-09500-4

Yenawine, P. (2013). *Visual thinking strategies: Using art to deepen learning across school disciplines*. Retrieved from http://search.ebscohost.com/login.aspx?direct=true&scope=site&db=nlebk&db=nlabk&AN=1285889

22

On the Recovery of Black Life

A Holistic Approach to Document Analysis

Wilson Kwamogi Okello

INTRODUCTION

Researchers are storytellers, charged with a responsibility to name, represent, and "reckon with loss, and to respect the limits of what cannot be known" (Hartman, 2008, p. 4). Part of how researchers maintain that responsibility to bear ethical witness is by a close, deep engagement with archives, broadly understood, in an effort to extrapolate their purpose, use, and significance. One method of deep reading that can accompany a research project is document analysis – a systematic process of reviewing, interpreting, and assessing various kinds of printed and electronic source material. The function of document analysis is to provide insight into past events. Documents can bear witness to the past and assist researchers in grappling with dominant narratives. Additionally, documents can engender new questions, recover suppressed narratives, and provide a rich source of supplementary data in research projects. In doing so, documents generate a trail that can outline a topic or ideas development. Finally, document analysis can corroborate findings and other evidence sources (Bowen, 2009). Following this procedure, this lesson plan may yield excerpts, quotations, passages, themes, and categories that contextualize a research problem and assist researchers in understanding the world(s) of Black people. This chapter outlines the process of engaging in holistic document analysis, which is characterized by three core ideas: skepticism, scarcity/absence, and annotations and redactions.

LESSON PLAN

Topic	Annotating texts in document analysis
Learning Objectives	• Students will practice deep reading and holistic analysis by dialoguing with text. • Students will strengthen their reflexive capacities as they pose critical questions of the text, the self, and context. • Students will evaluate and propose conclusions about the text.

DOI: 10.4324/b23320-28

Topic	*Annotating texts in document analysis*
Needed Materials	Du Bois, W.E.B (1960a). Brief notes: "Whither Now and Why." https://credo.library. umass.edu/view/full/mums312-b233-i005 Du Bois, W.E.B (1960b, March 31). Written speech: "Whither Now and Why." https://credo.library.umass.edu/cgi-bin/pdf.cgi?id=scua:mums312-b206-i050 Du Bois, W.E.B (1960c, April 2). Recording: "Whither Now and Why." https:// credo.library.umass.edu/view/full/mums312-b250-i003
Pre-lesson Preparation	The instructor will explain the function of document analysis as that which: • Provides insights into past events. • Grapples with dominant narratives. • Contextualizes the research questions. • Engenders new questions about research problem. • Corroborates findings and other evidence sources. In preparation for the document analysis exercise, the instructor will review the purpose of annotations in research. • The instructor can explain annotations as a process of deep reading that closely engages a text's public and, perhaps, hidden meanings (see Okello & Pérez, 2018; Scott, 1990). It is essential to convey that the students engaged in the exercise are not expected to draw similar conclusions to one another; instead, researchers ought to make meaning of a text from their lived positions, thereby centering the importance of one's positionality[1], or how they analyze and interpret documents. • When reflecting on one's positionality, researchers can consider Patel's (2016) questions: Why me/us? Why this topic? and Why now? In other words, why am I qualified to pursue this work? Why should or shouldn't I be analyzing this text? Why is this text, specifically, essential for my learning? What is the importance of this text and analysis to the current context? • Annotations are useful for uncovering patterns and making connections relevant to a research problem. • Annotations mark the text, allowing researchers to engage in dialogue with original author(s) of publications, orations, or other archival materials.

Activities	**Annotating Documents**
	• The instructor will provide handouts, electronic portable document files (PDF), or links to the following documents:
	  ○ Du Bois (1960a). Brief notes: "Whither Now and Why." https://credo. library.umass.edu/view/full/mums312-b233-i005
	  ○ Du Bois (1960b, March 31). Written speech: "Whither Now and Why." https://credo.library.umass.edu/cgi-bin/pdf. cgi?id=scua:mums312-b206-i050
	  ○ Explain that the speech and notes were prepared by W.E.B DuBois for the 25th Conference of the Association of Social Science Teachers at Johnson C. Smith University. Du Bois delivered this speech in the aftermath of the 1954 Brown v. Board of Education ruling. Following the ruling, non-Black education stakeholders were making decisions about the education of Black people, namely how they would be educated and on what grounds. In this speech, Du Bois contends that the future of Black education should be determined by Black people.
	  ○ If students are engaging the text as a PDF, I encourage them to use software that allows them to annotate documents (e.g., Mendeley).
	• I allot 45 minutes for students to dialogue with the text to stress the importance of *deep reading*, by which I mean, read and engage the text by annotating it with comments and/or questions. Students can write their responses directly on the transcript or in a research journal. Students will be in small groups, so the process of deep reading can involve verbal exchange about insights among group members as individuals read through the text.

Topic	Annotating texts in document analysis

	• I invite students to consider the following:
	   ◦ Author/Creator/Reader
	     ▪ Define and describe text? What form (photograph, pamphlet, government-issued document, newspaper article, diary entry, etc.) is it, and how has it been preserved? How is it being presented? Is it handwritten, typed? Are there edits (visible/undisclosed)? Are there markings?
	     ▪ Who wrote/created the text and when?
	     ▪ Who am I in relation to the writer and the text?
	   ◦ Context
	     ▪ Consider the social-political context of the writer/creator and the text. How does context shape, influence what is written/created? How does context shape and influence how the text is interpreted?
	     ▪ Importantly, instructors should have a firm understanding of the historical context that anchors this assignment such that they are able to probe students as they consider this set of questions.
	   ◦ Intended audience
	     ▪ Who is the audience for the text?
	     ▪ Why did the author/creator write/create the text? What evidence is driving your claim?
	   ◦ Purpose of the text
	     ▪ Why was the text written/created? What are some alternative reasons for its creation?
	     ▪ What are the main points as expressed by the writer/creator? What do I discern as the main points expressed in the text?
	   ◦ Significance
	     ▪ What contribution does the text make? Why is it important and to whom?
	   ◦ Embodied reactions
	     ▪ What do I feel in my body as I read the text (or speak it aloud)? What emotion does the text bring up for me?
	 Reflecting on Recording of Documents
	 • Next, I invite students to read and listen to the speech with the following link: Recording: Du Bois (1960c, April 2), "Whither Now and Why." https://credo.library.umass.edu/view/full/mums312-b250-i003
	   ◦ As students listen, I ask them to note the following in their individual research journals: What is being said? What is their tone? What am I feeling as I listen to and watch the reading/performance? Where do I feel what I feel? What is not being said? Where and how do I resonate with what is said as I listen?
	 • At the conclusion of the listening portion, I debrief with students about the various ways they engaged archives. Of importance here is encouraging students to consider the many ways that are available to them, and how various modes of engagement may raise differing perspectives.

Virtual Adaptations	• During each phase of analysis, groups may compile themes from their annotations on Google Jamboard.
Assessment	• Formative Assessment: During the initial reading period, check in on each group to gather how they are making sense of the assignment and tasks. What are their initial reactions? • Formative Assessment: After the first 45 minutes, gather to discuss findings and reactions as a class. • Summative Assessment: Invite students to journal about the skills they practiced during the document analysis assignment – how are they thinking differently about "deep reading" broadly, and document analysis in particular.

INTELLECTUAL PREPARATION FOR LESSON

Archives help preserve rare, delicate, scarce, and extraordinary materials. Their potential as open-access public records offer a pathway into the intimate, private, and withheld thinking, theorizing or contemplation of social actors and organizations. However, the archive, for all of its utility in creating a bridge to past moments and events, is never complete, and more specifically, decidedly discrete. Emerging researchers or those that would otherwise attempt to engage in document analysis face a complex and unrelenting conundrum: how does one understand, or make sense of materials, people, or lives at the limits of the archive? That is, the archive, that one might know as the carefully curated accumulation of historical records in digital or physical locations, is, by nature, the production of power and authority (Hartman, 2019). At face value, primary source materials that would spell out an individual's or organization's activities during a particular period, generally, are granted the benefit of doubt and privilege of verifiable truth. Authentication is determined in this way by the voices of the originator/producer of the source material (e.g., document, ledger, etc.) and by the "archivist"[2], who puts the source material in its rightful place in history to be read and engaged as such. Often, the assumption is that source materials are complete, which is to say that, whatever the story is, [that story] is true and being told in its fullness.

Core Ideas

Hartman (2008) troubles the assumed authority of the archive and primary source materials when writing about Venus, the name/term/stand-in for Black girls unremembered in and across trans-Atlantic slavery:

> What else is there to know? Hers is the same fate as every other Black Venus: no one remembered her name or recorded the things she said, or observed that she refused to say anything at all. Hers is an untimely story told by a failed witness.
>
> (p. 2)

That "no one remembered her name or recorded the things she said" is but one indication of the limits of the archive. Researchers fail to account for the lives of Black girls in particular and Black people generally, broadly, when they enter and leave the source materials presuming that a story is told in full, if it can ethically be told at all. Regarding ethics, I mean to suggest that any attempt to tell a story that one has not lived or experienced, is, at best, a rendition, and at its worst, a skewed portrayal. Researchers must be cognizant of this fact and approach an analysis accordingly. In reality, encounters with people via source materials amount to "little more than a register of [their] encounter with power" and "a meager sketch of [their] existence" (p. 2). It is, in many ways by chance, that archivists come upon the source material, which means that as researchers, using the case of Venus, for example, we only know what can be extrapolated through analysis of a document – a document offered by those in power (i.e., enslavers) over her (i.e., the enslaved). In this way, advancing a holistic approach to document analysis as a method, particularly as it relates to the "dispossessed, the subaltern, and the enslaved" (Hartman, 2019, p. xiii), ought to consider three core ideas.

ON THE RECOVERY OF BLACK LIFE

Core Idea #1: Skepticism

The archive, and by extension, the document(s) and artifact(s) that dominate collective memory, have limitations, raising questions of what can be known, whose perspectives have been centered and made to matter, and who, or what have been granted the prevailing authority of historical or historicizing actors. Following this premise, "it is doubtless impossible ever to grasp [these lives] again in themselves, as they might have been in a free state" (Hartman, 2008, p. 2). This sense of skepticism functions to evade the trap of western epistemology that would have one believe that stories can be recovered or told in their entirety by an objective observer. Beginning, not on firm, but shifting grounds enables the researcher to listen for "the unsaid, translating misconstrued words, and refashioning disfigured lives" (Hartman, 2008, pp. 2–3), with the intent of moving toward the impossibility that is "redressing the violence" that yielded fractured historical accounts of Black life and living.

Core Idea #2: Silence, Scarcity, Absence

Visiting the archives and source material presents an opportunity to sit with material artifacts in order to engage in deep reading. Researchers should take stock of what they notice/observe upon doing so. What are the document's physical characteristics, and what story is being told by those traits? How is the document or series documents organized for the reader? Was the intent that the document be read or repurposed by the originator? These questions can assist researchers in discerning the intended purposes of the source material and render complex inferences. To center the condition of Black life in document analysis is to encounter and reckon with "that * in the grand narrative of history; and, in the condition of Black life and death" (Sharpe, 2016, p. 33). The asterisk, Blackness (and the racialization process broadly that comes to bear on the lives of Black folks), throws into crisis conceptions of linearity, sequence, and fullness. Said differently, the archive, predicated on violence, is full of silences and absence. The violence over-determines, regulates, and constructs "subjects and objects of power" (Hartman, 2008, p. 10). Though the conditions of power and oppression repress the voice of Black life, the asterisk assumes that there is a different narration possible. This is not intended to suggest that an alternative reading can recover narratives that are not present. Yet, the work of exposing the gaps and absences that the archive/source material would tell about Black people and the device of history – beginning, middle, end, plot, setting, etc. – are useful. The shifting grounds of the archive give way to the question, how do we relinquish the goal/assignment of narrative to tell implausible stories?

Core Idea #3: Annotations and Redactions

Negotiating the limits of the archive infers speculation with the admission, as noted above, that re-telling (or conveying) the fullness of Black life through curated historical records is unrealistic. Alternatively, the aim is to attend to and represent those repressed by straining against the archive through narration, or what Hartman (2008) called critical fabulation:

> 'Fabula' denotes the basic elements of story, the building blocks of the narrative. A fabula, according to Mieke Bal, is 'a series of logically and chronologically related events that are

caused and experienced by actors. An event is a transition from one state to another. Actors are agents that perform actions. (They are not necessarily human.) To act is to cause or experience an event.'

(p. 11)

Where scarcity and absence exist, critical fabulation is one method of addressing the question of how to encapsulate life while simultaneously respecting what cannot be known. It represents the humble attempt to grapple with what is distorted, not named, and lost in the archive/source material in ways that can help testify to the complexity of how Black life is remembered, documented, and lived. It is a close reading approach that, in turn, may narrate a counter-history. Critical fabulation as an approach necessitates an analytic method by which a close narration might surface, of which annotations and redactions become useful.

Broadly, holistic annotations serve as a tool for close reading that can help researchers engaged in document analysis to identify patterns and note resonances and central ideas. Annotations are a process of adding to, explaining, or expounding on some physical or textual artifact; they mark a specific place in a document and offer further commentary to the original source material. Annotations accompany source material as supplemental information. Similarly, redactions also mark source material and bring attention to a specific area. Redaction describes a process of editing details toward experiencing material in excess on what is displayed (Sharpe, 2016). Here, I lift redaction, in its textual framing, as a process of blackening out portions as a way to bring something else into a sharper view. To put these deep reading practices in conversation with the limits of the archive/ source material discussed above engenders modes of writing and making sensible Black life against the absences of archival records.

Learners

Generally, document analysis is slow work. Source material that researchers will examine does not lend itself to cursory or superficial reviews (as noted above, we do so at the expense of counter-histories). For new researchers, balancing the rigors of coursework and reading expectations, skimming, and other adaptive learning models can become commonplace as part of their socialization. Accordingly, facilitators need to stress the importance of deep study – focusing time to read and carving out time to revisit the argument of a text in preparation to dialogue with others about one's ruminations. Relatedly, I do not assume that students have practiced this notion of deep study, and as a result, it may be helpful to explain the premise of such a practice.

I explain surface reading as the implicit approval of source material. This implied acceptance does not invite the reader/viewer into the material and lessens the potential for new learning to occur. Deep reading involves the readers/viewers attempting to analyze, which is to evaluate, break down, or dissect an argument for closer meaning-making. To accomplish the latter, placing students in pairs/small groups to read (aloud) a document can be a generative practice for helping students locate ideas that may lead to new understandings. Additionally, partnered study can be beneficial as students encounter new formats, framings, vocabulary, and scripts, and learn how to make sense of them in real time. This approach may create opportunities for questions to surface in the analysis process that would not otherwise do so. The instructor may offer critical questions to augment students' deep reading and analysis. On some occasions, students may query that they are unsure of what they ought to be looking for in an investigation. Instructors should be careful about leading students to prescribed endpoints. Instead, they might prompt students by providing open-ended questions tailored to the document/source material that can help direct students' learning and assist them in generating questions when they undertake their own analysis.

Context

Instructors can do some contextualizing as they present the assignment/approach by providing an overview of the method or the document under investigation. Concerning the documents for this lesson, Du Bois delivered his "Whither Now and Why" remarks in the aftermath of the Brown v. Board of Education ruling. These years were defined by public and political advances for civil rights. The speech is consistent with a strand of Black activism that advocated Black self-determination. Instructors might ask themselves, what was the significance of Black self-determination in this period of sweeping educational policy? This overview can acquaint students with the topic and direct them to call on their previous experiences and learning. Additionally, as instructors prepare students to encounter documents and the range of absences those encounters engender, instructors and students must contextually situate themselves in their analyses and meaning-making work.

Ethics and Reflexivity

In closing, two central ideas that will be important for students who engage in document/source material analysis are the notions of ethics and reflexivity. Ethics can be understood as forms of care that ask what it means to responsibly handle the violence of silence, absence, and abstraction – to gesture toward the belief that (Black) life is more than curated production. Care is the compulsion to look and look again, to look without turning away, and in our looking, mark the document for more profound meaning (annotate and redact). Care prioritizes the untold story, even if that story is not capable of being told. Reflexive engagement with a document obligates researchers to consider their identities before, during, and after encountering an archive. Here, reflexive practice builds on the notion of deep reading by questioning the assumptions one brings to research by considering how systems of oppression dictate one's viewing and assumptions. Reflexive engagement ensures recognition of the social and political context and how that influences how a document (and the broader assignment) is engaged. More than a cognitive endeavor, reflexivity in document analysis must be an embodied task as one considers what occurs in the body affectively when engaging the source material. A reflexive approach that attends to tensions, desires, fantasies, and indecision of the self as a researcher and the subject/s of the source material may yield richer, more ethical insight than attempts to reckon with material objectively. The goal, perhaps, is less about reparative readings of a document and more about developing an ongoing relationship with the source material for what it, in conversation with other materials, can teach us about a person, place, or phenomena.

NOTES

1 Positionality is the social and political context that creates your identity in terms of race, class, gender, sexuality, and ability status.
2 An archivist is an information professional who assesses, collects, organizes, preserves, maintains control over, and provides access to records and archives determined to have long-term value.

BIBLIOGRAPHY

Bowen, G. A. (2009). Document analysis as a qualitative research method. *Qualitative Research Journal, 9*(2), 27–40.

Du Bois, W. E. B. (1960a). Brief notes: Whither now and why, 1960. https://credo.library.umass.edu/view/full/mums312-b233-i005

Du Bois, W. E. B. (1960b, March 31). Written speech: Whither now and why. https://credo.library.umass.edu/cgi-bin/pdf.cgi?id=scua:mums312-b206-i050

Du Bois, W. E. B. (1960c, April 2). Recording: Whither now and why. https://credo.library.umass.edu/view/full/mums312-b250-i003

Golia, J., & Katz, R. M. (n.d.). What is document analysis? *Teaching Archives.* http://wwww.teacharchives.org/articles/document-analysis/

Hartman, S. (2008). Venus in two acts. *Small Axe, 26*(2), 1–14.

Hartman, S. (2019). *Wayward lives, beautiful experiments: Intimate histories of riotous black girls, troublesome women, and queer radicals.* WW Norton & Company.

Okello, W. K., & Pérez II, D. (2018). "Don't believe the hype." Complicating the thriving quotient for Latino undergraduate men at selective institutions. *About Campus, 22*(6), 27–31.

Patel, L. (2016). *Decolonizing educational research: From ownership to answerability.* Routledge.

Scott, J. C. (1990). *Domination and the arts of resistance: Hidden transcripts.* Yale Press.

Sharpe, C. (2016). *In the wake: On Blackness and being.* Duke University Press.

23

Emerging Approaches

Ensuring a Pyramid of Congruence When Using Critical and Poststructural Theories in Qualitative Educational Research

Antonio Duran and Alex C. Lange

INTRODUCTION

Students in educational research courses have increasingly displayed an interest in designing qualitative studies that seek to advance values of equity and justice. Jones et al. (2022) explain:

> As the need increases to understand the experiences of diverse populations and the policies, programs, and systemic structures that influence their experiences in education, the use of theoretical perspectives emerges as a useful approach to inform researchers in the conceptualization and analysis of data to convey findings through different lenses.
>
> (p. 43)

Specifically, these individuals aspire to critically analyze and contest the systems of power and oppression that influence the realities of minoritized students, staff, and instructors in various educational settings. Consequently, it is unsurprising that these researchers are using theoretical frameworks that align with critical and poststructural epistemologies (see Crotty, 1998 for descriptions of these perspectives) with greater frequency.

However, beyond simply naming these epistemologies as important to one's worldview, students must learn how to establish research congruence, also referred to as alignment (Bhattacharya, 2017), when designing studies with critical and poststructural theories in mind. Examples of critical and poststructural theories include critical race theory, queer theory, Indigenous and decolonizing paradigms, and feminist perspectives (see Jones et al., 2022 for brief descriptions of these frameworks). Congruence only occurs when researchers are able to convey how their chosen theoretical perspectives align with their methodological traditions, data collection, analysis, and dissemination strategies. This lesson involves the use of a study pyramid as a way to visually convey the concept of congruence, especially as it relates to critical and poststructural theories.

DOI: 10.4324/b23320-29

LESSON PLAN

Topic	*Establishing research congruence when using critical and poststructural theories in qualitative research*
Learning Objectives	• Students will articulate why it is important to establish study congruence in educational research. • Students will be exposed to how different theories provide different insights about data, meaning that they need to resist "the theory/practice binary by decentering each and instead showing how they *constitute or make one another*" (Jackson & Mazzei, 2012, p. 5, emphasis in original). • Students will learn how to align their chosen critical and poststructural theories with data collection methods, analytical strategies, and study outcomes.
Needed Materials	• Large Post-it notes • Markers • Prior to this seminar, students should have to read three scholarly journal articles, each utilizing a different theory that aligns with critical and poststructural epistemologies (e.g., Abes, 2012; Bowleg, 2008; Honan et al., 2000; Solórzano & Yosso, 2002).
Pre-lesson Preparation	• *How can I scaffold this lesson*? To engage this particular lesson, we typically would place this unit after students have had exposure to the concept of paradigms in qualitative research. Moreover, this lesson works best toward the end of an introductory research course in a graduate program after students have learned about the idea of congruence in qualitative studies. This lesson plan thus serves as an opportunity for students to explore research congruence specific to critical and poststructural theories. Alternatively, this lesson could also work in advanced methods courses or in a critical theories class offered in a graduate program. • *Do students have exposure to what critical and poststructural theories involve*? As noted above, this lesson builds upon previous classes that have introduced the concept of research congruence and paradigms. We would encourage students also to have the opportunity to learn about various critical and poststructural theories using chapters like the one written by Jones et al. (2022). Prior to this seminar, students should have to read and take notes on three scholarly journal articles that employ critical and poststructural theories.

Activities	• To begin this activity, it is critical that you first provide an example. In particular, you should use Figure 23.1, which displays a pyramid that is sectioned off by four different dimensions: Research outcomes, analysis, methods, and framework(s).
	• Explain that the purpose of the lesson is to illustrate how a theoretical framework should be the foundation for the decisions that a researcher makes with their data collection methods, analysis, and study outcomes. If the methods, analysis, or research outcomes do not appropriately align with the theoretical framework, it will make for an unbalanced pyramid and consequently, an incongruent study.
	• Offer an example of a pyramid that represents a study that utilizes a critical or poststructural framework. An illustration could involve writing the following (see Figure 23.2 for the visual):
	  a. Framework: Intersectionality (Crenshaw, 1989).
	  b. Data collection methods: Individual interviews informed by the concept of structural, representational, and political intersectionality (Crenshaw, 1991).
	  c. Analysis: Three rounds of coding informed by the different types of intersectionality.
	  d. Research outcomes: Work with the participants to develop an action plan on how to address inequities.

EMERGING APPROACHES

Topic	*Establishing research congruence when using critical and poststructural theories in qualitative research*

	• You can then provide an example of a pyramid highlighting a fictional project that claims use of a poststructural framework, but that does not adequately carry this throughout. You would represent this by having the pyramid top and the subsequent two shapes not aligning with the bottom shape. See Figure 23.3 for an example.
	 • If you assign three articles using critical and poststructural theories for homework, split the class into three groups or depending on class size, you may divide students into more groups (giving some groups the same article).
	 • Within 5–10 minutes, ask the groups to utilize the large Post-it notes to first identify the article's study design. They should include: the framework utilized, the data collection methods employed, the analytical process, and what outcomes the researchers achieved.
	 • Next, give students 10–15 minutes to discuss whether the study design was congruent. Within this time, they should also draw a pyramid that visually represents how congruent they perceived the study design using the three examples offered at the beginning of the lesson as guiding illustrations (see Figures 23.1–23.3). Encourage the students to consider: *How balanced is the pyramid for this study?*
	 • Afterwards, ask the students to review another group's Post-it notes for 10–15 minutes. Encourage them to ask the following questions:
	   a. How does this group's illustration of research congruence align with our analysis of the article?
	   b. What are some decisions that the authors could have made to better align with their selected critical or poststructural framework?
	 • Bring the class back to engage in large-group discussion using the following questions:
	   a. How did this activity enhance your thinking about research congruence, especially for studies using critical or poststructural theories?
	   b. What are some difficulties that authors encounter in establishing congruence with critical or poststructural theories?
	 • Homework: Students should develop a pyramid by the beginning of next class that reflects an original research study using a critical or poststructural framework.

Virtual Adaptations	For classrooms engaging virtual methods, this same lesson can be conducted using Google slides, a process further described below. • An instructor can create a Google Slide deck with four different shapes (i.e., trapezoids and a triangle on top) creating a pyramid on each slide. Next to the four shapes, instructors should include four text boxes displaying the following, from top to bottom: research outcomes, analysis, methods, and framework(s). • Students should then be directed to annotate their Google Slide based on the readings. They have to fill out the text boxes with the information from the articles. They can move the individual shapes to indicate how congruent they perceive the authors' study designs to be. • Each group can share their Google Slide by using the Share Screen feature on the video conference platform.
Assessment	• Formative assessment: As groups are working on their pyramids, an instructor should move throughout the room and assess how students are describing the study designs reflected in the articles. • Formative assessment: Students should submit a pyramid by the beginning of next class that reflects an original research study using a critical or poststructural framework. • Summative assessment: Students could have the opportunity to complete a research proposal for a study employing a critical or poststructural framework. The instructor should then utilize a rubric that assesses the degree to which their proposed study design displays the concept of congruence.

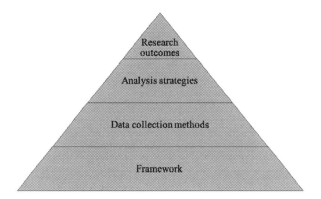

FIGURE 23.1 Pyramid of Congruence

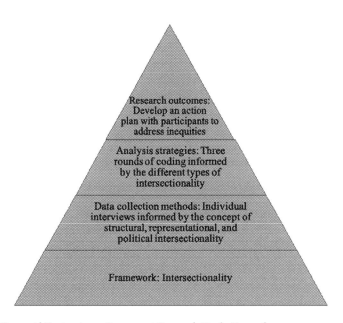

FIGURE 23.2 Pyramid Portraying a Congruent Research Study Example

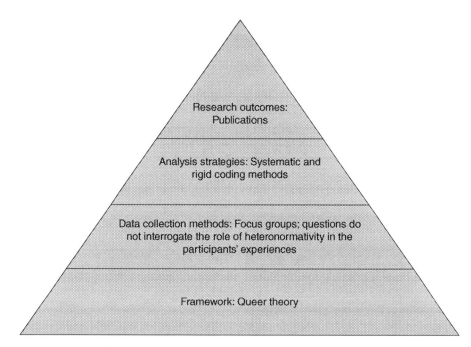

FIGURE 23.3 Pyramid Portraying an Incongruent Research Study Example

INTELLECTUAL PREPARATION FOR "PYRAMID OF CONGRUENCE" LESSON

Qualitative researchers frequently stress that theory is important to designing a rigorous study (e.g., Bhattacharya, 2017; Jones et al., 2022). Explicitly, theoretical frameworks and perspectives offer researchers a lens through which to view their phenomenon of interest. Consequently, theory should: guide how people frame their research questions, align with a methodological tradition, inform methods, and shape how people think about the outcomes of their study. However, ensuring congruence with one's theories, especially those that are critical or poststructural in nature, is a difficult task for the most experienced of scholars. Therefore, the "Pyramid of Congruence" activity is one that can be employed to help students (and instructors) learn how to establish congruence when employing critical or poststructural theories. To help illustrate the meaning behind this lesson, we describe the core ideas of this lesson, articulate the characteristics of the learners who will benefit from this activity, and speak to the context in which this lesson functions.

Core Ideas

The "Pyramid of Congruence" lesson will assist graduate students comprehend two core ideas. First, the activity underscores that theories need to be interwoven throughout a study design. Second, this lesson highlights that a study informed by critical or poststructural theories must advance equity and justice in its outcomes.

Interweaving Theories Throughout a Study Design
In the lesson plan, the "Pyramid of Congruence" activity demonstrates the skill necessary to maintain a rigorous qualitative study: interweaving theories throughout one's design. If a theory represents a lens that scholars employ to view a phenomenon, this lens must be present for the duration of the project. Figure 23.1 provides a tool that students can use as they orchestrate their own research. Specifically, in the "Pyramid of Congruence" activity, novice researchers examine how other scholars integrated their theoretical framework in their data collection, analysis, and study outcomes. In addition to developing greater competence with using critical or poststructural theories, this process will ensure that students propose study designs that are congruent once they complete the course.

Ensuring that Studies Informed by Critical or Poststructural Theories Advance Equity and Justice
The second core idea that the "Pyramid of Congruence" activity advances is most evident at the top of Figure 23.1: research outcomes. In particular, critical and poststructural theories are not only intended to analyze inequitable power dynamics, but also to move individuals and communities toward reimagining more just worlds. Through this activity, students will come to understand that engaging in critical and poststructural qualitative research must involve thinking about outcomes beyond what is considered traditional in the academy (e.g., publishing articles). A congruent critical or poststructural study should demonstrate how the project is attempting to further equitable educational environments by challenging the existing power structures, which may include working with participants to develop an action plan based on the study findings (see Figure 23.2 for an example). As a result, this lesson asks students to reflect on the central question: *How do I produce research that benefits minoritized communities and does not only result in positive outcomes for me?*

Learners

In order to effectively follow the "Pyramid of Congruence" lesson, an instructor must consider who their graduate students are, what their own positionality is, and what knowledge students bring with them to the classroom. In this section, we focus specifically on how the educator must keep in mind two different aspects that characterize the learners: what their understandings of critical and poststructural theories are, and how students view what constitutes a rigorous versus a simple study design.

Understandings of Critical and Poststructural Theories
As noted in the lesson plan, it is imperative that students engaging with this activity have a working knowledge of critical and poststructural theories. Graduate students taking an introductory research methods class may have a range of knowledge concerning critical and poststructural theories based on their previous coursework. Whereas some students may have been in a class that explored theories broadly or focused on a particular theory (e.g., queer theory), some may not have had this theoretical grounding. Therefore, an instructor must ensure that they strategically place this lesson within the context of the

EMERGING APPROACHES

course and provide opportunities for students to learn about critical and poststructural theories prior to this activity. Examples would include assigning readings that provide an overview of various critical and poststructural theories or having a class dedicated to this particular subject matter.

Views on What Constitutes a Publishable Study Using Critical or Poststructural Theories
In addition to holding differing understandings of critical and poststructural theories, students may also hold distinct views on what constitutes a publishable study based on their previous engagement with analyzing research articles. Some students may have read peer-reviewed journal articles that purport to utilize critical or poststructural theories but that have incongruent study designs. Therefore, some students may believe that it is not necessary to establish research congruence if peer-reviewed studies are published. As a result, instructors may have to challenge these pre-existing assumptions and emphasize that congruence is imperative to establish regardless of what has been published previously.

Context

The intention behind the "Pyramid of Congruence" activity relative to critical and poststructural theories is to help students build upon their previous knowledge related to increasing study alignment. Moreover, this lesson is intended to empower students to confidently deploy theories rooted in the knowledge of minoritized communities. In the sections that follow, we expand on these two points pertinent to our central argument.

Building Upon Students' Prior Knowledge of Epistemologies and Theories
The "Pyramid of Congruence" activity is useful for individuals who are building upon their previous understanding of epistemologies and theories in the context of qualitative research. This is particularly important for students learning how to employ critical or poststructural theories, because it challenges them to visually examine study designs to determine if they are congruent. This lesson plan draws upon knowledge that students would have explored earlier on in a course regarding the role of epistemologies and theories in qualitative research. The lesson is also structured such that students can analyze existing research studies and how congruent they perceive them to be.

Empowering Students to Utilize Theories Rooted in the Knowledge of Minoritized Communities
Although educators can utilize the "Pyramid of Congruence" activity to describe the concept of alignment in qualitative research broadly, including studies grounded in constructivist epistemologies, it is particularly meaningful for those rooted in critical and poststructural epistemologies. This lesson can help foster an equitable learning space by empowering students to confidently utilize theories like critical race theory, queer theory, Indigenous and decolonizing paradigms, and feminist perspectives. The "Pyramid of Congruence" activity emphasizes that it is important not only that critical or poststructural theories are invoked by name in a manuscript, but also that researchers must honor

these frameworks by accounting for power, privilege, and oppression in the study design. Ultimately, students need the valuable lesson of addressing how a project threads a particular theory, especially one that is attempting to advance equity and justice, throughout a research design.

The "Pyramid of Congruence" activity ultimately assists students in understanding a complex process that vexes the most experienced researcher: ensuring that critical or poststructural theories are employed in all aspects of a study. When deploying these theories, maintaining congruence allows researchers to produce studies that can further interrogate and deconstruct educational inequities.

BIBLIOGRAPHY

Abes, E. S. (2012). Constructivist and intersectional interpretations of a lesbian college student's multiple social identities. *The Journal of Higher Education, 83*(2), 186–216. https://doi.org/10.1080/00221546.2012.11777239

Bhattacharya, K. (2017). *Fundamentals of qualitative research: A practical guide.* Routledge.
Describes the basics of engaging in qualitative research and advances the term "alignment" to describe how one can create a study that is congruent with their epistemology and theoretical framework.

Bowleg, L. (2008). When Black + lesbian + woman ≠ Black lesbian woman: The methodological challenges of qualitative and quantitative intersectionality research. *Sex Roles, 59*(5–6), 312–325. https://doi.org/10.1007/s11199-008-9400-z

Crenshaw, K. (1989). Demarginalizing the intersection of race and sex: A Black feminist critique of antidiscrimination doctrine, feminist theory, and antiracist politics. *University of Chicago Legal Forum, 1989*(1), 139–167. http://chicagounbound.uchicago.edu/uclf/vol1989/iss1/8
Advances the concept of intersectionality, an example of a critical social theory referenced in the lesson plan above.

Crenshaw, K. (1991). Mapping the margins: Intersectionality, identity politics, and violence against women of color. *Stanford Law Review, 43*(6), 1241–1299. https://doi.org/10.2307/1229039
Represents an example of a critical social theory referenced in the lesson plan above.

Crotty, M. (1998). *The foundations of social research: Meaning and perspective in the research process.* Sage.
Introduces forms of operationalizing perspectives like critical theory and poststructuralism.

Honan, E., Knobel, M., Baker, C., & Davies, B. (2000). Producing possible Hannahs: Theory and the subject of research. *Qualitative Inquiry, 6*(1), 9–32. https://doi.org/10.1177/107780040000600102

Jackson, A. Y., & Mazzei, L. A. (2012). *Thinking with theory in qualitative research: Viewing data across multiple analytics.* Routledge.
Showcases how qualitative researchers can utilize theory to open up nuanced and complex views of qualitative data as opposed to viewing qualitative data analysis as a rigid and systematic process.

Jones, S. R., Torres, V., & Arminio, J. (2022). *Negotiating the complexities of qualitative research in higher education: Essential elements and issues.* Routledge.
Offers guidance on how researchers can use theories, including those under the critical and poststructural epistemological umbrella, to inform qualitative study designs.

Solórzano, D. G., & Yosso, T. J. (2002). Critical race methodology: Counter-storytelling as an analytical framework for education research. *Qualitative Inquiry, 8*(1), 23–44. https://doi.org/10.1177%2F107780040200800103

24

Exploring How Epistemologies Guide the Process of Coding Data and Developing Themes

Kari B. Taylor

INTRODUCTION

In 1998, Eisner reflected: "There is no codified body of procedures that will tell someone how to produce a perceptive, insightful, or illuminating study of the educational world. Unfortunately – or fortunately—in qualitative matters cookbooks ensure nothing" (p. 169). Although we as researchers may yearn for concrete recipes or sophisticated technologies for data analysis, the process of interpreting data ultimately requires our ability to make meaning of what we have seen, heard, and experienced. We must make decisions about what aspects of the data are most relevant, what lens works best for the research questions at hand, and how particular insights fit into a larger whole. Teaching students how to code data and develop themes for qualitative research requires them to learn how to make intentional decisions and participate in the innately human act of interpretation. I developed the following lesson as a way to engage students in the complex processes of coding data and developing themes for qualitative research. I draw upon grounded theory, a methodology characterized by analyzing data inductively rather than deductively (Jones et al., 2021), because it requires students to pay close attention to the data at hand and highlights how different epistemologies lead to different interpretations. Also, strategies associated with grounded theory such as the constant comparative method provide a structured way to help students move from generating specific codes to more abstract themes (Jones et al., 2021).

The purpose of this lesson is to help students gain hands-on experience with using different epistemologies to guide data analysis. It both challenges and supports students to make the types of decisions researchers must make as they grapple with interpreting data.

DOI: 10.4324/b23320-30

LESSON PLAN

Topic	*Using epistemologies to code data and develop themes inductively*
Learning Objectives	• Students will explore how different research epistemologies influence the process of coding data and developing themes. • Students will practice coding data and developing themes inductively based on a given research question. • Students will learn how to move from open/initial coding to axial/focused coding (see Jones et al., 2021, pp. 216–220).

Needed Materials	• 3–4 pages of raw, de-identified qualitative data that you have permission to share with students.
	  ◦ Several qualitative research textbooks include sample data you can use for this purpose. For example, Galletta's (2013) *Mastering the Semi-structured Interview and Beyond* provides excerpts from interview transcripts in Chapter 3.
	  ◦ Alternatively, you can use an excerpt from a published documentary or podcast transcript related to education. For example, *A Walk in My Shoes* – produced by the K-State College of Education (2018) – shares the stories of eight first-generation college students.
	• Paper copies of the data.
	• Pencils with erasers.
	• Markers.
	• Notecards.
	• For prior homework, students read Jones et al.'s (2021) Chapter 1 with particular attention to "Consideration Three: Contemplating the Nature of Knowledge, Reality and Existence, and Values" (pp. 17–23).

Pre-lesson Preparation	• *What research question and corresponding excerpt of data will be relevant to all students and allow for multiple interpretations?* I intentionally select an excerpt of data that focuses on a broad, multi-faceted aspect of higher education or a related discipline with which students will likely be familiar. Examples I have used or considered using include the decision of what major to pursue, socialization among peers, and interactions with faculty. I provide the context for the data in class and provide additional information as necessary. Also, I intentionally select an excerpt of data that includes information about a complex phenomenon that does not have one clean or clear explanation. • *What background knowledge regarding research do students have and need?* I conduct an informal assessment of students' understanding of how research paradigms and researchers' positionalities influence the research process. If this assessment indicates that students see the research process more as a universal set of steps to follow than a contextualized series of decisions to make, I spend more time providing scaffolding for this lesson plan. In particular, I engage students in readings and activities that show how the same methods can and do lead to different results.
Activities	• Engage students in discussion of Table 1.4 Comparing Epistemologies in Jones et al.'s (2021) chapter (p. 24). Prepare and provide students with abbreviated 1-page summaries of published qualitative research studies that use different epistemologies. For each summary, include the purpose, research questions, methodology, limitations, and any other information that highlights the researcher(s)' assumptions about the nature of knowledge. See Figure 24.1 for an example of a summary. Ask students to identify which epistemology guides each study. Ensure that students can accurately differentiate between each epistemology.

CODING DATA AND DEVELOPING THEMES

Topic	Using epistemologies to code data and develop themes inductively
	<ul><li>Divide class into groups of 3–4 students. Assign each group a different epistemology. *Notes:*<ul><li>In introductory courses or contexts, you may want to omit the postmodern/ poststructural epistemology from this activity as this epistemology is relatively complex to use in practice.</li><li>You may need or want to omit the positivism epistemology given that relatively few qualitative research studies in education use this epistemology.</li><li>Ultimately, the goal is to include at least two different epistemologies (e.g., positivism, post-positivism, constructionism, critical theory, and postmodernism) in the class as a whole.</li></ul></li><li>Provide all groups with the same 3–4 pages of raw, de-identified qualitative data (or text from a published transcript). Also, provide all groups with the same broad research question, which should correspond to the excerpt of data.</li><li>Ask each group to code the excerpt of data using the following process:<ul><li>As a group, identify 2–3 concepts to examine in the data based on the assigned epistemology and the given research question.</li><li>As individuals, carefully read through the excerpt of data once to gain an overall sense of what the data "says."</li><li>As individuals, read through the excerpt of data again; this time, underline in pencil key words or phrases that relate to the 2–3 concepts identified earlier.</li><li>As individuals, read through the excerpt of data a third time; this time, write codes in pencil that summarize the meaning of the underlined key words or phrases.</li><li>As a group, compare and contrast the codes each person created. Discuss how each person's perspective informed the codes they created. Collectively, identify 10–12 codes with which every group member agrees.</li></ul></li><li>Bring groups back together to debrief the coding process. As necessary, ask guiding questions such as:<ul><li>What did you find most rewarding about the coding process? In what ways was that rewarding?</li><li>What did you find most challenging about the coding process? In what ways was that challenging? How did you work through that challenge?</li><li>How did you use the group's assigned epistemology to guide the coding process?</li></ul></li><li>Ask students to return to their small group to develop themes using the following process:<ul><li>As a group, review what you want to know based on the assigned epistemology and given research question.</li><li>Work together to write each of the agreed upon codes on a separate notecard with a marker.</li><li>As a group, lay out the set of notecards on a flat surface (e.g., table, floor). Discuss how the notecards relate to one another. Group together notecards with similar codes or codes that speak to the same issue. Be willing to try out multiple arrangements of the notecards to reach an arrangement that works best.</li><li>Once you have the notecards arranged in groups, create a label for each group that captures what the codes in the group mean and how the codes in the group address the given research question. These labels represent themes.</li><li>Identify one group member to share the themes with the class as a whole and explain how the group's assigned epistemology influenced the development of the themes.</li></ul></li></ul>

Topic	Using epistemologies to code data and develop themes inductively

	• Bring groups back together to debrief the theme development process. Ask a representative from each group to share the themes their group developed and how their group's assigned epistemology influenced the development of themes. Then, as necessary, ask guiding questions such as:
	  ○ What did you find most rewarding about the theme development process? In what ways was this rewarding?
	  ○ What did you find most challenging about the theme development process? In what ways was this challenging? How did you work through that challenge?
	  ○ How did you use the group's assigned epistemology to guide the theme development process?
	  ○ How do the themes your group developed compare and/or contrast with the themes other groups developed? To what do you attribute these differences?

Virtual Adaptations	To adapt this activity for remote learning, I recommend making the following modifications: • Create a Google Doc version of the excerpt of data you want students to use for coding and theme development, and share the Google Doc with students in a secure fashion. Before granting students access to the data electronically, make sure to emphasize the importance of keeping the data confidential and not copying it or sharing it. • For coding the excerpt of data, as described in step 4 above, ask students to use text formatting options such as underlining, bolding, or highlighting to identify key phrases. Then, students can use the comment feature to create codes for the underlined, bolded, or highlighted phrases. • For developing themes, as described in step 6 above, ask students to generate a list of codes on a Google Jamboard by using the sticky note tool. Then, encourage students to rearrange the notes on the Jamboard to group the codes into broader categories. Students can also use the pen tool to illustrate relationships among groups of sticky notes. • The debriefing sections, as described in steps 5 and 7, can take place in breakout rooms via Zoom or on electronic discussion boards via a learning management system (e.g., Blackboard, Canvas, or Moodle).
Assessment	• Formative Assessment: During discussion of Table 1.4 Comparing Epistemologies in Jones et al.'s (2021) chapter (p. 21), assess students' abilities to identify the epistemology that guides each research study example. Also, listen for students' abilities to compare the purpose and type of knowledge claims associated with each epistemology. • Formative Assessment: During the debriefing sessions for the lesson, assess students' abilities to articulate clear and accurate ways in which a given epistemology guided their coding and theme development process. • Summative Assessment: Include a reflective component for a final research project that requires students to articulate a rationale for key decisions they made for data analysis; grade the reflection on intentionality, clarity, and alignment with the research design.

CODING DATA AND DEVELOPING THEMES

Purpose	Research Questions	Methodology	Limitations
To examine students' developmental readiness to engage in international service-learning (Taylor et al., 2017)	When are students ready to meet the developmental demands of international service-learning? What specific contextual conditions allow students to move toward more complex understandings of themselves and their worlds?	Case study informed by a "critical developmental theoretical framework" (Taylor et al., 2017, p. 688)	Researchers did not formally assess developmental readiness for each participant. Data were self-reported. Different perspectives may have emerged if data collection had included participant-observation. This study did not examine community partners' development.

FIGURE 24.1 Example of Qualitative Research Study Summary for Discussion of Different Epistemologies

Source: This figure summarizes key information from the following publication: Taylor, K. B., Jones, S. R., Massey, R., Mickey, J., Reynolds, D. J., & Jackson, T. (2017). Examining developmental readiness in an international service-learning context. *Journal of College Student Development*, 58(5), 685–703. https://doi.org/10.1353/csd.2017.0054

INTELLECTUAL PREPARATION FOR THE LESSON

Coding data and developing themes fit into a broader qualitative research process that requires researchers to make a series of informed decisions, not just follow a prescribed recipe. Learning to make informed decisions throughout the research process necessitates intentional scaffolding for researchers at all levels, even ones with prior research experience. To help educators provide intentional scaffolding, I discuss my intellectual preparation for the lesson plan shared above. In particular, I discuss the lesson's core ideas, key characteristics of learners involved in the lesson, and the context for effective learning.

Core Ideas

Three core ideas provide a foundation for the lesson plan shared above, which include: (1) identifying and applying epistemologies, (2) engaging in open/initial coding, and (3) moving toward axial/focused coding.

Identifying and Applying Epistemologies

Without a clear understanding of what epistemologies are and how they guide the research process from start to finish, learners tend to code data and develop themes haphazardly. In other words, they may learn the technical aspects of underlining and labeling key phrases within the data but often do not understand why they are doing so. To help learners understand that different rationales exist and lead to different but equally legitimate ways of interpreting data, it is important to discuss various epistemologies. Once learners have a foundational understanding of key epistemologies such as positivism, constructivism, critical theory, and postmodernism, they can begin to see how coding data and developing themes is part of a larger process that is informed by researchers' ways of knowing. Also, by differentiating among various epistemologies and seeing how they lead to different interpretations of the data, learners can begin to see that they, as researchers, are responsible for deciding how to code data and develop themes; in turn, learners begin to take ownership for how they interpret data.

Engaging in Open/Initial Coding
Another core idea for this lesson, which stems from grounded theory, is the process of open/initial coding (Jones et al., 2021). As learners engage in open/initial coding (i.e., analyzing data line by line or unit by unit), they immerse themselves in the data and experience first hand the process researchers use to interpret data inductively. This immersive experience allows learners to practice navigating challenges such as deciding what lines or units hold meaning for a given research question. Then, as learners compare and contrast their codes with classmates in other groups, they further recognize the inherently subjective nature of analyzing data. By debriefing the process with a group that used a different epistemology for the same data, learners also can see how researchers' assumptions influence data analysis.

Moving Toward Axial/Focused Coding
This lesson also centers on another level of coding associated with grounded theory known as axial/focused coding (Jones et al., 2021). Axial/focused coding starts the process of theme development because it involves making decisions about how initial codes fit into broader categories. Moving from open/initial coding toward axial/focused coding allows learners to practice identifying connections among specific codes and examining how key pieces of data relate to one another. Working together as a group to create axial/focused codes (i.e., themes) reinforces the inherently subjective nature of analyzing data. Simultaneously, this group process illustrates the iterative nature of data analysis whereby researchers continuously return to the data to question what it means for a given research question. Debriefing the process of creating axial/focused codes provides learners another opportunity to discuss how epistemologies influence data analysis and lead to different but equally legitimate ways of interpreting data.

Learners

To effectively facilitate the lesson described above, educators need to consider learners' developmental readiness. In particular, educators should consider whether or to what extent learners are ready to grapple with multiple perspectives and to see themselves as capable of generating knowledge. Also, educators need to recognize misconceptions or overly simplified conceptions learners might hold about qualitative research, which can range from believing there is only one right list of themes within the data to basing themes exclusively on the most frequent codes.

CODING DATA AND DEVELOPING THEMES

Developmental Readiness
Learners who want an authority figure such as an educator or established researcher to tell them the right way to conduct research are likely not developmentally ready to engage in this lesson and will need additional scaffolding prior to applying different epistemologies. Yet, even at more advanced developmental levels, learners may not bring a clear understanding of how coding data and developing themes fits into the broader research process. Thus, it will be important to help learners recognize that data analysis is not an isolated, stand-alone process but rather one that connects to other processes such as articulation of research questions, collection of data, and presentation of findings. Also, educators will likely need to emphasize that learners themselves are the experts for this lesson. That is, learners themselves have the opportunity to make decisions about what the data means.

Possible Misconceptions
From my experience, learners tend to bring two main misconceptions to the process of coding data and developing themes in qualitative research. First, learners often assume the process is clear cut and leads to one universal set of findings. Second, learners may see data analysis as a purely mechanical process or one that simply requires the latest and greatest technology; this misconception leads learners to miss the philosophical basis of generating codes and themes as well as the meaning-making processes necessary to interpret complex phenomena. Although technology can certainly assist with data analysis, this lesson is designed to help learners see that the essence of data analysis lies in decisions that researchers themselves make. Also, by working in groups to code data and develop themes and then debrief both processes, learners explore the philosophical and interpretive nature of data analysis.

Context

Because the process of coding data and developing themes inductively includes many challenges and requires learners to make meaning in complex ways, it is important to provide a high level of support. According to Baxter Magolda's (2004) learning partnerships model, which is based on a longitudinal study of college students' development, educators can balance the types of challenges inherent in qualitative data analysis with three key supports. These three key supports include drawing upon students' own experiences, portraying students as capable of generating knowledge, and collaborating with learners to make meaning. In this section, I explain how the lesson shared above incorporates each of these three key supports.

Drawing Upon Students' Own Experiences
The lesson draws upon students' own experiences through the intentional selection of an excerpt of data with which students can relate. By choosing an excerpt of data that describes a broad, student-focused aspect of higher education that learners are likely to have experienced or observed first-hand, educators ensure that students have a personal connection to the data and an internal basis for interpreting the data. In addition, this

lesson draws upon learners' own experiences in the debriefing sessions by asking students to reflect on and discuss their experiences coding data and developing themes. The questions in the debriefing sessions are designed to help students see the active role they played in data analysis.

Portraying Students as Capable of Generating Knowledge
Rather than showing students how other researchers code data and develop themes, this lesson positions students as researchers themselves and engages them in making key decisions such as determining what key phrases to underline in the data, what labels to use to summarize the data, and which codes to group together into themes. In essence, this lesson encourages students to develop their own process for analyzing data, which helps them build confidence in their research skills.

Collaborating With Learners to Make Meaning
This lesson involves two types of collaboration: (1) between the educator and learners, and (2) within groups of learners. The educator collaborates with learners by choosing a relevant excerpt of data for analysis and providing a basic structure for creating codes and developing themes while allowing learners freedom in how they apply the structure. The educator also collaborates with learners through the debriefing sessions by asking open-ended questions that prompt learners to make meaning of the processes they used to analyze the data. This lesson also encourages learners to collaborate with one another at various points, particularly when making meaning of the data on a broader level to develop themes. Both types of collaboration help learners see that interpretation of data requires them to consider multiple perspectives.

Ultimately, this lesson invites students to be researchers themselves and to experience the challenges as well as the rewards of making meaning of complex social phenomena. When facilitated successfully, this lesson allows students to embrace the subjectivity of data analysis and bring their own minds to the process of deciding what data means.

BIBLIOGRAPHY

Baxter Magolda, M. B., & King, P. M. (Eds.). (2004). *Learning partnerships: Theory and models of practice to educate for self-authorship*. Stylus.
> Provides an evidence-based model for designing developmentally appropriate educational experiences that foster meaningful learning. Chapters 3 and 8 discuss how to apply the model to educational contexts that are particularly relevant for research courses.

Crotty, M. (2021). *Foundations of social research: Meaning and perspective in the research process*. Routledge.
> Explains the major epistemologies that undergird current social science research and shows the link between epistemologies and methodologies; helps situate data collection and analysis within a broader philosophical context.

Eisner, E. W. (1998). *The enlightened eye: Qualitative inquiry and the enhancement of educational practice*. Prentice Hall.
> Examines educational research from an interdisciplinary lens by drawing upon methods and assumptions from the arts, humanities, and social sciences; helps researchers see and interpret what they see in innovative ways.

Galletta, A. (2013). *Mastering the semi-structured interview and beyond*. New York University Press.
> Provides in-depth guidance for conducting and interpreting semi-structured interviews. Chapter 2 includes excerpts of data from interview transcripts that educators can use for this lesson plan.

CODING DATA AND DEVELOPING THEMES

Jones, S. R., Torres, V., & Arminio, J. (2021). *Negotiating the complexities of qualitative research in higher education: Essential elements and issues* (3rd ed.). Taylor & Francis.

Provides a specific focus on qualitative research in higher education; highlights methodological challenges associated with designing and conducting high-quality, ethical research. Chapter 7 addresses issues related to analysis and interpretation of qualitative data.

K-State College of Education. (2018, January 3). *A walk in my shoes: First generation college students full documentary* [Video]. YouTube. https://www.youtube.com/watch?v=hQA5ahGFy5A

Provides a transcript from which educators can choose an excerpt for the purposes of helping students learn to code data and develop themes. A transcript from this type of documentary is useful if educators do not have access to raw, de-identified qualitative data.

Section VI

Mixed Methods

Section Editor: Chris Heasley

25

Introduction to Section VI

Mixed Methods

Chris Heasley

Gregory Corso, a well-known beat movement poet of the 1950s and 60s once posited, "If you have a choice of two things and can't decide, take both." Integrating components from both qualitative and quantitative approaches, mixed methods research finds itself in the middle of the research continuum (Creswell & Creswell, 2018). Fittingly, mixed method research uses both closed-ended (fixed response) and open-ended (void of predetermined response) questions to inform integrated data collection and analysis.

Philosophical assumptions informing the research paradigm is an important component of a research approach. Commonly situated in pragmatism, mixed methods studies are supported by an epistemology rooted in "practical understandings" of real-world issues and contexts (Patton, 2005, p. 153, also see Kelly & Cordeiro, 2020). However, it is important to recognize varying typologies are explored by some scholars. Stemming from its philosophical underpinning comes an intersection with design and specific methods (Creswell & Creswell, 2018).

Within mixed methods social science work, typically, we are centrally concerned with three considerations: interaction (e.g., parallel, explanatory, or exploratory), order (i.e., concurrent or sequential), and priority (Creswell et al., 2003). Here, priority (also called dominance) is relevant to which approach may be given more emphasis in the study; is it a large quantitative, small qualitative study, the inverse, or will both approaches be given equal weight? The chapters included in this section feature lessons with varying interaction and priority in mixed methods research with focus on how to frame, conduct, and interpret data within a specified approach. The last chapter in this section illustrates practices for presenting results and findings from data analysis within mixed methods work.

CHAPTER OVERVIEWS

Understanding in mixed methods research starts with contemplating the purpose of the approach. The chapter by Johnson and Fernandez, "Low Hanging Fruit, Ripe For Inquiry: Considering the Quantitative Dimensions of Mixed Methods Research," features a lesson plan that emphasizes quantitative data in mixed methods research. Employing an engagement and collaborative learning approach (Bruffee, 1999), they combine a case study

DOI: 10.4324/b23320-32

activity, focused on college access, with small group question and response exercises. Their aim is to help students explore the different ways quantitative questions and methods fit into research design. This lesson plan remains centered on developing questions that require quantitative methods and constructing quantitative strands that complement qualitative inquiry.

Sometimes unique approaches to learning can lead to wonderful new discoveries through knowledge and skill development. "Creating Your Masterpiece: Applying Brush Strokes to Qualitative Exploration of Mixed Methods Research," the chapter by Heasley, forces students to engage with difficult material starting with their imagination. The lesson prioritizes qualitative data in mixed methods research, using identified themes to create an instrument that best fits the expected sample of the study. In this way, qualitative data collection and analysis are contributory to subsequent quantitative methods. Purposefully, this chapter provides the learner with an innovative approach to discovery and sensemaking, emphasizing the qualitative component featured in exploratory sequential mixed methods design.

In the world of data visualization, the ways in which information can be presented is unending. Given this overwhelming availability of ceaseless options and the complexity of mixed methods research, it is easy to appreciate the struggle one might feel when trying to represent results in a visually meaningful way. The lesson provided by Garcia and Li, "Presenting and Visualizing a Mixed Methods Study," serves as an antidote to the aforementioned plight as they discuss how Joint Display Analysis (JDA) is helpful in data visualization of mixed methods findings. In group work, students come to experience how JDA may differ across iterations as it showcases a complement between both quantitative and qualitative methodological approaches. The end result of its use is a holistic representation of mixed methods findings presented in a palatable way for broad audience understanding.

Collective Contribution

Considering all three mixed methods lessons as a collective, there are four critical outcomes we wish the readership to appreciate. First, mixed methods research offers an alternative to single-approach studies. The power of mixed methods research is its ability to integrate two seemingly opposed research approaches into one study. Different from other methodologies, we are not restricted to stay in one lane. Second, these lessons remind us that appropriate study design is always guided by the research question(s), and for mixed methods, also by the interaction, order, and priority given in data collection and analysis. We have the ability to be beautifully creative and innovatively complex through flexible study design of mixed methods research. Third, the importance of discovery is amplified by engaging in learning through a variety of ways, techniques, and styles. Chapter authors' breadth of knowledge and approach to diverse instruction enhances new research skill development. Finally, their lessons advance understanding of mixed methods research in praxis, providing examples of varied research design, and presentation and visualization. The stones laid in these chapters build a pathway toward new confidence, skill development, and competency in mixed methods research.

INTRODUCTION TO SECTION VI

BIBLIOGRAPHY

Bruffee, K. A. (1999). *Collaborative learning: Higher education, interdependence, and the authority of knowledge.* Johns Hopkins University Press.

Creswell, J. W., Clark, V. L., Gutmann, M. L., & Hanson, W. E. (2003). Advanced mixed methods research design. In A. Tashakkori & C. Teddlie (Eds.), *Handbook of mixed methods in social and behavioral research* (pp. 209–240). Thousand Oaks, CA: Sage Publications.

Creswell, J. W., & Creswell, J. D., (2018). *Research design: Qualitative, quantitative, and mixed methods approaches,* (5th ed.). Thousand Oaks, CA: Sage.

Denzin, N. (2010). Moments, mixed methods, and paradigm dialogs. *Qualitative Inquiry, 16,* 419–427.

Kelly, L. M., & Cordeiro, M. (2020). Three principles of pragmatism for research on organizational processes. *Methodological Innovations, 13*(2), 1–10. https://doi.org/10.1177/2059799120937242

Patton, M. (2005). *Qualitative research & evaluation methods* (4th ed.). Los Angeles, CA: SAGE.

26

Low Hanging Fruit, Ripe for Inquiry

Considering the Quantitative Dimensions of Mixed Methods Research

Kayla M. Johnson and Frank Fernandez

INTRODUCTION

Mixed methods researchers combine quantitative and qualitative inquiry techniques and data sources in a single study to explore complex problems. When we teach research methods courses and advise graduate students, we begin by exploring the purposes of quantitative and qualitative research paradigms within our area of expertise, for example, across higher education topics. We suggest quantitative methods are best suited to "what" questions:

- *What* is the relationship between financial aid and graduation rates? (Identifying correlational relationships).
- In *what* ways does the relationship between campus racial climate and sense of belonging vary by students' racial identities? (Examining interactions or moderation in statistical relationships).
- *What* is the effect of an academic coaching intervention on student retention? (Estimating effects and supporting causal inferences).

In these ways, quantitative methods can estimate the statistical significance and relative size of relationships. However, quantitative approaches cannot tell us why those relationships exist; we rely on theory for that. Conversely, we counsel students that qualitative methods are best suited to address "how" questions that uncover processes, illuminate experiences, and describe their contextual significance:

- *How* do students experience atonement through restorative justice training?
- *How* do crisis counselors use intuition when supporting students who have experienced trauma?
- *How* do teachers stay motivated to teach when they lose face-to-face interactions with students?

As professors teaching introductory and advanced research methods courses in education, we work with many students who wish to answer both types of questions – *what*

DOI: 10.4324/b23320-33

happened and *how* did it happen? Those questions lead them to consider a mixed methods dissertation study. They are motivated by complex problems they believe require both quantitative and qualitative inquiry techniques to solve.

At the introductory level, we teach students that there are generally three ways qualitative and quantitative methods accompany each other in mixed methods studies (see Figure 26.1). (Although we offer these pragmatic categories, we recognize other scholars offer different typologies, and we recommend their readings at the end of this chapter.)

Most graduate students in education work, or aspire to work, in settings where they are surrounded by quantitative data. For instance, schools frequently keep demographic data, standardized test scores, attendance or discipline records, grade point averages, curricular experiences (individualized learning plans, gifted and talented education, dual enrollment, or even specific courses in high schools and colleges). These data are "low hanging fruit" and can often be used to begin a variety of different types of research projects (e.g., action research studies; program evaluations; course, program, or institutional assessments; etc.) and can provide insight for further quantitative or qualitative inquiry. For instance, if a researcher finds there is not a statistically significant relationship between enrollment in gifted and talented education and achievement (e.g., Bui et al., 2014), they could conduct a survey to measure parental involvement or other relevant variables. Alternatively, the researcher could interview students or teachers about how they experience gifted and talented education.

Alternatively, graduate students often draw inspiration from anecdotes and testimonies to ask whether qualitative data are generalizable beyond a small sample of participants. In this pattern, qualitative data precede quantitative data, and, in a sense, the qualitative data provide the conceptual framing for gathering or analyzing quantitative data. For example, a faculty member may repeatedly hear students talk about experiencing racialized micro- or macro-aggressions; the faculty member may then develop a survey to find out how frequently a representative sample of students experiences similar aggressions.

We work in an applied field, and many of our students are pursuing degrees that emphasize improving practice over building theory. The three arrangements in Figure

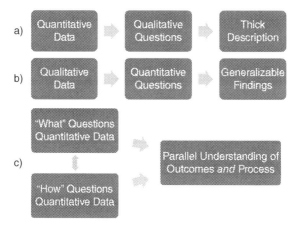

FIGURE 26.1 Three Combinations of Quantitative and Qualitative Methods

26.1 are all common in educational research where we use data to improve practice. In education, data and findings must often be practical if they are to be fundable or influence decision-making. Attending to these challenges of using multiple types of data to address problems requires action and reflection that gets students thinking about the kinds of data required to answer certain questions, and how all the data fits together in one cohesive design. Whether collected initially, secondarily, or in parallel to qualitative data, quantitative data help document how prevalent problems are in schools, record experiences or outcomes, and bolster claims to administrators, funders, and policymakers about influencing outcomes.

The lesson detailed below asks students to: a) reflect on a research problem that would be best addressed with both quantitative and qualitative data, and b) design the quantitative dimension(s) of a mixed methods study. It is a practical exercise – with connections to both K–12 and higher education – that mirrors how many graduate students in education select and design their dissertation studies. To further emphasize to students the importance of both quantitative and qualitative dimensions of mixed methods research design, we encourage readers to follow this lesson with its qualitative counterpart in this book, or to repeat this exercise with a focus on the qualitative dimensions of the study.

LESSON PLAN

Topic	*Designing the quantitative dimension of a mixed methods study*
Learning Objectives	• Students will consider a kind of research problem that necessitates mixed methods inquiry. • Students will develop research questions that require quantitative methods. • Students will articulate and justify the interaction, sequencing, priority, and integration of the quantitative dimension(s) of their design in relation to the qualitative dimension(s). • Students will begin to consider how to successfully integrate quantitative and qualitative data.
Needed Materials	• Printed case study prompt (at least one sheet per group); see Appendix A for a provided case study. • Big Post-it paper and markers (minimum of two sheets per group) • (*Optional*) Printed copy of Figure 26.1 (one sheet per group)
Pre-lesson Preparation	• *How can I scaffold this lesson?* This lesson is most appropriate for an introductory level research design course. For this lesson to be effective, students should have been introduced to both quantitative and qualitative research design, as well as to mixed methods design more generally. We recommend beginning this lesson with a brief recap of mixed methods design configurations (see Figure 26.1 as an example), as well as a review of the four key elements of mixed methods design: interaction, order/sequencing, priority, and integration. • *Do all students have the cultural context to understand the case study prompt?* The prompt we have created deals with the issue of college access in the rural United States, a topic that is relevant to graduate students pursuing degrees in K–12 and higher education. Although the case study prompt is meant to be self-contained, international students or students not pursuing graduate degrees in education may need additional information to understand this issue. This could be addressed by encouraging peer discussion and asking students in the class to share their own experiences.

LOW HANGING FRUIT, RIPE FOR INQUIRY

Topic	*Designing the quantitative dimension of a mixed methods study*

Activities	• Divide the class into groups of 3–4 students. If possible, make sure each group is composed of students interested in and/or knowledgeable about qualitative and quantitative methods.
	• Distribute big Post-it paper and markers to each group.
	• On the board or screen, recap the basic mixed methods design configurations and their main differences, as well as the four key concepts of mixed methods design: interaction, order/sequencing, prioritization, and integration. Give students an opportunity to ask clarifying questions. (*Optional*: Distribute Figure 26.1)
	• Distribute and introduce a case study prompt to the class. We have provided a case study in Appendix A and built the lesson around this case, but instructors can create their own cases as needed. Give groups 5 minutes to read the prompt, discuss it, and seek clarification.
	• On the board or screen, display the following prompt: "In your groups, develop a series of questions you think need to be addressed to better understand this situation. Write your questions on the first sheet of big paper and post it on the wall."
	• After 10 minutes of generating questions, have each group read their questions aloud to the class. For each group's list, have the class determine whether each question is better suited (or how well suited it is) to quantitative or qualitative methods. Label each one accordingly. If needed, ask probing questions such as:
	  a. Are you asking about relationships between variables or between experiences and outcomes (e.g., the relationship between school attendance and standardized test scores)?
	  b. Are you asking about the effect or influence of an intervention (e.g., an after-school tutoring program)?
	  c. Are you trying to develop a standard measure of an experience (e.g., sense of belonging)?
	  d. Are you trying to examine the ways that a relationship varies across groups of students (e.g., whether the relationship between attendance and odds of being recommended for gifted and talented education varies by student race)?
	  e. Are you trying to understand someone's lived experience (e.g., what it is like to receive recognition for exceptional work)?
	  f. Are you examining how groups of people cultivate shared meanings (e.g., how students develop school pride)?
	• Next, display the following prompt on the board or screen: "Reflect on the questions we have all posed. Revisit your original list of questions and revise it as needed." Sometimes students may think they are asking a quantitative question, but they are actually asking a qualitative question, or vice versa. They may need to revisit/revise their questions and consider how the ways they ask research questions informs their methods.
	• After 5 minutes of revising their questions, display the following prompt: "Separate your quantitative questions from your qualitative questions. Then, ask yourselves the following:
	  a. Which questions are most important?
	  b. How do these questions relate to one another?
	  c. Do any of these questions need to be answered before the others can be?"
	Explain that these questions relate to the interaction, order/sequencing, and prioritization of strands of data in a mixed methods research design.
	• After 15 minutes of group discussion, display the following prompt: "Now that you have determined a rough order for answering your questions and which questions are most important, turn your attention to the QUANTITATIVE questions you have developed. Thinking about your plans for interaction, sequencing, and prioritization, draw your research design on the second sheet of big paper. Following Figure 26.1, be sure to illustrate the sequencing of qualitative and quantitative data collection and the goals of the mixed method design."

Topic	*Designing the quantitative dimension of a mixed methods study*
	• After 10 minutes of group work, prompt students to: "Consider the types of data collection and analysis approaches you will need for the quantitative portion of your design. For instance, do you need access to institutional data your school has already collected? Is there a planned data collection effort you could join or 'piggyback' off (e.g., use as a starting point)? Do you need to collect new data (e.g., via a survey)? How would you analyze the quantitative data (e.g., calculating descriptive statistics; correlational regression methods; quasi-experimental approaches)? Add these details to your visual." • After 20 minutes of group work, ask students to discuss in their groups: "What will you gain from the quantitative findings? How will they substantially complement your qualitative findings? How will the mixed-method approach support research-to-practice implications?" • Give each group 5 minutes to show, explain, and justify their design decisions. Facilitate discussion after each group. • *(Optional)* Conclude by previewing the next activity, which will ask them to focus on the qualitative portion of their planned study. • Homework: Each student considers the kinds of quantitative questions they might pose and the methods they might use in their study/dissertation and how those questions might inform or be informed by other qualitative questions and methods.
Virtual Adaptations	This lesson is easily executed in a virtual learning environment and could be successfully implemented in a synchronous or asynchronous virtual classroom with minimal adaptation. *For synchronous classes:* • Prior to class, create a PDF document or Learning Management System (LMS) (e.g., Canvas) assignment page with the case study prompt and instructions. • Send each group to their own virtual breakout room for discussion between each activity. • Rather than big Post-it paper, students use Google Jamboard, Slides, or a similar tech tool to record their designs. Allow 5 additional minutes at the beginning for groups to get organized, create and share access to the tech tools, and so on. • Students share their designs and justifications using the Share Screen function in Zoom. *For asynchronous classes:* • Create an LMS module that contains: the case study prompt, group assignments and meeting instructions, and a discussion forum. • Instruct groups to find a time to meet synchronously via Zoom to discuss and create their design plans. • Rather than big Post-it paper, students use Google Jamboard, Slides, or a similar tech tool to record their questions and designs. • Each group posts their designs, and a brief justification (with options for written, audio, or video submissions), to the discussion forum. • Students engage in asynchronous discussion.
Assessment	• Formative Assessment: During group work time, move about the room to assess their understanding of why we use quantitative data and their ability to design a mixed methods study with a quantitative component. • Summative Assessment: Review homework which asks students to apply the day's lesson to their own emerging research interests.

INTELLECTUAL PREPARATION FOR LESSON

A sound mixed methods research design requires attention to four key details: the level of interaction between quantitative and qualitative strands, the order/sequencing of strands, the prioritization of strands, and the integration of strands. Appropriate planning of these details requires students to understand the rationales for basic mixed methods design configurations and when different kinds of data are needed. Students should read Creswell et al. (2003) prior to the lesson. If students have not taken introductory statistics or research design courses, they should be able to reference Trochim and Donnelly (2006) or its online component available from https://conjointly.com/kb/. Note instructors can register to use the Trochim and Donnelly online knowledge base here: https://run.conjoint.ly/account/login.

Core Ideas

In addition to the key concepts outlined above, this lesson focuses on two core ideas for designing the quantitative dimensions of a mixed methods study, as follows:

Developing Questions that Require Quantitative Methods
We sometimes work with students who plan to use quantitative methods but who pose qualitative questions, or vice versa. This lesson gets students thinking about the kinds of questions that require quantitative methods (i.e., "what" questions) and the kinds of quantitative methods and data collection efforts they could use to address those questions. In doing so, it facilitates learning that goes beyond mixed methods research design.

Designing Quantitative Strands that Complement Qualitative Strands
Mixed methods research should be intentional, with thoughtfully planned quantitative and qualitative strands that complement one another in meaningful ways. By beginning with a set of questions, then sorting them into quantitative and qualitative questions, and then considering which are more important, which may need to be answered first, and so forth, students think more intentionally about the ways quantitative data can complement qualitative data. However, research is also a series of compromises, and we must think about the practical realities of qualitative and quantitative data collection and analysis. At the end of this lesson, as time permits, students could reflect on the feasibility of their plans and how various circumstances may require adaptations without compromising the integrity of their overall design.

The Learner

We find students' plans to engage in mixed methods research are often foiled by two problems: a) not all research problems require a mixed methods design, and b) students often prioritize one method and tack on the other as an afterthought. We believe these challenges stem from the failure of graduate programs to provide adequate training in *both* quantitative and qualitative research designs – and the ways they can complement each other – which leads to a superficial understanding of mixed methods research.

Deepening Superficial Knowledge

This lesson confronts students' potential superficial understandings of mixed methods by pushing them to apply key components of mixed methods research design and explore different ways quantitative questions and methods fit in those key components. It also pushes learners to think about the purpose(s) for including quantitative methods in mixed methods research beyond the common refrains: because administrators or policymakers see them as more convincing than qualitative methods, because quantitative research is more fundable, or because quantitative researchers can publish more quickly.

Context

Our lesson on the quantitative dimensions of mixed methods uses two key strategies to facilitate student learning, as follows:

Practical Application

We learn best when we can readily apply new concepts to known situations (Neumann, 2005). Our college access case study is relevant for graduate students in a broad array of subdisciplines in education. Providing students with the opportunity to practice new skills in a way that connects with their experiences and interests can increase motivation, engagement, and learning.

Collaborative Learning

Drawing on Bruffee's (1999) work on engagement and collaborative learning, we recommend having students work in small groups throughout the lesson. Students, especially minoritized or underrepresented students, cannot merely be told they need to adopt new perspectives. Students should be led through experiences that allow them to learn through engagement and, ultimately, acculturate to academic norms – like principles of research design and research team collaboration. Bruffee (1999) found when students struggle, they learn better when they can connect esoteric or abstract ideas to their prior experiences. We offer the scenario of evaluating a college access program as something that should connect with personal and professional experiences in educational institutions, but alternate scenarios can be used to follow Bruffee's principles for collaborative learning. Additionally, mixing groups to include both quantitatively- and qualitatively-oriented students gives them experience in collaborating in teams that may share different paradigms, possess different skills, and have different goals.

APPENDIX A

CASE STUDY PROMPT: "INCREASING COLLEGE ACCESS"

You have been hired as a college access consultant for Nittany Public School District. NPSD is a rural district with two high schools: Beaver Tech and Atherton Central. NPSD has already provided you with basic demographic data, GPAs, standardized test scores, and postsecondary enrollment rates for all students at both high schools. You immediately

LOW HANGING FRUIT, RIPE FOR INQUIRY

notice students who attend Beaver Tech generally have higher GPAs and test scores and enroll in college at twice the rate of students from Atherton Central.

Your task is to design a research study that will help NPSD improve their students' postsecondary enrollment rates. You have determined you will need both quantitative and qualitative data to understand the issue and to convince the NPSD Board that your recommendations will be effective.

As you plan your research study, consider the following:

- What QUESTIONS do I have about this situation that can be answered with quantitative data?
- What QUESTIONS do I have about this situation that can be answered with qualitative data?
- What STRATEGIES for collecting data are at my disposal?

BIBLIOGRAPHY

Bruffee, K. A. (1999). *Collaborative learning: Higher education, interdependence, and the authority of knowledge*. Johns Hopkins University Press.

Bui, S. A., Craig, S. G., & Imberman, S. A. (2014). Is gifted education a bright idea? Assessing the impact of gifted and talented programs on students. *American Economic Journal: Economic Policy*, 6(3), 30–62. https://doi.org/10.1257/pol.6.3.30

Coulson, H. L., Zou, Y., & Fernandez, F. (2022). *Transformational university leadership: A case study for 21st century leaders and aspirational research universities*. Emerald Publishing.

Creswell, J. W., & Clark, V. L. P. (2018). *Designing and conducting mixed methods research* (3rd ed.). SAGE.

Creswell, J. W., Plano Clark, V. L., Gutmann, M. L., & Hanson, W. E. (2003). Advanced mixed methods research designs. In A. Tashakkori & C. Teddlie (Eds.), *Handbook of mixed methods in social and behavioral research* (pp. 209–240). SAGE.

Ertesvåg, S. K., Sammons, P., & Blossing, U. (2021). Integrating data in a complex mixed methods classroom interaction study. *British Educational Research Journal*, 47(3), 654–673. https://doi.org/10.1002/berj.3678

Goertz, G., & Mahoney, J. (2012). *A tale of two cultures: Qualitative and quantitative research in the social sciences*. Princeton University Press.

Neumann, A. (2005). Observations: Taking seriously the topic of learning in studies of faculty work and careers. In E. G. Creamer & L. Lattuca (Eds.), *New directions for teaching and learning: No. 102. Advancing faculty learning through interdisciplinary collaboration* (pp. 63–83). Jossey-Bass.

Trochim, W. M. K., & Donnelly, J. P. (2006). *Research methods: The essential knowledge base* (3rd ed.). Atomic Dog.

Whitehurst, G. (2014). Relying on evidence. In C. E. Finn Jr. & R. Sousa (Eds.), *What lies ahead for America's children and their schools* (pp. 177–189). Hoover Press.

27

Creating Your Masterpiece

Applying Brush Strokes to Qualitative Exploration of Mixed Methods Research

Chris Heasley

INTRODUCTION

The *Mona Lisa* is arguably "the best known, the most visited, the most written about, the most sung about, the most parodied work of art in the world"(Lichfield, 2005, para.1). The work of Italian polymath, Leonardo Da Vinci, the *Mona Lisa* painting is an archetypal masterpiece of the Italian Renaissance. Another piece of worthy artistry drawn by Da Vinci is *L'uomo vitruviano*, more commonly known as *Vitruvian Man*. The drawing is what Leonardo Di Vinci believed to be the ideal human body proportions and is based on the notes of Vitruvius, a 1st century BC Roman architect. So, what does all this talk of art have to do with mixed methods research?

Vitruvian Man is an integrated work of art and mathematics, a blend of two distinct disciplines used to illustrate deep knowledge of proportions. Mixed methods research, like *Vitruvian Man*, demonstrates a combination of qualitative and quantitative methodologies. Using Da Vinci's technique as inspiration, the purpose of this lesson is to provide an interactive approach where students are artists of their own masterpiece, one in which they explore the qualitative dimensions of mixed methods research.

LESSON PLAN

Topic	*Exploring qualitative dimension of mixed methods research design*
Learning Objectives	• Students will explore the central mixed methods components: interaction, sequencing, prioritization, and integration within the lesson, expressing their design in relation to the quantitative dimension(s). • Students will create a data source from which they will gather, organize, and categorize information into themes (qualitative design). • Students will integrate qualitative data in constructing a survey for the quantitative phase of exploratory sequential mixed methods research. • Students will experience the interconnectedness between qualitative and quantitative data as complements of one another in mixed methods.

DOI: 10.4324/b23320-34

CREATING YOUR MASTERPIECE

Topic	*Exploring qualitative dimension of mixed methods research design*
Needed Materials	• Each student will need a surface upon which they will create their portrait (e.g., flat canvas board, newspaper print, butler block paper, sketchbook paper, cutting board, etc.). • In order to promote choice, varying art supplies are needed. Recommendations include: markers, colored pens and pencils, water colors, acrylic paints, charcoal, chalk, modeling clay, and Lego blocks. The instructor will also need dry-erase markers for posting prompts on the classroom white board. • (*Online*) Students may construct their image using art supplies they have at their location and share their piece via their online computer camera. Alternatively, students may also choose to illustrate in a graphic program of their choice using an integrated electronic touchpad and stylus tool.
Pre-lesson Preparation	• *How can I scaffold this lesson?* The "Create your Masterpiece" experience is one that requires no professional skill or expertise in artistry. In fact, I have found those with little or no formal art training do better with this experience as they are not seeking to create the perfect product (i.e., image or sculpture), and instead, are more interested in the overall process. Importantly, this lesson is meant to follow an introduction to both qualitative and quantitative research epistemologies, ontologies, and axiologies. Students should also have a working knowledge about appropriate data collection and analysis techniques for both qualitative (e.g., focus groups, thematic coding, etc.) and quantitative (e.g., survey construction, variables, etc.) approaches. Lastly, this lesson is meant to take approximately 2.5–3 hours to complete. It could be divided over two interactions, but works best if started and finished in the same setting. • *Do all students have the cultural context to appreciate the "Create your Masterpiece" experience?* Students are asked to be creative in illustrating a self-portrait. No specific artistic technique or style is requested. In fact, the art itself is of little importance in comparison to the process and synthesizing of the experience.
Activities	• Students are informed they will take part in a self-portrait exercise as part of a qualitative data collection process. The primary research question guiding the way students draw/create their self-portrait is: *How do graduate students experience this academic program through their lived experiences (e.g., identities, social roles, or personality traits, among others)?* along with the secondary question: *What factors are most salient to this student experience?* These questions should be visible for the duration of this lesson. • Now students will be creating a self-portrait. They may use any art supplies made available for this class project. • Give the students 45 minutes to craft their masterpiece using any medium or combination of mediums they want. Emphasize there is no "one" technique or style being sought here. They are merely trying to create a representation of self through art. Perfection is not the goal. • After 45 minutes, ask students to look at their self-portrait. On a separate piece of paper, have students list up to 10 characteristics (words, statements, or complete sentences) they would use to describe what they see in the image they have constructed. Specifically, what identities, social roles, or personality traits have they captured in their artwork? Would they describe an adult learner, graduate student, parent, first generation college student, Black, Hispanic, transgender, and so on? These will serve as part of the initial data in the qualitative data collection process.

Topic	*Exploring qualitative dimension of mixed methods research design*

- After composing a list of the identities, roles, and traits, students will "show and tell" their artwork in small groups of 3–4 people. This will give everyone a turn to share in a focus group (FG) setting. When a student is sharing their work, they are the acting "moderator" of the FG.
- Each moderator will answer the following questions in their FG setting (the instructor provides prompts on a distributed flier, a dry-erase board, or questions projected via a pre-loaded PowerPoint slide deck):
  a. Why did you choose the medium that you selected to illustrate yourself?
  b. How did you select your colors?
  c. What stylistic representation did you use to do your portraiture (e.g., impressionism, abstract art, or realism, among others)? Why?
  d. What facial or body expression (pose) did you give yourself? Why did you give yourself that expression?
  e. Did you provide a background? If so, what background did you choose, and why?

These initial questions guide the students through a reflective exercise to begin to make meaning as to why they illustrated themselves the way they did. These low-risk questions allow the student to become comfortable discussing their work with others.

- Once the student moderator's presentation is over, they are silent while others in the group provide the characteristics they see in the student's image (the identities, social roles, or personality traits captured in the artwork). Here, the group shares how they interpret the moderator's identities (e.g., race, gender, religious, age, etc.), social roles (e.g., caregiver, students, career, etc.), and personality traits (e.g., friendly, apprehensive, pensive, etc.) captured in the masterpiece.
- During this process the moderator is actively listening to the group feedback and taking notes to accurately summarize the critical words and thoughts of others. Later, the moderator will compare the group's observations with their previously written list of characteristics.
- Within the FG setting, the purpose is to have students begin to understand how they view themselves and how others view them. Each student's turn as moderator should last no more than five minutes.

NOTE: After everyone has been a moderator, the next steps in the lesson are individual work.

- Students are asked to reflect on the FG feedback given to them about their self-portrait. What thoughts and statements resonated from the FG participants? Each student will generate a complete list of phrases from the comments (e.g., identities, roles, personality traits, etc.), shared by the FG participants. This list should be inclusive of the characteristics the moderator developed about their art before commencing the FG activity. Some examples of phrases might include: parent of young children, working adult balancing career and school, life-long learner seeking advanced degree, first-generation Latina from rural community, among others. This is not an exhaustive list.
- Serving as their qualitative data source, students will begin sorting and categorizing their data (see the "Candy Sort" lesson for ideas on how to properly organize data). This exercise is expected to take no more than 20 minutes. The end result is a list of words and phrases placed into 3–5 named themes.
- To complete the aforementioned task, students will synthesize data (their words and phrases), grouping statements into categories. For example, from the following statements/phrases: parent to 3 elementary-aged children, community service oriented, and nurturing growth in others, one might derive "caregiver to others" as a named theme.

CREATING YOUR MASTERPIECE

Topic	Exploring qualitative dimension of mixed methods research design

	• The final step in the qualitative analysis process is creating *statements of inquiry* using the named theme. These statements will be used in the quantitative survey construction process. Utilizing the example given in the previous bullet point, a statement of inquiry could be: "The role of caregiver is salient for me as a graduate student and shapes my view of the world."
	 NOTE: The next steps in the lesson utilize the analyzed qualitative data to create a survey for use in quantitative data collection, thereby illustrating the qual to quant nature of mixed methods research.
	 • The statements of inquiry should be drafted in a way so they can be answered using an itemized rating scale (such as a Likert scale). Students will utilize their statements of inquiry to derive rated responses from participants. Using the previous example, the instructions and statement on a survey might read:
	 Please indicate your level of agreement (1= strongly disagree, 2= disagree, 3= neither disagree nor agree, 4= agree, 5= strongly agree) with the following statement: "The role of caregiver is salient for me as a graduate student and shapes my view of the world."
	 Students may choose to use a consistent itemized scale for all statements or may select varied itemized rating scales. Approximately 20 minutes is given to draft a survey instrument using qualitatively themed statements of inquiry.
	 • With the time remaining in class, provide a mini-discussion/lecture detailing the exploratory sequential (i.e., exploring qualitative data collection and analysis with the intent for use in completing quantitative data collection) mixed methods design. Probe students for comprehension using guided questions:
	   a. How is each component of mixed methods actualized in this lesson (i.e., interaction, sequencing, prioritization, and integration)?
	   b. What data sources were created through this lesson? What process was used to collect and analyze data?
	   c. How was qualitative data used for quantitative data collection?
	   d. Lastly, ask students to articulate the interconnectedness between qualitative and quantitative data as complements of one another in mixed methods.
	 • Homework: Students finish drafting their surveys by adding demographic questions and by comparing their work with others in the class (suggested through an online sharing program). The instructor may also include an extended assignment, in which the student finds a published survey for comparison, so as to check validity of the student's work. An online search of the dissertation/thesis library might prove helpful to the latter portion of this homework as dissertations typically include a copy of survey instruments in their appendices.
	 Suggested Lesson Timeline

Sharing research questions; giving instructions for self-portrait.	5 minutes
Creating self-portrait.	45 minutes
Developing <10 characteristics.	10 minutes
Focus Groups (3–4 ppl in each group).	20 minutes
Listing all characteristics (combining all data).	10 minutes
Sorting and organizing data. Creating 3–5 statements from key themes.	25 minutes
Survey construction, turn qual themes/statements into quant survey questions.	20 minutes
End of class discussion on exploratory sequential mixed methods design.	15 minutes

Topic	*Exploring qualitative dimension of mixed methods research design*

Virtual Adaptations	Whether teaching in a synchronous or asynchronous virtual classroom, this lesson can be easily modified for learning with minimal adaptations.
	For synchronous instruction:
	• Prior to class, create a PowerPoint slide deck with all the prompts available for students to review as they navigate through this lesson.
	• Students can craft their self-portrait at their location and upload a picture of their artwork. Tech savvy students may choose to illustrate in a graphic program of their choice using an integrated electronic touchpad and stylus tool.
	To facilitate focus groups, utilize the breakout rooms feature on the virtual application.
	• Students may choose Google Jamboard, Google Slides, or a similar application or tool for recordkeeping. Remember to allow additional time for utilization and access of files in a virtual realm.
	For asynchronous instruction:
	• Prior to class, create the PowerPoint slide deck.
	• Students upload their artwork.
	• To simulate focus groups, there are several worthy options for consideration.
	   ○ Utilize a *discussion post* with students' written responses to focus group prompts. Classmates then respond asynchronously with feedback.
	   ○ Students can also use Google Jamboard, Google Slides, or a similar application or tool for providing their narrative response and giving feedback.
	   ○ Students may pre-record a short video or audio response to focus group questions. Feedback is then provided through the same means.

Assessment	• Formative Assessment: Throughout the duration of the lesson, it is important to formatively assess student understanding and commitment to the process. This can be done successfully by relocating oneself in different parts of the learning space while practicing active listening and providing clarity to inquiries given by participating students. • Summative Assessment: Review homework, the quantitative survey for completion.

INTELLECTUAL PREPARATION FOR LESSON

With confidence, graduate students often declare their methodology before knowing their topic. Of course, this proclamation is implausible without the research question(s) to inform appropriate methodological process. While many experts are familiar with the role research questions play in dictating the appropriate method of discovery, it seems our students often remain unfamiliar with this process. Furthermore, students face an even more challenging predicament when adding in the complexity of a mixed methods approach. To help alleviate this challenge, I describe this lesson's core ideas and considerations of the learner and the context.

Core Ideas

This chapter gives attention to two core ideas: (1) understanding the importance of the research question(s) and their role in selecting an appropriate methodology; and (2) acknowledging the worth of both qualitative and quantitative research approaches in mixed methods design.

CREATING YOUR MASTERPIECE

Role of the Research Question(s)
Given a plethora of mixed methods research designs for consideration (e.g., convergent parallel, transformative mixed, embedded mixed, explanatory sequential, etc.), selecting the appropriate approach can be daunting. However, the correct study approach is always determined by the research question(s). Consider how, in a sea of complexity, we find our direction by first asking where we want to go. Similarly, our research question(s) provides direction to our approach. Give thought to the four components in mixed methods design: interaction, sequencing, prioritization, and integration (Creswell et al., 2003; also see Tashakkori & Teddlie, 2010). How do we envision these components being mapped to answer our study inquiry?

Worthiness of Qual and Quant Approaches in Mixed Methods Design
What happens when our inquiry takes us beyond just a single-mode methodological approach? In these cases, we find ourselves interested in exploring mixed methodological design. Here, we acknowledge the need to extend beyond either a qualitative or quantitative approach. Pluralistic processes allude to intentionality, intricacy, and integration. Worthiness is given to all parts of the process. Similarly, mixed methods studies are not meant to showcase one approach with complexity and the other with simplicity. All components of the study, both qualitative and quantitative, are given equal time and development as there is a reliance on each to complete the whole. This core idea is given further attention in the misconception section of this lesson.

The Learner

The effectiveness and value of the lesson amounts to little if the learner's needs are not considered in the planning process. Included in this practice is understanding the prior competency and skills the learners bring into the learning space. What follows are two central thoughts about the learner. First, I reflect on what knowledge students should master prior to attempting this lesson; and second, I discuss seemingly common misconceptions of mixed methods design.

Previous Learning and Misconceptions
In preparing this lesson, the content was developed based on the assumption students have had cursory instruction and learning on research paradigms and their epistemological, ontological, and axiological foundations; specifically, how knowledge is formed, reality shaped, and values inculcated within each. Differentiating between philosophical underpinnings of common research approaches is essential learning upon which this lesson builds. In academic programs with which I am familiar, mixed methods instruction follows single approach design and therefore, foundational knowledge of the separate parts will help in understanding their interconnectedness within mixed methods design. Creswell and Creswell (2018) provide a broad overview should students need additional readings in this area of understanding.

Frequent misconceptions learners often make about mixed methods research lie in the rigor and structure of the study. For some, perhaps emphasis placed on interaction, sequencing, prioritization, and integration suggests the qualitative research approach is more important than the other. This ill-informed misconception reduces study value. Evidence of this practice is seen when students who favor qualitative methodologies, subsequently add an incomplete or insubstantial quantitative portion to their mixed methods study. This is a cautionary tale. Equal attention must be given to both the quantitative and qualitative aspects of the study design. Working through this lesson, students are asked to confront their misconceptions about qualitative to quantitative mixed methods research. They are pushed to think beyond false impressions, and experience the full scope and possibilities of exploratory sequential mixed methods design.

The Context

"Creating your Masterpiece" is a lesson on the qualitative dimensions of mixed methods research and relies on two factors to support student learning: *creative learning and reflective practice*, and *enriched sensemaking*. Both are discussed in greater detail below.

Creative Learning and Reflective Practice

Borrowing from Maxine Greene (1995), this lesson invites students to cultivate their own source of data and meaning in context. Application of the imagination through art can be a freeing experience; one where the voiceless can speak and the marginalized claim power (Greene, 1995). Being in the presence of art and participating in its creative process makes transactions between the artist and the viewer possible. In this learning space, we share knowledge and understanding; we deepen our relationship with one another through artistry and reflective practice. Within this place, we also avail ourselves to humble critique from peers while undergoing deep introspective discourse examining our identities, social roles, and character traits.

Enriched Sensemaking

A cornerstone for qualitative research is the process by which we explore participant experiences. Specifically, we collect data and analyze others' personal experiences, in an attempt to understand the "meaning individuals or groups ascribe to a social or human problem" (Creswell & Creswell, 2018, p. 4). In essence, we engage in this form of inquiry for sensemaking. An asset of this lesson is helping students visualize sensemaking (skill) development as an integral element in developing a quantitative process. This lesson allows students to confront their misunderstandings about scholarly research and practice. It engages students in building a bridge, linking two seemingly contradictory research approaches. Sensemaking is enriched when we more clearly see mixed methods research situated in the middle of the research spectrum, where one approach is accountable to another.

Similar to the integrative process used by Leonardo Da Vinci in his artistry, mixed methods research blends components from two research approaches to paint a beautiful picture (Creswell & Creswell, 2018).

BIBLIOGRAPHY

Creswell, J. W., & Creswell, J. D., (2018). *Research design: Qualitative, quantitative, and mixed methods approaches,* (5th ed.). Thousand Oaks, CA: SAGE.

Creswell, J. W., & Plano Clark, V. L. (2018). *Designing and conducting mixed methods research* (3rd ed.). SAGE.

Creswell, J. W., Plano Clark, V. L., Gutmann, M. L., & Hanson, W. E. (2003). Advanced mixed methods research designs. In A. Tashakkori & C. Teddlie (Eds.), *Handbook of mixed methods in social and behavioral research* (pp. 209–240). SAGE.

Goertz, G., & Mahoney, J. (2012). *A tale of two cultures: Qualitative and quantitative research in the social sciences.* Princeton University Press.

Greene, J. C., Caracelli, V. J., & Graham, W. F. (1989). Toward a conceptual framework for mixed-method evaluation designs. *Educational Evaluation and Policy Analysis, 11*(3), 255–274.

Greene, M. (1995). *Releasing the imagination: Essays on education, the arts, and social change.* San Francisco, CA: Jossey-Bass.

Lichfield, J. (2005, April). The moving of the *Mona Lisa. The Independent.* London. Retrieved from https://www.independent.co.uk/news/world/europe/the-moving-of-the-mona-lisa-530771.html

Morse, J. M., (1991). Approaches to qualitative-quantitative methodological triangulation. *Nursing Research, 40*(1), 120–123.

Plano Clark, V. L., & Creswell, J. W. (2008). *The mixed methods reader.* Thousand Oaks, CA: SAGE.

Tashakkori, A., & Teddlie, C. (Eds.). (2010). *SAGE handbook of mixed methods in social and behavioral research* (2nd ed.). Thousand Oaks, CA: SAGE.

28

Presenting and Visualizing a Mixed Methods Study

Hugo A. García and Xinyang Li

INTRODUCTION

Typically, a purely quantitative or qualitative study follows a "standard form" of presentation and visualization. For instance: (a) a table that reports the parameter estimations with standard errors, p-values, and effect size in a regression analysis, (b) a path diagram that visualizes the best-fitted model with all the variables (latent and manifest) as well as the directional casual path in a SEM analysis, or (c) a cluster of emerged themes followed by representative quotes that allude to the themes in a qualitative case study. However, the presentation and visualization in a mixed methods study could vary dramatically due to the study's planning and designing. Referring to Creswell and his colleagues' (2003) summary on timing, weighting, mixing, and theorizing when designing a mixed methods study, the presentation of the results and findings should also reflect the early planning and strategizing of the study, just as it does for other procedures (e.g., data collection, management, manipulation, analysis, and interpretation). More specifically, when designing the study, are there ways to integrate both approaches that better convey the findings to an audience? In this chapter, we discuss how instructors can work with students on how to present mixed methodological studies.

Writing and presenting the results and findings of qualitative or quantitative studies has a long tradition; however, presenting/visualizing the results from a mixed methods design study in a coherent manner could be a challenge, especially for emerging scholars. Indeed, a common approach is to follow the conventional way of presenting qualitative and quantitative results separately, each abiding by standard practices prescribed by associations or institutions. Then, relying on the writings to convey how each part works in tandem to address the study's findings/results. However, we take a different approach by discussing and illuminating how utilizing a Joint Display Analysis (JDA) can enhance the presentation of mixed methodological approaches, as it allows for the presentation of both approaches simultaneously instead of separately (Fetters, 2020; Gutterman et al., 2015; Johnson et al., 2017). A proper JDA would include the quantitative data (e.g., parameter estimates), the qualitative data (e.g., quotes from participants), and more importantly, be arranged in a way to paint a clearer picture of the phenomenon being explored to

DOI: 10.4324/b23320-35

PRESENTING AND VISUALIZING A MIXED METHODS STUDY

better understand how the different methodological findings complement each other. An adapted example is included in Appendix A. Students will understand the process of developing a visual presentation through joint display, which is a process that may differ across iterations, and thus different from a pure qualitative/quantitative study or traditional way of presenting mixed methods when one just has two separate parts. This showcases how each methodological approach complements another and sketches a better picture of what was discovered.

LESSON PLAN

Topic	*Presenting/Visualizing a Mixed Methods Study through Joint Display Analysis*
Learning Objectives	• Students will learn how to create and organize Joint Display Analysis (JDA). • Students will learn what is it, how it works, and the value of presenting data via JDA. • Students will learn different ways to present various types of information with tables, diagrams, and wheel charts. • Students will utilize paper and software to organize and present data.
Needed Materials	• Standard easel and 25 x 30-inch flip chart for each group. • Various color markers. • Identify a few published mixed-method studies in the field that present qualitative and quantitative findings separately and which allow students to use the study's findings to apply JDA and understand how JDA can improve the presentation of data.

Pre-lesson Preparation	• *How can I scaffold this lesson?* This lesson is most appropriate for a mid-level research design course. For this lesson to be effective, students should already have a solid understanding of both qualitative and quantitative research. Since the JDA is about communicating and disseminating the results, we recommend beginning this lesson by recapping the results and findings of data collected or obtained from secondary sources. This will allow the instructor to prepare students for the creation of a JDA. This lesson is meant to take approximately 1.5–2 hours to complete.
	• *Do all students have the cultural context to understand the JDA adapted example?* Students are asked to be creative in integrating the qualitative and quantitative data in a figure. For our JDA example, we used data from a study exploring mid-level staff satisfaction utilizing empowerment theory. Students who lack work experience may not completely understand the role or experience of mid-level staff. Thus, a brief explanation of the challenges that employees who have mid-level positions within complex organizations, such as colleges and universities, have to confront may be warranted.
	• Students should read mixed method research studies that present qualitative findings and quantitative results separately to better understand how they are traditionally presented. Here are three examples:
	   ◦ Fong, C. J., and J. M. Krause. 2014. Lost confidence and potential: A mixed methods study of underachieving college students' sources of self-efficacy. *Social Psychology of Education*, 17, 249–268. doi:10.1007/s11218-013-9239-1.
	   ◦ Potnis, D., Deosthali, K., Zhu, X., & McCusker, R. (2018). Factors influencing undergraduate use of e-books: A mixed methods study. *Library and Information Science Research, 40*(2), 106–117. https://doi.org/10.1016/j.lisr.2018.06.001.
	   ◦ Strayhorn, T. L. (2015). Factors influencing black males' preparation for college and success in STEM majors: A mixed methods study. *Western Journal of Black Studies, 39*(1), 45–63.

Topic	Presenting/Visualizing a Mixed Methods Study through Joint Display Analysis

Activities	Overall, the class is divided into three stages:
	• The first stage starts with a review appraising the design of mixed methods study, which should guide the reasoning for every following step of the study. Hence, the visualization/presentation of the results and findings are no exception. Students will participate in an activity sketching a joint display on a flipchart to visually organize the presentation of qualitative and quantitative results. This stage focuses on linking what has been taught in the mixed methods study design, and developing a draft for each group to work on throughout the following stages.
	• The second stage includes a lecture on Joint Display Analysis (JDA), in which the instructor will formally introduce JDA with provided examples (see supplementary materials in Appendix A), including concepts, usual forms of the display, and things to consider when implementing JDA. An activity updating the previous draft is arranged. This stage focuses on enhancing students' understanding of JDA, especially within the examples. Moreover, it is vital for the instructor to emphasize that JDA should be an iterative process.
	• The third stage includes a final discussion regarding the software (PowerPoint, Prezi, Lucidchart, MAXQDA) to use when building different JDAs, given the form of visualization (tables, diagrams, wheel-charts, flowcharts) and the context of the presentation (e.g., printed poster vs. online lecture/presentation).
	• Prior to class, students will read assigned mixed methods journal articles (see Needed Materials section).
	• In a whole class setting, the instructor will lead a discussion (15–20 mins) on the results of assigned mixed methods articles (see Creswell and his colleagues' (2003) work on typologies). Probe how the results were presented in these articles. The discussion could involve:
	  ◦ Is it a sequential or concurrent design (i.e., timing)?
	  ◦ Is it a qual-first or quant-first structure (i.e., timing)?
	  ◦ Is it a study concentrating on qualitative, quantitative, or equally-weighted (i.e., weighting)?
	  ◦ What is the function of each part? Comparing, supporting, connecting, embedding (i.e., mixing)?
	  ◦ What visualization/presentation did the author(s) use?
	• Divide the class into groups of 3–5 students.
	• For the next 15–20 minutes, ask students to brainstorm and sketch the possible visualization/presentation that incorporates both qualitative and quantitative on the flipchart. More specifically, students need to decide:
	  ◦ What information to include in the display
	  ◦ How to arrange the information to reflect the timing, weighting, and mixing of the study
	• The instructor could observe the class during the session and give hints or suggestions, if needed, such as:
	  ◦ Encouraging multiple drafts.
	  ◦ Rearranging the layout in the space.
	  ◦ Using different colors to categorize themes.
	• Then, for the next 15–20 minutes, ask each group to share their draft of the data presentation they sketched on paper. They then discuss and reflect on the rationale, advantages/disadvantages of their draft, as well as the challenges they may have encountered. Typically, the discussion revolves around:
	  ◦ How can we make sense of the visualization/presentation while accommodating the design of the mixed methods study (timing, weighting, mixing)?
	  ◦ How might groups come up with different solutions (e.g., table with qual and quant side by side, flowchart to connect qual and quant, etc.)?
	  ◦ How can we incorporate colors, shapes, and so on, in the drawing for an extra layer of information?
	  ◦ How can we balance the JDA between including meaningful information and avoiding a convoluted display?

PRESENTING AND VISUALIZING A MIXED METHODS STUDY

Topic	Presenting/Visualizing a Mixed Methods Study through Joint Display Analysis
	<ul><li>Wrap up the first stage of the activity by explaining that what students have done is build a joint display for a mixed methods study. Then, provide a 15–20 minutes lecture on Joint Display Analysis with adapted examples (see Appendix A). The lecture will focus on exploring:<ul><li>What is Joint Display Analysis (JDA)?</li><li>What are some usual forms of joint display?<ul><li>Tables.</li><li>Diagrams.</li><li>Wheel chart.</li><li>Flow chart.</li></ul></li><li>Why is it important to present mixed methods in an integrated way?</li></ul></li><li>For the next 15 minutes, ask students to discuss in groups and update their drafts of the visualization/presentation. The update could potentially include:<ul><li>Changing thedisplay form.</li><li>Rearranging the position of qual and quant part.</li><li>Trimming excessive information.</li></ul></li><li>During the activity, the instructor could guide the developmental process when needed. Then, wrap up the second stage of activity by emphasizing that the JDA should:<ul><li>Follow the design of the study (timing, weighting, mixing).</li><li>Have no "standard form" or have a "one size (format) fits all" design: be creative in using JDA for storytelling.</li><li>Have an iterative nature.</li><li>Balance the amount of information to be included for readability and interpretation.</li></ul></li><li>In the last stage of the course (15–20 mins), the instructor will discuss the tools and software that could be used for building different types of joint displays (non-exhaustive list):<ul><li>Word/Excel for tables.</li><li>PowerPoint/Google Slides for wheel charts.</li><li>Prezi for diagrams (also suitable for interactive display in presentation).</li><li>Lucidchart for flow chart/diagrams.</li><li>MAXQDA/NVIVO.</li></ul>For instance, the Insert Chart function in Excel could be utilized to generate multi-layered wheel charts, and further text and/or integration with other forms of presentation could be added in PowerPoint. The availability of software might vary across institutions, so we suggest the instructor seek advice from their IT department. There are no standard tools for making the JDA and the list above is subject to change given the instructor's needs, as well as the programs or software that students are trained to use in their classroom.</li><li>Homework suggestion: Students create a joint display for their own study based on their (proposed) mixed methods design. Alternatively, students create a joint display for a (self-identified or instructor-assigned) published study. Students are encouraged to be creative when it comes to the tool/software selection for the homework because there is no "fixed" or "standard" form of JDA.</li></ul>
Virtual Adaptations	The virtual adaptations of this course may be made with two alterations:<ul><li>Instead of a group activity, in stage one, each student develops a joint display in Microsoft PowerPoint. Then, a follow-up discussion ensues with volunteers sharing their screens, preferably those who developed different forms of joint display.</li><li>Instead of using markers and flip charts, the blank template of different types of joint displays such as tables, diagrams, and wheel charts will be shared/assigned to students in stage two. Students could either choose to update their joint display with the provided template or come up with their version.</li></ul>

Topic	Presenting/Visualizing a Mixed Methods Study through Joint Display Analysis
Assessment	Grade students' homework project (or final if applicable) based on the following rubrics: • Alignment: The joint display aligns with the mixed methods design in the proposal/study and fits the timing, weighting, and mixing of the design. • Arrangement: The joint display is arranged in a readable, presentable, and meaningful way. • Articulation: The joint display sufficiently answers the research questions (in the context of paper/poster/reports).

INTELLECTUAL PREPARATION FOR LESSON

Most scholars and researchers tend to gravitate towards a specific area of methodological experience (either quantitative or qualitative) and assume most of the traditions and expectations of presenting quantitative findings within a qualitative study or vice versa. These traditions and expectations may hinder our ability to truly present a mixed methodological study in a way that best showcases the strengths of mixed methods. To help overcome some of these obstacles, we discuss the core ideas presented in this chapter, what the learner may have previously experienced that may create challenges when thinking about how to present mixed methods data, and how to facilitate the process of developing a joint display.

Core Ideas

The use of Joint Display Analysis (JDA) is a very useful way to display mixed method data to various audiences. We have discussed how it can be utilized for visual presentation for a mixed methods study with real examples. The instructor can modify the different types of examples of JDA provided in this chapter, which allows the instructor to: (a) form their own example that fits the needs in their field, (b) teach students the strategies to adapt the JDA to different designs of mixed methods study, and (c) teach students the process of JDA. Overall, students should takeaway from this lesson that: (1) there are various ways to present findings, (2) there are various programs and software that enables them to create a JDA, and (3) JDA can enhance how they present mixed method findings by sketching one figure with information that can clarify connections between the quantitative numbers and qualitative emergent themes.

The Learner

The challenge for students is that many methodological courses tend to focus exclusively on quantitative or qualitative ways of presenting data. These traditional ways of disseminating data may not be the most effective, given today's technology and stakeholders' priorities. Thus, there are challenges requiring discussion that instructors may encounter when working with students on presenting mixed methods results and findings. In the following section, we provide some examples of potential obstacles that could arise when instructing JDA visualization on mixed methods:

PRESENTING AND VISUALIZING A MIXED METHODS STUDY

- Students might face an inability to conceptualize results in mixed methods due to the complexity of the study.
- Students might lack confidence and/or knowledge in one method over the other (quantitative vs. qualitative), which could prevent meaningful representation of both methods in the visualization.
- Students might misunderstand mixed method sequence, weight, mixing, and theorizing of the study, which could impede the development of an appropriate joint display for the study.
- Students might have a hard time keeping the joint display concise and try to force too much information into a single joint display, especially at the early stage of the development.

Reflecting on the list mentioned above, some suggestions are discussed to address these challenges, as follows:

- Revisiting the Creswell and his colleagues' (2003) summary on timing, weighting, mixing, and theorizing, which is the foundation for building the JDA in a mixed method study.
- Breaking down the broader scope into smaller, more manageable parts. For instance, only discuss how timing alone could affect the conceptualization of the JDA (e.g., a table joint display for concurrent triangulation design so the qualitative and quantitative parts could be listed side-by-side vs. a flowchart joint display for a sequential design so the qualitative part could follow the qualitative part to reflect the timing of data collection/analysis).
- Ruminating on the planning, design, data collection, and data analysis of the study, and checking if the joint display has accommodated these aspects.
- Acknowledging there is more than one "standard" form, and that the JDA is a dynamic and iterative process which requires multiple revisions to achieve the final product.
- If the information does not fit in one chart/figure, do not force it. It could be done as a group of visualizations (e.g., use a flowchart to illustrate themes that emerged throughout the interview and their corresponding parameter estimation and p-value, plus a color-coded table to display the actual quotes and corresponding weights within the sample).

Context

Presenting results of mixed method research can be intimidating if we subscribe to traditional ways of dissemination. However, as Neumann (2005) notes in her discussion on learning: "as changed cognition, [learning] involves the personal and shared construction of knowledge; it involves coming to know something familiar in different ways, or to know something altogether new…" (p. 65). The lesson plan in this chapter centralizes constructing a new way of presentation and visualization on top of the traditional way of displaying quantitative and qualitative results separately.

Lessons learned from this chapter illustrate the importance of re-calibrating what it means to display findings from research projects. Specifically, this means unshackling ourselves from the "standard form" of presentation and visualization that we have been trained to follow. With regard to the aforementioned challenges and suggestions, students and other emerging scholars should understand and embrace the fact that they have freedom of interpretation, which is exhibited through the innovation and creativity that we emphasized when utilizing JDA. As Greene (2000) illustrated through a series of essays, responding to problems with an imaginative approach is essential to cultivate the ability to see and interpret the world in a novel way.

APPENDIX A

JDA ADAPTED EXAMPLE

In this appendix, we offer an example of sequential mixed methods research adapting JDA for data presentation and visualization. With pseudo-data, we present a combination of wheel chart and flow chart JDA that incorporates quantitative and qualitative data for an integrated presentation of findings. We encourage the instructor to utilize this example, or other forms of JDA as mentioned in the activities, to create examples that fit to the scope of their course.

BACKGROUND

This pseudo research focuses on the empowerment of mid-level staff in the higher educational institutions. The quantitative data are collected though surveying mid-level staff in the higher educational institutions across the States. The data reflect a sample (n = 300) of mid-level staffs' demographics, sense of empowerment, working condition, and sense of satisfaction. The follow-up qualitative data (n = 30) are collected by inviting volunteer mid-level staff (from the aforementioned sample) to a semi-structured interview, which revolves around the topics (i.e., relationships) that have been revealed in the quantitative part.

Quantitative Part

Assuming a moderated mediation model is fitted to the data and an adequately fitted model with standardized factor loadings and statistical significance reported as in Figure 28.1:

Qualitative Part

A set of preliminary codes are generated through inductive and then deductive analysis of the qualitative data (i.e., semi-structured interviews). Intercoder reliability is achieved through coding discussion, and saturation is achieved through adjusting and refining codes until no new codes emerge. Last, the emerged themes are finalized as below:

1. Meaning
2. Trust
3. Self-efficacy
4. Self-determination

PRESENTING AND VISUALIZING A MIXED METHODS STUDY

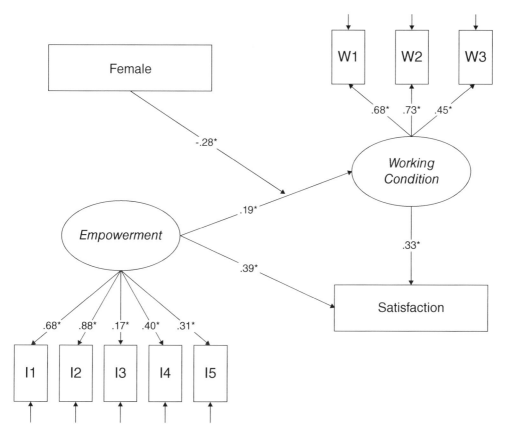

FIGURE 28.1 Fitted Moderated Mediation Model.

Note: Empowerment model with standardized loadings. * = statistically significant at .05 alpha level. CFI = .93; TLI = .91; RMSEA = .04.

5. Personal consequence
6. Staffing
7. Workspace
8. Work–life balance
9. Fulfillment
10. Belonging
11. Gender disparity

JDA Wheel Chart

Conventionally, the figure in the quantitative part and finalized themes (and selected quotes) are reported to convey the results of this study. The instructor could discuss how the conventional way of presentation and visualization could potentially hinder efficiency in information dissemination. For instance, explaining the moderated mediation model, an exhaustive list of emerging themes, and lengthy pages of quotes that support these themes might not suit a report to stakeholders, or a poster presentation. Therefore, a JDA could be useful in presenting the results in a nutshell.

Following the steps in the activities, we consider/decide:

1. Timing: quant-first, qual is guided by the results of quant.
2. Weighting: emphasize qual.
3. Mixing: how the qual data supports and explains the quant model.

A final version of our JDA presentation highlights the quantitative result in the center. The four quadrants of the first circle represent different latent variables (i.e., empowerment and working condition) and observed variables (i.e., gender and satisfaction). The second wheel represents the emerging themes that correspond to each variable. Moreover, the percentage under each theme exhibits how many of our participants (out of 30) alluded to the theme based on the coded interview. Lastly, the extended four quadrants include selected quote(s) that reflect the corresponding themes, as well as the potential reasoning behind the statistical significance of the moderated mediation model (see Figure 28.2):

Given the timing, the JDA wheel chart illustrates the sense of quant-first from center to outside. For weighting, we trimmed the quant model to fit the display and added a percentage under each emerged theme so as to put more emphasis on the qual part. For mixing, we only included the themes that connect to the quant model and the quotes that help to explain the statistically significant relationship in the quant model.

The underlined flexibility in JDA could create equitable learning spaces by promoting different ways of presenting, through which students could better understand by incorporating different perspectives and views.

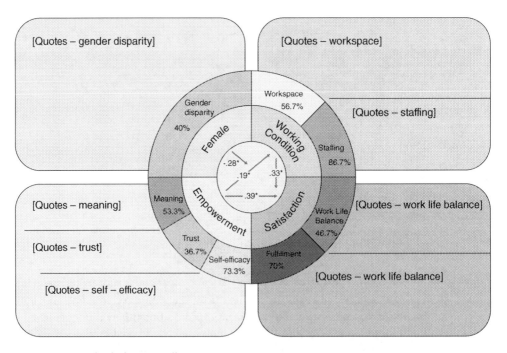

FIGURE 28.2 Wheel Chart JDA Illustration

BIBLIOGRAPHY

Bustamante, C. (2019). TPACK and teachers of Spanish: Development of a theory-based joint display in a mixed methods research case study. *Journal of Mixed Methods Research, 13*(2), 163–178. DOI: 10.1177/1558689817712119

Fetters (2020). *The mixed methods research workbook*. Sage.

Creswell, J. W., Plano Clark, V. L., Gutmann, M. L., & Hanson, W. E. (2003). Advanced mixed methods research designs. In A. Tashakkori & C. Teddlie (Eds.), *Handbook of mixed methods in social and behavioral research* (pp. 209–240). SAGE.

Greene, M. (2000). *Releasing the imagination: Essays on education, the arts, and social change*. John Wiley & Sons.

Guetterman, T. C., Fetters, M. D., & Creswell, J. W. (2015). Integrating quantitative and qualitative results in health science mixed methods research through joint displays. *Annals of Family Medicine, 13*(6), 554–561. https://doi.org/10.1370/afm.1865

Johnson, R. E., Grove, A. L., & Clarke, A. (2019). Pillar integration process: A joint display technique to integrate data in mixed methods research. *Journal of Mixed Methods Research, 13*(3), 301–320.

Neumann, A. (2005). Observations: Taking seriously the topic of learning in studies of faculty work and careers. *New Directions for Teaching and Learning, 2005*(102), 63–83.

Sage Publishing. (2020). *Joint display analysis for mixed method research* [Video]. YouTube. https://www.youtube.com/watch?v=jnJe0Vo2vVM&list=WL&index=15

Section VII

Findings and Discussion

Section Editor: Erin Doran

29

Introduction to Section VII

Findings and Discussion

Erin Doran

There's a famous scene in the sitcom "Schitt's Creek" where David and his mother Moira are making enchiladas even though clearly neither one can actually cook (West, 2016). Moira reads the recipe to David, and she tells him the next step in the directions says, "Fold in the cheese." David, who is frantically stirring, does not understand what folding means in cooking and repeatedly asks his mother Moira to explain it to him, to which she simply replies, "You fold it in" like it is an obvious statement. As they both get increasingly agitated, Moira says, "I don't know how to be any clearer!" while continuing to repeat some version of "You just fold in the cheese."

When I started teaching qualitative research methods, I have to admit that I probably reacted more like Moira than I like to admit, especially about teaching students about the backend of research studies: writing the findings, discussion, and implications. Within a typical semester, there is so much content to cram into one methods course, and I found that I was so focused on the earlier stages of a study (e.g., choosing a theoretical framework, writing interview protocols) that I did not leave students enough time for the steps they should take once data collection and analysis winds down. So, I confess with some bashfulness that when students would ask for directions on how to write a findings or discussion section, I likely gave them a version of "You just fold it in."

An underlying assumption of teaching the components of findings and discussion in research is that students have data that they can analyze or interpret in order to make meaning and significance of and then communicate to various audiences. In the chapter on quantitative findings, Ewinghill and colleagues walk instructors through group activities using linear regression that will give students small-group, hands-on experience with data analysis and interpretation. They emphasize the critical thinking aspects of generating findings in ways that are also mindful of some students' anxieties or trepidation about working with quantitative data. On the qualitative side, Pifer's chapter encourages the development of findings through visual storytelling, which may help students get out of their heads in order to think about where they are going with their analysis in a creative manner. Both of these chapters capture a sentiment that Pifer articulates very eloquently: "These final steps in the journey towards independence as a scholar can be isolating,

DOI: 10.4324/b23320-37

vulnerable, and intimidating" (p. 234). Each of the lessons described in these chapters offer suggestions for how to teach students to craft their findings section in a way that is communal and constructive.

Whether talking about the fifth chapter of a traditional dissertation or the discussion section of a journal-length manuscript, I have told my own students that the discussion section can be the trickiest to write. For dissertation students in particular, the discussion section is written last when students are tired and ready to be done. They may not be able to see the forest for the trees – that is, to see how their study fits into the broader scholarly conversation. I think that students may also be intimidated by being hit with any study's kiss of death: the dreaded question, "So what?" Drawing on a model article, the chapter by Brandenberg and colleagues walks readers through the major components of the discussion section as a foundation for building their own.

Finally, in education in particular, we are concerned with the implications of our studies – that is, providing a roadmap for how other researchers, policy makers, and practitioners may pick up where we left off to enact change, to promote certain practices, and/or to conduct further research on the given topic. The chapters by Coviello and Marsicano and colleagues both offer specific ways that novice researchers can speak directly to implications for theory and policy, respectively. In my own teaching, I encounter students who are nervous to offer implications for theory – perhaps thinking that they are not qualified to challenge or critique theory. What is so strong about Coviello's lesson is the way that he urges instructors to create lessons about theory through a practical lens. This is especially helpful for master's students or Doctor of Education (EdD.) students who may be taking up research projects that are meant to be more practice-oriented but still need theory to ground their study. Finally, Marsicano and his colleagues make the implications for policy fun by marrying the ideas of generation processes with donuts.

Taken together, the lessons in these chapters demystify some of the more challenging aspects of the research and writing processes – the ones where students really start to take ownership of their labor to answer their research questions and walk their reader through what they found and why it is important. Once those researcher muscles are developed, it may be hard to remember what the process was for learning how to make sense of data and to communicate to others why the findings matter. It may be even harder to break down tasks and mental processes that are well-established in a seasoned researcher's repertoire – so much so that they fail to adequately explain what their students should do beyond a terse, "You fold in the cheese." It is my hope that instructors and students will find these lessons both fun and useful for building confidence in the research process.

BIBLIOGRAPHY

West, D.R. (Writer), & Ciccoritte, J. (Director). (2016, January 16). Family Dinner (Season 2, Episode 2) [TV series episode]. In E. Levy, D. Levy, F. Levy, A. Barnsley, B. Feigin, & K. White (Executive Producers), *Schitt's Creek*, Not a Real Company; Canadian Broadcasting Company.

30

An Introduction to Regression Using Critical Quantitative Thinking

Terrace Ewinghill, Adam Lazarewicz, Cindy Meza, Brent Gambrell, Diana Guerrero and Jameson Lopez

INTRODUCTION

Our goal is to teach linear regression, which is a statistical technique that predicts relationships between predictor/independent variables and outcome/dependent variables. The lesson is couched within critical quantitative theory, which uses data to reveal inequities and institutional complicity in perpetuating inequities in educational processes and outcomes, and challenge, question, and improve models, measures, and analyses of quantitative research to better describe the experiences of underrepresented populations (Stage, 2007).

To pursue critical quantitative work, we need to expand the population of people engaged in scholarship and data science to include those who hold marginalized identities such as Indigenous people (Lopez, 2020). The first statistics class introduced to students in a series can act as a "gateway class" – a barrier for students to continue pursuing STEM pathways (Zhang, 2022). Students often decide whether they view themselves working within quantitative research within their first semester of statistics. Many leave with a personal declaration of whether statistics is for them or not. To make the world of quantitative research inclusive, we must provide a sense of belonging, an understanding that mistakes are part of the journey, and a belief that we all have something to contribute. The field of quantitative research will be improved if it addresses educational equity and inclusion issues so that more students who hold marginalized identities find space in mathematics and data science classes and perhaps even enjoy them (Chestnut et al., 2018).

In this chapter, we share a model for highly structured, collaborative learning called "complex instruction," a term coined by Cohen and Lotan (2014), who describe ways that students (un)consciously judge and rank one another. Cohen and Lotan call those rankings "status" and they explain that students tend to over- or under-participate depending on their status in a classroom. In math classrooms, this can take the form of white, straight, cis students over-participating and students who hold marginalized identities contributing less. In the K–12 setting, numerous studies have been published on the positive impact of their complex instruction model (Crespo, 2016; Davidson, 1990).

DOI: 10.4324/b23320-38

LESSON PLAN

Topic	*Introduction to regression using critical quantitative methods in a collaborative learning model.*
Learning Objectives	Students will be able to: • Identify characteristics of a balanced and equitable math collaboration between team members and their personal area(s) for growth through highly structured collaborative learning (Cohen & Lotan, 2014). • Explain the relationship between the slope-intercept equation and the linear regression equation. • Identify the components of the linear regression equation and use the equation to solve for Y_i, given a value of X_i. • Apply the concept of regression to an area of interest while maintaining a critical perspective. • Define critical quantitative reasoning and discuss representation of race and gender within quantitative research.
Needed Materials	This lesson was designed for use online, but can be adapted for the classroom. Teachers will need Desmos, an interactive website, and to create a "Teacher" account: https://teacher.desmos.com Create a copy of the activity: https://teacher.desmos.com/activitybuilder/custom/6196f6cfcf94371f7e3e9eae If using only this one lesson on Desmos, click "Assign" and create a single-session code. It is recommended that teachers create a link for each class and select the option to keep the code active for one year. Teachers can share the student link or students can go to https://student.desmos.com and type in the code.

Pre-lesson Preparation	**Teacher**
	• Review examples from this lesson, to help students apply linear regression principles to real-world situations.
	• Review prior related course material (e.g., linear formula, slope and intercept, goal of regression).
	  ◦ Possible resources:
	    ▪ Charles Wheelan's (2014) *Naked Statistics: Stripping the Dread From Data* (Chapter 11, Regression Analysis)
	• Set up Desmos teacher account and classroom (see instructions).
	Student
	• The exercises are created with a low-floor, high-ceiling approach (Cohen & Lotan, 2014). The "low-floor" means any student (even with a long gap between college and high school) will be able to contribute to the conversation. Throughout the lesson, students can refer to helpful graphics, content refreshers and friendly resources like MathIsFun.com. (The "high-ceiling" will be covered later in the lesson.)

Activities	• Divide the class into small groups. Explain the goal is to talk through the lesson's content and make meaning of it together. The priority is rich conversation, not speed. • In the spirit of highly structured collaborative learning (Cohen & Lotan, 2014), students begin by reading the collaborative reminders within the Desmos lesson plan and setting an intention to improve their own teamwork by selecting an answer to the following question. "Which of these is an area of growth for you that you can be intentional about during this activity?" (Select one) • Helping balance conversations • Asking questions of group members

AN INTRODUCTION TO REGRESSION

Topic	Introduction to regression using critical quantitative methods in a collaborative learning model.

- Being helpful to others
- Being compassionate during math tasks
- In small groups, students review slope-intercept equation $y = mx + b$, where m is the slope and b is the y-intercept by doing the following:
  - Students "brain dump" what they know about slope and the y-intercept. Encourage them to look online if they don't remember and provide MathIsFun.com as a resource.
  - Linked in activity: https://www.mathsisfun.com/algebra/linear-equations.html.
- Students are provided a new version of the linear equation with beta coefficients: $Y_i = \beta_0 + \beta_1 X_i$
  - X_i: value of the predictor/independent/explanatory variable.
  - Y_i: value of the outcome/dependent/response variable.
  - β_0: Y-intercept (value of Y when $X = 0$).
  - β_1: rate of change coefficient (slope of the regression line). (predicted increase/decrease in Y, given a one-unit increase in X).
- Following Slide 4 of Desmos, students will discuss with their group members the following regression equation prompt:
- **Example 1:** "With the Campus Recreation center under renovation, a college student is looking for a gym near their home. They found one with a start-up fee of \$100 and a monthly membership fee of \$25." Clarify for students that X_i represents the number of months that a person has been a member and Y_i represents the total cost.
  - **Questions for Example 1**:
    - "Write the regression equation, including beta values."
    - "How much will a person pay in gym membership fees after 6 months in this scenario?"
    - In this student-centered activity, it is important that students are relying on one another rather than the instructor for solutions (Cohen & Lotan, 2014). Mistakes should be highlighted as positive moments for maximum learning (Boaler, 2014, 2015; Moser et al., 2011; Steuer et al., 2013, Stanford Graduate School of Education, 2019).
    - Rather than providing answers, encourage teamwork with phrases like:
      - "Have y'all checked in with one another lately?"
      - "Two common answers that I am seeing are ____ and ____. If you haven't already, take a moment to talk about possible answers with your group."
      - "My favorite 'wrong' answer is ____! Why does that answer make sense?"
  - **Graph for Example 1**: Independently, each student should sketch a graph of the regression equation from the previous example. (See Figure 30.1)
  - Following Desmos Slide 6, students will compare graphs with their group members and share mistakes, questions, and "ah-ha" moments.
  - **Example 1: Visualizing "messy" real-world data**.
    - Real-world data isn't perfect. It'll look more like a graph of messy dots. Imagine that you have a survey of local gyms. Figure 30.2 shows a graph of the monthly cost for each gym and its corresponding number of members.
    - On Desmos Slide 7, students individually attempt to draw a "line of best fit" through imperfect data and write a possible linear equation and then share with group members. Affirm that answers will likely vary among students.
    - Graphs may vary and will hopefully spark an appreciation for software that creates a "perfect" regression line.

Topic	*Introduction to regression using critical quantitative methods in a collaborative learning model.*
	<ul><li>○ Desmos Slide 8 concludes Example 1 by introducing students to the term "linear regression"<ul><li>■ "What you just saw was an example of linear regression. We drew a best fit line to represent the data we collected. We can use that regression line to make future predictions about an outcome."</li></ul></li><li>• Now students will turn to Example 2:</li><li>• **Example 2**: A researcher finds a relationship in their community between years of postsecondary education and annual income. They found that people in this community with 0 years of postsecondary education earn an average of US \$28,000. However, each year of postsecondary education predicts an average increase in income of US \$3,000. Clarify that X_i represents years of secondary education and Y_i represents annual income.<ul><li>○ **Equation for Example 2**: "Write the regression equation, including beta values and graph the equation. What do each of those beta values tell us?"</li><li>○ **Graphing Calculator Equation: Example 2**: Using the Desmos graphing calculator, write the equation, including beta values.<ul><li>■ YouTube instructions: https://www.youtube.com/watch?v=RKbZ3RoA-x4</li></ul></li></ul></li><li>• **Appreciating Mistakes**: On Desmos Slide 12, students reflect on appreciating mistakes and asking questions.</li><li>• **Example 3: Application to Area of Interest**<ul><li>○ The instructor says: "Now is your chance to make this your own! Work as a group to write down an example that has a negative *y*-intercept and a negative slope. Try to apply it to your area of study or something you care about."</li><li>○ **Desmos Slides 13–15**: Students identify a scenario with a negative *Y*-intercept and negative slope; they share their scenarios, graphs, and equations in Desmos and with one another.</li></ul></li><li>• **Example 4: Critical Quantitative Methods**: A study found that years of postsecondary education (X_i) predicts a person's annual income (Y_i).<ul><li>○ This is the "high-ceiling" portion of the lesson where students are asked to think critically and apply content to a larger problem (Cohen & Lotan, 2014).</li><li>○ On Desmos Slide 15, students, with their group members, will think critically about studies such as this example, making connections to ethnicity, gender, disability status, and age. Encourage them to think about what variables should be included in a study like this. This integrates critical quantitative methods, in which students are asked to explore issues of inequity. Explain that "critical quantitative methods" center these social issues within research.</li><li>○ Conversations among the groups will vary. The intention of the final prompt is to organically generate curiosity about future topics of exploration in quantitative methods including demographic data collection and multivariate regression. After the group discussion, debrief as a class about the importance of centering social issues and identity, especially when interpreting research results.</li></ul></li></ul>
Virtual Adaptations	<ul><li>• This lesson was taught live using Zoom and Desmos. Find tutorials on using the Desmos teacher features here: https://www.youtube.com/c/Desmos</li><li>• If used in-person, use whiteboards to display concepts and work through examples.</li></ul>
Assessment / Evaluation	<ul><li>• Students will be informally assessed based on their group discussions and contributions to class understanding. Once the activity ends, teachers will review the lesson and respond to questions or requests for further clarification.</li><li>• If the instructor wants a more formal assessment, they can use the Teacher Dashboard in Desmos to view each student's progress.</li></ul>

AN INTRODUCTION TO REGRESSION

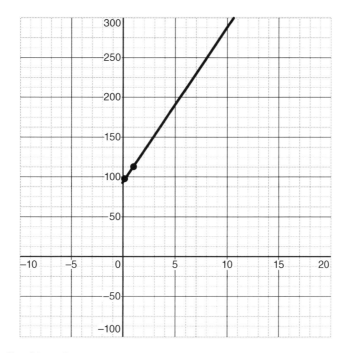

FIGURE 30.1 Sketching a Scenario

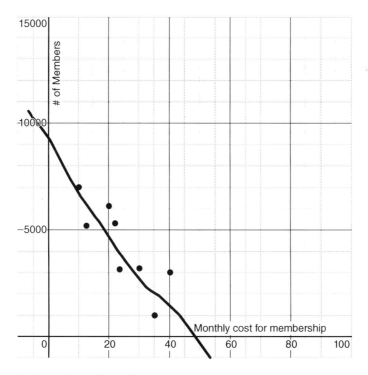

FIGURE 30.2 Intuiting a Line of Best Fit

INTELLECTUAL PREPARATION FOR A "LINEAR REGRESSION" LESSON

Core Ideas

This lesson seeks to introduce the foundational concept of linear regression and critical quantitative theory. Mathematically, students will develop a better understanding of independent and dependent variables, and the idea of a "line of best fit" to data. As classmates, they will be challenged to be mindful of the space they take up in discussion, attending to equity of voice and thoughts in group work. An end result is for students to understand the regression equation and expand their critical thinking by addressing omitted variables in a regression model. Often when selecting variables within a regression equation, variables or identifiers are chosen due to longstanding preferences or biases, while other identities that could directly affect results are omitted, such as gender preference, race, and/or ableism. By looking at what is included and critically asking what is not, the hope is that the structure of the lesson and the content allow for the development of critical quantitative reasoning.

Learners

Students in an introductory statistics course enroll with varying academic experiences. Some may have different knowledge than others, or perhaps a long span of time has passed since their last course. Students with a stronger background (e.g., having completed advanced math courses) may negatively influence peer learning as they speed through lessons, potentially causing others to feel confused or less confident. A student's confidence plays a major role. Helping students shift from a fixed mindset to a growth mindset (Rattan et al., 2015) increases confidence and improves capacity for learning.

Previous Learning and Misconceptions
A potential misconception about linear regression is that the term sounds advanced and extremely difficult. Math generates anxiety in many students. Some have experienced math trauma (Allen, 2016) in prior educational settings. Feelings that they "don't know math" and consequently feel incompetent lead to thoughts that they will be unable to learn linear regression. Reassure students that they have a foundational understanding that aids in comprehending linear regression.

Another misunderstanding entails what linear regression outputs indicate. Students may experience uncertainty about how linear regression can provide insight into research questions. Determining if they are accurately measuring what was intended is another challenge. Students must be conscious of the purpose of the research and potential benefits or injury. Data analysis has the potential to impact those who are invisibilized (un)intentionally. For further reading on social justice approaches and critical quantitative methods, see the Bibliography (e.g., Cokley & Awad, 2013).

The lesson fosters an equitable learning space through group activities that enable students to learn from each other while solidifying their own knowledge. Smaller groups create space to discuss how terms, references, and concepts are culturally different. Students less comfortable are able to contribute or ask questions in smaller groups, thus reducing fear or embarrassment in front of the class.

AN INTRODUCTION TO REGRESSION

The Context

As previously mentioned. in order to have critical quantitative work, we need to expand the population of people engaged in scholarship and data science to include those who hold marginalized identities. This lesson finds connections to students' prior knowledge of math and how they might approach statistical concepts from a critical quantitative framework.

To expand understanding and use of quantitative analysis, instructors must encourage students to find solutions to historically problematic ways that researchers conduct quantitative analysis. Researchers are often tempted to use quantitative methods in traditional ways. In our examples, we used simple scenarios, such as the cost of gym membership and the annual expected income based on educational attainment, with the intention of having students understand the statistical concepts before engaging in critical quantitative thinking. In the end, we want them to ask themselves, "who is being excluded in this model?" One activity above prompts students to critically think about how to capture gender identity. Binary understandings of gender identity are problematic in research and encourage narrow representations (Garvey et al., 2019; Dockendorff, 2019), although variables can be operationalized to better represent identity (Garvey et al., 2019). To be inclusive, quantitative learners and researchers must examine how characteristics such as gender or race are measured and counted, and how identity manifests within the ecology of higher education campuses.

Equitable Learning Space

This lesson fosters an equitable learning space through several methods. First, the lesson is designed to help students, regardless of level and past experience, to start from a common initial entry point, leaving no one behind in the learning. Students have many different entry points about linear regression and use funds of knowledge, such as bringing their own experiences, as well as familial and community knowledge into the classroom to enhance a communal learning space (Kiyama & Rios-Aguilar, 2018). Doing so promotes educational equity for all involved to share common terminology and concepts, something that can often be overlooked or assumed prior to the lesson.

Confidence Building

The examples provided as building blocks are meant to be situations that many students may experience or recognize. Such illustrations help students ground the concepts and show how elements of their learning are already embedded within their daily lives, revealing possible experiential knowledge of the material unknown to the students initially. In addition, through the shared learning model presented within the lesson (both in small groups as well as sharing with the larger class), students not only learn from each other, but also through their shared experiences and interactions. Through such communal learning and group work, students establish a learning group to share previous, and create new, funds of knowledge where each small group's common experiences are learned from, about, and incorporated into the lesson and learning of all those involved through culturally responsive pedagogy – intentionally incorporating and making space for student's cultural knowledges and strengths (Ladson-Billings, 1995; Kiyama & Rios-Aguilar, 2018).

Such learning helps to promote overall student engagement, which can benefit them both inside and outside the classroom, through a positive influence on overall performance markers and student outcomes like persistence (Harper & Quaye, 2014).

Conclusion

This chapter introduced the foundational concepts of linear regression and critical quantitative practices. Students who go through this lesson will be able to use and interpret the regression equation, while simultaneously critiquing examples through the gaze of critical quantitative methods. After the lesson, the students should be able to infuse their critical understanding throughout the research process. Our hope is that quantitative learners and researchers will move beyond traditional quantitative methods. By seeing how they are enriched through an expanded understanding of variables in statistical models, we hope students will be able to critically think about how such models can support underrepresented communities and be more aware of problematic approaches in quantitative research from the past.

BIBLIOGRAPHY

Allen, K. (2016). *Math trauma: Healing our classrooms, our students and our discipline.* https://www.bigmarker.com/GlobalMathDept/Math-Trauma-Healing-Our-Classrooms-Our-Students-and-Our-Discipline

Boaler, J. (2014). *The mathematics of hope: Moving from performance to learning in mathematics classrooms.* Youtube at Stanford University. https://bhi61nm2cr3mkdgk1dtaov18-wpengine.netdna-ssl.com/wp-content/uploads/The-Mathematics-of-Hope-5.pdf

Boaler, J. (2015). *Mathematical mindsets: Unleashing students' potential through creative math, inspiring messages, and innovative teaching.* Jossey-Bass.

Boaler, J. (2016). Mistakes grow your brain. *Youcube at Stanford University Graduate School of Education.* retrieved December 3, 2021 from https://www.pdst.ie/sites/default/files/Mistakes-Grow-Your-Brain-Revised.pdf

Chestnut, E. K., Lei, R. F., Leslie, S-J, & Cimpian, A. (2018) The myth that only brilliant people are good at math and Its implications for diversity. *Education Sciences*, 8(2):65.

Cokley, K., & Awad, G. H. (2013). In defense of quantitative methods: Using the "master's tools" to promote social justice. *Journal for Social Action in Counseling & Psychology*, 5(2), 26–41.

Cohen, E. G., & Lotan, R. A. (2014). *Designing groupwork: Strategies for the heterogeneous classroom third edition.* Teachers College Press.

Crespo, S. (2016). *Why are you asking for these impossible math lessons? Cases for mathematics teacher educators: Facilitating conversations about inequities in mathematics classrooms*, Information Age Publishers, 63–69.

Davidson, N. (1990). *Cooperative learning in mathematics: A handbook for teachers.* Addison-Wesley Publishing Company, Inc.

Dockendorff, K. J. (2019). Queering data collection: Strategies for reimagining survey instruments in student affairs. *Journal of Student Affairs*, 29, 16–27.

Garvey, J. C., Hart, J., Metcalfe, A. S., & Fellabaum-Toston, J. (2019). Methodological troubles with gender and sex in higher education survey research. *The Review of Higher Education*, 43(1), 1–24.

Harper, S. R. & Quaye, S. J. (2014). Making engagement equitable for students in U.S. higher education. In S. R. Harper & S. J. Quaye (Eds.), *Student engagement in higher education* (pp. 17–30). Routledge.

Kiyama, J. M., & Rios-Aguilar, C. (2018). *Funds of knowledge in higher education.* Routledge.

Ladson-Billings, G. (1995). Toward a theory of culturally relevant pedagogy. *American Educational Research Journal*, 32(3), 465–491.

Lopez, J. D. (2020). Indigenous data collection: Addressing limitations in Native American samples. *Journal of College Student Development*, 61(6), 750–764.

Moser, J. S., Schroder, H. S., Heeter, C., Moran, T. P., & Lee, Y. H. (2011). Mind your errors Evidence for a neural mechanism linking growth mindset to adaptive post error adjustments. *Psychological Science*, 22(12), 1484–1489.

Rattan, A., Savani, K., Chugh, D., & Dweck, C. S. (2015). Leveraging mindsets to promote academic achievement: Policy recommendations. *Perspectives on Psychological Science*, 10(6), 721–726.

Stage, F. K. (2007). Answering critical questions using quantitative data. *New Directions for Institutional Research, 2007*(133), 5–16.

Stanford Graduate School of Education. (2019, May 24). Mistakes grow your brain. *YouCubed.* retrieved November 22, 2022, from https://www.youcubed.org/evidence/mistakes-grow-brain/

Steuer, G., Rosentritt-Brunn, G., & Dresel, M. (2013). Dealing with errors in mathematics classrooms: Structure and relevance of perceived error climate. *Contemporary Educational Psychology, 38*(3), 196–210.

Wheelan, C. J. (2014). *Naked statistics: Stripping the dread from the data.* W. W. Norton.

Zhang, Y. L. (2022). Early academic momentum: Factors contributing to community college transfer students' STEM degree attainment. *Journal of College Student Retention: Research, Theory & Practice, 23*(4), 873–902.

31

Show the Story

Presenting Qualitative Findings

Meghan J. Pifer

INTRODUCTION

I find that students often struggle to present findings from their qualitative studies. Many students assume a descriptive approach that over-relies on general summaries and long participant quotes. What is lacking is evidence of deep analysis guided by the study purpose, research questions, theoretical framing, and methodological choices. Students struggle to connect their findings to the reason they wanted to find something out in the first place, and as the result of the hard work they did to get answers.

I observe several reasons for this, which are not mutually exclusive or exhaustive. First, students' intellectual curiosity is satiated as a result of a successful research study. It can be challenging to maintain the focus needed to prepare findings for dissemination. Second, students have completed many prior steps of a study and may feel intellectually fatigued, typically after sustained periods of learning and growth, rounds of feedback, late nights and early mornings, and races against due dates and timelines. Third, responsibilities, expectations, and years of well-meaning questions from family, colleagues, and others can influence degree completion above all else. This can compete with guidance from faculty members to work carefully, often in time-consuming ways, in the final stages of a study. Fourth, writing up one's findings is an act of courage and decision-making in a research project, to be followed by discussing the significance of that new knowledge and then sharing it with the world. These final steps in the journey towards independence as a scholar can feel isolating, vulnerable, and intimidating.

There is at least one more reason why some students struggle with the presentation of findings: they were never taught how. It takes familiarity with the literature, clear purpose and process, deliberate strategy, and evidence-based conclusions to effectively determine the most salient findings from a completed study and present them in a compelling way. It also takes active learning to prepare for analysis, interpretation, and communication.

When I reflect on the student experience, I find all these reasons to be understandable. They are opportunities for meaningful supervision and support from faculty. After all, teaching is the facilitation of learning and we admit students into our programs to prepare them for membership in disciplinary and professional communities. Instructors can help

DOI: 10.4324/b23320-39

SHOW THE STORY

ensure that students learn the needed skills for presenting their findings so that students may employ them in later coursework, collaborative research, dissertation studies, and eventually their own independent scholarship. I developed the following lesson on visual storytelling to help students cultivate the skills and confidence needed to present qualitative findings.

LESSON PLAN

Topic	*Presenting qualitative findings through visual storytelling*
Learning Objectives	• Students **identify** connections between study findings and study purposes, research questions, and frameworks. • Students **explore** tools, resources, and strategies for visualization. • Students **compose** visual representations of study findings to **illustrate** connections to study purposes, research questions, and frameworks. • Students **experiment with** using their scholarly voice and creativity to communicate with others. • Students **review** peers' presentations of findings to give and receive feedback within the norms of knowledge production.

Needed Materials	• Students' prior work on a qualitative study including study purpose and significance, research questions, conceptual framework, review of relevant literature, data, and completed analysis.
	  ◦ The lesson assumes that students have collected and analyzed qualitative data, perhaps as part of a research team or through a prior course assignment. As an alternative with some modifications, select or have students locate qualitative research articles and task students with creating visual stories of the findings from those articles and cross-checking findings with study purposes, research questions, and frameworks.
	• Sample data visualizations and visual stories
	  ◦ If using this lesson for the first time, consider sharing examples from your own scholarship, research articles that relate to the course topic or students' disciplinary areas, or exemplars in visual storytelling from other contexts. See Cardel et al. (2020) in the Bibliography for one example.
	  ◦ At the end of the lesson, consider asking for permission to use de-identified examples in future courses.
	  ◦ Examples are helpful, but may limit creativity as students seek to mitigate ambiguity. Consider showing examples in class rather than distributing them.

Pre-lesson Preparation	• Inform students of the nature of the lesson so they can prepare effectively. Students should bring:
	  ◦ Preliminary findings from their own data analysis.
	  ◦ Any materials they wish to use based on personal preferences –common examples would be pens or markers; a notebook, sketch pad, electronic tablet for drawing; or a laptop that allows for the use of software or online tools.
	• Encourage students to explore tools that will allow for downloading, sharing, and future editing of their visual stories (e.g., Canva, Piktochart, Vengage; PowerPoint, Adobe Creative Suite).

Activities	**Activating Discussion** (10 minutes) • Ask students to describe in their own words why it is important to effectively communicate study findings. • Review the importance of effectively presenting qualitative findings, drawing from relevant disciplinary and methodological texts (seeBibliography).

Topic	*Presenting qualitative findings through visual storytelling*
	<ul><li>Conduct a brief check of prior knowledge to learn about students' firsthand experiences with presenting qualitative findings, and to identify student questions.</li><li>Acknowledge that students may have received little training on the skill of presenting one's findings, and that each research study requires its own creative process.</li><li>Provide students with a simple printed or online worksheet to help them demonstrate connections between findings and study purposes, research questions, guiding theoretical or conceptual frameworks, methodological choices, and intended audiences or consumers. Briefly describe the structure and purpose of the worksheet. Note that some students may not be able to demonstrate all these connections; possibly identifying areas of needed improvements or lessons learned for future research. Remind students that they are engaged in the iterative learning process of becoming qualitative researchers. Missing connections need not prevent students from moving forward with the lesson activities.</li><li>Discuss data visualization as both a strategy for presenting findings, and as a tool for preparing more traditional presentations of findings. Include examples and supporting resources (see Bibliography).</li></ul>

Visual Storytelling Workshop (25 minutes)

- Task students with completing the guiding worksheet, then drawing from that to prepare a visualization that tells the story of their study findings. The focus should be on presenting the findings, though students should draw from aspects of the study to inform that work based on their completed worksheets.
- Examples include a process chart, a concept map, a heat map, a cartoon or comic, or an infographic.
- Encourage students to be creative in their storytelling. Provide examples such as visualizations of navigation or journeys, landscapes or planetary systems, bodies or ecosystems, manufacturing or growing, group interactions, and simple shapes and arrows.
- Remind students that their visualizations need not be text-free, and that labels and other brief text will likely be important in effective visualizations.
- Students may wish to use technological resources or low-tech approaches. Encourage students to try new tools. Inform them that they will have to show their work to peers at the end of the session so they can factor that into their choice and planning.

Peer Review (10 minutes)

- Working in pairs, students exchange visual stories *without commentary*.
- Students prepare to share their peer's findings using only the visual story as a guide. Provide a standard set of questions that should be answerable after reviewing the data visualization:
  - What are the key findings from the study?
  - How do the findings fulfill the purpose of the study?
  - What answers to the research questions were generated?
  - How is the guiding framework evident in the visualization?
  - What are the key takeaways from the study?
- Task students with providing 2–3 targeted areas for improvement, noted strengths, or questions to their peers through brief discussions.

Report Out (20 minutes; adjust as needed depending on class time and size)

- Individually, students take one minute to share their peer's data visualizations with the class and describe the findings of their peer's study based on the prompts included in the **Peer Review**. You may wish to call on some students rather than having every student present.
- Students may feel rushed to present findings in under a minute. Use this as an opportunity to emphasize the amount of preparation that goes into effective brevity.

Topic	Presenting qualitative findings through visual storytelling
	Wrap Up (10 minutes) • Open the discussion and invite students to share their observations, reflections, and lessons learned. Were there exemplars that were effective visualizations of findings? Were there any themes in common errors or opportunities for improvement? What were the more difficult aspects of sharing your own findings? What was learned about visual storytelling, tools and processes, or the experience of hearing someone else describe your work? • Conclude by helping students understand how data visualizations may serve as presentations of findings, as well as planning tools for enabling more traditional textual presentations of qualitative study findings. Encourage them to approach the presentation of findings as a skill that can be developed and provide additional supports or resources.
Virtual Adaptations	**This lesson can easily be adapted for virtual learning environments**: • Set up student breakout rooms within your existing learning management system (e.g., Blackboard Collaborate) or create a modified schedule that supports one-on-one breakouts and full-class meeting space within the lesson (e.g., Facetime, Teams meetings, Zoom). • Consider tools that may help facilitate the lesson when taught virtually (e.g., Google Jamboard, photos of sketches). • Begin the session in a large group, then facilitate breakout groups for the **Peer Review**. Return to the large group for the **Report Out** and **Wrap Up** components.
Assessment	• Formative Assessment: Students receive peer feedback from each other during the workshop phase. • Formative Assessment: Circulate through peer dyads to offer feedback to students during the workshop phase. • Formative Assessment: Each student presents their peer's infographic to the class, allowing for an additional round of peer feedback from the collective group. • Summative Assessment: Grade the student's submitted infographic using a rubric or a clear description of objectives for assessment. • Summative Assessment: As a secondary assignment or part of a participation grade, you may wish to grade the student's engagement in the **Peer Review** workshop using a rubric or a clear description of categories for assessment; do this based on your own observations and/or informed by students' submissions of brief self-evaluations and peer evaluations of providing and receiving meaningful peer feedback.

INTELLECTUAL PREPARATION FOR LESSON

Core Ideas

It takes a complex understanding of study findings to effectively present them in a simple manner. This lesson guides students through developing and demonstrating that understanding through qualitative data interpretation, narrative, and reporting. The major goals of the lesson are to: (1) help students rely on prior research steps to inform and interpret findings in ways that fulfill study purposes, (2) provide students with experiences of telling the story of their research findings, centered on approaches to visual storytelling or data visualization, and (3) equip students to transition to strong discussions of their findings and implications for research, theory, and practice. Major et al. (2016) provided an effective synthesis of the research around graphic organizers as learning tools that help students organize new knowledge, which the instructor might consider when preparing this lesson.

The purpose of qualitative research is "ultimately to reveal, clarify, and construct significant awareness, understanding, and meaning" (Miles et al., 2014, p. 343). Patton (2015) reminded the qualitative researcher that purpose not only guides analysis, it also guides writing. As Babbie (2016) wrote, "[u]nless research is properly communicated, all [prior] efforts…will go for naught." He summarized three purposes of scientific reporting: communicate specific data and ideas, contribute to the body of knowledge, and inform future inquiry through the presentation of specific conclusions generated by qualitative analysis. To meet those purposes, Babbie emphasized the importance of providing enough detail to allow the reader to trust and understand data interpretations and findings. He also emphasized the use of materials that enhance communication of findings.

In his consideration of academic writing as storytelling, Pollock (2021) overlayed the components of a qualitative article with the arc of a story. He referred to the findings section as the story's climax and the journey toward the catharsis that comes from knowing. Cormick (2019), too, encouraged scientists to consider storytelling as an important skill in communicating their research. This lesson plan builds on the idea of academic storytelling by emphasizing visual storytelling. Patton (2015) predicted the subsequent importance of being able to create "meaningful and powerful visuals" (p. 608). Although this lesson focuses on visual storytelling, it may be scaffolded or translated to include an emphasis on tables, charts, word clouds, and other traditional and emergent data visualization tools within academic papers. It may also be extended to consideration of other research products beyond academic papers or dissertations, such as infographics, executive summaries, blog posts, white papers, and social media posts. As methods of research dissemination and digital communication continue to evolve, it is important for researchers to share their work quickly, effectively, and meaningfully. Rodrigues (2021) emphasized this need in educational research in her summary of strategies for visual abstracts, which have been identified as effective tools for sharing information (Ibrahim et al., 2017).

The Learner

Understanding students' prior learning and knowledge is important for successfully implementing this lesson. Students will demonstrate differing levels of prior experience, reactions to the lesson, and artistic and creative skills. Welcome that creativity as students explore ways of depicting findings. Using an app to create a path diagram with geometric shapes may work well for one student, while another student may wish to illustrate a cartoon by hand.

Students may experience imposter syndrome (Clance, 1985) when comparing drafts of their findings to published research articles, or when having to demonstrate to others that their research generated meaningful findings and new knowledge. Students may also feel uncomfortable having their work presented by a peer, or when presenting someone else's work. If you observe these reactions, address them in the wrap-up discussion and invite students to reflect on their learning, introducing a component of metacognition (Major et al., 2016).

Harness the creative energy of the activity and bring some levity to help students keep a positive perspective. Reinforce the learning environment as a space for vulnerability, peer support, and active learning for skill development. Acknowledge that students worked in

SHOW THE STORY

a short time frame, and possibly with new tools. Help students focus on a growth mind-set (Dweck, 2008) and remind them that these are skills that can be mastered through experience. Encourage them to reflect on the reasons they decided to become researchers. Remind them that effective studies, and effective communication of findings, can be powerful tools for making a positive difference.

Developing one's scholarly perspective and voice is an intended outcome of this lesson, and something that Patton (2015) identified as important for conveying authenticity and trustworthiness in qualitative research. The lesson is a counterpoint to rigid and prescribed aspects of research activity. It emphasizes excellence in presenting one's findings, but in a way that centers authenticity, self, and creativity. Consider sharing your own experiences with finding your scholarly voice and learning how to share the story of your research study findings with others. Encourage students to employ culturally relevant approaches (Ladson-Billings, 1995), existing funds of knowledge, and diverse ways of knowing when preparing their visual stories.

Context

Course level, sequence, and student population should be taken into consideration. For example, if the lesson is in the later part of a qualitative methods course for doctoral students, students will likely have had opportunities to collect and analyze their own data as well as to engage in socialization around qualitative research studies and publications. If the lesson is part of a unit in an undergraduate course that focuses on disciplinary topics rather than methodological topics, students will be at an earlier stage of development.

I first used a version of this lesson plan years ago and have adapted it over time. Research, how-to guides, communication norms, and technology have all developed in ways that have supported its evolution. I encourage instructors to modify it in ways that work for their students and courses, and in line with continued advancements related to connecting research with audiences and stakeholders, an important skill in the social sciences (American Psychological Association, 2022). For example, Bresciani and Eppler (2015) provided a comprehensive synthesis of "the pitfalls and potential disadvantages of visual representations" (p. 1), which is a helpful guide and may be included as prior reading for this lesson.

The ways that we consume and communicate information have changed. One thing I like about this lesson is that it helps students to prepare for engaging with multiple audiences. This might include members of academic disciplinary communities, policy makers, practitioners, or the public. Visual storytelling guides students through the intellectual work of identifying, synthesizing, and demonstrating the key findings of their studies. It equips students to share that story broadly and in multiple creative formats. Finally, the effective generation and communication of findings is both independent and collaborative. It is important for students to gain experience in presenting their findings as an act of engagement with the community of scholars, including both offering and receiving peer review.

To paraphrase something a student once said to me, when students have completed data collection in qualitative studies, they see the light at the end of the tunnel but they can't tell whether or not it's the train. This lesson is meant to guide students through the creative process of initiating a presentation of findings from their qualitative research in ways that foster authenticity, credibility, and voice while relying on structure and purpose. I hope it will remind students that they are the powerful trains carrying valuable information, and that they are capable of developing the knowledge, skills, and abilities required to meet the destination.

BIBLIOGRAPHY

American Psychological Association. (2022). *Demonstrating the public significance of research*. https://www.apa.org/pubs/journals/resources/translational-messages

Babbie, E. (2016). *The practice of social research* (14th ed.). Cengage Learning.

Bresciani, S., & Eppler, M. J. (2015). The pitfalls of visual representations: A review and classification of common errors made while designing and interpreting visualizations. *Sage Open, 5*(4), 2158244015611451.

Cardel, M. I., Dhurandhar, E., Yarar-Fisher, C., Foster, M., Hidalgo, B., McClure, L. A., … & Angelini, C. (2020). Turning chutes into ladders for women faculty: A review and roadmap for equity in academia. *Journal of Women's Health, 29*(5), 721–733.

Clance, P. R. (1985). *The impostor phenomenon: Overcoming the fear that haunts your success*. Peachtree.

Cormick, C. (2019). *The science of communicating science: The ultimate guide*. Csiro.

Dweck, C. S. (2008). *Mindset: The new psychology of success*. Random House.

Ibrahim, A. M., Lillemoe, K. D., Klingensmith, M. E., & Dimick, J. B. (2017). Visual abstracts to disseminate research on social media: A prospective, case-control crossover study. *Annals of Surgery, 266*(6), e46–e48.

Ladson-Billings, G. (1995). Toward a theory of culturally relevant pedagogy. *American Educational Research Journal, 32*(3), 465–491.

Major, C. H., Harris, M. S., & Zakrajsek, T. (2016). *Teaching for learning: 101 intentionally designed educational activities to put students on the path to success*. Routledge.

Miles, M. B., Huberman, A. M., & Saldaña, J. (2014). *Qualitative data analysis: A methods sourcebook* (3rd ed.). Sage.

Patton, M. Q. (2015) *Qualitative research and evaluation methods* (4th ed.). Sage.

Pollock, T. G. (2021). *How to use story telling in your academic writing: Techniques for engaging readers and successfully navigating the writing and publishing processes*. Edward Elger.

Rodrigues, J. (2021). Get more eyes on your work: Visual approaches for dissemination and translation of education research. *Educational Researcher, 50*(9), 657–663.

32

Block by Block

Building the Discussion Section

Maire Brandenberg, Tamara Hoffer, McKenzie Rabenn and
Cheryl Hunter

INTRODUCTION

The importance of the discussion section is well established (Allen, 2017; Cals & Kotz, 2013; Drisko, 2005) with the purpose clearly being to explain and interpret what was found and how it relates to research that has already explored similar phenomena. However, there is variability in what to include within the overall discussion section. For example, depending on the scholar, between three to six subheadings or components are recommended. Across the literature the only common component suggested is the significance of findings. Additionally, the order in which these components are presented also varies widely. For example, both Cals and Kotz (2013) and Drisko (2005) recommend comparing findings with other studies. However, Cals and Kotz (2013) recommend making this the second component while Drisko (2005) recommends this be included in the first. We argue that the order of the components is most relevant to how the article or chapter is constructed and should primarily be considered in the overall structure provided in the body of the article.

LESSON PLAN

Topic	Block by Block: Building a Discussion Section
Learning Objectives	Students will be able to: • Identify the components of a discussion section of a journal article as measured by their completion of a *Test your Knowledge Activity*. • Evaluate the supporting details required for various components of a discussion section of a journal article as measured by their participation in the *Discussion Group Activity*. • Demonstrate their knowledge of the components of a discussion section by creating the discussion section of a research article provided in the *Guided Application Activity*.

DOI: 10.4324/b23320-40

Topic	Block by Block: Building a Discussion Section
Needed Materials	*Activating Activity*: • Paper • Writing Utensils *Instructional Activity*: • Copy of article: "A Multilevel Examination of Racial Disparities in High School Discipline: Black and White Adolescents' Perceived Equity, School Belonging, and Adjustment Problems" Bottiani, Bradshaw, and Mendelson (2017). *Discussion Group Activity*: • Electronic devices with access to library databases. *Guided Application Activity*: • Instructor-selected research article with discussion section removed. The article should be relevant to course material/student concentrations.
Pre-lesson Preparation	*Activating Activity*: • Prepare personal drawing using shapes to demo for students (based on directions in the Activities section). *Instructional Activity*: • Select format and prepare a presentation on core components of a discussion section that includes examples of alternative components and uses information provided in the Activities section. • Create interactive *Test Your Knowledge Activity* using the questions/responses provided in Activities. *Discussion Group Activity*: • Ensure students bring devices and have access to a library database. • Encourage students to bring articles that they want to explore at a deeper level. *Guided Application Activity*: • With (or without) students, select a relevant article that students must read ahead of class. Remove the discussion portion of the article prior to providing students with the article to read.

Activities	**Activating Activity (5–10 minutes):**
	• Provide students with a piece of paper to draw on.
	• Give students 3–5 minutes to draw an image where they must use a specific set of shapes with the option to select additional shapes from a second list.
	  ◦ Required shapes: 2 squares, 2 circles, 2 triangles, 2 rectangles.
	  ◦ Alternate shapes: diamond(s), star(s), octagon(s), and/or trapezoid(s).
	• Once completed, call on 2–4 students to share their images and their inspiration for their images.
	• Explain that discussion sections of journal articles are constructed in a similar fashion to the drawings. There are components that must be included in a discussion section, but there are other components that can be included at the writer's discretion. Ultimately, the discussion section is a unique interpretation and presentation of these components as they relate to research findings and relevant prior studies.
	Instructional Activity (20–25 minutes):
	• Briefly introduce the four key discussion components that reflect the "required shapes" from the activating activity: Prior studies, significance of findings, implications, and limitations. Include information on optional components of a discussion section that relates to the "optional shapes" from the activating activity. A model of what the instructor's presentation could look like is featured below:

BLOCK BY BLOCK

Topic	Block by Block: Building a Discussion Section
	<ul><li>○ **Slide 1**: Introduction<ul><li>▪ Establish the connection between the introductory activity and writing a discussion section in a journal article.</li><li>▪ Introduce the notion that there are generally four agreed upon and required parts of a discussion (description of what is found in relation to prior studies, significance of findings, implications, and limitations). Explain that there are several additional components that can be added to a discussion section that are typically determined by the researcher's field, discipline, or where the journal an article is submitted.</li></ul></li><li>○ **Slide 2**: Prior Studies<ul><li>▪ Provide context regarding where your research fits in with current research.</li><li>▪ Discuss how results agree or dispute existing research.</li></ul></li><li>○ **Slide 3**: Significance of Findings<ul><li>▪ Discuss correlations (or lack thereof) that exist in the data.</li><li>▪ Provide explanations for correlations (or lack thereof).</li><li>▪ Provide generalizations that can be made based on the data.</li></ul></li><li>○ **Slide 4**: Implications<ul><li>▪ Explore underlying meaning of data.</li><li>▪ Make theoretical connections.</li><li>▪ Discuss practical application of findings.</li></ul></li><li>○ **Slide 5**: Limitations<ul><li>▪ Discuss notable and/or potential problems with methodology and findings.</li><li>▪ Discuss impact of limitations on validity.</li></ul></li><li>○ **Slide 6**: Alternatives<ul><li>▪ Interpretations – alternative explanations for data.</li><li>▪ Future Studies – areas for further development.</li><li>▪ Expanding Themes – distinctly highlight connections/patterns between data relationships to research questions.</li><li>▪ Conclusion – concise summary of findings and why important.</li></ul></li><li>○ Upon completion of the lecture, provide the following *Test Your Knowledge Activity*. The first four questions focus on the core features of a discussion section and the remaining four questions are optional examples of alternative features of discussion sections. Be sure to discuss keywords/phrases within the quotes that drove the students' decision regarding which component the quote belongs to.</li></ul>*Test Your Knowledge Activity* The following is a series of quotes selected from the article: "A Multilevel Examination of Racial Disparities in High School Discipline: Black and White Adolescents' Perceived Equity, School Belonging, and Adjustment Problems" Bottiani, Bradshaw, and Mendelson (2017). Match the quote with the appropriate component of a discussion section: **Core Discussion Components** 1) "The present study is, to our knowledge, the first quantitative analysis to explore the contextual effects of discipline disparities on students' perceptions of themselves and their schools, regardless of whether they have been suspended or not." (p. 539)<ul style="list-style-type:none"><li>A. Future Studies</li><li>B. Implications</li><li>C. **Significance of Findings**</li><li>D. Conclusion</li></ul>2) "This study's findings suggest that, in addition to introducing alternatives to suspension (e.g., restorative justice programming) and equity-focused interventions to eliminate the gap (e.g., culturally responsive classroom behavior management), more immediate supports for Black youth in schools with highly differential discipline practices may be needed." (p. 542)<ul style="list-style-type:none"><li>A. Future Studies</li><li>B. **Implications**</li><li>C. Significance of Findings</li><li>D. Conclusion</li></ul>

Topic	Block by Block: Building a Discussion Section

3) "A large and growing literature examines the potentially harmful effects of out-of-school suspension, which disproportionately removes Black youth from U.S. schools (e.g., Fabelo et al., 2011)." (p. 539)
   A. Conclusion
   B. Expanding Themes
   C. Implications
   D. **Prior Studies**

4) "First, the results should be interpreted with caution because of the potential that the degree of discipline disparity may have changed during the 1-year time lapse between the collection of discipline disproportionality data and student-reported outcomes." (p. 541)
   A. Interpretation of Findings
   B. **Limitations**
   C. Implications
   D. Conclusion

Alternative Discussion Components

5) "The results highlight the need for more research on interventions that can ultimately eliminate the discipline gap." (p. 542)
   A. Implications.
   B. Significance of Findings
   C. **Future Studies**
   D. Limitations

6) "This finding suggests that, when Black students are more frequently removed from the school than their White classmates, it may send a message to all students (suspended or not) about the degree to which Black students are welcome and accepted in the school social context." (p. 540)
   A. **Interpretation of Findings**
   B. Prior Studies
   C. Significance of Findings
   D. Conclusion

7) "It is novel in its use of multilevel analysis to examine school discipline disparities as a feature of the school context negatively associated with protective factors such as *perceived equity* and *school belonging*, and positively associated with *adjustment problems*." (p. 539)
   A. Conclusion
   B. **Expanding Themes**
   C. Implications
   D. Prior Studies

8) "Initiatives to broach the issue of the discipline gap with Black students in high-disparity schools have potential to disrupt harmful perceptions of the school social context as unfair and unaccepting by demonstrating respect for the perspectives of Black youth and some readiness to change." (p. 542)
   A. Prior Studies
   B. Interpretation of Findings
   C. **Conclusion**
   D. Expanding Themes

Discussion Group Activity **(20–30 minutes):**
- Divide students equally into four groups and assign them one of the four core sections of the discussion section.
- Direct each group to access their institution's library database to find a brief, relevant research article for analysis.

BLOCK BY BLOCK

Topic	Block by Block: Building a Discussion Section

	• Direct students to answer the following questions regarding their assigned section:
	  ◦ How was your section represented in the discussion section?
	  ◦ What details from the article are included under your assigned section? How do those details shape the meaning of your assigned section and the discussion as a whole?
	  ◦ What details are included in your section that is NOT represented in another section of the article? How does this information contribute to the discussion section and overall message of the article?
	  ◦ What key vocabulary does the author use to inform your understanding of the assigned section?
	  ◦ What writing style does the author use to communicate information included in this section?
	  ◦ How is the author's voice represented in this section of the discussion section? What is the author communicating?
	• Call on each group to present the findings on their assigned section and one "optional" section.
	• Encourage students to share their thoughts on the presentations, what is involved in creating a discussion section, and if they have any questions about the construction of a discussion.
	Guided Application Activity (25–30 minutes):
	• Students should have read an assigned research article prior to class, with the discussion section removed. Provide time to write a discussion section for the article.
	• Provide students with the actual discussion section of the research article that was written by the authors.
	• Give students time to reflect on the discussion section they prepared and the discussion section written by the authors. Provide the following guiding questions:
	  ◦ How does what you wrote compare with the discussion created by the researchers?
	  ◦ What made you select the components you chose to represent in your discussion section?
	  ◦ Where was there room for improvement of the author(s)'and the self-generated discussion sections?
	• Direct students to turn in their self-written discussion section.
	• Wrap up by gaining feedback from students.

Virtual Adaptations	Each component can easily be adapted for virtual environments: • *Activating Activity* – https://sketch.io/sketchpad/ is a virtual sketchpad. • *Instructional Activity* – an outside quiz maker, such as Kahoot, can be used in virtual adaptations. Players answer on their own devices, while questions are displayed on a shared screen. • *Discussion Group Activities* – for these small group settings, we recommend utilizing the breakout rooms in Zoom. Each group can create a Google Slide with their component and then share their screen using the Share Screen Zoom feature. For asynchronous adaptations, we use the Voice Thread discussion platform. • *Guided Application Activity* – again we recommend having students break into Zoom Breakout Rooms. Each group will work together on a Google doc to write their discussion section.
Assessment	Formative Assessment: Interactive Jigsaw Quiz Formative Assessment: Discussion Analysis Presentation Summative Assessment: Independent Discussion Writing Sample

INTELLECTUAL PREPARATION FOR LESSON

Core Ideas

A professionally written discussion section helps the audience interpret the significance of the present study in context with past literature, then map out recommendations for future research (Shon, 2015). The foundational concepts students should gain from this lesson include knowledge of: (1) the key components common across research articles or chapters for a discussion section; (2) diverse ways to organize these components in a discussion section; and (3) optional components of a discussion section that can also be incorporated. The key components for any discussion section include a description of what was found in relation to prior studies, significance of findings, implications, and study limitations. Depending on the field or journal, other components such as interpretation, future studies, expanding themes, and a conclusion may be relevant.

Learners

We have found that novice researchers struggle to move past simple data summary into integrating current findings with previous scholarship and offering future vision. This is often attributed to inadequate reading, both in quantity (broad) and quality (critically), and to learners having underdeveloped writing skills and styles (Shon, 2015). Learning to situate current results of findings within the context of past works requires students to read broadly and critically so that integration of past, present, and future develop into a well-crafted story (Shon, 2015). Students must have read enough literature to understand the discussion for which they are contributing and do so with a critical eye to be cognizant of the gaps in the scholarship they might address with their contribution.

Students must also learn to insert their voices into the scholarly community and develop their writing styles. By deconstructing the discussion section with their peers, then building a discussion of their own, and finally comparing it to the original article, we help students to identify the foundational components of most discussion sections and expose them to a variety of writing styles and voices.

We use explicit instruction, making the learner aware of the processes for learning a skill, then reverse engineering that skill into a series of small steps (Rosenshine, 1987). When novice writers are made aware of critical scholarly writing skills, like taking a stance or making an argument, by identifying these key features in exemplars, instructors help emerging scholars to learn and apply these skills more effectively in their own academic writing (Zhang & Zhang, 2021). We draw attention to the variety of components that can be present in a discussion with our opening shape-building activity, then we make transparent authors' use of style when presenting their findings within the backdrop of previous works and how they insert themselves into the scholarly community during the *Test Your Knowledge Activity*. Students must identify vocabulary used as well as style components when they defend how they matched their component with an item from the article. By identifying specific structural and style components in journal articles, students transfer this knowledge to develop their own style.

We try not to make assumptions about learners' prior knowledge of writing conventions or skills; we try to anticipate prerequisite skill gaps and use explicit teaching to address these missing or underdeveloped skills. For example, inserting oneself into the scholarly community requires using voice. Students may not understand what "voice" means or how to insert their voices into scholarly writing. We make the use of voice transparent for students by showing them how authors use their own in the articles we have chosen. Then, students practice using their own voices when building the discussion in the *Guided Application Activity*. By explicitly teaching writing style conventions, showing examples and non-examples, having students identify stylistic applications in articles, and then applying these style conventions as they construct a discussion section with their peers, we are supporting diverse learners with varying skills and expertise across the learning continuum. We are not making assumptions that students have the prerequisite skills or language necessary for artfully constructing a well-written discussion section. Rather, we are bridging the gap between prior knowledge and new knowledge.

Context

For students to move from concept awareness to integration, research recommends providing opportunities for collaborative practice of writing skills to help learners assimilate abstract knowledge through concrete application and practice of newly learned concepts (Barzilai, et al. 2018; Darowski, et al., 2020). We use collaborative practice in small groups to dissect article discussion sections. Students first identify the four components, any additional components added for meaning, and stylistic applications. Groups then practice building their own discussion sections that incorporate the four key components, experiment with adding their own stylistic elements, and conclude with a class discussion where they reflect on whether the written section they constructed enhances meaning for their intended audience. Students defend their choices of vocabulary and style during these discussions and receive feedback from peers. This collaborative learning approach allows students to learn and grow from one another and promote higher order thinking (Gates, 2018).

Throughout this lesson, students work together and spend time immersed in rich literature; one of which will be an assigned culturally relevant article about racial disparities as well as an article of choice selected by students to account for alternative perspectives. Students have diverse backgrounds, capabilities, vocabulary, language, and experiences with writing. Making assumptions about students' prior knowledge when learning something new can leave learners in disequilibrium and render them ill-equipped as they try to construct meaning without a sturdy foundation to build upon. The instruction activity section utilizes explicit instruction to ensure all students understand the main components of a discussion. Afterwards, students are tested on their knowledge using a culturally relevant article that focuses on racial disparities. Any misunderstandings can be addressed at that time. During the discussion and guided group activities, students practice collaboratively to help address any missing or lagging skills necessary for scholarly writing and to bridge students' prior knowledge with newly learned concepts in a low-stake setting. By honoring and accounting for students' funds of knowledge, addressing previous misconceptions, incorporating student choice, and honoring alternative perspectives, students will be able to successfully write a discussion section.

BIBLIOGRAPHY

Allen, M. (2017). Writing a discussion section. *The SAGE encyclopedia of communication research methods*, pp. 1883–1886. SAGE Publications, Inc. 10.4135/9781483381411

Barzilai, S., Zohar, A. R., & Mor-Hagani, S. (2018). Promoting integration of multiple texts: A review of instructional approaches *and practices. Educational Psychology Review, 30*(3), 973–999.

Bottiani, J.H., Bradshaw, C. P., & Mendelson, T. (2017). A multilevel examination of racial disparities in high school discipline: Black and white adolescents' perceived equity, school belonging, and adjustment problems. *Journal of Educational Psychology, 109*(4), 532–545.

Cals, J. W. L., & Kotz, D. (2013). Effective writing and publishing scientific papers, part VI: Discussion. *Journal of Clinical Epidemiology, 66*(10), 1064. https://doi.org/10.1016/j.jclinepi.2013.04.017

Darowski, E. S., Helder, E., & Patson, N. D. (2020). Explicit writing instruction in synthesis: Combining in-class discussion and an online tutorial. *Teaching of Psychology, 49*(1), 57–63.

Drisko, J. W. (2005). Writing up qualitative research. *Families in Society: The Journal of Contemporary Social Services, 86*(4), 5.

Fabelo, T., Thompson, M.D., Plotkin, M., Carmichael, D. Miner, P.M., & Booth, E.A. (2011). Breaking schools' rules: A statewide study of how school discipline relates to students' success and juvenile justice involvement. Report by Council of State Governments Justice Center No. 235311.

Gates, S. (2018). Benefits of collaboration. *National Education Association*. https://www.nea.org/professional-excellence/student-engagement/tools-tips/benefits-collaboration

Rosenshine, B. (1987). Explicit teaching and teacher training. *Journal of Teacher Education, 38*(3), 34–36.

Shon, P. C. (2015). *How to read journal articles in the social sciences: A very practical guide for students*. Sage. [Kindle version]. Retrieved from Amazon.com

Zhang, L., & Zhang, L. J. (2021). Fostering stance-taking as a sustainable goal in developing EFL students' academic writing skills: Exploring the effects of explicit instruction on academic writing skills and stance deployment. *Sustainability, 13*(8), 4270.

33

Making the Theoretical Practical

Implications for Theory

James C. Coviello

INTRODUCTION

As a research methods instructor in an educational leadership doctoral program that serves current practitioners and emerging scholars, one of the most difficult aspects of writing a discussion section is the Implications for Theory section. Theory in general is often misunderstood or maligned, with feelings of "It's *just* a theory" or "That theory sounds fine, what do I do *tomorrow* at school?" hiding just below the surface in class discussions. Students often gravitate towards aspects of their studies they see as more practical and applicable to their current and future positions in the field. Given this background, implications for practice are perhaps a bit clearer to consider; implications for theory, perhaps less so. The purpose of this lesson is to present a structured, practical lesson to help students consider how theories utilized in a study are confirmed, challenged, or complicated by a study's findings when writing an Implications for Theory section.

LESSON PLAN

Topic	Brainstorming, making connections, and writing an Implications for Theory section
Learning Objectives	• Students will brainstorm ideas for connecting findings to theory. • Students will consider how a theoretical framework is confirmed, challenged, or complicated by a study's findings. • Students will examine previous examples of implications for theory in empirical studies and balance under- and over-stating their contributions to present genuine additions to the field.
Needed Materials	• A published empirical study (of the instructor's choice) with the Discussion section removed. For homework before the lesson takes place, students would read this abridged article and summarize the main elements of the theoretical framework used in the study and the study's main findings (see Coviello & DeMatthews (2021) for an example that utilizes an accessible theoretical framework).

DOI: 10.4324/b23320-41

Topic	Brainstorming, making connections, and writing an Implications for Theory section
	• A worksheet consisting of a table (either printed or technology-based, e.g., word processing software) with two columns labeled as: "Main Elements of Theoretical Framework and Findings." Under these columns should be a set of "Questions to Consider," and then under these questions a row for potential "Implications for Theory" (see Appendix A).
Pre-lesson Preparation	• *What is the purpose of theory and a theoretical framework?* I make sure that students are on the same page when it comes to the purpose of a theoretical framework in a research study, given its connection to the Implications for Theory. These topics are sometimes presented in different courses, so it is helpful to refresh these ideas in the minds of students (see the Activities section below for some key points an instructor might include). • *How do you make the Implications for Theory practical? How can students practice writing this section without conducting their own study?* Finding useful examples of empirical articles with a well-written Implications for Theory section is important for emerging researchers to see how the authors connected theory to findings (see DeMatthews, 2018). Choosing a study that has a topic, theory, and method that is easily accessible for students is therefore key. To be sure, students will not have the same familiarity with this study, its theoretical framework, findings, and implications as they would their own research. Yet, this lesson provides an opportunity to work with examples from the field and compare their work to a published Implications for Theory section.

Activities	• Provide students an example of a published empirical study (of the instructor's choice) with the Discussion section removed (I would advise choosing one that is not too long). For homework before the lesson takes place, students read this abridged article and summarize the main elements of the theoretical framework used in the study and the study's main findings
	• Begin class with a brief discussion or lecture on the purpose of a theoretical framework and a study's implications section. Explain that:
	  ○ A theoretical framework is used to establish the basis for a study's problem or question and helps provide a rationale for the researcher's choices in structuring their study (see Lederman & Lederman, 2015). Ask students to reflect on past lessons relating to theory and the use of theoretical frameworks in research.
	  ○ Building, testing, and refining theories is an important function of empirical research for a field of study.
	  ○ As emerging researchers, students have an opportunity to add to the field's understanding of theory and its explanatory and predictive usefulness.
	  ○ The Implications for Theory section of a dissertation or published article provides researchers this opportunity to contribute to the field by connecting the study's findings to the theory that was tested or explored.
	  ○ This section asks researchers to consider how the findings connect to the theory used in the article (and to theories in the field as a whole). It can address the answers to multiple questions (see Appendix A).
	• Distribute to each student a copy of a blank, editable worksheet consisting of a table (either printed or technology-based, e.g., portable document format [pdf] or word processing software) with three columns labeled as: "Main Elements of Theoretical Framework" and "Findings." Under these columns should be a set of "Questions to Consider," and then under these questions a row for potential "Implications for Theory" (see Appendix A).

MAKING THE THEORETICAL PRACTICAL

Topic	Brainstorming, making connections, and writing an Implications for Theory section
	<ul><li>Students will do an activity called "Think/Pair/Share"</li><ul><li>"Think": Allow students approximately 15–20 minutes to independently fill in the chart with the main elements of the theoretical framework used in the study and the study's main findings (their homework) and reflect on what possible implications these findings have for theory.</li><li>"Pair": Then, for approximately 10–15 minutes, have students partner with a classmate to share their interpretation of how the findings extended or challenged the theories used in the study. What similarities or differences do they notice in their possible implications for theory?</li><li>"Share": Finally, invite students to come back to the larger group and engage in a discussion on their thought processes and experience in considering Implications for Theory.<ul><li>Ask each pair to list the different Implications they produced.</li><li>Inquire about the practical difficulties of connecting the findings to the theoretical framework. What did they learn from this exercise and what lessons would they bring to their future work? How might they balance under- and over-stating their contributions in order to present genuine additions to the field?</li><li>Finally, as a class, reveal the study's actual Implications for Theory from the published work. How were they similar to what the class discovered? How well did their work match that of the actual research (understanding that they are less familiar with the study than the actual authors)?</li></ul></li></ul></ul>
Virtual Adaptations	This lesson can be easily adapted as a virtual lesson using a synchronous video conferencing application (like Zoom, Google Meet, Skype, or Microsoft Teams).<ul><li>For the "Think/Pair/Share":</li><ul><li>The worksheet can be distributed electronically beforehand or during the lesson itself (some video-conferencing applications allow for the posting and sharing of files).</li><li>Breakout rooms can be used when students are asked to pair with one another to discuss their work.</li><li>For sharing with the larger group, instructors can conduct the discussion as they would for an in-person lesson. An additional option would be to consider using a virtual whiteboard application. These allow the entire class to post their responses onto a virtual whiteboard (during the "pair" part of the activity) which can then be viewed by the entire class and serve as the basis for discussion.</li></ul></ul>
Assessment	<ul><li>Formative Assessment: For the pair discussion, instructors should walk around the room (or, in a virtual adaptation, drop into breakout rooms) in order to listen to student discussions, determine the level of comprehension, and address any common questions students might have as part of the subsequent large group discussion.</li><li>Summative Assessment: Students can be assessed through a similar exercise as the in-class lesson. Present students with an abridged study (or a simulated theoretical framework and set of findings created by the instructor) and assign them to write an Implications for Theory section. The rubric for this assignment can be based on how effective the Implications addressed the questions included as part of the practice lesson.</li></ul>

INTELLECTUAL PREPARATION FOR IMPLICATIONS
FOR THEORY LESSON

Core Ideas

Though theory can be abstract and esoteric, as Kurt Lewin is said to have stated, "Nothing is as practical as a good theory" (Greenwood & Levin, 1998, p. 19). As I have often repeated to my students, we all use theory to understand, explain, and make predictions about the world around us, whether we are aware of it or not (and whether or not we give these theories fancy, intellectual-sounding names).

With this in mind, one of the most effective ways of communicating the overall purpose of theory – and the important contributions that they can indeed make to this part of the field – is the consideration of the theories that they all, as practitioners, carry around with them every day. Those based on their experience, both professionally and personally, are what researchers such as Sugrue (1997) refer to as "lay theories." Given that most of our doctoral students have a desire to change and fundamentally improve education, an understanding of the inescapable, tacit presence and use of theory is significant.

I try to impart to students the idea that learning and research are, in part, analogous to entering into a conversation and dialogue within the field. This is also true for theory, where students can apply theory in their roles as practitioners and contribute to theory through their research. In their study about the theory-practice gap in educational leadership, Roegman and Woulfin (2019) wrote "Neo-institutional theorists suggest that administrators' lay theories, having been developed within their institutional contexts and often unconsciously, are more likely to support leadership action that maintains the status quo rather than challenge it" (p. 14). Lay theories, left unexamined, can result in the recreation of an organization and will not result in change, which is a goal that most of my students bring to their studies. The study of theory, and students' contributions to it, are one way of bringing about the reform and change they seek.

Learners

Yet, despite its importance, theory can also be intimidating. Students who are emerging scholars and establishing their identities as scholars (see Chapter 37 in this book) are not always comfortable expounding on the efficacy or nuances of a theory, resulting in understating their theory contributions. Or, on the other hand, feelings of insecurity may manifest in students overstating a study's theoretical contributions. So how should students go about considering the implications of a study to theory?

One way is to make it practical. As mentioned previously, students' perceptions of theory are often rooted in its seemingly abstract or esoteric nature. Emerging scholars and practitioners often have little patience for ideas or concepts that do not have an immediate, practical application to their professional lives. This is understandable, given the complex and demanding nature of working in schools, a fact made even more pressing during the Covid-19 pandemic. Rather than considering implications for theory as a purely philosophical and open-ended exercise, I tried to design this lesson in a way that gives students a starting point and provides some structure for their work. I therefore included the use of a worksheet that requires students to first list the important aspects of the theoretical

MAKING THE THEORETICAL PRACTICAL

framework and a summary of the main findings. Rather than simply instructing the student to consider how the study contributed to theory, I also included several questions to consider in order to spur some reflection and deeper thought. This approach provides students some level of organization and direction that might otherwise be missing.

Additionally, using a published study is key in order for students to see an example of this section of a study and allow them to "practice" without having to conduct a research project beforehand. Certainly, a researcher is more familiar with their study and would have greater insight into these theory implications, but students will likely have some level of concurrence with the actual article and will also allow themselves practice in doing what would be a difficult activity that would otherwise be done only by doing their own study. It is also useful to reveal the actual implications for theory that the original author composed in order to compare students' responses, reflect on their process, and build their confidence to critique established theories and scholars in the field.

Though I suggest using a published empirical study and leave open the choice of the specific article, instructors could also use an exemplary dissertation, either from their own program or outside of their institution. Instructors could also choose to create a shortened study utilizing a theory covered in another of the students' courses and connect a set of fictitious findings to this theory to allow for further practice of writing implications.

Context

This lesson is rooted in a consideration of the importance of learning as a reflective and social process, especially for adult learners. As mentioned previously, these students often come to the classroom with a wealth of practical experience that instructors should respect and consider when designing a lesson. Writing about adult learning, Merriam (2008) states, "Encouraging reflection and dialogue, whether with the self, another, or a group, enables learning to take place" (p. 97). In the context of this activity, asking students about past lessons on theory – either those in their current course or in previous courses – is an important aspect of the initial review of prior knowledge that begins the brief lecture on theory and its uses. Specifically, instructors should ask students to reflect on previous lessons on the use and inclusion of a theoretical framework in research, which will provide a basis for discussions on how theory serves as the lens through which researchers base their study and decide their approach was appropriate (see Lederman & Lederman, 2015). Evaluating a theory in relation to these two ideas is a key consideration when reflecting on possible implications for theory.

Additionally, "Think/Pair/Share" exercises are incredibly useful to "encourage dialogue and reflection." Writing a study's implications for theory requires some amount of reflection and dialogue on the contributions this study made for a larger field, of which an emerging scholar is just beginning to appreciate and consider. In that vein, creating spaces for this reflection and dialogue is incredibly important. However, a lesson of this kind without organized purpose can often lead students to feel overwhelmed and lost, so structures like a worksheet or specific reflection questions will give students more direction and feel as though they have a solid foundation from which to consider their study's contribution to theory. Use of a table (like the one that I propose) or other graphic organizer will help to be explicit and systematic in considering how each of a study's findings connect with theory. It is also good practice to explicitly connect each of the implications to a finding from the study when writing up this section, so an organizer will help to provide a clear template for students to follow.

Though theory may continue to get a bad rap from students, this lesson is intended to provide a practical method for considering the importance of theory and allow emerging scholars the space to reflect on how a study they conduct might contribute to the field's understanding of theory. They might also reflect on the lay theories they use every day and appreciate the important role they place as practitioner-scholars in conceptualizing change in the world.

APPENDIX A

EXAMPLE WORKSHEET – CONNECTING THEORETICAL FRAMEWORK AND FINDINGS

Main Elements of Theory/Theoretical Framework	Summary of Findings

Questions to Consider

How effective was the theory in explaining or predicting the phenomenon under study?
Did it make sense to use this theory and apply it in this study? Could another theory or theories have worked better?
Did the findings support or undermine any aspects of the theory?
Did the findings add any nuance or further a more detailed understanding of any aspects of the theory?
Where did the theory come from? Was it used in other fields (business, sociology, etc.)? If so, did it work in the field of education? If not, could it be used on other fields or for other purposes (based on what you learned in your findings)?
How might the theory be improved?
Should the field consider creating a new theory or combining this theory with another?
How might future researchers use this theory now that there is additional understanding of it?
Given what was found, could this theory inform an understanding of different units of analysis (e.g., teachers, parents, community, school, leadership, district)? Could it be applied in other contexts or other populations/ participants? Or other methods (quant/qual/mixed) or methodological approaches (e.g., narrative, case studies, quasi-experimental)?
How do you know if you have struck a balance in not over- or under-stating your contribution to theory?

Implications for Theory

BIBLIOGRAPHY

Coviello, J., & DeMatthews, D. E. (2021). Failure is not final: Principals' perspectives on creating inclusive schools for students with disabilities. *Journal of Educational Administration, 59*(4), 514–531.
DeMatthews, D. (2018). Social justice dilemmas: Evidence on the successes and shortcomings of three principals trying to make a difference. *International Journal of Leadership in Education, 21*(5), 545–559.
Greenwood, D. J., & Levin, M. (1998). Action research, science, and the co-optation of social research. *Studies in Cultures, Organizations and Societies, 4*(2), 237–261.
Jaeger, A. J., Dunstan, S., Thornton, C., Rockenbach, A. B., Gayles, J. G., & Haley, K. J. (2013). Put theory into practice. *About Campus, 17*(6), 11–15.
Practical discussion of understanding theoretical frameworks and how to apply them in research.
Lederman, N. G., & Lederman, J. S. (2015). What is a theoretical framework? A practical answer. *Journal of Science Teacher Education, 26*(7), 593–597.
Attempts to demystify an broaden an understanding of theoretical frameworks and how theory underpins research.

MAKING THE THEORETICAL PRACTICAL

Merriam, S. B. (2008). Adult learning theory for the twenty-first century. *New Directions for Adult and Continuing Education, 119*, 93–98.

Brief primer on adult learning theory and new conceptions and applications.

Roegman, R., & Woulfin, S. (2019). Got theory? Reconceptualizing the nature of the theory-practice gap in K–12 educational leadership. *Journal of Educational Administration, 57*(1), 2–20.

An examination of the specific factors related to the theory-practice gap, particularly in educational leadership.

Sugrue, C. (1997). Student teachers' lay theories and teaching identities: Their implications for professional development. *European Journal of Teacher Education, 20*(3), 213–225.

Provides a discussion of lay theory and its relationship to teacher professional development.

Whetton, D.A. (1989). What constitutes a theoretical contribution? *Academy of Management Review, 14*(4), 490–495.

Discusses writing theoretical articles, but is applicable to empirical articles and implications for theory.

34

The Donut Memo

Writing for Policymakers and Practitioners

Christopher R. Marsicano, Rylie Martin, Ann F. Bernhardt and Emilia G. Rounds

INTRODUCTION

Mark Twain once joked, "Reader, suppose you were an idiot. And suppose you were a member of Congress. But I repeat myself." To write for a policymaker, one has to think like a policymaker; doing so is difficult – especially for graduate students who have more likely than not never held public office or worked in government. Although graduate students may have had previous experience as educators or other practitioners, the incentive structures for writing in the research and practical world are grossly misaligned. Neither policymakers nor practitioners are subject-matter experts. They do not know what they do not know. They rely on quality research from scholars to enable evidence-based decision-making. Translating "researcher" into "policymaker" or "practitioner" can be a daunting task.

The world of politics and policymaking moves slowly… until it doesn't. During long periods of political inertia, position papers and think pieces are tolerable – even welcome. Yet, when the government begins to move, policymakers lose what little appetite they had for long-form research. They have no time to read your magnum opus dissertation. Neither do practitioners; they want to know what can help their students immediately, without delay. To have an impact, scholars must distill the most important parts of their work into easily digestible pieces. Turning 8,000 words into 80 is a difficult skill to master. First-year PhD students and seasoned full professors alike struggle with cutting precious paragraphs into focused chunks resembling campaign ad soundbites.

The purpose of "The Donut Memo" lesson is to provide students with some insight into the ways policymakers and practitioners think about interventions while also bolstering student mastery of clear, concise, relatable writing. Also, donuts are delicious.

DOI: 10.4324/b23320-42

THE DONUT MEMO

257

LESSON PLAN

Topic	*Thinking like (and writing for) policymakers and practitioners.*
Learning Objectives	• Students will learn how to write clear, concise analytic memos for policymakers, practitioners, and a general audience. • Students will critically analyze a simplistic policy decision, then apply lessons learned to a more complex policy problem. • Students will translate the core concepts of analytic memo writing to the implications section(s) of their research work.
Needed Materials	• Donuts procured from a nearby location (location matters for the exercise), and hidden somewhere in class. The instructor will need enough for each student to have a donut. • Printed copies of "The Donut Memo" (example provided at the end of the chapter). • White board with dry-erase markers (though screen or a chalkboard will do). • For prior homework, students should read Part I of: Bardach, E., & Patashnik, E. M. (2019). *A Practical Guide For Policy Analysis: The Eightfold Path to More Effective Problem Solving.* CQ press.
Pre-lesson Preparation	• *How can I scaffold this lesson?* We use "The Donut Memo" in introductory policy analysis classes, but it could be used in any introductory research methods course as a "change of pace" activity or as a way to teach policy implications writing. Upper level courses can revisit this lesson by asking students to think about the criteria used for policy analysis in gauging the policy relevance of their work. • *Do all students have the cultural context to appreciate" The Donut Memo"?* "The Donut Memo" exercise requires students to shout out the names of snacks for class. We have found that preferred snack choice is culturally and geographically dependent. For example, when teaching this class in Nashville, students yelled out "Goo Goo Clusters" – a common candy from the region. In a class with several students of Latin American descent, "churros" was a popular option. Note that the choice of primary snack used for the lesson – donuts – could easily be any snack that is inexpensive, easily transportable, and sweet. The instructor is welcome to change the snack to whatever is most culturally relevant to the class. Instructors may also want to take into account participant dietary restrictions.
Activities	• Require students to read Part I of the Bardach and Patashnik book prior to class. • Before class begins, place the donuts you will eventually give to students at the end of class out of sight. • Distribute paper copies of "The Donut Memo" facedown and ask students not to turn over the paper until told to do so. • Start the class by telling students the purpose of the lesson: to learn how to write for policymakers. Point out that writing on a specific policy topic like "how to ameliorate the effects of climate change" or "how to ensure literacy for all children in the United States" can be a daunting task, so instead, we will be using a simpler policy question as an example: "what snack should the class get today?" • On the board or screen, write the policy question: "What snack should the class get today?" • For around five minutes, ask students to shout out snack options. Write each option on the board. Given enough time, students will inevitably shout out three – donuts, fruit, and ice cream. While rare, it is possible that students will not hit all three of the options, in that case, force the choice by saying something like, "And for the gluten-free and health conscious among you, let's add a nice fruit option." I have never not had a group of students say "donuts."

Topic	*Thinking like (and writing for) policymakers and practitioners.*
	• Tell students that for the purposes of class, you will focus on those three snack options. Then, begin to go over a policy analysis using each of the snack options as "alternatives" in the Bardach parlance. Start by listing the problem – the professor wants to give students a snack. Work with students to add additional caveats to go into the "problem" statement in the written *Donut Memo*: 　◦ The snack must be affordable (professors aren't rolling in the dough). 　◦ The snack must be easy to transport, ensuring that it gets to class without a problem. 　◦ The snack must be sweet; we often use language around a class snack being an opportunity to eat something delicious and sugary (see the memo example at the end of the chapter for guidance). 　◦ There is no time to gauge class preferences before choosing the snack. • After fully listing the above caveats in the problem statement, ask students to use active verbs to shout out criteria to analyze each of the alternatives (snack options) based on the statement of the problem. Guide the students to use active verbs in their criteria (e.g., control costs, limit expenses, etc) and relate each criterion to a section of the problem statement (the snack must be affordable → limit expenses). • Once students and the instructor agree on the alternatives (snack choices) and criteria, draw a large matrix on the board that looks like this:

	Limit expenses	Transport easily	Sweet treat
Ice Cream			
Fruit			
Donuts			

• Begin the policy analysis task by weighing each of the snack options against each of the criteria. Ask students to make a case for whether each snack meets each criterion. We recommend using a check (✔), cross (✘), neutral mark (–) system, whereby checks show that the snack meets the criterion, crosses show that the snack does not meet the criterion, and neutral marks show that the snack only partially meets the criterion. Students may either make this determination in small groups (with each group assigned to a given snack) or as a whole class. The end result should look something like this:

	Limit expenses	Transport easily	Sweet treat
Ice Cream	–	✘	✔
Fruit	–	✔	✘
Donuts	✔	✔	✔

• Then ask students which option provides the best option for a snack based on the criteria. The answer will overwhelmingly be "donuts" as donuts meet all three criteria.
• Tell students to turn over their hard copies of "The Donut Memo". Walk through with them each section of the memo, asking students to tie each section with a component of the group exercise above. We recommend asking a different student to read each section of the memo aloud (with each paragraph in the analysis being read by a different student).

THE DONUT MEMO

Topic	*Thinking like (and writing for) policymakers and practitioners.*

- Provide students with a mini-lecture/guided discussion on the importance of different sections of the memo. Be sure to mention the following:
  - The main takeaway of the memo is listed three times: in the subject line, in the overview, and in the recommendation. Policy makers have short attention spans and rely on repetition to fully comprehend a recommendation.
  - The background section includes not only what we know about the problem (the instructor wants to eat something sweet) but also what we do not know (we cannot take into account student preferences). Choosing donuts as the class snack satisfies all three criteria set forth by the instructor. It is important to point out to the class that in the world of policymaking, it is unlikely that a policy decision will so neatly satisfy all criteria. Policymakers will have knowledge constraints and the potential solution to every policy problem has some limitations. Acknowledging these limitations builds trust and provides caveats for any recommendations given.
  - Nearly every sentence is written in the active voice, assuring clarity and concision. Passive voice constructions mask the actor, making the analysis difficult to follow.
  - By combining the text of each alternative (e.g., donuts) with each criterion (e.g., limit expenses), the reader can all but determine what the analysis will say. For example, "donuts limit expenses" and "ice cream does not transport easily." Again, this all but guarantees concise and clear writing.
  - The three criteria represent three very common issues policymakers face: cost constraints (professor's salary), infrastructure/logistical issues (transportation to class), and political concerns (wanting to eat something sweet). Policymakers think about these issues all the time.
- When finished with the mini-lecture, ask students if they want donuts. Revel in the joy and wonderment on their faces when you reveal you had hidden donuts in the class the entire time.
- While students begin to select and eat their donuts, give another mini-lecture tying this exercise to policy implications sections in research. Focus on the following core concepts:
  - The policy implications section, along with the abstract, may be the only components of a research paper that a policymaker's staff may read… if they read research papers at all. Therefore, the writing of that section should reflect an active voice with short, snappy, bold sentences.
  - Caveats to the research findings should be few in number in these sections and placed in a dedicated limitations section of every work.
  - Students should identify each research finding as a criterion or an alternative that meets student-identified criteria. Policymakers may not use these terms, but they think in this manner. Here are some examples:
    - If a student's research findings bolster a call for greater equity in higher education, students should frame building equity as a criterion for future analysis of potential policies.
    - If students have evaluated a program or intervention, that program or intervention should be treated as an alternative, with students providing to policymakers the criteria that intervention meets (e.g., "Free community college is a politically popular policy program that bolsters state economies, increases the likelihood of degree attainment, and costs little to state governments").
- Break the students into groups and ask them to follow the same process of "The Donut Memo" with a new policy topic. Some topic examples include:
  - How can the state of California increase postsecondary educational attainment?
  - How can the federal government lower student loan debt?

Topic	Thinking like (and writing for) policymakers and practitioners.
	◦ How can UNC – Chapel Hill reduce binge drinking on campus? ◦ How can the Charlotte-Mecklenburg School District integrate its schools along racial/ethnic lines without busing? • Homework: Ask students to write up the policy implications of a research work of theirs using what they've learned in class. The section should be no longer than 350 words.
Virtual Adaptations	Almost the entirety of "The Donut Memo" (with the exception being able to actually eat donuts) is transferable to an online setting. • Rather than write the check matrix on a white board, using Zoom's white board function or sharing a screen with a Google Slide matrix works just fine. • "The Donut Memo" can be uploaded to course management systems like Moodle, Sakai, Canvas, or Blackboard for student viewing when appropriate. • Breakout rooms easily facilitate discussion at the end of the class.
Assessment	• Formative Assessment: During group discussion time, visit each group and assess students' ability to connect the key components of "The Donut Memo" to student work on policy implications. • Formative Assessment: Review homework requiring students to write a policy implications section of a research work. Provide feedback on work received. • Summative Assessment: Grade the final academic paper using a rubric based on the style of policy analysis adopted by Bardach and Patashnik.

INTELLECTUAL PREPARATION FOR "THE DONUT MEMO" LESSON

Writing for practitioners and policymakers is a challenge. Translating normally cave-at-filled research text into prose that policymakers can understand to inform their work is difficult. To write about policy implications of research findings, one must think like a policymaker. To help students identify the policy implications of their work, we describe our intellectual preparation for "The Donut Memo" by identifying the lesson's core ideas, learners, and context.

Core Ideas

"The Donut Memo" focuses on two major core ideas with respect to the writing of policy implications: clear and concise writing and thinking through research findings as criteria or alternatives in a format with which policymakers are familiar and a Bardach-style policy analysis.

Clear and Concise Writing
"The Donut Memo" lesson consistently exposes students to key principles surrounding clear and concise writing, namely active constructions, short sentences, and language for a general audience. Students are then encouraged to use these principles when completing their writing assignments – both the short-term homework assignment and the long-term final research paper.

THE DONUT MEMO

Identifying Research Findings as Criteria or Alternatives for Analysis

A more important core idea of "The Donut Memo" is helping students frame their research in the terms of criteria or alternatives for policy analysis. Policymakers and practitioners make value tradeoffs consistently in their work as they weigh potential decisions against latent or realized political and institutional constraints. Framing each snack as a policy alternative for analysis by several criteria (ease of transportation, containing costs, satisfying sweet tooths, etc.) allows students to use a low-stakes approach to determine the potential implications of each decision. For example, choosing to transport ice cream over donuts may lead to a melty mess instead of a delightful snack. Furthermore, the exercise helps students identify three key considerations against which policymakers and practitioners will weigh their research findings: cost constraints (professor's salary), infrastructure/logistical issues (transport to class), and political concerns (ignoring the dentist's advice). Indulging in sugary sweets could easily be a political scandal worthy of the "-gate" suffix added to nearly all American political scandals. You've heard of Watergate, but "donutgate" or "cavitygate" could easily be just as impactful in the micropolitics of a dentist's office.

The Learner

While some learners may have previous work experience as classroom teachers or student affairs professionals, they are unlikely to be familiar with the ways in which policymakers understand research writings. They are likely to be unfamiliar with the lingua franca of the policy-making world of criteria and alternatives used in a policy analysis. That lack of knowledge lends itself to "The Donut Memo"; rather than focus on a major policy issue, which can seem overly complex and difficult to understand, "The Donut Memo" simplifies the problem into a relatable issue – a snack for class.

We often find that students come into the course with vastly different levels of preparation for policy-focused writing. Some come from academic backgrounds that include study in disciplines such as English that privilege more long-winded and descriptive writing styles. In another example, legal scholars often use the passive voice, which makes sense in the context of their work. If your client committed a crime, you do not want to identify your client as the culprit when talking about the crime. Instead of "my client robbed the bank," a lawyer might say, "the bank was robbed." This previous learning could hamper the instruction of more direct forms of written communication. Policymakers and practitioners do not have the time to hunt for the actor in every sentence obscured by passive voice. As such, "The Donut Memo" attempts to offset previously learned behavior by hammering home the use of active voice and short sentences.

Learning research methods necessitates learning a new language – one of caveats, stipulations, and careful writing. For the vast majority of every research article, acknowledging limitations is without a doubt the best approach. Writing for a general audience or policymakers and practitioners, however, requires balancing caveats with more declarative, simplistic statements. The irony of a research methods class is that it is likely to have taught the learner to be careful, thereby instilling a habit that makes writing implications sections more difficult. "The Donut Memo" helps learners realize that not every section of writing benefits from cautious or passive language. By lowering the stakes of the decision – it is easy to decide between donuts and ice cream, but not so easy to decide between the child tax credit and student loan forgiveness – "The Donut Memo" allows students to practice more declarative sentences and sentiments befitting an "implications for policy and practice" section. Donuts are the clear best choice based on the criteria put forth in the exercise. While no policy decision will be without its limitations, the addition of too many caveats would muddle the writing and the message. Applying the same logic to more complex research findings suddenly becomes easier after a sillier (and sweeter) example.

The Context

"The Donut Memo" provides an exemplar of scaffolded learning. A silly exercise that ties student conceptualization of problems with a snack leads to a written exercise on the same topic, which leads to a conceptual exercise on a more complex topic, which leads to a written exercise on more complex research findings. With each step, "The Donut Memo" exercise builds upon mastery (or at least familiarity) with an easier, more digestible previous step. The lesson's strength is in its reliance on each previous step. Students don't try to run before they can walk, and the exercise starts them at a nice crawl.

APPENDIX A

EXAMPLE "DONUT MEMO"

MEMORANDUM

To:	Class
From:	Dr. Marsicano
Date:	19 April, 2022
Subject:	Donuts are the best option for a class snack

OVERVIEW

Dr. Marsicano should bring donuts to class because donuts are cheap, easy-to-transport, and sweet.

Problem

Dr. Marsicano wants to bring a snack to class. He wants to pick up the snack right before class and bring it directly to class. Dr. Marsicano cannot use departmental funds for the food, so he will have to pay for anything he provides. Furthermore, Dr. Marsicano has not had a sugary snack in a while and has been craving something sweet. For this reason, Marsicano wants to use the class snack as an opportunity to satisfy his sweet tooth. While he cares about student preferences, Dr. Marsicano cannot poll the class before writing this memo.

THE DONUT MEMO

Criteria

1. Limit expenses
2. Transport easily
3. Allow Dr. Marsicano to eat a sugary treat

Alternatives

A. Ice Cream
B. Fruit
C. Donuts

Analysis

Depending on the brand, ice cream can be either very expensive or very cheap. Dr. Marsicano can, however, contain costs by buying grocery store brand ice cream. Because of its need to stay frozen, ice cream is difficult to transport even with a grocery store near campus. Ice cream has very little nutritional value, satisfying Dr. Marsicano's sweet tooth. Ice cream meets some, though not all, of the criteria for analysis.

Like ice cream, fruit varies in price. Dr. Marsicano can limit expenses by buying apples and bananas in bulk at Costco. Both apples and bananas are easy to transport and are healthy alternatives to junk food. While fruit as a snack option sounds delicious, it does not meet Dr. Marsicano's wish to eat a sugary treat. Fruit meets two of the three criteria.

Donuts cost about ten dollars per dozen, thereby keeping costs low. Because a Dunkin' Donuts location is close to campus, donuts are easy to transport. Donuts will enable Dr. Marsicano to eat a sweet treat during class. Donuts meet all three criteria.

Recommendation

Donuts are a low-cost, easy-to-transport option for someone wanting to eat something sweet. Dr. Marsicano should bring donuts to class.

BIBLIOGRAPHY

Bardach, E., & Patashnik, E. M. (2019). *A practical guide for policy analysis: The eightfold path to more effective problem solving.* CQ Press.

Section VIII

Special Topics

Section Editor: Vicki L. Baker

35

Introduction to Section VIII

Special Topics

Vicki L. Baker

As Boyer (1990) so aptly noted:

> The most important obligation now confronting the nation's colleges and universities is to break out of the tired old teaching versus research debate and define, in more creative ways, what it means to be a scholar. It's time to recognize the full range of faculty talent and the great diversity of functions higher education must perform.
>
> (p. xii)

This volume answers Boyer's call by supporting current and future scholars as they engage in the diverse contexts in which scholarly learning occurs.

Faculty across the academy continue to be rewarded for achieving traditional scholarship metrics (e.g., publications). Yet, calls to broaden our views of scholarship continue. I argue for the need of an additional important framework – how well current scholars prepare the next generation of scholars and scholar-practitioners through their teaching of scholarship in and beyond classrooms and laboratories. This "Special Topics" section provides said framework by highlighting other critical areas in which scholarly identity development and learning occur. The chapters included in this section feature lessons situated in the context of high-impact practices including undergraduate research, community-engaged learning, global learning, and writing-intensive experiences aimed at broad audiences for diverse purposes (Kuh, 2008). In addition, a focus on the "so what?" question is addressed in a lesson focused on policy implications.

CHAPTER OVERVIEWS

Important to scholarly development is learning how to craft a compelling narrative that highlights the outcomes of engagement. The chapter by Baker and McCaffrey features a lesson plan for a professional development workshop delivered as part of an intensive 10-week undergraduate research experience at Albion College. The aim of "Building a Portfolio to Support Professional Advancement and Scholarly Learning," is to help students craft a narrative that translates their scholarly work into a portfolio of work products

DOI: 10.4324/b23320-44

and experiences. As part of the lesson, students are asked to think about their discipline-specific engagement and contribution, and highlight the soft skills developed as part of their research experiences and how that translates in other settings.

As conversations about scholarly development continue to expand globally, so too does the need to support students' scholarly learning in and for global contexts. The chapter by Lunsford and Jutta, "Developing Students' Cultural Competence Through Video Interviews," focuses on the importance of developing students' cross-cultural competence. Through a global partnership with Soliya Connect, an intercultural exchange program, students at Campbell University connect with peers from global partners. The aim is to help students build an understanding of research practices in other cultures and exchange ideas about cross-cultural research. The chapter features a lesson plan about the interview component in which students interview global peers to increase their cultural awareness and competence.

In a post-pandemic world, the significance of community-engaged scholarship is even more paramount as members of the academy seek to develop future generations of scholars eager to tackle social problems. The chapter by Corbin, Hartfield-Méndez, and Ward highlights the role of community engaged scholarship, and the importance of such scholarly engagement to students, communities, and institutions. The featured lesson plan, "Developing Awareness of Self and Others," equips students with the vital capacity for appreciating narrative (one's own and others') through the practice of story circles. As the authors note, the lesson plan represents a critical first step for engaging students in a collaborative mode of inquiry directly with community partners. Such engagement offers promise for harnessing the resources of educational institutions, through collaborative processes.

Thinking broadly about the implications of scholarship is a critical, yet often under supported area of scholarly development. Lane's chapter highlights the role of policy implications in the research process. By engaging in the featured "Equity Cake Exercise," students must think about how others conceptualize and view equity depending on the perspective(s) from which they are viewing it. To explore these diverse views, students are asked to distribute portions of cake based on varied policy models, with the caveat they cannot agree to split the pieces of cake equally among team members. Rooted in the critical connection between intention and outcomes, students can devise more robust, equity-minded policy implications.

While academic writing is important within and outside the academy, this near singular focus on scholarly skill development fails to acknowledge the power of public writing and the role of that writing in engaging in and advancing public discourse. Hennessy bring this issue to the forefront through her featured lesson, "Disseminating Research Through Public Writing for Mainstream Publications." By engaging in this lesson, students begin to understand the difference between academic writing and public writing by focusing on the power of the op-ed as a means of highlighting critical issues and diverse stakeholders.

COLLECTIVE CONTRIBUTION

As a collective, there are four critical outcomes of the featured lessons in the "Special Topics" section. First, the authors highlight the varied and diverse outcomes that result

INTRODUCTION TO SECTION VIII

from engagement in scholarly and creative activity. Their lessons advance the conversation, and subsequent practice, to account for the scholarly learning that happens beyond the classroom. Second, long gone are the days where wisdom is imparted by a teacher who professes in front of a room full of students. The work of these section contributors highlights the role of diverse partners and stakeholders as co-creators and co-disseminators of knowledge and facilitators of scholarly learning. Third, the lessons encourage us all to think broadly about the implications of our scholarly and creative endeavors beyond dissemination. We must ask ourselves, who does this work benefit, and how does it provide a benefit? Finally, each of the section contributors provide a roadmap on how to develop confidence and needed skills to engage in a scholarly world; a world that exists outside the confines of the academy.

BIBLIOGRAPHY

Boyer, E. L. 1990. *Scholarship reconsidered: Priorities of the professoriate*. Princeton, NJ: The Carnegie Foundation for the Advancement of Teaching.

Kuh, G. D. (2008). Excerpt from high-impact educational practices: What they are, who has access to them, and why they matter. *Association of American Colleges and Universities, 14*(3), 28–29.

36

Scholarly Identity Development of Undergraduate Researchers

A Lesson Plan for Professional Development

Vicki L. Baker and Vanessa McCaffrey

INTRODUCTION

Undergraduate research (UR) is regarded as a high-impact practice (Kuh, 2008) that spans all disciplines. Engagement in UR is shown to benefit the students who engage and the faculty who serve as mentors (Baker et al., 2018; Donohue-Bergeler et al., 2018; Easley, 2017). The overall goal of the Foundation for Undergraduate Research, Scholarship and Creative Activity (FURSCA) at Albion College is to fund and support undergraduate research. Formalized in 1999, FURSCA has supported more than 1500 students in all disciplines to work on creative projects and present the results of those projects at both local and national conferences. UR is supported through funding for research/scholarly supplies during the semester, fellowships for ten weeks of work on campus during the summer, conference travel for students or through fellowships for first- and second-year students to work during the semester.

The summer research fellowship program is the flagship program of FURSCA. To receive funding, students identify and collaborate with a faculty mentor and submit a three-page proposal outlining their scholarly plans. After the proposal is reviewed by an internal committee, students receive a stipend for up to ten weeks of work, housing for the duration of their project and money for supplies to complete their project. The FURSCA program funds 40+ students every summer.

An important aspect of the summer program is the use of professional development (PD) workshops to supplement and complement the skill and scholarly development that occurs as a result of engaging in UR. These workshops span a range of topics including *Crafting a Compelling Personal Statement, Effective Interviewing Techniques*, and *Mental Health for the Schola*r. They are hosted and run by campus experts or college alumni with graduate or advanced training in these areas.

For the purposes of this chapter, we highlight a specific PD workshop titled, *Building Your Portfolio*, otherwise referred to as a body of work, developed and delivered by the lead author of this chapter. The aim of the workshop is to provide students with the needed support as they develop a portfolio of scholarly or creative works and other professional accomplishments that help to characterize their academic experiences while at Albion College.

DOI: 10.4324/b23320-45

SCHOLARLY IDENTITY DEVELOPMENT

LESSON PLAN

Topic	*Building a portfolio to support professional advancement and scholarly learning*

Learning Objectives	• Students will be able to define a "portfolio" and its elements.
	• Students will learn to clearly communicate work products that are part of their portfolio (with a particular focus on engagement in the summer FURSCA experience in this example; instructors can substitute their own relevant programs/workshops).
	• Students will walk away with an ability to:
	  ○ Tell their story about *why* FURSCA (or other relevant program)?
	  ○ Explain *what/who* they are studying / what they are creating and *why*.
	  ○ Communicate the benefits, and who benefits, from their scholarship/creative inquiry (implications for knowledge creation and practice).
	  ○ Articulate how this experience supports professional goal achievement in college and beyond; how it contributes to their scholarly learning.
	• Students will have the skills to craft a related narrative that connects the dots among work tasks, activities, and professional pursuits that make up one's portfolio.

Needed Materials	For Students: • FURSCA proposal • Current resume • List of academic activities (e.g., student organizations, co-curricular engagement, athletics). • Google Drive (or similar) as a place to upload content for the portfolio. For Instructors: • Basic understanding of a portfolio and related concepts (see resources offered in "Activities").
Pre-lesson Preparation	• *How can I/we scaffold this lesson?* This PD workshop is part of a series of workshops aimed at fostering a UR pipeline starting with the first year and equipping students with the needed skills and competencies to develop their scholarly learning. Throughout the full FURSCA program, topics of workshops build on and reinforce each other. • *Does this activity have cross-disciplinary appeal?* FURSCA is open to and includes students from all four divisional areas across the college. Therefore, I/we ensure the content starts broadly making a case for how/why this topic is relevant regardless of disciplinary area, diverse disciplinary examples of how to achieve the learning outcomes are shared throughout the workshop.

Activities	This lesson is modeled in a PD workshop style, in which the instructor guides attendees through the steps outlined, while offering examples, support, and dialogue facilitation.
	One of the goals of the workshop is to help students compile elements of their portfolio.
	• The workshop begins with a review of the definition, elements, and benefits of portfolios, including key points:
	  ○ Why this topic/focus on building a portfolio?
	  ○ Define portfolio; discuss the originations and context of the term.
	  ○ Clarify what is included in a portfolio and why (e.g., work samples, creative works, white papers, presentations, personal narrative).
	  ○ How this serves as "Your Albion [institution] Story" (e.g., why you chose Albion, why participate in FURSCA, how engagement in chosen curricular, co-curricular, experiential activities supports your goals, passion, purpose).
	*See for example "What is a Work Portfolio?" and "How to Build a Work Portfolio." https://www.indeed.com/career-advice/resumes-cover-letters/build-your-work-portfolio

Topic	Building a portfolio to support professional advancement and scholarly learning
	https://www.linkedin.com/pulse/how-build-work-portfolio-get-hired-by-linkedin-news/ • For the next 15–20 minutes, ask students to respond to a series of independent reflection questions about their educational, professional, and personal lives, including: 　○ What are your values (e.g., what matters to you, what grounds your decisions, what grounds your action)? 　○ What identities shape (e.g., demographics, athlete, first-generation) your interactions? What identities are most important to you? 　○ What engagement brings you the most joy? What are you most passionate about? • After independent reflection, the instructor calls on volunteer students to share their answers. The instructor provides follow-up questions to students' responses. • For the next 20–25 minutes, with support from the workshop facilitator, students begin to "connect the dots" as they seek to first answer the following question independently –How are your values, joy, and passion connected to your (a) academic/curricular pursuits, (b) co-curricular pursuits, (c) experiential, extra-curricular, co-curricular engagement, and (d) professional roles. In time, the facilitator asks students to share their reflections with nearby peers, and eventually volunteer students share with the whole group. • For the next 30 minutes, students are asked to individually craft statements, sentences, visualizations, or document evidence, to be included in their portfolio about their FURSCA experience using a PSEI framework (Purpose, Scope, Evidence of Impact); they answer the questions below as part of the "Evidence of Impact" component of the framework: 　○ How did you grow, evolve, develop, learn by participating in FURSCA? 　○ What opportunities and hindrances confront you in your growth?
Virtual Adaptations	This workshop can be adapted to be fully virtual or hyflex (in-person and online attendees). To engage virtual attendees, the use of breakout rooms, discussion/jam boards, 1-minute/1-question quizzes, and polls all work well.
Assessment	Formative assessments that ground this PD workshop are outlined below: • To support scholarly learning and PD assessment, students are reminded of the goal(s) of the workshop which is to: Tell your "Albion story"/ build your portfolio by addressing the WHY, WHAT, HOW, and associated outcomes of the UR experience • Articulate the WHY 　○ Why Albion [insert institution/program]? 　○ Why that particular major? 　○ Why this particular activity? (focus on FURSCA) • Articulate the WHAT 　○ What activities? 　○ What learning opportunities? • Articulate the HOW 　○ How did you engage in those "WHATs?" 　○ What were the broader outcomes? • Students share examples of their written statements, goals, and ideas crafted using the PSEI framework. On the spot feedback is offered to students to help refine their thinking. • Student and faculty examples are shared,(with permission) with students so that they can refer to them post-workshop. • 1:1 mentoring sessions are offered to students as a follow up.

INTELLECTUAL PREPARATION FOR LESSON

The Council for Undergraduate Research (CUR) published an edited volume titled, *Characteristics of Excellence in Undergraduate Research (COEUR)* in which volume contributors outlined critical areas necessary to ground and support a successful UR program (Hensel, 2012). The contribution of Rowlett, Blockus, and Larson (2012) is particularly germane to this chapter in that it highlights the critical considerations institutional leaders, program directors, and faculty mentors are encouraged to consider. One such area offered for strong consideration is the inclusion of professional development opportunities that support faculty mentors and student researchers to sustain development while engaged in UR. It was this insight, coupled with our own research into the successes of the FURSCA program at Albion College (McCaffrey et al., 2019), which informed our investment in a professional development workshop series. In the following section of the chapter, we highlight the intellectual preparation that informed the featured workshop and the overall PD series.

Core Ideas

The inclusion of a professional development series, including the featured PD workshop, is to support and enhance participating students' skill and competency development and to encourage sustained engagement in UR. Building a portfolio is grounded by three core ideas aimed at helping students better articulate their story, including how, and in what ways, participation in UR contributes to that story. The core ideas that undergird the featured PD workshop are: (a) what is a portfolio?, (b) values, joy, and passion, and (c) articulating your value add.

What is a Portfolio?

We deliberately chose the word "portfolio" as the core idea or concept from which to ground this PD workshop. Traditionally, a portfolio characterizes a range of investments held by an individual or organization. Although students are not building or managing a financial portfolio, they are in fact developing a portfolio of scholarly or creative works and other professional accomplishments that help to characterize their academic experiences while at Albion College. This body of work helps to define and clarify their scholarly experience with undergraduate research at Albion College and lays the foundation for how they proceed in life after they graduate.

By offering the workshop *during* their summer research experience, as opposed to after, students are given the chance to continually reflect and keep track of what they are doing and what they are learning from the experience. The descriptions that they write in real time are more detailed and better reflect their experiences. Because many of our students have aspirations for graduate or professional school, having an accurate record of their experiences helps when it comes to filling out applications that require them to list professional experiences and when writing personal statements. Furthermore, many of our students apply for a summer research fellowship in the following year to continue their research project. A properly written portfolio can serve as the seed of a research proposal, growing from the work of a previous summer.

Values, Joy, and Passion

Building on the notion of a portfolio, the other core ideas that ground this PD workshop are values, joy, and passion. Students are asked to think about their values, joy, and passions to determine how, and in what ways, they serve as influences that guide their professional and personal choices while at Albion. Additionally, students are guided through reflective exercises to think about how their values, joy, and passions are accounted for in their portfolio broadly *and* in the context of their summer UR experience. Two simple questions guide this discussion and subsequent reflection – Why do you do the things you do (e.g., major, co-curricular, student activities, FURSCA) and how does that engagement help tell your story? What does this "portfolio" of experiences and outcomes mean to you and your own learning?

For many of our students, this is a challenging part of the portfolio for them to address and it can take a great deal of time and discussion. Students are not used to thinking more broadly about the reasons why they are doing the work that they are doing, beyond seeing it simply as a tool or step to get them to their next academic destination. Further, students often do not think about how their engagement contributes to the development of their own scholarly and creative identities. By asking students to reflect on their experiences and frame them within their values and passions, we are helping to create lifelong learners who are more likely to persist in their academic endeavors.

Articulating Your Value Add

As individuals engaged in UR (e.g., faculty mentors, administrator) for nearly two decades, we have come to realize that students struggle to communicate the value add of their UR experience and to think critically about how their engagement in an intensive summer UR experience, for example, contributes to their professional and personal growth. When asked to describe the outcomes of their summer UR, many of the students default to a simple recitation of the mechanics of their project, leaving out the broader skills that they developed, like teamwork, communication, and focus. This PD workshop strives to help students communicate not only the scholarly or creative implications of their work, but to reflect on how it contributes to their evolving personal narrative and skill and competency development (e.g., emotional intelligence, reflexivity in short and long-term goals). In addition, we encourage students to think about how their current engagement contributes to disciplinary and professional advancements in their respective fields.

Learners

When students arrive at the College, many have had limited (or no) prior experience with conducting research or pursuing creative inquiry. Through their coursework, they gain a deeper knowledge in a subject area and become motivated to move beyond what the classroom can offer them. They then identify a research mentor and start the UR process. The UR program directors and faculty mentors then teach students the needed skills, techniques, and methodologies to succeed in their project.

SCHOLARLY IDENTITY DEVELOPMENT

Students often have misconceptions about what constitutes "research." They have pictures in their heads of scientists in white coats staring at test tubes or a writer actively creating a manuscript, but they do not appreciate that in order to be able to do those things, basic skills have to be learned and the background reading must be done. From surveys done at Albion College, students also do not understand that data cleaning and analysis is also part of the UR process. Further, they often do not understand the broader outcomes and the skills that they have learned.

The students also need help understanding what their engagement means in the broader context of their academic experience and how that engagement contributes to their scholarly learning. The success of this PD workshop is seen when students are able to articulate a more clear definition of UR and creative inquiry, the associated activities and learning, and how to thoughtfully describe the importance of what might seem like menial tasks to broader audiences.

Misconceptions and Challenges in Undergraduate Research and Creative Inquiry
The biggest misconception students bring to UR and creative inquiry experiences is a lack of understanding about the extrinsic *and* intrinsic outcomes that can result from engagement. Throughout our tenure working with students in UR, they are often unclear about what is meant by terms such as "research" or "creative inquiry." In instances when there is a baseline understanding of these concepts, students are singularly focused on their disciplinary domains, lacking an ability to understand what these ideas "look like" in other contexts, settings, and disciplines. Therefore, all PD workshops, including the one featured in this chapter, must account for this lack of awareness by offering disciplinary-relevant examples (e.g., helping students understand what this looks like in their field) of what scholarship looks like both in terms of how students discuss their experience, and in how their experience is transferable in other settings.

Students are traditionally clear on the intended outcomes of their engagement (e.g., publication, presentation) given they describe these as part of the proposal submission process. However, students need guidance on how that engagement helps them grow professionally and personally. For example, while frustrating at the moment, a great deal of learning and development occurs from failed laboratory experiments or not receiving approval to enter archives to secure data. These "failures" require students to think of other ways to achieve intended goals. The ability to adapt, to re-envision, and stay focused in the face of setbacks are skills that transcend academic and professional boundaries; they are skills employers are seeking. Helping students understand this and make the needed connections is vital to scholarly learning and identity development.

To facilitate engagement of diverse students, who represent diverse disciplines, we schedule the PD workshops during work/campus hours. Using the workshop format with short interactive discussions, followed by hands-on activities, as opposed to simply lecturing or watching videos, students have the opportunity to exchange ideas as they share samples of their portfolios for review and feedback. Because the projects that the students are working on are personal examples of their interests and discipline-specific scholarly methods, participants are able to gain an appreciation for understanding of the different modes of inquiry that exist across the academy.

Context

In 2019, a comprehensive assessment of the program was undertaken by the authors to understand student usage patterns and student outcomes of the various aspects of the program (McCaffrey et al., 2019). Data from 20 years of participation, along with the results of paired student/faculty surveys administered recently, were analyzed and resulted in two publications. The results of these studies made it clear that both students and faculty who participated in the various FURSCA administered programs wanted support beyond simply the money that was being distributed for research support.

The surveys showed that there were significant differences in the way students vs. faculty/staff mentors described and defined "research" or "scholarship." Students who were participating in these projects did not see themselves as "researchers" due to the perceived menial nature of the tasks and would often stop participating because of this. The FURSCA leadership saw these (and other) comments as an opportunity to create programming that would help bridge this understanding gap. The workshop described here is one of many that have been introduced during the summer fellowship program. This one specifically addresses the assumption that students know what research/scholarship/creative inquiry are.

The tasks and goals in this lesson plan help students who are participating in UR understand the experience, define their skill development, and learn how UR relates to and supports academic and professional goals, and their learning in general. One of the goals of this workshop is to help them craft a compelling narrative that accurately describes both their research project and also the broader skills that they have developed as a result of the UR participation.

By training them to think more critically about the "soft" skills they are developing (collaboration, communication, time management, and so on, as opposed to the "hard" skills such as programming, pipetting, painting, or other discipline specific skills) as part of their summer fellowship participation, we are equipping the students to continue to find and identify these skills in other work that they do on campus, including classwork, community service and participation in sports.

BIBLIOGRAPHY

Baker, V. L., Greer, J., Lunsford, L.G., Ihas, D., & Pifer, M. J. (2018). Supporting faculty development for mentoring in undergraduate research, scholarship, and creative work. In *Excellence in Mentoring Undergraduate Research* (Eds. Maureen Vandermaas-Peeler, Paul C. Miller, and Jessie L. Moore). Council on Undergraduate Research.

Donohue-Bergeler, D., Goulet, C., & Hanka, D. (2018). Flattened hierarchy through drama-based pedagogy: A graduate student instructor and two undergraduates partner on classroom research. *College Teaching, 66*(2), 104–110.

Easley, J. A. (2017). 5 reasons why undergraduates should do research. UC Davis Blog. https://www.ucdavis.edu/majors/blog/exploring-options/reasons-why-undergraduates-should-do-research/

Hensel, N. (Ed.) 2012 *Characteristics of Excellence in Undergraduate Research.* Washington, DC: Council on Undergraduate Research. http://www.cur.org/assets/1/23/COEUR_final.pdf

Kuh, G. D. (2008). Excerpt from high-impact educational practices: What they are, who has access to them, and why they matter. *Association of American Colleges and Universities, 14*(3), 28–29.

McCaffrey, V. P., Baker, V. L., & Manning, C. (2019). "Divisional Trends in Undergraduate Research: A Data-Driven Dialogue in the Creative Arts." Special Issue: Mentoring Undergraduate Creative Scholarship. PURM (8.1). Elon University. ISSN 2157-7307.

Rowlett, R. S., Blockus, L., & Larson, S. (2012). *Characteristics of Excellence in Undergraduate Research* (COEUR). Washington, DC: Council on Undergraduate Research, 2–19.

37

Developing Students' Cultural Competence through Video Interviews

Laura Lunsford and Jutta Street

INTRODUCTION

We seek to prepare students for careers in increasingly global research settings. Most undergraduates have limited experience abroad (NAFSA, n.d.), and 90% of undergraduates at our university are from North Carolina, where our institution is located. Exposure to people from other cultures is a formative activity to develop cultural competence. Yet, travel abroad is challenging for many undergraduates, for financial and personal reasons.

Thus, when Campbell University was contacted about participating in a virtual, international exchange program, we agreed to pilot it in our courses. The Soliya Connect program (https://soliya.net/connect-program) offers four-to-eight-week virtual, international exchanges. We have embedded the program in two of the authors' courses: Social Psychology and an honors course on Global Encounters. Students participate in discussion groups with eight students from the Middle East/North Africa region. One of the assignments is for each group to select a question of interest and then video interview two people, exchange the videos with others in their group and reflect on the commonalities and differences in responses. We recommend the full experience; however, this lesson plan highlights one element of that activity.

For the purpose of this chapter, we have adapted the interview assignment to be completed as a stand-alone activity in any course. The lesson supports the development of aspiring researcher's cultural competence as part of required course activities.

LESSON PLAN

Topic	*Video interview to enhance students' cultural competence.*
Learning objectives	Students will: • Use more culturally inclusive language. • Recognize psychological concepts used by people from other countries. • Increase their awareness about the influence of culture on research.

DOI: 10.4324/b23320-46

Topic	*Video interview to enhance students' cultural competence.*
Needed materials	• Camera on a cell phone or computer with video recording capability. • Internet connection to access YouTube or similar video storage. • Set up a YouTube channel in which students can upload their videos. It is easy to set up a channel with these instructions: https://support.google.com/youtube/answer/1646861?hl=en • Questions (approved by instructor) to use in the interview.

Pre-lesson preparation	*Pre-lesson reading and discussion:*
	• We assign the two articles below that focus on cultural and psychological scales beyond Western, Educated, Industrial, Rich, and Democratic (WEIRD) for this lesson:
	  ○ Henrich, J., Heine, S. J., & Norenzayan, A. (2010). Most people are not WEIRD. *Nature, 466*(7302), 29–29.
	  ○ Muthukrishna, M., Bell, A. V., Henrich, J., Curtin, C. M., Gedranovich, A., McInerney, J., & Thue, B. (2020). Beyond Western, Educated, Industrial, Rich, and Democratic (WEIRD) psychology: Measuring and mapping scales of cultural and psychological distance. *Psychological Science, 31*(6), 678–701. https://doi.org/10.1177/0956797620916782
	• In advance of class, the following questions are given to the students and they write their responses while reading the articles before class.
	  ○ What is a WEIRD sample?
	  ○ Why would we be concerned about generalizing findings from WEIRD samples to non-WEIRD populations?
	• In a class session, students will share their responses to the questions in small groups. One student leader from each group will share their responses with the class, while the instructor facilitates the class discussion.
	Pre-lesson discussion on critical thinking and research questions:
	• Have a class discussion about the importance of critical thinking and culturally inclusive language in developing research questions. We ask students what it means to think critically and compare their answers with Halonen's (1996) broad definition: "the propensity and skills to engage in an activity with reflective skepticism focused on deciding what to believe or do."
	• Students will be asked to invite a student from a country other than their own country of origin to participate in a short, one-question interview. Discuss how to respectfully identify and invite students from another country to participate in the lesson. For additional support, the instructor could invite relevant offices (i.e., Office of International Students, Student Life, Residence Life) to speak to the class, as well as support students while they invite a student from another country.
	Pre-lesson preparation on video logistics
	• Provide students with the informational link on how to make YouTube short (60 seconds or less) videos: https://support.google.com/youtube/answer/10059070
	• Google "Soliya Connect videos" and show examples in class, such as these:
	  ○ What is love? https://www.youtube.com/watch?v=xRQ65br0_Lg
	  ○ How do you define climate change? https://www.youtube.com/watch?app=desktop&v=vqlJIjzMmV4

DEVELOPING STUDENTS' CULTURAL COMPETENCE

Topic	*Video interview to enhance students' cultural competence.*

Activities	This is a multi-week activity that will take three weeks to complete.
	Week 1
	• For 10–15 minutes, ask students to brainstorm questions for the interview. Ask them to write down 1–2 broad questions that relate to the course topics and recent world events. Then, have students share their questions in small groups and select the best question. Ask a group representative to write their question on the board. The instructor then facilitates a discussion to select the best question for everyone to ask. If the instructor approves all the questions, then students can either vote on the best question or they can be divided into groups of 5–10 and have each group select their question of interest.
	    ○ Be sure to record the question or, if using groups, have each group submit a paper with their names and their question.
	• Students will invite a person from a different country to participate in a 50–90 second interview of the selected question above. Note: if a student in the class is not US born, then they should invite a US-born student to participate in the interview. All students are asked to invite participants who are not enrolled in the class.
	    ○ Students submit the name and country of origin of the person they plan to interview. This assignment ensures that the person is from another country.
	Week 2
	• Students record their interview of their one question with their counterpart from another country. The interview should be posted to the YouTube channel set up by the professor. (10–15 minutes out of class activity.)
	Week 3
	• Students watch at least two other interviews from the YouTube link that the professor set up. Ask students to record notes about commonalities and differences among the responses to the same question. (5–10 minute out of class activity)
	• Students submit a journal reflection of 200–300 words. Ask students to answer these prompts and provide examples for their assertions:
	    ○ What question did you ask? Describe if you believe this was a good question or not.
	    ○ Describe if respondents answer the question the way you intended [expected?] or not?
	    ○ Compare and contrast the responses from other interviews; were there similarities or differences in the responses?
	    ○ What implications does this activity have for how you study human behavior in other cultures?
	    ○ (20–30 minutes, out of class submission.)
	• Hold a 15–20-minute class discussion on the generalizability of their "findings" from their interviews after the journal is submitted. Explore what it means to be a culturally competent researcher. See Bibliography for ideas of key themes to discuss.

Virtual adaptations	Students can use free teleconference software, such as Zoom for the interviews, which can be recorded and uploaded to the YouTube channel for online viewing.

Topic	Video interview to enhance students' cultural competence.
Assessment	• Formative Assessment: Submitting the name and country of the interviewee should be graded pass/fail; students who have trouble locating someone can ask for help from the instructor or another relevant office. The goal is to have everyone pass this benchmark assignment. • Formative Assessment: Students should receive a pass/fail grade for uploading a video to YouTube. You can ask them to submit the URL of their video to you to confirm it was submitted. • Summative Assessment: The journal reflection would be weighted like a course quiz. Suggest 25% for each of the four prompts. ○ Grade of A: addresses all four questions and provides an example for each point. ○ Grade of B: addresses all four questions but has spelling/grammatical errors or did not provide evidence for one prompt. ○ Grade of C: did not address one of the prompts, may have spelling/grammatical errors, and lacked evidence for two of the prompts. ○ Grade of D: only addressed two of the prompts: may have spelling/grammatical errors; and/or did not provide evidence for three of the assertions. ○ Grade of F: little to no effort to address the prompts; poor writing; little to no evidence presented.

INTELLECTUAL PREPARATION

Core Ideas

Increased globalization and continuous social change within individual cultures require researchers to stay informed and relevant within and across cultures in four areas: language, social science researchers, representative samples, and cross-cultural studies. Each area is discussed in the section on core ideas.

Culturally Inclusive Language
Students need more exposure to language standards in education and the social sciences. The American Psychological Association's (APA, 2021) revised standards illustrate cultural change and emphasize that "words matter" and that words are "key to creating psychologically safe, inclusive, respectful, and welcoming environments." The APA introduced terms related to equity and power (e.g., bias, equity, privilege etc.), terms that illustrate person-first language (e.g., "person with a substance use disorder" rather than "addict"), recommendations to avoid stereotypes, and identity-first language for references to age, disability status, race, ethnicity and culture, socioeconomic status, and sexual orientation and gender diversity. The APA's guidelines for inclusive and appropriate language also include examples of pejorative language that should be avoided, such as conversational microaggressions, inappropriate use of violent language and language that does not say what we mean. For example, the term "died by suicide" is preferable to "committed suicide" because the latter implies that a crime was committed. The APA language standards are course content that is covered prior to the assignment. The interview provides the opportunity to practice, apply, and possibly compare these language standards.

DEVELOPING STUDENTS' CULTURAL COMPETENCE

Culture-specific Social Issues that Researchers Need to Consider/Address
The revised *Multicultural Guidelines*, published by the APA in 2017, seek to represent an ecologically valid model of diversity and multiculturalism that includes context, identity, and intersectionality. Intersectional researchers can attend to the dynamics of self-definition and relationships with quantitative, qualitative, or mixed-method research designs as long as they monitor their own conceptualizations, lack of knowledge, and possible biases about individuals and communities (Clauss-Ehlers et al., 2019). Effective strategies to do so include interdisciplinary research teams and collaborations with individuals of diverse backgrounds and diverse communities. Prior to the interview assignment in our courses, students examine the relevant research issues related to context, identity, and intersectionality of diversity and multicultural issues within and across cultures.

Representative Samples
There is a concern about an overuse of western, educated, industrial, rich, and democratic (WEIRD) samples in psychological research (Muthukrishna et al., 2020; Pollet and Saxton, 2019). Thus, this lesson supports students' engagement in cross-cultural communication to increase their cultural competence and awareness of non-WEIRD populations. We know that only about 40% of US citizens have a passport and COVID restrictions have presented further challenges to international travel (US Department of State, n.d.).

Virtual interaction with individuals from other countries increases students' familiarity with and knowledge about individuals and social issues from cultures other than their own. They will become more comfortable with and more aware of the need for recruiting diversified samples in order to include different perspectives and to increase ecological validity. Such considerations are critical in cross-cultural as well as culture-centered investigations.

Cross-Cultural Studies
As they are just beginning to formulate their research identity, it is important to introduce undergraduates to the concept of international research collaboration, an activity that is becoming increasingly essential in a globalized world. In support of this message, the APA (2015) published *Engaging in International Collaborative Research*. The basic message of this booklet is that research conducted by several individuals from different places, with various perspectives, can accomplish more than work done by one individual alone. The results of such collaborations are new expertise, new perspectives, and new international relationships. This APA publication also provides advice on how to get involved with international research projects and how to navigate the process of international collaboration. They focus on the importance of developing intercultural competence in order to understand the customs and psychological research in the host country. They summarize the benefits of international collaboration as follows:

> These collaborations enable researchers to go beyond a view of culture as a static variable to be examined in isolation or controlled in an analysis.... They can mobilize a global network to consider and refine important ideas concerning education and psychological interventions, as well as social policies.
>
> (National Research Council, 2008, p. 1)

With this lesson, students can take the first exploratory steps and start to consider how their own scholarly identity may one day lead them to become a member of this global research network.

Learners

This interview lesson takes into account various elements of being a learner of research, including the development of a scholarly identity and potential misconceptions about intercultural research work, both of which are discussed next.

Scholarly Identity
James Marcia's (1993) concept of the four identity statuses (see Table 37.1) emphasizes that identity formation is an ongoing process. In terms of scholarly identity, most undergraduates are at the diffusion level because they have neither explored research activities nor committed to any particular direction. During their undergraduate years, we hope to help them move their scholarly identity to the moratorium level by exposing them to new experiences and new concepts related to cultural competence in research.

Given that most undergraduate students do not see themselves as researchers, exposing them to active exploration in this domain generally requires an introduction to research activities, research concepts, ethics guidelines, and cultural considerations. With this interview lesson, they can explore cross-cultural perspectives on such topics as sample selection (Why are WEIRD samples a problem? Do researchers in other countries face similar problems?), acceptable degrees of deception, acceptable language, preference for qualitative or quantitative research, favorite topics of research, and so forth. The lesson will help some students move from scholarly identity diffusion, where they are not exploring or committing, to moratorium, where they actively explore research options and cultural considerations.

Previous Learnings and Misconceptions
Before the interview, we ask students to share what they are worried about and what they hope to learn. This discussion provides the opportunity to encourage perspective taking, for example, by reminding the students that they are also the strangers to their potential interviewee. We have learned that some interviews will be better than others and that students are often initially nervous to talk with strangers. Students are concerned about

TABLE 37.1
Identity statuses and associated levels of exploration and commitment

	Exploration – Yes	*Exploration – No*
Commitment – Yes	*Identity Achieved* Alternatives explored and commitments made.	*Foreclosure* No exploration, but commitments made.
Commitment – No	*Moratorium* Still exploring, no firm commitment yet	*Identity Diffusion* No exploration and no commitment.

DEVELOPING STUDENTS' CULTURAL COMPETENCE   283

offending others who may have different worldviews, religious preferences, and other apparent differences.

In response, we emphasize that the lesson is meant to provide an opportunity for them to engage with people from a different country in a respectful manner. It is important that the professor normalize feelings such as nervousness or anxiety and ask students to trust the process.

Context

Two assignments scaffold the learning to support the development of cultural competence: a journal reflection and class discussion.

Scaffolded Learning: Journal Reflection

The journal reflection is an important tool to provide developmental feedback. We find that feedback that poses questions or recognizes student learning is more effective than evaluative statements. For example, one student wrote this statement, "In some cases, I found my own underlying prejudice towards Middle Eastern groups to be far greater than I had first initially thought, and that alarmed me." One of us replied with this comment, "I appreciate the deep level of reflection and candor. Where do you think this prejudice came from?"

Other times students write very little. In these cases, we ask questions like, "how did the interview relate to the content we are covering in class?" and provide an expectation that more in-depth reflection is expected.

In the classes where we require the full eight-week discussion experience we have students journal weekly and review those journals at the end of the course. For a one-journal reflection, a professor might also ask students to review their reflection and discuss it in a final exam, short answer question. This assignment would give students the opportunity to integrate the interview assignment with the entire course.

Asking students to review their prior writing and reflect on it promotes their metacognition about their cultural competence. In the eight-week experience, one student wrote:

> After going over my journals, I could see the gradual progression of my growth in communication through acknowledging my own biases and prejudices and my ability to listen and observe the people I was interacting with. In the beginning, I admit I was timid in voicing my opinions and asking questions of other people who were different than me.

Scaffolded Learning: Class Discussion

The class discussion should occur after students have made a journal reflection. Students can work in small groups of four–five students and share what they learned about their topic from their interview. The question prompt, described above in the lesson plan, asks students to summarize what their group learned from the interview responses and to decide how much those responses would be true for others (generalizability). Each group's appointed spokesperson shares their responses and the professor can facilitate the discussion. It is important to highlight the cultural similarities and differences in responses to enhance students' cultural competence and awareness of other cultural norms.

BIBLIOGRAPHY

American Psychological Association. (n.d.). *Learning goals & outcomes. APA Guidelines for the Undergraduate Psychology Major Version 2.0.* http://www.apa.org/ed/precollege/about/learning-goals.pdf

American Psychological Association. (2002). *Guidelines on Multicultural Education, Training, Research, Practice, and Organizational Change for Psychologists.* https://www.apa.org/about/policy/multicultural-guidelines.pdf

American Psychological Association. (2015). Going international: A practical guide for psychologists. Book 2: Engaging in international collaborative research. https://www.apa.org/international/resources/publications/research

American Psychological Association. (2017). Multicultural guidelines: An ecological approach to context, identity, and intersectionality. https://www.apa.org/about/policy/multicultural-guidelines.pdf

American Psychological Association. (2021). Inclusive language guidelines. https://www.apa.org/about/apa/equity-diversity-inclusion/language-guidelines.pdf

Clauss-Ehlers, C.S., Chiriboga, D.A., Hunter, S.J., Roysircar, G., & Tummala-Narra, P. (2019). APA multicultural guidelines Executive summary: Ecological approach to context, identity, and intersectionality. *American Psychologist, 74*(2), 232–244. http://dx.doi.org/10.1037/amp0000382

Erikson, E. (1968). *Identity youth and crisis.* Norton.

Haag, A. M., Boyes, A., Cheng, J., MacNeil, A., & Wirove, R. (2016). An introduction to the issues of cross-cultural assessment inspired by Ewert v. Canada. *Journal of Threat Assessment and Management, 3*(2), 65–75. http://dx.doi.org/10.1037/tam0000067

Halonen, J. S. (1996). On critical thinking. APS Observer, 9. Retrieved: https://www.psychologicalscience.org/observer/on-critical-thinking

Marcia, J. E. (1993). The ego identity status approach to ego identity. In J. E. Marcia, A. S. Waterman, D. R. Matteson, S. L. Archer, & J. L. Orlofsky (Eds.), *Ego identity: A handbook for psychological research.* Springer. https://doi.org/10.1007/978-1-4613-8330-7_1

Muthukrishna, M., Bell, A. V., Henrich, J., Curtin, C. M., Gedranovich, A., McInerney, J., & Thue, B. (2020). Beyond western, educated, industrial, rich, and democratic (WEIRD) psychology: Measuring and mapping scales of cultural and psychological distance. *Psychological Science, 31*(6), 678–701. https://doi.org/10.1177/0956797620916782

NAFSA. (n.d.). Trends in U.S. study abroad. https://www.nafsa.org/policy-and-advocacy/policy-resources/trends-us-study-abroad#:~:text=Nationally%2C%20the%20number%20of%20U.S.,participation%20starting%20in%20March%202020

National Research Council. (2008). *International collaborations in the behavioral and social sciences: Report of a workshop.* Washington, DC: National Academies Press.

Pollet, T. V., & Saxton, T. K. (2019). How diverse are the samples used in the journals 'Evolution & Human Behavior' and 'Evolutionary Psychology'? *Evolutionary Psychological Science, 5,* 357–368. https://doi.org/10.1007/s40806-019-00192-2

U.S. Department of State. (n.d.). *Reports and statistics: U.S. Passports.* http://travel.state.gov/content/travel/en/about-us/reports-and-statistics.html

38

Preparing Students for Community-engaged Scholarship

A Lesson Plan for Collaborative Inquiry Grounded in Awareness of Self and Others

Gene Corbin, Vialla Hartfield-Méndez and Elaine Ward

INTRODUCTION

The growing movement of community-engaged scholarship refers to a range of mutually beneficial partnerships between educational institutions and communities to collaboratively generate, disseminate, and apply knowledge for the purpose of addressing public issues (Carnegie Classification, n.d.; da Cruz, 2018; Saltmarsh, et al., 2021). Applied specifically to community-engaged methods of research, the emphasis on collaboration ensures that researchers and community partners engage in shared and equitable decision-making for reciprocal benefit throughout the research process (Cox, 2010; Horowitz et al., 2009). Thus, knowledge is co-created in a manner that respects the contributions of communities rather than privileging the knowledge of the educational institution (Saltmarsh et al., 2021). Furthermore, rather than solely advancing the needs of the researcher and academy, mutually beneficial relationships are formed which address the concerns of community partners (Saltmarsh & Hartley, 2012). In this mode of inquiry, "knowledge is co-created for the purpose of social change" (Jacquez et al., 2016, p. 77).

Many community-engaged researchers note the demands of meeting both the norms of community-engagement and the rigor of academic research (Hale, 2008; Strand et al., 2003; Warren et al., 2018). Researchers must interrogate their own identities and biases and develop the capacity to listen to and understand others to engage in a more equitable and collaborative mode of inquiry (Dunlap, 2018; Jacquez et al., 2016; Ward & Moore, 2010). Therefore, the development of these capacities for collaborative inquiry is the essential first step in teaching community-engaged research methods.

DOI: 10.4324/b23320-47

LESSON PLAN

Topic	*Developing Awareness of Self and Others*
Learning Objectives	*Learning takes place at three different points in time: (1) during the preparation for the lesson, (2) during the lesson activity, and (3) through post-activity reflection.* ***Intellectual Preparation (3 hours prior reading)*** Students will increase their: • Understanding of the concept of "worldview". • Understanding of epistemology and ontology. • Understanding of theoretical paradigms that contribute to the development of our worldview. ***Activity (1 hour)*** Students will develop: • Self-awareness including perceptions. • Awareness of others. • Awareness of mutual influences, resonances, and possibility of co-created knowledge. ***Post-Activity Reflection (2–4 hours, depending on reflection)*** Students will be able to articulate in writing: • Their own worldviews identifying their values, beliefs, and assumptions as it relates to the collaborative, community-engaged research process. • The importance of the role of listening in collaborative co- construction of knowledge.

Needed Materials/ Resources	• A facilitator and timekeeper.
	• A space prepared with chairs in a circle.
	• Suggested story circle prompts:
	  ○ Tell the story of a time when you made up your mind about something, a fundamental belief that you now hold. What happened?
	  ○ Examples from a prior activity: a decision about a career path (perhaps going against others' expectations or prior choices); a decision about a religious stance or affiliation. These are simply examples, not meant to be prescriptive.
	  ○ In setting up the story circle, the facilitator should not offer examples. Rather, the stories should emerge from the group assembled in the circle.

Pre-lesson Preparation	**For students/participants**:
	• Read the assigned selection of Research Paradigms (see Intellectual Preparation section below):
	  ○ Written reflection about research paradigms (see Worldview Intellectual Preparation section below); minimum 500 words approximately.
	• Read Ganz (2009), Public Narrative: Self, Us, and Now.
	For facilitators/teachers:
	• Review carefully the Roadside Theater (n.d.-b.) story circle guidelines.
	• Set up the chairs for the story circles.
	• Ask for a volunteer to be the timekeeper.
	• A few lessons learned from prior experiences:
	  ○ It is important to follow the protocol of the story circles:
	    ■ Ensure that everyone agrees to respect the silence between stories (no crosstalk).
	    ■ Emphasize that participants are to actually tell a story (a narrative, with scene, characters, plot) rather than simply expressing an opinion.
	    ■ Establish signals for timekeeping and stick to the allotted time for each story.
	  ○ Pay attention to the circle dynamics. If, for some reason, a participant has difficulty with the process, it is important to allow space for this in the most appropriate manner, with the goal of completing the circle with the least possible amount of disruption.

PREPARING FOR COMMUNITY-ENGAGED SCHOLARSHIP

Topic	*Developing Awareness of Self and Others*

Activities	• The activities section of the lesson plan has two distinct components to complete in one session:
	  ○ Story circle.
	  ○ Reflection immediately upon completion of the story circle.
	• Both components function to help students develop their understanding of their worldview through awareness of self and awareness of others.
	• Allow approximately **10 minutes** to organize the circle(s), explain the protocol, and attain group agreement.
	Story Circle(s) (30 minutes)
	• Ideally, a story circle consists of 5 to 15 people. Time management is necessary; the facilitator will keep track of the time allotted to each participant for the story.
	• Following the story circle guidelines of Roadside Theater (n.d.-b.), create one or more groups of people. There must be a facilitator for each circle if more than one circle is created.
	• Explain the story circle prompt and the purpose of the circle (to share stories that help us to better understand our worldview and the experiences of others).
	• Using the Roadside Theater (n.d.-b.) guidelines (see URL link in Bibliography), explain the protocol of a story circle and ensure that everyone is in agreement to participate following the protocol.
	• Ensure that the participants review the elements of a story (narrative arc, setting, characters, etc.) and agree to tell a story rather than simply express an opinion.
	• Finally, as the guidelines emphasize, the most important action in a story circle is listening. The facilitator should underline this and also attain group agreement that there will be no crosstalk and no commentary on a story. Rather, silence is held in the group until the next person begins their story.
	Reflections (20–30 minutes)
	If the group has been divided into more than one story circle, each circle should complete the first reflection. The second reflection can be done with all the groups reconvened.
	• Once the story circle is complete, allow time for **two stages** of reflection:
	  ○ The first stage is the reflection contemplated in the guidelines: what the participants observed about the stories or the process. This first stage can be solicited with a simple question: "What happened and what did you notice?"
	  ○ The second round of reflections is in response to a question about what this process reveals about worldview. In our stories, what are some of the assumptions that we can notice? Each person should have the space to reflect on their own assumptions, values, and beliefs as these were revealed in the story circle. There may also be assumptions that several participants have in common. This stage of the reflection can focus on how our worldview might have changed in the process of sharing our own stories and listening intently to the stories of others. What effect do we observe of the act of intentional listening and the absence of commentary or immediate response to a story? Finally, consider the protocol followed for the story circle. What is the effect of using a practice that is rooted in community for the purposes of understanding self and others?
	• As a follow up to the story circle experience, ask participants to extend, through written journaling, the second stage of reflection about worldview and the use of story circles, a practice drawn from multiple community-based traditions, to deepen awareness of self and others.

Virtual Adaptations	Story circles can be adapted for videoconferencing platforms (Zoom, Microsoft Teams, or other similar platforms). For remote sessions, it is best to utilize the breakout rooms feature to foster social presence in groups of approximately five persons for the story circle and first reflection.

Topic	*Developing Awareness of Self and Others*
Assessment	• *Short-term* – Pre- and post-activity surveys
	○ Up to four survey questions, on a five-point scale, based on these prompts: Before the story circle, with regard to "worldview," what did you know about yourself and about everyone else? After the story circle, what do you know about yourself and about everyone else?
	• *Short-term* – Reflection
	○ Prompt: Using Ganz (2009) as a point of departure, write about the relationship between the story of self and the story of us as it played out in the story circle. Think about the collaborative nature of the story circle, and co-construction of knowledge through the sharing of different worldviews via narratives. How might this new awareness of worldview and the effect of others' worldviews inform our approaches to research with community partners?

OVERVIEW OF LESSON

The "Developing Awareness of Self and Others" lesson plan is designed to help students understand themselves and others more fully as researchers and to engage in a collaborative mode of inquiry. Each student will prepare by connecting their own principles, values, and beliefs to an existing research paradigm. The identified paradigm can be understood as the "worldview" or guiding principles, values, and beliefs that shape the research process; it is the lens through which the researcher sees the world (Creswell, 2007). Students will also prepare by gaining an understanding of the public narrative framework which will enable them to communicate this worldview and connect it with the principles, values, and beliefs of others for purposeful collective action (Ganz, 2009). Through this preparation, students will come to a deeper understanding of what informs and motivates their decision making as researchers. As a result of this preparation, students can take this deeper self-understanding into the activities session where they develop the capacity to convey their worldview and to listen to the worldviews of collaborative research partners.

The activities session includes two components: (1) an experiential component (the story circle process) that facilitates self-knowledge and collaboratively constructed knowledge; and (2) a space for reflection on why an understanding of self in relation to others is vital in community-engaged research. The first component utilizes the format of story circles as derived from community-based and indigenous practices and codified by Roadside Theater (n.d.-a.). Thus, this activity provides students with a concrete example of how researchers in higher education can benefit and learn from the knowledge and practices developed in community settings which are often passed along orally. This activity also draws upon Ganz (2009) and the three elements of a public narrative plot. In Ganz's articulation, the story of self is a necessary first step toward collective civic engagement when linked with the collective story of "us" which leads to the story of "now" or the space of public and collaborative action.

The second component utilizes two reflection prompts designed to deepen the transformational learning of the story circle experience. Students are asked to reflect upon both the collaborative process and their increased understanding of self and others. Reflection on the study circle process builds the skills necessary to collaborate with community partners. Reflection on understanding one's own guiding principles, values, and beliefs and the worldviews of others provides students with important knowledge necessary for effective and equitable partnerships. This reflective process can be further scaffolded with application to the collaborative inquiry resulting in ongoing cycles of experience and reflection which continually deepen learning and strengthen research relationships.

INTELLECTUAL PREPARATION FOR LESSON

Core Ideas

"Developing Awareness of Self and Others" introduces students to three core ideas: (1) community-engaged scholarship is grounded in democratic practices and is an equitable, collaborative process between the academic researcher and the community member/s to address public problems; (2) research practice is shaped by who we are – our identity, values, and lived experiences; and (3) awareness of others is fundamental to the effective practice of community-engaged scholarship.

Democratic Practice

Community-engaged research is grounded in democratic values such as equity, inclusion, and reciprocity. Equity because the co-created research process legitimizes the sources of expertise and the assets of all partners (Carnegie Classification, n.d; da Cruz, 2018; Saltmarsh et al., 2021). Inclusion because the participation of community members, including traditionally marginalized cultural traditions and perspectives, is valued (da Cruz, 2018; Dunlap, 2018; Jacquez et al., 2016). Reciprocity because the benefits of the collaboration are multi-directional (Carnegie Classification, n.d.).

To effectively deliver on these values, students must become familiar with theoretical paradigms that guide research practice. Students should recognize that the positivist paradigm views knowledge as objective and absolute, relies on controlled studies for discovery, and separates the researcher from the community to conduct unbiased research (Crotty, 1998). Thus, positivism is often driven by elitist, hierarchical, and patriarchal assumptions that center academic knowledge over community knowledge. Such a paradigm is antithetical to the democratic values of community-engaged research since it establishes a hierarchical power dynamic (Horowitz et al., 2009; Saltmarsh & Hartley, 2012). Community-engaged research seeks to rebalance such power asymmetries and recast the process of knowledge generation in a more equitable and inclusive manner (Naples, 2003; Reinharz, 1992; Ward & Lortan, 2021).

Knowledge of Self/Researcher Identity

We each hold values and beliefs – our philosophical view of the world. Our worldview influences the decisions we make and the directions we take in the work we do. Thus, the researcher's worldview influences and shapes the research process and practice (Creswell, 2007). There are many influences on the development of our worldview including our personal, academic, and community experiences. We need to have a more than partial understanding of self as a researcher. Greater understanding of our values and beliefs can lead to a deeper impact of our research.

Worldview Intellectual Preparation
The student researcher:

1) Reads various philosophical paradigms in Creswell (2007) and pulls out aspects of the paradigms that align with their own values and beliefs.
2) Adds the aspects of the paradigm to the table in bulleted format.
3) Synthesizes the bullet points into a brief statement that captures the essence of their worldview.

Example:

Research Paradigm	Aspects of the paradigm that align with my values and beliefs
Postmodern	• Knowledge claims set within current world conditions based in multiple perspectives of class, race, gender, ability, sexual orientation.
Feminist	• Gender domination exists within a patriarchal society. • Collaborative and non-exploitative relationships.
Critical	• Concerned with empowering human beings to transcend race, class, gender, sexual orientation, ability constraints.
Constructivist	• Meanings are multiple and varied. • Goal of research is to rely on the participant's view of the situation.

Source: Adapted from *Qualitative Inquiry and Research Design: Choosing Among Five Approaches*, by J. W. Creswell, 2007, Sage Publications.

This activity prepares students to come to a deeper understanding of themselves and what drives their research choices and decision making. Students do this examination of self in preparation for them to connect with and learn from others more fully.

Awareness of Others
A critical aspect of storytelling is listening. Active listening is emphasized as equally important as the telling. Listening to others' stories sparks the telling of one's own story – either how one tells a "self" story, or even which "self" story one chooses to tell. Listening is fundamental to community-based scholarship that we need to learn how to "do" well. This lesson plan offers an approach that focuses on the process of both telling one's story (and understanding better one's own perspective) and listening carefully to the story of others allowing for transformation of one's perspectives.

Learners

The "Developing Awareness of Self and Others" lesson plan is intended for both undergraduate and graduate students who are preparing for engagement with community partners to complete community-based research projects. This learning is especially important for students with limited experience with research or a community engaged approach to research. Such students often pursue opportunities to participate in community-engaged forms of scholarship while possessing the misconception that their desire to do good is sufficient. These learners must develop greater awareness of self and others to avoid doing harm. The understanding developed through story circles and reflection prepares learners to engage in collaborative inquiry in a manner that reflects democratic practices and embraces equitable and collaborative processes.

Context

Versions of story circles and reflections have been used at the undergraduate and graduate levels of higher education and could easily be adapted to other settings such as K–12 classrooms. For example, members of the national consortium Imagining America: Artists and Scholars in Public Life, have explored story circles as a way to build a sense of community across the consortium and between community partners and faculty and student researchers (Bott et al., 2015). At Emory University, through ETHOS (Emory Telling and Hearing Our Stories) story circles have been used in a variety of ways to extend classroom learning, including preparation for engaging with community partners. Building on these experiences, the "Developing Awareness of Self and Others" lesson plan is adaptable to community engaged scholarship courses in a range of disciplines and settings to introduce students to the ideas that: (a) knowledge-gathering practices in community settings (through activities such as story circles) can inform scholarly inquiry within the academy, and (b) awareness and understanding of self and others is fundamental to successful collaborative research with community partners.

BIBLIOGRAPHY

Bott, K., Avila, M., Hartfield-Méndez, V. (2015, Spring). Finding our way to organizing culture change in higher education. *Organizing. Culture. Change.* 3(1). https://public.imaginingamerica.org/blog/article/finding-our-way-to-organizing-culture-change-in-higher-education/

Carnegie Foundation for the Advancement of Teaching (n.d.). *Defining community engagement.* https://carnegie electiveclassifications.org/the-2024-elective-classification-for-community-engagement/

Cox, D. (2010). History of the scholarship of engagement movement. In A. E. Austin, H. E. Fitzgerald, C. Burack, & S. D. Seifer (Eds.), *Handbook of engaged scholarship. Volume 1: Institutional change. Contemporary landscapes, Future directions.* (pp. 25–38). Michigan State University Press. http://www.jstor.org/stable/10.14321/j.ctt7ztb0c.6

Creswell, J. W. (2007). *Qualitative inquiry and research design: Choosing among five approaches.* Sage Publications.

Crotty, M. (1998). *The foundations of social research: Meaning and perspective in the research Process.* Sage Publications.

da Cruz, C. G. (2018). Community-engaged scholarship: Toward a shared understanding of practice. *The Review of Higher Education,* 41(2), 147–167. https://doi.org/10.1353/rhe.2018.0000

Dunlap, M. R. (2018). Four community engagement lessons from Detroit to Connecticut. *Metropolitan Universities,* 29(4), 60. https://doi.org/10.18060/22835

Ganz, M. L. (2009). *What is public narrative: Self, us & now (Public Narrative Worksheet).* Working Paper. http://nrs.harvard.edu/urn-3:HUL.InstRepos:30760283

Hale, C. R. (2008). *Engaging contradictions: Theory, politics, and methods of activist scholarship.* University of California Press.

Horowitz, C. R., Robinson, M., & Seifer, S. (2009). Community-based participatory research from the margin to the mainstream: Are researchers prepared?. *Circulation,* 119(19), 2633–2642. https://doi.org/10.1161/CIRCULATIONAHA.107.729863

Imagining America: Artists and Scholars in Public Life. (n.d.). https://imaginingamerica.org/

Jacquez, F., Ward, E., & Goguen, M. (2016). Collaborative engagement research and implications for institutional change. In M. A. Post, E. Ward, N. V. Longo, & J. Saltmarsh (Eds.), *Publicly engaged scholars: Next generation engagement and the future of higher education* (pp. 76–95). Stylus Publishing.

Naples, N. (2003). *Feminism and Method: Ethnography, discourse analysis, and activist research.* Routledge.

Reinharz, S. (1992). *Feminist reserach in social research*. Oxford University Press.

Roadside Theater (n.d.-a). *About: Story Circles*. https://roadside.org/asset/about-story-circles?unit=117

Roadside Theater (n.d.-b). *Story Circle Guidelines*. https://roadside.org/asset/story-circle-guidelines?unit=117

Saltmarsh, J., Corbin, G., & Kehal, P. S. (2021, November 16). *Why community engaged scholarship needs a clear definition*. Scholars Strategy Network. https://scholars.org/contribution/why-community-engaged-scholarship-needs-clear

Saltmarsh, J. & Hartley, M. (2012). Democratic engagement. In J. Saltmarsh & M. Hartley (Eds.), *To serve a larger purpose: Engagement for democracy and the transformation of higher education*, (pp. 14–26). Temple University Press.

Strand, K., Cutforth, N., Stoecker, R., Marullo, S. & Donahue, P. (2003). *Community-based research and higher education*. Jossey-Bass.

Ward, E., & Lortan, D. (2021, December). Decolonial dreamers and dead elephants. *Gateways: International Journal of Community Research and Engagement*, 14(2) https://doi.org/10.5130/ijcre.v14i2.8016

Ward, K., & Moore, T. L. (2010). Defining the "engagement" in the scholarship of engagement. In A. E. Austin, H. E. Fitzgerald, C. Burack, & S. D. Seifer (Eds.), *Handbook of engaged scholarship: Contemporary landscapes, future directions. Volume 1: Institutional change* (pp. 39–54). Michigan State University Press. http://www.jstor.org/stable/10.14321/j.ctt7ztb0c.7

Warren, M. R., Calderón, J., Kupscznk, L. A., Squires, G., & Su, C. (2018). Is collaborative, community-engaged scholarship more rigorous than traditional scholarship? On advocacy, bias, and social science research. *Urban Education*, 53(4), 445–472. https://doi.org/10.1177/0042085918763511

39

Teaching Policy Implications

Can You Have Your Cake and Eat It Too?

Jason E. Lane

INTRODUCTION

As student research projects end, whether as theses, dissertations, or seminar papers, writing the policy implications that extend from the research results can often be done in an afterthought-like, rushed manner. It can be challenging to think critically and analytically about the impact and further recommendations in the final overwhelming days before a project is due. As a professor teaching policy analysis in both the domestic and global contexts to graduate students in education, I have seen too many students with well-thought-out theses finalize their work without a thorough policy implication section. And many times, those implications might center on making something more equitable, with superficial analysis and limited discussion of the inevitable tradeoffs.

The *Equity Cake Exercise*, which is modified from Deborah Stone's (2011) book *Policy Paradox: The Art of Political Decision Making*, highlights the complexity of policy implications using an example from one of today's most current issues: equity. One might wonder about the connection between cake and policy implications. But how we devise rules to divide a cake for eating is not too dissimilar to creating a policy to allocate public resources. The purpose of the *Equity Cake Exercise* is to push students to think about how others may conceptualize and view equity depending on what angle they are viewing it from - and then to apply a similar level of analysis to their own policy implication section.

In the exercise, students are asked to distribute portions of a cake based on different rules (or policy models). [*Note*: you can substitute other edible products or non-edible items, such as beads]. The exercise demonstrates the connection between intention and outcomes and invites students to explore both the opportunities and challenges with different approaches. In doing so, students can begin to envision their own research from different angles; and from these varying perspectives, brainstorm potential implications. What is equitable to one person may not seem equitable to another, and it turns out that having students split a cake is an efficient means to illustrate this point and encourage critical thinking to blossom. Exploring different visions of equity in this exercise builds a foundation for devising policy implications that take varying visions, viewpoints, and nuances into account.

DOI: 10.4324/b23320-48

LESSON PLAN

Topic	*Teaching policy implications: Can you have your cake and eat it too?*
Learning Objectives	• Review different perspectives on equity and resource distribution. • Discuss the impact of policy/resource allocation decisions. • Identify tradeoffs between policy options and the differential impact of those policy options on different groups. • Understand and identify the connection between research findings and policy implications. • Write and review policy implications.
Needed Materials	• One cake per group (or other edible products or easily divisible items, such as beads). • Utensils, napkins, and small paper plates. • Presentation slides. • Handout with good practice examples of policy implications (examples can be drawn from the recommended readings in the Bibliography; see also example about holiday gifts below).

Pre-lesson Preparation	• Instructor should read Chapters 1 & 2 of Stone (2011) to provide background on policy development and implications, with a focus on:
	  ◦ How does one conceptualize society?
	  ◦ How are policy goals determined?
	  ◦ What is the relationship between self-interest and public interest?
	  ◦ What is the difference between equality and equity?
	  ◦ What are the 8 outcomes of Stone's plan to distribute the cake?
	• Bring copies of Chapter 2 (Equity) in Stone (2011).
	• Assign pre-reading that provides clear examples of policy implications. This could be a strong example from a dissertation completed by a student in the department. One scholarly option is to assign Brown et al. 2002.
	• Ask students to bring three written policy implications based on a research project they have completed or are currently working on. If they do not have their own research to use, they can develop them based on a peer-reviewed journal article. The product would likely be a bulleted list of policy implications. They do not have to be in-depth; but substantive and specific enough to demonstrate they are informed by the research and relate to a specific policy arena. Refer them to the Brown et al. (2002) reading for examples.
	• To embody cultural responsiveness in the lesson, recall that understanding how policy is implemented and its implications may vary based on the backgrounds of students. If possible, encourage students to focus on a policy arena that they have some familiarity with and where they believe their analysis might have some impact. Different cultures also have different conceptions around food and the celebration of birthdays. If you refer to the cake as a birthday cake, that may need to be explained. Further contextualization preparation is provided below in the section on learners.

Activities	• Start by asking for a group of volunteers (5–7 students) to be the policymakers – you can also assign the group ahead of time – and then designate the other class members as the silent populace who will observe their work. (Alternative: split the class into small groups and have each do the exercise below with no observers.) • Next, share with the class that they will be enjoying cake (or brownies, chips, or other edibles of your choice) because it is your birthday (or some other celebration).

TEACHING POLICY IMPLICATIONS

Topic	*Teaching policy implications: Can you have your cake and eat it too?*
	• Invite the group to develop a policy for distributing the cake among their colleagues. The only rule is that they cannot simply divide the cake equally among everyone in the group; they have to use a different set of criteria. Have each member of the group write down their recommendation for how to divide up the cake. Once everyone has done this, each person should share. Then the group will need to decide on one approach. You may need to set a time limit and force a vote at the end.
	• Instruct the observers (if used) to listen to the conversation and to make notes about what they heard in the discussion.
	• Have the policymakers explain why they split the cake in the way they did, and if they thought about other ways of doing it. Discussion prompts can include:
	○ Would anyone like to explain the thinking behind their initial recommendation?
	○ How did your thinking change as you heard others describe their recommendation?
	○ What was the goal of the group? Do you think that was achieved?
	○ How did you feel about making a decision that would affect others?
	• Have the observers describe what they heard. Discussion prompts can include:
	○ What were some of the key discussion points that you heard?
	○ Did anything surprise you about the conversation?
	○ What other options might the group have considered?
	○ How did the final recommendation make you feel? (*Try to have folks with different sizes of cake comment.*)
	○ How did it make you feel that others were deciding the amount of cake you would have?
	• After the discussion, distribute Chapter 2 from Stone and have them review. Then turn to the presentation slides and present each of Stone's ways for dividing the cake up, including:
	○ By rank.
	○ By gender.
	○ By previous food consumption.
	○ On a first-come, first-served basis, etc.
	• The scenarios demonstrate the different approaches that might be used to distribute the cake equitably. For each scenario, ask the students about the pros and cons of dividing the cake in that way and if they think it is equitable.
	• Explain the difference between process, item, and membership-based forms of equity and probe the students as to which cake-sorting methods fit into each type. One option is to provide the students with a definition of terms via a PowerPoint or a handout and have them identify/discuss the differences.
	• Then provide a short lecture about how the *Equity Cake Exercise* relates to devising and writing policy implications about research outcomes. See the Stone and Baradach books in the Bibliography for lecture content.
	• Ask students to pull out the policy implications they wrote in advance of the lesson, share these with small groups, and discuss how each of the implications may be interpreted in different ways by different groups of people.
	• Ask the students to work independently for 5–15 minutes on updating their policy implications to integrate their learning from the *Equity Cake Exercise*. Prompts for this exercise may include:
	○ Ask them to consider what angles they may not have considered in drafting their policy implications and how they might be improved.
	○ Encourage them to consider how any policy suggestions would lead to their envisioned desired outcome or what unintended consequences might ensure.
	○ Have them reflect on the policy from a standpoint of a person/group that may be different from them and directly affected by the policy.
	○ Explore the connection between their research findings and their policy implications.

Topic	Teaching policy implications: Can you have your cake and eat it too?
	• After they have finished, bring the group together for a final discussion about the lesson and provide information about how to submit the before and after policy implications as an assessment activity. • Students revise and edit their previously formulated policy implications as a follow-up assignment to the class.
Virtual Adaptations	• This lesson should be easy to move into a virtual environment without too much adaptation. For synchronous sessions, online break-out rooms can be used. For asynchronous sessions, groups could collaborate using discussion boards. • While it would not be possible to physically share the cake, tools such as Miro or Canva can be utilized to create digital cakes that students can divide up using shared screens.
Assessment	• Formative Assessment: During the group discussion time, move around the room and listen to students' ability to relate the lessons from the activity to their groups' individually presented policy implications. • Formative Assessment: The improvement between the policy implications they wrote before the class and their written policy implications after the class and/or their arguments for removing certain proposed solutions based on the class activity. • Summative Assessment: Assuming that a product of the course is a final research paper/outline/proposal/presentation, include a concrete focus on policy implications in the grading rubric.

INTELLECTUAL PREPARATION FOR LESSON

The idea behind developing a policy implications section for a research project is to demonstrate how the research findings may help us better understand the impact of certain policy decisions. Implications can take several different forms and may entail: (a) evaluation of the intended and unintended implications of the current policy; (b) proposed revisions to current policy, often to achieve a different outcome; and/or (c) analysis of the differential impact of policy based on group membership. Moreover, each of these should be clearly grounded on the research outcomes of the project. However, many students, while experts on their topic can struggle with identifying policy implications, and instructors of research writing may not always be experts in the policy arena. In this section, I provide insights to assist instructors with preparing for this lesson.

Core Ideas

The idea behind the *Equity Cake Exercise* is to provide students with an opportunity to develop a policy that determines the allocation of a limited resource (i.e., cake). The idea of identifying how best to distribute cake amongst themselves and their classmates is likely an occurrence that each has encountered in their lives. It also reflects what happens as policymakers make policy to distribute limited governmental resources (e.g., federal financial aid for students, Medicaid, or state aid to localities). For each situation, there is typically more need than available resources.

TEACHING POLICY IMPLICATIONS

The Complexity of Equity

The focus on equity for this exercise is often relevant to many students in educational research. Equity tends to be included in their work in some form or fashion and it is not unusual to read policy implications that state that policy needs to be more equitable. However, it is not usual for students to consider equity as a relative concept – meaning that what might be understood as equity by some does not necessarily mean such understanding is shared among multiple groups. The *Equity Cake Exercise* exposes students to a more nuanced understanding of equity with the hope that they will bring the same nuanced understanding to their own work as they develop policy implications.

Appreciating the Perspective of the Silent "Other"

Very often we each view the implications of decisions through our personal lens. However, when developing policy implications, it is important to be clear about which lens is being applied and to acknowledge that there are "others" who may be impacted differently. The *Equity Cake Exercise* is set up to include silent observers of those deciding how to distribute the cake. These individuals represent those members of our community who often do not have a voice in decisions but must live with the consequences. In the same way, researchers can reflect on their policy implications and how their research may aid in understanding differential impact, particularly for those not often represented in policy-making decisions.

Tying Policy Implications to Research Findings

One of the most glaring gaps that occur in policy implication sections is the lack of clear connection back to the research findings. For example, a research project may focus on the environmental impact of feral cats in Zanzibar. The policy implications may suggest that a policy is needed to require the spaying and neutering of cats in Zanzibar, without clearly explaining the linkages to the research findings. Rather than simply assuming the reader understands the connection, the author needs to present a logical set of arguments that the unchecked proliferation of cats may have led to a detrimental decline in mice. Therefore, a policy around spaying and neutering is needed. What is critical is that it is clear how the policy implications are clearly derived from or informed by the research findings.

Learners

In terms of the *Equity Cake Exercise*, it is likely that most students will understand the concept of sharing food; however, students may bring different understandings of equity to the discussion. Some students, particularly those from other countries, may conceptualize equity in different ways or not be used to it being part of policy discussions. In these cases, the instructor may need to be prepared to talk about why equity matters.

In fact, a lesson on policy implications may assume that students have a familiarity with policy – policy development, policy implementation, and the like. The level of applicable knowledge, however, will vary based on the student's experiences and academic preparation. Some students may have previously interned in the state capital and others may have had almost no academic or applied experience in the policy domain. On more than one occasion, I have had students tell me they cannot write about policy implications as they do not understand policy. In addition, the ability to influence policy or the opportunity to criticize policy may also vary based on experiences. Students from countries with different governmental arrangements may not feel comfortable criticizing government policy. In this case, you may need to help them understand that in the US context, this is a common and accepted exercise to try to create a more effective policy.

In preparation for the lesson, it can be helpful to gauge students' prior experiences and comfort level with policy. Some academic programs require a course on policy. If that is your situation, then you may want to link the lesson to that curriculum. If that is not the case, then you need to be prepared to deal with students with different experience levels.

One way to prepare students for the lesson is to have them reflect on their research projects and try to identify any type of policies that they may have come across in their research – this can be at the institutional, state, or federal level (or other levels). Reminding them of previous interactions with policies can ease them into the conversation. If that does not work, then prompt them to think about what policies might be relevant to their research project. For example, if their project is focused on identifying successful activities that reduce the melt in the number of graduating high school seniors who intended to go to college but did not, then they might consider what high school or college policies inhibit or support the implementation of those activities.

Because of the differing levels of experience and expertise, it can also be easy for those comfortable with policy to dominate the discussions. It will be important for the instructor to ensure that there is enough space in the discussion for everyone to have the opportunity to engage, share, reflect, and learn.

Context

Writing about the connection between their research findings and policy implications can require faculty to first support students in understanding the connection between the two. As noted, one of the challenges in this lesson is that students may enter the classroom with different levels of knowledge and experience with policy. The *Equity Cake Exercise* can provide students with a common experience on which to ground their discussion as well as explore the implications of policies.

For many students, policy development can be seen as something that they do not have influence over and is done far off by elected officials or institutional leaders. The *Equity Cake Exercise* is intended to show students that policy is developed all the time in contexts in which they are likely familiar, such as in families, classrooms, and organizations. Policy is ultimately about making decisions between tradeoffs that are likely to impact different people differently. The *Equity Cake Exercise* has students develop the policies to distribute a cake among their classmates. The distribution of food is likely something they can quickly understand and see the implications of their decisions. Be sure to have them consider the tradeoffs of their different options.

If you receive pushback from the class suggesting that they do not understand why the cake cannot simply be divided equally among all present (or think they would benefit from additional discussion), you might invoke the following example to push the conversation forward. Assume there is a set of grandparents who have a limited budget and

TEACHING POLICY IMPLICATIONS

saved $500 to spend on Christmas presents for their children and grandchildren. The grandparents have three children, each is married. One child, a son, has no children. A second child, a daughter, has three children. And, a third child, a son, has two children. How should the grandparents distribute the $500? Should it be evenly divided between the families of their children (three)? Should it be divided based on the number of grandchildren (five)? What if one of the spouses is disabled and they have no money to buy gifts for their children? What if one family never sees or helps the grandparents while the grandparents live with another family? What if one child converted to Islam and no longer celebrates Christmas? As an instructor, you can add on any type of scenario that reflects situations in society. What is important is not so much to come to a consensus on what to do, but to have the students explore the implications of the choices.

One of the objectives of the *Equity Cake Exercise* is to help students understand that policy is all around them and they have the ability to assess and discuss the implications of the tradeoffs that are part of policymaking. This then provides them with the foundation and confidence to look at policies that may be beyond their immediate control; but for which their research equips them with expertise to evaluate and discuss the implications. Throughout the entire lesson, you will want to continually come back to discuss the implications of the policy.

As a final note, policies are often not devoid of political and ideological influences – discussion can become heated, particularly those policies that relate to broader public policy issues and those that might be hotly debated at the time of the course. The *Equity Cake Exercise* seeks to provide an environment where students can focus on implications without having to grapple with those other issues. However, as the discussion turns to other policies, particularly public policies, the instructor should be aware that his/her/ their own potential biases, as well as those of students, are likely to seep into the conversation. The instructor should take time before the exercise to reflect on how they might handle such discussions as well as be prepared to be the devil's advocate on different sides of an issue. Again, the point of the exercise is not to have students develop policy, per se, but to consider the implications and tradeoffs of policy based on their research expertise.

BIBLIOGRAPHY

Baradach, E. S. & Patashik, E. M. (2019). *A Practical Guide for Policy Analysis. The Eightfold Path to More Effective Problem Solving* (6th ed.). CQ Press.

Brown, M. C., Lane, J. E., & Rodgers, K. R. (2002). Walking a Policy Tightrope: Balancing Educational Opportunity and Criminal Justice in Federal Student Financial Aid. *Journal of Negro Education 71*(3), 233–242.

Stone, H. (2011). *Policy Paradox* (3rd ed). W.W. Norton & Company.

40

Introducing Scholars to Public Writing

Erin A. Hennessy

INTRODUCTION

Scholars and students undertaking research in their field are often singularly focused on the markers of academic success – the publication of the fruits of their work in their dissertation or in a prestigious, peer-reviewed journal. While these academic outlets are important, particularly for those seeking tenure and promotion within the academy, focusing solely on them minimizes the impact of the scholar's work. Preparing students to disseminate their work more widely through public writing for mainstream publications offers them a vital skill that will complement their ability to write for academic publication.

In this lesson, readers will be exposed to the purposes and conventions of public writing through the op-ed. By exposing current and aspiring scholars to op-eds based in academic research, they will hopefully be inspired to look at their own research with an eye to what findings may be relevant and interesting to lay audiences interested in education. This lesson also provides an opportunity to workshop a piece of public writing with peers so that students feel supported as they explore this type of writing, possibly for the first time. Lastly, it surfaces and gives space to conversation about students' concerns or reluctance to engage with the popular press and offers resources that can help navigate those challenges.

LESSON PLAN

Topic	*Disseminating research through public writing for mainstream publications*
Learning Objectives	• Students will be able to articulate the difference between academic and public writing. • Students will explore ways in which they can use public writing to contribute to discussions relevant to their field of research. • Students will demonstrate understanding of how to conceive of and write pieces related to their research findings for mainstream audiences.

DOI: 10.4324/b23320-49

INTRODUCING SCHOLARS TO PUBLIC WRITING

Topic	Disseminating research through public writing for mainstream publications
Pre-class Preparation	In advance of class, ask students to identify research finding(s) from their own work or from a recently published scholarly article that they believe has interest for a mainstream audience. For example, op-eds related to Florida's "Don't Say Gay" bill (Cochran & Davis, 2022) and online standardized tests (DeSantis, 2022) were published in mainstream outlets based on researchers' expertise in these areas.
Readings/ Assignments	Prior to class, ask students to read: • Guest Pryal, K. R. (2019, December 1). *10 Questions Every Academic Should Ask Before Writing for the Public*. Chronicle. com. Retrieved February 12, 2022, from https://www.chronicle.com/ article/10-questions-every-academic-should-ask-before-writing-for-the-public/ • Ray, V. (2019, July 12). *How to Start Writing for the Public*. Advice for writing effectively for the public (opinion). Retrieved February 12, 2022, from https://www. insidehighered.com/advice/2019/07/12/advice-writing-effectively-public-opinion • The OpEd Project. (n.d.). *Op-ed writing: Tips and tricks*. The OpEd Project. Retrieved February 14, 2022, from https://www.theopedproject.org/ resources#structure • Dumitrescu, I. (2021, April 19). *How to Cope With a Fear of Public Writing*. Chronicle.com. Retrieved February 12, 2022, from https://www.chronicle. com/article/how-to-cope-with-a-fear-of-public-writing?cid2=gen_login_ refresh&cid=gen_sign_in In recent years, many academics have seen success in public writing and have begun to offer advice and encouragement to others as they consider similar work. These articles are among the many that have been published and will introduce students to the skills necessary to begin writing for mainstream audiences, familiarize them with the basic structures of the op-ed form, and help them overcome concerns they may have about putting their work into the public arena through this form of writing. Because many of the pieces are written by academics, they take into consideration the challenges of public writing and offer relevant guidance to academics as they navigate the challenges of public writing. As they read, ask students to pay particular attention to the stylistic and structural differences between academic and mainstream writing, consider their comfort level engaging with the public in this way, and think about ways in which their areas of research could connect to ongoing conversations among the public.
Lesson Activities	This lesson will require two class sessions to complete. ***Session One*** Brief discussion/lecture (20 mins.) to: • Provide a definition of public writing: "Public writing is a broad category that includes a wide variety of genres: opinion pieces, letters to the editor, blogs, newspaper reports, magazine features, letters to elected officials, memoirs, obituaries, and much more. All these genres share common features. Public writing aims to be accessible." (Plotnick, n.d.). • Review purposes of public writing and how they differ from academic writing. Public writing seeks to inform, persuade, and provide context while speaking to a lay audience of non-specialists, whereas academic writing is most often geared toward an audience of specialists and seeks to lay out new knowledge or theories and convince readers of its primacy. (University of Southern California). • Review classic op-ed structure: In an op-ed, the author makes their argument in the first paragraph (also known as the lede) and uses the following three to four paragraphs to outline supporting points. The author then acknowledges counterarguments, provides a synthesis that bolsters the argument they are making despite counterarguments and ends the piece with a concluding paragraph.

Topic	Disseminating research through public writing for mainstream publications
	• Review op-ed best practices: The Op-Ed Project website lays out best practices for op-ed writing. With students, emphasize that short, punchy lede paragraphs will draw in both the editor reviewing their piece for publication as well as their eventual reader. Remind them that long words and convoluted sentence structure are out and aiming for a seventh-grade reading level is in; in addition, if they are writing for a business audience, they should emphasize numbers and data while a piece written for a more general audience might include pop culture or current events references. For all outlets, authors should avoid jargon and acronyms that might otherwise be appropriate for a specialized academic audience.

Split class into small groups and give each an example of a recent op-ed based on research to review and critique (30 min.). Good sources for op-ed examples include the opinion pages of daily newspapers like the *New York Times*, the *Washington Post*, or *USA Today*; online publications like *Slate*, *Salon*, or *Vox*; or magazines like *The Atlantic*.

Sample discussion prompts:

- What is the author's opinion?
- Does the lede paragraph grab the reader's attention?
- Are they effective in their argument?
- Which points resonated most strongly for you?
- Does the author give sufficient space to counterarguments?
- How would you rebut this piece in your own op-ed?
- Are there other forms of public writing through which the author could make their case?

Bring class back together and ask each group to summarize and share their reactions to the op-ed they reviewed (15 mins.).

<u>Homework:</u> Ask students to outline an op-ed piece that incorporates the finding they selected from their own research or from a recently published journal article and to draft a lede paragraph following suggestions from The OpEd Project.

Session Two

In small groups or together as a class, ask students to share their outlines and lede paragraphs and solicit feedback from the group (35 mins.). Sample discussion prompts:

- Is the author expressing an opinion?
- How can their argument be sharpened?
- What other data or supporting information might make the piece stronger?
- Are they appropriately acknowledging the strongest or most prevalent counterargument?
- Did their lede paragraph capture attention? Can it be further sharpened?
- In what kinds of publications can you imagine this piece appearing?

Review op-ed submission process and follow-on steps (20 mins.):

- Use research to identify target outlets that have run pieces on this and/or similar topics.
- Check submission guidelines published by the outlet and ensure piece conforms.
- Draft pitch note that summarizes the piece and why it is relevant to the outlet's audiences.
- Send pitch and draft pieces to one outlet at a time – submissions must be exclusive.
- Work through edits.
- Push published pieces to networks through social media, professional/academic organizations, and employer networks.

Discussion of concerns about engaging in public writing and identification of resources that can help address those concerns, including (20 mins.):

- Institutional/organization communications professionals.
- Mentors/colleagues with experience.
- The OpEd Project.

<u>Homework:</u> Students complete a full draft of an op-ed and a list of possible outlets for placement. Consider offering additional participation points for those who offer evidence of having submitted their piece to a publication.

INTRODUCING SCHOLARS TO PUBLIC WRITING

Topic	Disseminating research through public writing for mainstream publications
Virtual Adaptations	These lessons will adapt easily to virtual settings. Conduct the lecture/discussion portions with the class before randomly or manually creating small groups using breakout rooms. Sample op-eds can be shared via links in the chat portion of the video conferencing platform.
Assessment	Formative assessment: During small group and independent work, engage with students to assess their understanding of the purposes and structures of public writing. Sample prompts include: • What is the opinion you are expressing in this piece? • Are there current events or conversations you can use as a news hook in the piece? • How are you thinking about making this topic resonate with a lay audience? • What outlet would you like to see this piece in? Is it written appropriately for that outlet's audience? Summative assessment: Grade the submitted op-ed based on a rubric that requires appropriate structure and language as well as a strong argument based in research. Possible categories for the rubric include: • Piece expresses an opinion in the first paragraph. • Piece includes supporting arguments and acknowledges counterarguments. • Piece is written in language appropriate for mainstream audiences and avoids jargon. • Piece uses active voice and has a goal of persuading its audience.

INTELLECTUAL PREPARATION

While academia holds sacred academic publishing, a scholar's willingness to engage with mainstream media will almost certainly bring far more attention to their ideas and their research than solely publishing in academic journals. Preparing scholars with public writing skills and introducing them to the process of writing and placing an op-ed in popular media is useful. Further, helping them navigate the possible negative repercussions of public writing will position scholars to share their research with a broad audience and help rebuild trust in media by bringing additional expert voices into public conversation about critical issues.

Core Ideas

While more than 1.5 million peer-reviewed articles are published annually, it is estimated that the average paper in a peer-reviewed journal is accessed just ten times. A recent survey published by *The Journalist's Resource* indicates that while peer-reviewed research is important to some journalists, 25 percent report rarely accessing academic papers as part of their own research (Ordway, 2022). Meanwhile, vital conversations about policy and practice in the field of education are ongoing and in need of informed, rigorous, and relevant research to ensure the field continues to advance. This lesson is grounded in the concepts of: (1) introducing scholars to the concept of public writing, particularly the op-ed, to extend the reach and influence of their scholarship, and (2) providing students with an introduction to the form and conventions of op-ed writing as well as the process of pitching a piece to a mainstream outlet.

Public Writing

Academia holds up academic publishing as the gold standard and often disincentivizes engagement with the mainstream media by disregarding those publications in tenure and promotion criteria (Heleta, 2016). However, writing for the mainstream press is an important complement to academic publishing for scholars who wish to inform public policy and public conversation.

Introducing scholars to the opportunities public writing provides should be part of their research training so that more – and more diverse – voices enter conversations in these public spaces. As education is increasingly positioned as a proxy for ever more polarized and extreme political views, it is vital to ground conversation about education policy in rigorous and peer-reviewed research. However, if that research never makes it beyond the pages of academic publications in which experts are essentially talking to other experts, it stands little chance of having a real and tangible impact in the classrooms of our country, where the children who most directly benefit from sound and thoughtful policy are learning every day.

By sending scholars prepared only for academic writing into the world, we are hamstringing administrators, faculty members, students, and their families as well as graduates of education programs who have the knowledge and expertise to positively influence policy, if only they can find the right outlets through which to do so.

Writing Skill Development

In addition, this lesson plan introduces the writing skills needed to engage in public writing. Scholars spend years learning the rules and expectations of academic writing, which are often in direct conflict with writing for the mainstream press. But that style of writing in many ways limits the accessibility of the information contained within, confining the results of research to academic journals that are rarely accessed by anyone outside of academia. By helping scholars become comfortable with yet another form of writing, we are setting the expectation that they contribute to broader societal conversations and debates while providing them the skills they need to do so. At the same time, we are removing roadblocks to successful public writing and giving them an advantage that students in other programs may not have upon completing their training, and which will set them apart in professional settings throughout their careers.

Learners

Because we all interact with mainstream media in our daily lives, students will come to this lesson with a set of experiences and beliefs about the trustworthiness of media, as well as having observed recent debates about academic fields like critical race theory and having absorbed attitudes and perceptions of mainstream publishing from professors and other academic leaders. Being prepared to hear and acknowledge these beliefs and experiences of students while respectfully challenging them is vital to presenting this material.

Declining Trust in Media

As our society has become more and more polarized, Americans are increasingly distrustful of the media. According to an October 2021 poll conducted by Gallup, "Americans' trust in the media to report the news fully, accurately, and fairly has edged down four percentage points since last year to 36%, making this year's reading the second lowest in Gallup's trend" (Brenan, 2021). Among those who identify as Republican, the figure is even lower – just 11 percent have a great deal or fair amount of trust in the media. Our students are not immune to these perceptions and so we may need to counter them in our classrooms.

Weaponization of Research

Students also will arrive in our classrooms having watched academic concepts and research being weaponized to serve political ends in recent years. Those whose research touches on potentially controversial issues may be understandably wary about engaging in public writing for fear that their work will be willfully misinterpreted, and their reputation may be impacted. These scholars, especially those who are part of historically marginalized groups, may also fear for their personal safety. Pointing scholars to institutional and external resources that can help them prepare for possible pushback may help alleviate some of their fears.

Perceptions of the Value of Public Writing

It is also possible that students will have absorbed a belief that publishing in the mainstream media is less valuable than academic publishing, particularly for those who are pursuing a PhD and an academic career. Because most institutions do not assign value to public writing in the hiring, tenure, and promotion processes, some students may feel it does not behoove them to engage with mainstream press but instead stay focused solely on academic publishing (Alperin et al., 2019). However, institutions are beginning to see value in professors who help elevate the university's profile with alumni and prospective students through op-eds and expert citations in mainstream publications so faculty who can excel in both forms of publishing are in increasing demand.

Instructors can help bridge these concerns by sharing their own experiences, offering resources, and engaging with external experts in media and public writing. These experts can add to the instructor's lesson plan by sharing additional insight in the popular press, suggesting ways to approach topics of interest to students that present less chance for public criticism or misinterpretation, and surfacing outlets that provide less risk for scholars who are new to public writing.

Context

Students will come to these lessons with deeply held beliefs about the trustworthiness of the media and the value of engaging with it. At the same time, they will be in the process of devoting considerable time and energy to creating new and original research related to a topic about which they care deeply. By presenting public writing as an opportunity to bring additional attention to their work and to influence conversations that are already happening, it is hoped that students will be inspired to see the value of going beyond speaking to other experts through academic publishing.

There are many opportunities for students to test out their skills in public writing. Faculty can help simply by including discussion of public writing as equally valuable as academic writing throughout their programs. Including public writing assignments in various research and policy focused classes will also help build familiarity and skills. Creating a class website or blog on Medium which students can populate with op-eds and other pieces offers a low-stakes sandbox in which to play. LinkedIn and local news outlets offer a bit more of an audience when students are ready to go to the next level, and for many, publishing in national outlets is the long-term goal. Having opportunities to stretch and develop these writing skills will be enormously helpful for those seeking to bring the fruits of their research to bear on conversations in the mainstream media.

CONCLUSION

Introducing students to public writing offers them an opportunity to develop an important, additional skill set that complements their academic writing. Conversations about education are happening in all corners of the popular press, frequently led by those who can only access personal anecdote. These conversations cry out for the involvement of scholars who can tap into their own well-designed, rigorous research. As I often remind scholars, there are many voices contributing to these conversations – why should not yours be one of them?

BIBLIOGRAPHY

Alperin, J. P., Muñoz Nieves, C., Schimanski, L. A., Fischman, G. E., Niles, M. T., & McKiernan, E. C. (2019). How significant are the public dimensions of faculty work in review, promotion and tenure documents? *eLife*, *8*. https://doi.org/10.7554/elife.42254

Brenan, B. M. (2021, November 20). *Americans' Trust in Media Dips to Second Lowest on Record*. Gallup.Com. https://news.gallup.com/poll/355526/americans-trust-media-dips-second-lowest-record.aspx

Cochran, B., & Davis, K. (2022, March 3). *"Don't Say Gay" Bill Will Be Detrimental to LGBTIQ+ Youth | Opinion. Newsweek*. https://www.newsweek.com/dont-say-gay-bill-will-detrimental-lgbtiq-youth-opinion-1684323

DeSantis, J. (2022, February 4). *Moving the SATs online won't restore them to relevance*. MSN. https://www.msn.com/en-us/news/politics/moving-the-sats-online-won-t-restore-them-to-relevance/ar-AATugtB

Heleta, S. (2016, March 9). *Academics can change the world – if they stop talking only to their peers*. The Conversation. https://theconversation.com/academics-can-change-the-world-if-they-stop-talking-only-to-their-peers-55713

Ordway, D.-M. (2022, February 24). 1 in 4 journalists surveyed rarely, never use research to learn about issues. *The Journalist's Resource*. Retrieved April 15, 2022, from https://journalistsresource.org/home/user-survey-journalists-research-habits/

Plotnick, J. (n.d.). *Writing for the Public*. Writing Advice. Retrieved April 15, 2022, from https://advice.writing.utoronto.ca/types-of-writing/public-writing/#:~:text=Public%20writing%20is%20a%20broad,writing%20aims%20to%20be%20accessible

University of Southern California. (2015). Research Guides: Organizing Your Social Sciences Research Paper: Academic Writing Style. Usc.edu. https://libguides.usc.edu/writingguide/academicwriting

Closing Words

Helping Students to Learn Research and Become Researchers

Anna Neumann and Aaron M. Pallas

We have been teaching master's and doctoral students and post-doctoral scholars since the 1980s – mostly apart, but occasionally together. We agree on some matters, disagree on others, but nearly always struggle to understand each other's thinking. In this way, we have learned from each other. Anna, trained as an educational researcher, engages in qualitative research, though her earliest work included survey research. Aaron, trained as a sociologist, is an expert in quantitative methods, but over the years, has carried out numerous interview-based studies. Our differences matter, as does the learning in which we have engaged in working through them. To explain our shared view of teaching research, we begin with how we differ. For starters, we do not agree on the terms we use to describe what we seek to accomplish in our teaching.

Anna's preference is to say that we teach research, and more specifically, educational research. She uses the word "research" to denote a way of inquiring about the educational world – to see, think, ask, and pursue, and to make claims about educational phenomena that are tempered by judgments about their fit with the available evidence. She is attentive to the strengths and limitations of study design, the depth and richness of individuals' cognitions, the power of culture in research, and the inherent subjectivity of inquiry. In this view, teachers strive to help students learn – expanding on what they do and can know, and helping them probe the intrapersonal, interpersonal, and other contextual dynamics of education, from pre-K to graduate and professional school and beyond. Still, there is an acknowledgement that even more lies beyond their ken.

Aaron is more comfortable saying that we teach *about* research, or that we teach *approaches to* or *methods of* research. In this view, research is a set of practices developed by professional communities of researchers, typically discipline-based, thus representing a way of inquiring unique to that discipline. Different communities may share in some of what they study and how they study it, but a community's research ethos can be viewed as distinctive. This is not to say that views of research within such a community are homogeneous; they are not, and clearly scholars within the same community argue vehemently with one another, often forming identifiable subcommunities. Through this lens, graduate courses typically expose students to core practices, including ways of knowing and inquiring, for a particular community or subcommunity.

DOI: 10.4324/b23320-50

The two of us *do* agree that a focus on research, which we view as a practice (much as teaching and leading are practices), and on the teaching of that practice, joins our two perspectives. And we have come to believe that teaching stands to benefit from their joining. We also acknowledge that there are fault lines in the combined view, with some graduate programs aligned more with one perspective than the other. For example, some graduate programs are oriented towards preparing students to *produce* research, whereas others seek to prepare students to be competent *consumers* of research. Drawing on what we bring to our teaching, our own goal has been to develop what educational researcher Christopher Clark (Clark & Peterson, 1984) calls "well-started novices," that is, individuals acquiring basic skill in both reading and making sense of research, and in generating new research. Well-started novices know that research evolves over time, and that their learning of research will continue, too, through the full length of their research careers. They may even begin to learn how to help others learn, thereby initiating their own careers of teaching research.

The joint view we have just described draws heavily on notions of communities of practice, a term introduced by Lave and Wenger (1991), and extended by Wenger (1998). Pallas (2001) makes the argument that education research comprises multiple overlapping communities of practice (often, discipline- or field-based), in which individuals are mutually engaged in a joint enterprise, relying on a shared set of communal resources to guide their efforts. The members of these communities engage jointly in a practice (or practices) of research fit to the community's goals, interests, and reasons for being. In their early work, Lave and Wenger saw novices becoming full members of communities of practices through legitimate peripheral participation, taking on authentic but peripheral tasks in service to developing identities as full members of the community, and trying out the practices amidst more knowledgeable community members who can offer support, guidance and correction.

What then do the members of a community of the practice of research learn in the name of practice? While in most fields there are many straightforward things to master (e.g., factual knowledge, bedrock ideas), there also are other things to learn that are less clear cut (Bransford, et al., 2000; Schon, 1984), including some that call for complex judgment that textbooks cannot address. Textbooks – including books such as this one! – are nonetheless useful in encoding (Lave and Wenger use the term, "reifying") the knowledge, and the modes of thought, held by a community. Inevitably, though, there are ambiguities that cannot be resolved via referencing a text, as texts cannot possibly anticipate all the idiosyncrasy and complexity that the non-routine facets of inquiry present. In his later writings, Wenger (1998) described a duality of reification and participation, implying that each holds the capacity to repair the ambiguity of meaning lodged in the other.

We are making the obvious point that one cannot learn to engage in education research, and in the various phases of the research process this volume considers, solely via textbooks, and by extension, coursework. We contend that novices do indeed need to study textbooks and take courses on research – they need knowledge *about* research – but they must also participate, with guidance, in one or more communities of research practice that extend beyond the graduate school classroom. Such participation provides novices the opportunity to learn practices via observation, spontaneous conversation,

CLOSING WORDS

internalizing local lore and jargon, and working together to solve specific problems of practice. How can coursework simulate this kind of authentic participation? Below, we offer some suggestions.

Instructors can develop authentic classroom tasks and assessments that engage students in real-world problem-solving connected to students' professional identities as scholar-practitioners. Consider, for example, the distinction between education students learning about the statistical technique of analysis of variance (ANOVA) via a lecture and textbook chapter, and then each being assigned a problem set in which they use ANOVA to analyze crop yields, versus their learning about the analysis of variance in a situation in which teams of students are provided a batch of per-pupil school expenditure data for all of the elementary schools in their county, and asked to write up and justify an analysis of what those data mean, using statistical tools they select and deploy for reasons they can defend. Consider the difference, too, between teaching students the logic of sample construction for interview studies by having them read textbook representations of this phase of research, as opposed to asking them to design a study sample fit to research questions pertinent to their scholarly interests, and, in collaboration with others, to weigh its strengths and shortcomings. We suggest using the classroom not only to expose students to research, but also to guide them toward expanded engagement in it. The classroom can be a site of such learning.

Instructors can lead with the idea that research entails judgment. Another way to say this is that while researchers need to have deep knowledge of the purpose of research, its designs and methods, the various phases of the research process, and the substantive content of their discipline or field, they also must be able to make sound, thoughtful, and balanced judgments about what to do in situations that cannot always be spelled out in advance. In making a judgment, one must be aware of and acquainted with the knowledge pertaining to a particular problem (e.g., deep understanding of observational methods). But that is not enough. One also must know when and how to use that knowledge, including its contributory powers and limitations in various situations.

Education researchers are constantly making decisions, and these decisions rest on their judgments about the merits and consequences of various alternatives. Do I choose to study this topic, or some other one? Which theoretical and conceptual frameworks will work well for my study? Do I choose an observational design, or a field experiment? How many cases do I need, and how do I select them? What do I do when my best-laid plans break down? Who is the audience that I'd like to target as recipients of what I've learned in carrying out a study? All of these questions require complex judgments, deployed at various points in the research process. The majority of responses to such questions cannot simply be plucked from the reifications of textbooks or lectures.

The heart of the matter is that doing research about education is a personal *and* a social process, drawing on the collective knowledge of communities of education research practitioners and the interests, identities, and expertise of individual researchers. That knowledge has evolved over time, as new ways of knowing, methods, theories, and findings have developed. In some cases, these extend prior knowledge and understandings; in others, they fundamentally call it into question.

Instructors can restrain themselves from presenting the research process only in its ideal form, as clear-cut, linear, and tidy in its unfolding. They can and should illuminate its messy insides, spotlighting the ambiguities that researchers experience, the mistakes they make, and the back-tracking in which they often engage, even as they strive for processual ideals. Moreover, instructors should do this across various study designs. Toward this end, we champion the reading of texts that reveal the mistakes that expert researchers have made as they have carried out their studies.

Mistakes are a real part of doing research. Many research methods textbooks lay out images of research as a rational ideal, unfolding in a neat and orderly way, as do most published research articles and monographs. These texts largely elide the personal, social, and political dynamics of bringing research into being in researchers' and research participants' lives, in political organizations, and in the highly unpredictable environments of everyday life. Editorial premiums on space, at least in the era when these texts were printed on paper, have meant that researchers' experiences of research as they carry it out, and especially their thinking and the choices they make, were rarely exposed to public view. Students embarking on research for the first time, and seeking guidance from methodological texts, miss out on what really happens as researchers conceptualize studies, enter the field, work through data analysis, and present their work in public venues, including in writing. The path is rarely uncomplicated.

Although we admire and have made good use of texts representing the research process in ideal form, we especially value texts in which researchers reflect openly, deeply, and critically on their own practices and experiences, sharing insights on the often disordered insides of research, how they worked through them, mistakes they have made, and what they have learned. These authors know a great deal about how experts in a disciplinary domain think about their subjects of study and ways of inquiring into them; they understand where the ideal of research falls short in the face of real-life research dilemmas. They also know a great deal about how novices approach their early forays into research. There is often a big difference between the two.

Though alert to challenges that newcomers to research can face, and the mistakes they can make, reflective researchers are aware, too, of the strengths that novices often bring to research. They know how to identify and use them to enhance learning, organizing classrooms and research groups so that students learn to rely on each other's knowledge rather than just on that of the instructor or lead researcher. They also often are in touch with how they themselves learned research, the low points as well as the highs, using that knowledge to support novices' efforts. Moreover, they publish texts – real life experiences in and with research – that speak to these realities of teaching and learning research.

Two types of readings have been prominent in classes we have taught bearing on students' learning of educational research. First are reflexive texts that active researchers have written about their own "lessons learned" while carrying out their studies. These may be partially autobiographical, with authors speaking openly in first-person voice about the challenges they have encountered and their struggles to address them; insights they have formulated; and principles of good practice they have invented based on mistakes they made through study design, data collection or analysis, or public presentation of findings. We think of these writers as reflective methodologists. Their methods derive directly from their own (and sometimes others') real-world experiences of doing research. Five authors, exemplifying this approach, stand out among our favorites: Annette Lareau, Kathleen Gerson, Sarah Damaske, Kristin Luker, and Howard Becker.

CLOSING WORDS

Annette Lareau's methodological writing – about her struggles (including mistakes) in the field, with tips for learners encountering similar challenges – includes a stand-alone guidebook on how to carry out interview and observational studies (*Listening to People: A Practical Guide to Interviewing, Participant Observation, Data Analysis, and Writing It All Up*). She also has written self-revelatory appendices to two of her monographs on social class and parents' activation of cultural capital in American schools (*Home Advantage: Social Class and Parental Intervention in Elementary Education*) and on the class-based cultural logic of child-rearing (*Unequal Childhoods: Class, Race, and Family Life*). These texts reveal Lareau's behind-the-scenes research struggles, conundrums, and errors, and how she responded, as well as what she learned. Our own students have relished Lareau's honesty and her portrayal of mistakes as intrinsic to learning. They learn, for one thing, that researchers are not born, they are made, often amid travails of "learning while doing," and struggling to figure it out.

Kathleen Gerson and Sarah Damaske share equally useful insights on the conduct of interview research. Like Lareau, they draw heavily on lessons learned amid fieldwork, data analysis, and other research phases (see *The Science and Art of Interviewing* (2020)). While in this section we have emphasized processes of qualitative research (interviewing, observation), we must point as well to the methodological contributions of Kristin Luker, a sociologist who portrays herself as constructing an approach to research that "aims to hit that sweet spot between the rigor and theory-building capacities of canonical quantitative social science research, and the emergent, open-ended, and pragmatic capabilities of traditional field research" (p. 2). Thus Luker's conception of research, documented in *Salsa Dancing: Research in an Age of Info-Glut*, is undeterred by popular distinctions between quantitative and qualitative research. She makes it a point to say that her view of research speaks more broadly to the nature of inquiry in the social sciences. Drawing on her experience of teaching research, Luker presents key challenges that doctoral students often face in designing and conducting research (e.g., taking charge of a sprawling literature review, navigating "canonical social science" without losing oneself, articulating what counts as "a case," developing meaningful and productive study samples, generalizing, and others), and she follows with thoughtful advice. There is much to be appreciated about Luker's true-to-life portrayal of the utter complexity of conducting research in an information-saturated era. Still another long-time favorite of ours, attuned less to specific methods than to the thinking behind research, is Howard Becker's (1986) *Writing for Social Scientists*. Like Luker, Becker draws on his experiences of research, and research mentoring, to speak directly to beginning scholars about topics at the heart of learning research – for example, in chapters about researcher persona, risk in writing, and learning to use the literature rather than being used by it.

Final words: In their recent work, Jal Mehta and Sarah Fine (2019) define deeper learning in terms of mastery, identity, and creativity. We believe that these concepts, applied to students' learning in high schools, may also guide college and university teachers seeking to support graduate students in their efforts to learn research. Mastery refers to the learning of the basic knowledge of a domain, organizing that knowledge so that it can be applied both to routine cases that do not require much thought – often referred to as *near transfer* – and, ideally, to new, or more complex, situations or problems that cannot be resolved through rote application of an automatic skill. This kind of application is called *far transfer*, and it is much more challenging to cultivate. Teaching research requires attention to both.

Identity, the sense of how we see ourselves in combination with how others see us, is a critical source of internal motivation and engagement. Ideally, students in education research classes will come to see themselves as producers of new knowledge about education, and internalize the view that they are education researchers themselves. This, too, is facilitated by classroom activities that enable students to engage in research practices in scaffolded and supported ways.

Creativity involves creating something new. In research classes this may involve positioning students to identify topics, imagine frameworks, invent study designs, and plan analyses that intentionally feature novel content – unexpected (yet well-defended) ways to construct the elements of research. All of these components of the education research process can be constructed in courses. The lesson plans in this volume are chock full of examples of tasks that do so.

A final word brings us back to the realization that what we teach is reflective of who we are, just as it reflects who our students are. This view may, indeed, yield differing perspectives on research. Resolving differences that may at first seem ominous often involves melding them. Doing so demands that teachers use everything they know about research to become learners themselves, seeking to grasp what others know. What emerges in the end, as it has for us, is an enriched view of how to teach research, and how to engage it as well.

BIBLIOGRAPHY

Becker, Howard S. (1986). *Writing for social scientists: How to start and finish your thesis, book, or article*. University of Chicago Press.

Bransford, J. D., Brown, A. L., & Cocking, R. R. (2000). *How people learn: Brain, mind, experience, and school*. National Academy Press.

Clark, C.M., & Peterson, P.L. (1984). *Teachers' thought processes*. Institute for Research on Teaching, Michigan State University.

Gerson, K., & Damaske, S. (2020). *The science and art of interviewing*. Harvard University Press.

Lareau, A. (2000). *Home advantage: Social class and parental intervention in elementary education*. Rowman & Littlefield Publishers.

Lareau, A. (2014). *Unequal childhoods: Class, race, and family life*. University of California Press.

Lareau, A. (2021). *Listening to people: A practical guide to interviewing, participant observation, data analysis, and writing it all up*. University of Chicago Press.

Lave, J., & Wenger, E. (1991). *Situated learning: Legitimate peripheral participation*. Cambridge University Press.

Luker, K. (2010). *Salsa dancing into the social sciences: Research in an age of info-glut*. Harvard University Press.

Mehta, J., & Fine, S. M. (2019). *In search of deeper learning: The quest to remake the American high school*. Harvard University Press.

Pallas, A. M. (2001). Preparing education doctoral students for epistemological diversity. *Educational Researcher* 30(June/July), 6–11.

Schon, D. A. (1984). *The reflective practitioner: How professionals think in action*. Basic Books.

Wenger, E. (1998). *Communities of practice: Learning, meaning, and identity*. Cambridge University Press.

Index

Pages in *italics* refer to figures; pages in **bold** refer to tables and pages followed by n refer to notes.

1987 EITC expansion 132
1993 Earned Income Tax Credit (EITC) expansion 132

Abutabenjeh, S. 69
ACPA 143
additive impact 138
Adelman, Cliff 66
Ahmed, S. 52
Ahn, Soyeon 104, 120–129
Alvesson, M. 12
American Psychological Association (APA), The 280–281
analysis of variance (ANOVA) 104, 110, 309
Anderson, Gillian 146
Andrade, H. 94
Angelini, C. 235
APA Publications and Communications Board, The 121
Arminio, J. 85n2, 171–172, 180, 182
articulating a research problem: asynchronous online adaptations 23; class-wide discussion 20–23; equitable learning environment 25; examples 22; formative assessment 23; funds of knowledge 25; graphical depictions 19, 22, 24–25; narrowing, alignment, evidence and importance 23–24; prior knowledge and possible misconceptions 24–25; problem and purpose statements 20–22; small-group discussion 22–24; summative assessment 23; synchronous online adaptations 23
assessment, evaluation, and research (AER) 143
Atherton Central 200–201
axiology, axiological 53, 207

Bain, K. 50
Baker, Vicki L. 267–276
Baldwin, L. 20–21
Bardach, E. 257

Bartlett's test 127–129
Baxter Magolda, M. B. 185
Beaver Tech 200–201
Becker, H. S. 46, 310–311
Bernhardt, Ann F. 224, 256–263
bias 13, 24, 31, 51, 59, 80, 82, 86–88, 98, 124–125, 133, 136, 230, 281, 283, 285, 299
bivariate and simple multivariate methods 103
Bizup, J. 20
Black girls 166
Black self-determination 169
Blalock, A. E. 144, 154–161
Block by Block: activating activity 242; alternative discussion components 244; context 247; core discussion components 243–244; core ideas 246; discussion group activity 244–245; formative assessment 245; guided application activity 245, 247; instructional activity 242–243; learners 246–247; learning objectives 241; needed materials 242; summative assessment 245; test your knowledge activity 243, 246; virtual adaptations 245
Blockus, L. 273
Bolitzer, L. 2
Booth, W. C. 20
Bottiani, J.H. 243
Boyer, E. L. 98, 267
Bradshaw, C. P. 243
BRANCH OUT criteria 31–32
Brandenberg, Maire 224, 241–247
Brayboy, B. M. J. 52
Brazelton, G. Blue 66, 94–99
Bresciani, S. 239
Brown, M. C. 294
Brown v. Board of Education ruling 164, 169
Bruffee, K. A. 200
Bukoski, Beth E. 66, 86–92
Byrd, J. A. 37–38

Cals, J. W. L. 241

Campbell University 268, 277

candy sort 38, 46–51; alternative perspectives and contributions 49; book report format 50; confidence building 51; creating and naming categories of themes 49; formative assessment 48; Google Slide 48; Halloween trick-or-treating 47; needed materials 46; organizing literature review 46–48; scaffolded learning 50–51; stream of consciousness approach 50; summative assessment 48; virtual adaptations 48

Card, D. 132–133, 139

Cardel, M. I. 235

causal/causation: effect 136–138; inference 135–137, 194; research questions 27–30

Cavafis, Contantino 77

Characteristics of Excellence in Undergraduate Research (COEUR) 273

Chiseri-Strater 91

coding data and developing themes: axial/focused coding 184; collaborating with learners to make meaning 186; different epistemologies 180–182, *183*; engaging in open/initial coding 184; formative assessment 182; identifying and applying epistemologies 183–184; learners' developmental readiness 184–185; learning objectives 180; needed materials 180; possible misconceptions 185; pre-lesson preparation 180; students as capable of generating knowledge 186; students' own experiences 185–186; summative assessment 182; virtual adaptations 182

Cohen, E. G. 225

collective contribution 10, 192, 268–269

Collins, C. S. 56

Collins, Patricia Hill 88

Colomb, G. G. 20

community-engaged research 285–286, 288–289

comparison 203, 205; comparison group(s) 136–138; comparison variables 133

congruent decision-making: assessment 57; close 57; congruence review 55; data analysis methods 54; data collection methods 54; debrief 56–57; definitions 53; Google Jamboard Activity 57, *58*; paradigmatic/onto-epistemological approaches 53; prior homework 54; research methodologies 54; small group activity 1 56; small group activity 2 56–57; theoretical coding 56, 60; theoretical frameworks 53–54; theoretical *vs.* conceptual frameworks 55; theory nuggets 55; timing and scaffolding 54; virtual adaptations 57; what is theory? 54–55

congruent research design: importance of theoretical and 59–60; pervasiveness of theory 58–59

constructivism 53

control(s) (and controlling, controlled through variable) 98, 117–118, 281, 299; control costs 258; control group 132, 135, 137; controlled studies 289; time controls 136

convergent teaching 2

Conway, Katie 9–10

Corbin, Gene 268, 285–291

Cormick, C. 238

correlation(al), correlations 29, 70, 104, 114–115, 127–129, 194, 198, 243; correlation coefficient 115; correlation design 70; correlation matrix 127, 129

Corso, Gregory 191

Council for Undergraduate Research (CUR), The 273

counterfactual 135; *see also* hypothesis testing and theory testing

COVID-19 pandemic 94, 122, 252

Coviello, James C. 224, 249–254

Covrig, D. M. 20

Creswell, J. D. 69, 207

Creswell, J. W. 20–24, 27, 69, 199, 207, 210, 215, 290

critical and poststructural theories 171; congruent research study *174*; formative assessment 173; incongruent research study *175*; learning objectives 172; needed materials 172; pyramid of congruence 172–173, *174*; research congruence and paradigms 172; summative assessment 173; understandings of 176–177; views on what constitutes a publishable study 177; virtual adaptations 173

critical fabulation 167–168

critical quantitative theory 225, 230

critical self-reflexivity 42

Cunningham, S. 132

Damaske, S. 310–311

Da Vinci, Leonardo 202, 208

Deosthali, K. 211

dependent variable 114

descriptive 27 157, 234, 261; analysis 133; images 160; interpretations 32; research questions 32–33; statistics 114–115, 198

"Developing Awareness of Self and Others" 268; awareness of others 290; context 291; democratic practice 289; facilitators/teachers 286–287; knowledge of self/researcher identity 289–290; learners 290–291; learning objectives 286; needed materials/resources 286; reflections 287; short-term–pre-and post-activity surveys 288; short-term–reflection 288; Story Circle(s) 287; students/participants 286; virtual adaptations 287

Dhurandhar, E. 235

difference-in-differences in quasi-experimental design 131; advanced concepts not covered 136; counterfactual 135; equitable learning space 138–139; exogenous change 135; exogenous variation and timing 137; experimental design 135; formative assessment 134; foundational concepts 135; fully synchronous online adaptation 134; hybrid online adaptation 134; internal and external validity 136; learners participating in course 136–137; natural experiment 135; needed materials 132; parallel trend assumption 136; prior

INDEX

knowledge and disciplinary background 138; regression models with interaction terms 137–138; research design 132; summative assessment 134; Week 1: activity 132–133; Week 2: activity 133; weights, weighting 136

"Disseminating Research Through Public Writing for Mainstream Publications" 268

Doctor of Education (EdD) 224

document analysis: annotations 164–165; archives 166; authentication 166; Black Venus 166; core idea #1: skepticism 167; core idea #2: silence, scarcity, absence 167; core idea #3: annotations and redactions 167–168; critical fabulation 167–168; ethics and reflexivity 169; formative assessment 165; function of 164; learning objectives 163; needed materials 164; preparation for exercise 164; reflecting on recording of documents 165; summative assessment 165; virtual adaptations 165

Donnelly, J. P. 199

"Donut Memo, The": alternatives 263; analysis 263; clear and concise writing 260; context 262; criteria 263; criteria/alternatives for policy analysis 261; formative assessment 260; "Goo Goo Clusters" 257; learner 261–262; learning objectives 257; memorandum 262; needed materials 257; policy analysis 258; policy makers 259; policy question 257; politics and policymaking 256; pre-lesson preparation 257; problem 262; process of 259–260; recommendation 263; summative assessment 260; virtual adaptations 260

Doran, Erin 223–224

Drisko, J. W. 241

Du Bois, W. E. B. 164–165

Dumford, A. D. 104, 113–118

Dumitrescu, I. 301

Duran, Antonio 144, 171–178

Dynarski, S. 132–134, 139

eigenvalue(s) 126–129

Eisner, E. W. 179

Eissa, N. 132

Emerson, R. M. 157–158

Emory Telling and Hearing Our Stories (ETHOS) 291

Emory University 291

Engaging in International Collaborative Research 281

epistemology/epistemological 5, 12–13, 53–56, 59, 85n2, 87–88, 91, 167, 180–182, 184, 191, 207, 286

Eppler, M. J. 239

Equity Cake Exercise, The 293, 296–299

equity 171, 175–176, 178, 225, 228, 230–231, 242–244, 259, 268, 280, 289, 293–295, 297; equity, diversity, inclusion and accessibility (DEIA) 143–144

ethical and trustworthy research 96; individual learners 98; Lang's model 99; learning community 98; reflexivity as a practice 97–99

Ettl, K. 12

evidence 10

Ewinghill, Terrace 223, 225–232

experiment 70, 132, 135, 235, 247, 275; experimental (also randomized experiment) 70, 87, 133, 135; field 309; non-experimental 70; quasi-experimental 70, 87, 104, 131–137, 198, 254; randomized experiment 70, 133

exploratory factor analysis (EFA) 3, 104, 120; Bartlett's test 127–129; Block 1: students critique published sample EFA articles 123; Block 2: instructors demonstrate EFA application 123; Block 3: students apply EFA to their datasets 124; eigenvalue(s) 126–129; flowchart 126; instructional scaffolding 125; Kaiser-Meyer-Olkin (KMO) test 127–129; learning blocks 122; maximum likelihood (estimation) 120, 126, 128; opportunities for inclusive research design 125; previous learning and misconceptions 124–125; principal axis factoring 120, 126; principal component analysis 124, 126–127; using IBM SPSS 28, 127; using R, demonstration of 127–129; scree plot 126–128; supportive learning environment 125; template for 129; varimax (or varimax rotation) 127–128

Fabula 167–168

factor analysis 104, 120; confirmatory factor analysis 127; exploratory factor analysis *see* exploratory factor analysis

faculty 103, 267

Fain, J. A. 20–21

Fernandezm Frank 191, 194–201

Fitzgerald, W. T. 20

Fong, C. J. 211

Foster, M. 235

Foundation for Undergraduate Research, Scholarship and Creative Activity (FURSCA) 270

Freire, P. 97

Fretz, R. I. 157–158

Gagné, R. M. 69

Gambrell, Bren 223, 225–232

Ganz, M. L. 286, 288

García, L. 160

Gerson, K. 310–311

Getty, Paul J. *159*

Gilbert, Chelsea 37–38

Glesne, C. 97

Gonzales, Leslie D. 37–38

Goodman-Bacon, A. 132

good teaching 28–29; exercise 31

Google Forms 107, 109

Google Scholar and ResearchGate 40–43

Google Slide 31, 48, 173, 206, 213, 245, 260

Google spreadsheet 40, 42, 107

Graefe, Beck 104, 120–129

graphical depictions 19, 22, 24–25

Greene, M. 208, 216

Groenewald 68

Guerrero, Diana 223, 225–232
Guest Pryal, K. R. 301
Gutmann, M. L. 199, 210, 215

hands-on application of exploratory factor analysis
(EFA): EFA procedures review 121; formative
assessment 122; group activity: apply EFA to sample
peer-reviewed articles 121; group activity: applying
EFA 122; learning objectives 120; needed materials
121; principal component analysis (PCA) 121;
pre-lesson preparation 121; review of EFA 121;
summative assessment 122; virtual adaptations 122
Hanson, W. E. 199, 210, 215
Harris, M. S. 237
Hartfield-Méndez, Vialla 268, 285–291
Hartman, S. 166–167
Heasley, Chris 191–192, 202–209
Hennessey, Erin A. 300–306
Hidalgo, B. 235
Hoffer, Tamara 224, 241–247
Hokusai, Katsushika 155, 159
Hollingworth, L. 22
hooks, b. 52
hot topics 11, 14
Housen, A. 161
Hunter, Cheryl 224, 241–247
hypothesis/es (hypothesis testing) 28, 66, 77–82, 84,
108–112

implications for theory: context 253–254; formative
assessment 251; lay theories 252; learners 252–253;
learning objectives 249; needed materials 249–250;
pre-lesson preparation 250; summative assessment
251; theoretical frameworks 250, 254; "Think/Pair/
Share" 251, 253; virtual adaptations 251
independent variables 114
institutional databases 42–43
institutional library: page 40–41; website 42
institutional research board (IRB) 96
intellectual preparation 1–2; articulating a research
problem 23–25; Block by Block 246–247; "candy
sort" lesson 49–51; congruent research design 58–60;
connecting pieces to puzzle 42–44; "Developing
Awareness of Self and Others" 289–291; difference-
in-differences 135–139; document analysis 166–170;
"Donut Memo, The" 260–262; generating research
questions 31–33; hands-on application of EFA
122–125; implications for theory 252–254; joint
display analysis 214–216; Let's Road Trip 82–85; linear
regression 116–118, 230–232; multivariate analysis
111–112; positionality artifact 90–92; professional
development 273–276; public writing 303–306;
Pyramid of Congruence 175–178; qualitative
dimension of mixed methods 206–208; quantitative
dimensions of mixed methods 199–200; teaching
policy implications 296–299; video interview to
students cultural competence 280–284; visualize your
research design 73–75; visual storytelling 237–240;
writing what you see 159–161

interpretivism 53
intervention 138, 194, 197, 244, 256, 259, 281;
equity-focused intervention 243; pre-intervention
138; post-intervention 138
Irlbeck, S. A. 20

Jaradat, R. 69
Johnson, Kayla M. 191, 194–201
joint display analysis (JDA) 4, 192, 210; adapted
example 216; assessment 214; context 215–216; core
ideas 214; create and organize 211; fitted moderated
mediation model 217; instructing visualization on
mixed methods 214–215; needed materials 211;
pre-lesson preparation 211; pseudo research 216;
qualitative and quantitative data 211; qualitative and
quantitative part 216–217; tools and software 213;
virtual adaptations 213; visualization/presentation
212–213; Wheel Chart 217–218, 218
Jones, Sosanya 11–17
Jones, S. R. 85n2, 171–172, 180, 182
Jones, Willis A. 103–105

K–12 setting 225
Kahlo, Frida 155
Kamimura, Aurora 66, 77–85
King, P. M. 185
Knight, Gwendolyn 155
Kotz, D. 241
Krause, J. M. 211
Krieg, Eric J. 107
Krueger, A. 132–133, 139

Lane, J. E. 268, 293–299
Lange, Alex C. 144, 171–178
Lang, J. M. 98–99
Lareau, A. 66, 160, 310–311
Larson, S. 273
Lazarewicz, Adam 223, 225–232
lesson plans 1–2; context 4–5; core ideas 4; learners 4;
standard template 4; vetting criteria 3
Let's Road Trip: crosswalk table for quantitative and
qualitative research study 84–85; diversity of
learners 83; ensuring alignment 81–82; fostering
equitable learning spaces 84; overall directions
78–79; Part I directions 79; Part II directions 79;
previous learning and misconception 83; virtual
adaptations 81–82
Lewin, Kurt 252
librarian's tutorial 40
library database 40
Liebman, J. B. 132
linear regression 116; actual regression model 113;
causation to use with 115; correlation coefficient
115; experiential learning and application 118;
formative assessment 116; multiple linear regression
113, 117; online 116; previous learning and
misconceptions 117; Qualtrics 114; regression
coefficient 115; simple linear regression 113, 115,
117; simpler quantitative analyses 114; statistical and

INDEX

survey software 114; team-based learning 118; team breakouts 116; variables 113, 115

listening deeply: activating prior knowledge 148; basic interview facilitating skills 147; being attentive to shared humanity 151; being present 150–151; engaging in self-reflection 151; formative assessment 150; grounding practice 147–148; learners and context 152; learning objectives 147; needed materials 147; perfect questions 146; practicing restatement 149; practicing silence 148–149; sense of shared humanity 147; students to engage in self-work 147; summative assessment 150; virtual adaptations 150

literature review and theoretical/conceptual framework 3, 37–38

Lopez, Jameson 223, 225–232

Lotan, R. A. 225

Luker, K. 310–311

Lucidchart 212–213

Lunsford, Laura 268, 277–284

Major, C. H. 237

Marcia, J. E. 282

Marsicano, Christopher R. 224, 256–263

Martin, Rylie 224, 256–263

MAXQDA 212–213

McCaffrey, Vanessa 267, 270–276

McClure, L. A. 235

McCusker, R. 211

Mendelson, T. 243

Merriam, S. B. 21–22, 66, 253

Meza, Cindy 223, 225–232

Michaelsen, L. K. 104

Microsoft Teams 23, 251, 287

MindMeister 72–73

Mona Lisa painting 202

Morandi, Giorgio 155

MS Excel 40, 42, 107, 213

multiple linear regression 104, 113, 117; *see also* regression

multivariate analysis: activity #1: data collection 108–109, 111; activity #2: analyzing the data 110; assessment 111; bivariate and simple multivariate methods 103; critical thinking skills 111; developing the scenario 107–108; math phobia 106; online survey platform 107; quantitative data analysis 112; real-world applicability of 111; real-world scenarios 107; statistical software 107, 110; statistical tests 110; students' anxieties 112; teaching methods 112; virtual adaptations 110

Murnane, R.J. 132, 134

narrative 50, 54, 59–60, 65, 70, 97, 144, 159, 163–164, 167, 206, 237, 267–268, 271, 274, 276, 286–288

NASPA 143

National Center for Educational Statistics (NCES) 121

Natow, Rebecca S. 10, 19–25

Neumann, A. 2, 215, 307–312

Newman, I. 20

Nittany Public School District (NPSD) 200–201

Okello, W. K. 144, 163–170

Ononuju, Ijeoma 66, 94–99

ontological, ontology 85n2, 53, 207, 286

Op-Ed Project website, The 301–302

Pallas, A.M. 2, 307–312

Pasque, P. A. 37–38

Patashnik, E. M. 257

Patel, L. 164

Patton, M. Q. 238–239

Peer Review workshop 237

Pérez II, David 143–145

Peshkin, A. 12, 97

Pifer, M. J. 223, 234–240

Pillow, W. 91

placebo tests 136; *see also* control

Plano Clark, V. L. 199, 210, 215

Policy Paradox: The Art of Political Decision Making 293

Pollock, T. G. 238

Porter, C. J. 37–38

positionality 12, 15–16, 154–155, 170n1; definition of 87; with examples **89**; politics and ethics of 88; researcher's 87, 93n1; statement 87, 89, 91–92; work of 86–87, 91

positionality artifacts 87; activity 1: lecture-chat 87; activity 2: subjectivity, power and politics 88; activity 3: subjectivity 88; activity 4: politics and ethics of positionality 88; confidence building 92; formative assessment 89; insider and outsider statuses 90, **90**; opening 87; positionality work *see* positionality; reflexivity 91–92; student-provided, artifacts 87; subjectivity 90; summative assessment 89; Venn diagram 88; virtual adaptations 89

post-positivism 53

Poth, C. N. 20–24, 27

Potnis, D. 211

PowerPoint 149, 204, 206, 212–213, 235, 295

praxiology 53

previous learning and misconceptions: articulating a research problem 24; candy sort 50; exploratory factor analysis 124–125; Let's Road Trip 83; linear regression 117; regression using critical quantitative methods 230; research questions 32–33; visualize your research design 74–75

Prezi 212–213

principal component analysis (PCA) 124

privilege 37, 60, 87–88, 92, 136, 147–149, 151–152, 166, 178, 261

problem statements 20–22

professional communities of researchers 307

professional development (PD) 270; articulating your value add 274; assessment 272; building a portfolio to support 271; FURSCA experience 271–272; needed materials 271; pre-lesson preparation 271; "soft" skills 276; UR process 274–275; values, joy and passion 274; virtual adaptations 272; what is a portfolio? 273; workshop 271, 273

public writing: assignment 305; declining trust in media 304–305; faculty 305; formative assessment 303;

Journalist's Resource, The 303; learning objectives 300; lesson activities: Session One 301–302; lesson activities: Session Two 302; perceptions of the value of 305; pre-class preparation 301; readings/assignments 301; summative assessment 303; trustworthiness of media 304; virtual adaptations 303; weaponization of research 305; writing skill development 304

purpose statements 20–22

puzzle pieces connecting: assessment 42; determine terms and search functions 40–41; find and maintain resources 39; Google Scholar and ResearchGate 40–43; higher value/perceptions of quality 44; inclusionary and exclusionary boundaries 41–43; institutional databases 42–43; institutional library 44; key terms and language 43; library database 40; literature synthesis 42; methodological approach 42; phrase searching 40; qualitative research inquiry 44; stop searching 44; virtual adaptations 41

"Pyramid of Congruence" activity 175; advance values of equity and justice 171, 176; critical and poststructural theories 176–177; *see also* critical and poststructural theories; interweaving theories throughout a study design 176; students' prior knowledge of epistemologies and theories 177; utilize theories 177–178

qualitative and quantitative methods 196–197

qualitative dimension of mixed methods: asynchronous instruction 206; "Create your Masterpiece" experience? 203, 208; creative learning and reflective practice 208; FG setting 204; formative assessment 206; learning objectives 202; needed materials 203; previous learning and misconceptions 207–208; qualitative analysis process 205; role of research question(s) 207; self-portrait exercise 203; sensemaking 208; suggested lesson timeline 205; summative assessment 206; synchronous instruction 206; worthiness of qual and quant approaches 207

qualitative methods 3, 143–145, 195–196

qualitative research 38, 223; code data and develop themes for *see* coding data and developing themes; critical and poststructural theories in *see* critical and poststructural theories; pervasiveness of theory in 59

Qualtrics 107, 114

quantitative and qualitative data 195–196

quantitative dimensions of mixed methods 3, 191–192; asynchronous classes 198; case study prompt: increasing college access 200–201; collaborative learning 200; deepening superficial knowledge 200; developing questions require quantitative methods 199; formative assessment 198; needed materials 196; practical application 200; pre-lesson preparation 196; quantitative dimensions of 196; quantitative/qualitative question 197–198; quantitative strands complement qualitative

strands 199; summative assessment 198; synchronous classes 198

quantitative methodology course 116

quantitative methods 103–105, 194–195

Rabenn, McKenzie 224, 241–247

Ray, V. 301

Reddy, Vikash 10, 27–33

Reddy. Y. M. 94

reflexive engagement 169

reflexivity 11–12, 14–17; positionality artifacts 91–92

reflexivity exercise 14–15, 17; epistemological 12–13; personal 12–13; positional 12–13

regression 104, 113–115, 131–133, 198, 226–228, 232; *see also* linear regression; analysis 135, 137, 210; model(s) 137, 230; multiple linear regression 104, 113, 117; training 138; techniques 135, 137

regression coefficient 104, 113, 116–117

regression using critical quantitative methods: apply linear regression 226; assessment/evaluation 228; confidence building 231–232; critical quantitative methods 228; critical quantitative reasoning 230; Desmos lesson plan 226–227; equitable learning space 231; graph of regression equation 227–228, *229*; learning objectives 226; line of best fit *229*, 230; needed materials 226; previous learning and misconceptions 230; virtual adaptations 228

reliability, reliable 66, 98, 216

research design 3; categories of 65; components 85n3; road map approach in 80; trustworthiness 66

research design based on research question(s): activity 1: reading discussion 69–70, 72; activity 2: visualizing and mind mapping 70–73; activity 3: research design speed interview 71–73; activity 4: journaling your decision 72–73; formative assessment 73; learning objectives 68; mind mapping 69; needed materials 69; opening 69; summative assessment 73

researcher reflexivity statement: asynchronous learning 96; formative assessment 96; learning objectives 95; needed materials 95; rubric for evaluating 96; summative assessment 96; synchronous learning 96; trustworthiness 95

research paradigm 12, 17, 180, 192, 207, 286, 288, 290

research questions: causal questions 27–30; class exercise–formulating 31; confidence building 33; correlational questions 29; descriptive questions 29; discussion of 30–31; formative assessment 31; generating and refining 27; introduction of research tree 30; learning objectives 28; misconceived questions 33; previous learning misconceptions 32–33; to research design *see* research design based on research question(s); scaffolded learning 33; scaffolding opportunity 29; summative assessment 31; tree exercise 32; virtual adaptations 31; "what is good teaching?" 28–30

research topic selection: asynchronous online discussion 14; culturally responsive framework 14; formative

INDEX

responses 14; hot topics 11, 14–16; own interests and experiences 17; positionality 12, 15–16; reflexive exercises *see* reflexivity exercise; reflexivity 11–12, 16–17; research paradigms 12, 17; research question 12, 15, 17; role of relevance 15–16; topic "hot" exercise 14

Rivers, Ishwanzya 65–66, 68–75

Rizga, Kristina 28, 30, 33

road mapping: formative assessment 82; frameworks, hypotheses, researh questions and research design 78–82; "Let's Road Trip" exercise *see* Let's Road Trip; summative assessment 82; US Planning Road Maps 78, 81; "warming up our voices" exercise 78

Rodgers, K. R. 294

Rodrigues, J. 238

Roegman, R. 252

Rounds, Emilia G 224, 256–263

Rowlett, R. S. 273

Sandberg, J. 12

SAS 114, 121

Schleutker, E. 103

scientific sociology 68

self and research 86–89, 91; *see also* positionality artifacts

sense of belonging 59–60

Shalka, T. R. 144, 146–152

Shaw, L. L. 157–158

Shulman, L. 2

simple linear regression 113, 115, 117

simpler quantitative analyses 114

small-group discussion 22–24

Smith, Johnson C. 164

social markers 13

Soliya Connect program 268, 277–278

Special Topics 267

speed interview 71–72

SPSS 107, 114, 121, 123, 127, 132

SPSS Technology Manual for Statistics and Data Analysis for Social Science 107

STATA 107, 121, 132–134

Stata statistical software 104

statistical software 107, 110, 114

statistical tests 110

statistics 113, 116

Stockton, C. M. 56

Stone, H. 293–294

Street, Jutta 268, 277–284

student affairs and higher education (SAHE) 143

Sugrue, C. 252

Sun, Jeffrey C. 65–66, 68–75

SurveyMonkey 107, 114

survey software 114–115

Sweet, M. 104

Taylor, Kari B. 144, 179–186

teaching policy implications: activities 294–296; appreciating perspective of silent "other" 297;

assessment 296; complexity of equity 297; *Equity Cake Exercise*, the 296–299; learning objectives 294; needed materials 294; pre-lesson preparation 294; tying policy implications to research findings 297; virtual adaptations 296

team-based learning 3, 104; linear regression 113, 118

team breakouts: linear regression model 116, 118; visual storytelling 237

Terosky, Aimee LaPointe xiii–xiv, 1–5, 37–38, 46–51

theory testing 250; counterfactual 135

Thiebaud, Wayne 155

"Think/Pair/Share" exercises 251, 253

Thomas Tobin, Courtney S. 103, 106–112

Thornton, N. 20

Tisdell, E. J. 21–22, 66

topics, problems and research questions 3, 9–10

Torres, V. 85n2, 171–172, 180, 182

treatment 90, 131–138; pre-treatment 133, 136, 138; post-treatment 133; treatment effect 136; treatment group(s) 135–136, 138

Trochim, W. M. 199

trustworthiness 59–60

Tuck, E. 92

Twain, Mark 256

undergraduate research (UR) 270; and creative inquiry 275; experience 274; FURSCA leadership 276; process 274–275

US Planning Road Maps 78

validity, validate, validated 66, 80, 84, 91, 98, 125, 133, 144, 205, 243, 281; evidence 13; external 133, 136; internal 133, 136; threats to 131–132, 134

variables 113, 115

variance inflation factors (VIF) 115

Venet, A. S. 152

video interview to students: class discussion 283–284; cross-cultural studies 281–282; culturally inclusive language 280; culture-specific social issues 281; formative assessment 280; journal reflection 283; learning objectives 277; multi-week activity 279; needed materials 278; pre-lesson preparation 278; previous learnings and misconceptions 282–283; representative samples 281; scholarly identity 282; summative assessment 280; virtual adaptations 279

visual arts, performing observations and writing field notes: elements of art and questions to 158, *159*; formative assessment 158; framework *154*, 154–155; images and paintings 155; *La Lotería as Creative Resistance* 160; learning objectives 155; learning to see in different ways 156–157; making sense of what you see 156; method of observation 159–160; needed materials 155; personal creativity 161; prior and new knowledge 161; recognizing what you know 155; student's creativity 160; summative assessment 158; virtual adaptations 158; Who We Are Shapes How and What We See 160; writing is the visual record 160; writing what you see 157–158 visualize your research design 68–69; active learning and critical thinking 75; identifying research design 74; mind map topic 70–71; MindMeister 72–73; previous learning and misconceptions 74–75; reflection 74

visual storytelling 223; activating discussion 235–236; context 239–240; core ideas 237–238; formative assessment 237; learner 238–239; learning objectives 235; needed materials 235; Peer Review 236; pre-lesson preparation 235; Report Out 236; summative assessment 237; virtual adaptations 237; workshop 236; Wrap Up 237

Vitruvian Man 202

Waddington, R. Joseph 104, 131–139
Wallace, W. 68
Ward, Elaine 268, 285–291
Watt, D. 95
weight(s), weighted, and weighting 136, 191, 210, 212–215, 218, 258, 261, 280, 309

western, educated, industrial, rich, and democratic (WEIRD) samples 281
"what is good teaching?" 28–30, 32
What the Best College Teachers Do 50
Willett, J.B. 132, 134
Williams, J. M. 20
Wilson, S. 146
word document 40–42
world(s) of Black people 163
worldview 42, 60, 171, 283, 286–290
Woulfin, S. 252

Yang, K. W. 92
Yarar-Fisher, C. 235

Zakrajsek, T. 237
Zhu, X. 211
Zoom 14, 23, 31, 48, 82, 110, 122, 134, 150, 182, 198, 228, 237, 245, 251, 260, 279, 287

Printed in the United States
by Baker & Taylor Publisher Services